P9-CRQ-846

The Reality
of Christian Learning:

Strategies for Faith-Discipline Integration

Edited By
Harold Heie
David L. Wolfe

**CHRISTIAN
UNIVERSITY
PRESS**

A subsidiary of the
Christian College Consortium
and
William B. Eerdmans Publishing Company

Available from Wm. B. Eerdmans Publishing Co.
255 Jefferson Ave. SE, Grand Rapids, Mich. 49503

Library of Congress Cataloging-in-Publication Data

The Reality of Christian learning.

1. Learning and scholarship — Religious aspects — Christianity.
I. Heie, Harold, 1935-   . II. Wolfe, David L., 1939-
BR115.L32R43 1987   261.5   86-19631

ISBN 0-8028-0233-8

Dedicated to the memory of Ronald R. Nelson, whose life, scholarship, and teaching exemplified the commitment to Christian learning expressed in these pages.

Contents

Preface   vii
Notes on Contributors   xi

PART I INTRODUCTION   1

    David L. Wolfe The Line of Demarcation between
        Integration and Pseudointegration   3

PART II DISCIPLINARY ESSAYS   13

    POLITICAL SCIENCE   15
        Commentary   15
        James W. Skillen Can There Be a Christian
            Approach to Political Science?   17
        Richard J. Mouw Alternative Christian Approaches
            to Political Science: Toward a More
            Comprehensive Perspective   38

    SOCIOLOGY   53
        Commentary   53
        Robert A. Clark and S. D. Gaede Knowing
            Together: Reflections on a Holistic Sociology of
            Knowledge   55
        Ronald Burwell Epistemic Justification, Cultural
            Universals, and Revelation: Further Reflections
            on the Sociology of Knowledge   87

    PSYCHOLOGY   101
        Commentary   101
        Bert H. Hodges Perception Is Relative and
            Veridical: Ecological and Biblical Perspectives
            on Knowing and Doing the Truth   103
        James E. Martin Toward an Epistemology of
            Revelation   140

    BIOLOGY   153
        Commentary   153
        D. Gareth Jones The Human Brain and the
            Meaning of Humanness   155
        William Hasker Brains and Persons   181

MATHEMATICS   204

   Commentary   204
   Harold Heie Mathematics: Freedom within
     Bounds   206
   Gene B. Chase Complementarity as a Christian
     Philosophy of Mathematics   231

THE ARTS   247

   Commentary   247
   Harold M. Best God's Creation and Human
     Creativity   249
   Mark Coppenger Creativity and Analogy: Some
     Limitations   268

PHILOSOPHY   290

   Commentary   290
   C. Stephen Evans Could Divine Rewards Provide
     a Reason to Be Moral?   292
   Malcolm A. Reid Is There an Alternative Reason
     to Divine Rewards for Being Moral? 303

PART III CONCLUSION   315

   Ronald R. Nelson Faith-Discipline Integration:
     Compatibilist, Reconstructionalist, and
     Transformationalist Strategies   317

Preface

Over the years a number of books have been published on the relationship of faith and learning.[1] The clear emphasis in these works has been on the foundational concerns (theological, philosophical, historical) that formulate the program for attempts to integrate faith and learning. The time has come to move boldly in attempting those programmatic designs within the various academic disciplines. Unfortunately, in most of the literature and workshops where concrete integration is discussed there is great difficulty translating foundational concerns into something helpful to teachers, researchers, and students. There is a distinct need for excellent examples of concrete integration, informed by earlier foundational studies, carried out with a clarity and explicitness that is instructive to students and professional scholars. The purpose of this volume is to present a series of such models. Our hope is that this book will inspire other Christian scholars to commit themselves seriously to integrative tasks within their respective disciplines, thereby leading to further refinement and elaboration of the positions presented in the following pages.

To suggest that the essays in this book are examples of integration is to presuppose a common understanding of the word *integration*. In the introduction we explain more fully the way in which we intend to use this word. Here let us simply state that our use of the word *integration* emphasizes the fundamental search for commonalities between the Christian faith and the substantive, methodological, and value assumptions that underlie activity in the academic disciplines, as well as attempts to systematize academic learning into an overarching Christian schema. As the title of the book suggests, we propose that at this fundamental level it is proper to talk about the reality of Christian learning. We do not dwell on the characteristics and attitudes of the Christian

1. Such books include: Harry Blamires, *The Christian Mind* (New York: Seabury Press, 1963); Frank Gaebelein, *The Pattern of God's Truth* (Chicago: Moody Press, 1968); Nicholas Wolterstorff, *Reason Within the Bounds of Religion* (Grand Rapids: Eerdmans, 1976); L. Kalsbeek, *Contours of a Christian Philosophy* (Toronto: Wedge Publishing, 1975); Arthur F. Holmes, *All Truth is God's Truth* (Grand Rapids: Eerdmans, 1977); Arthur F. Holmes, *Contours of a World View* (Grand Rapids: Eerdmans, 1983); Arthur F. Holmes, ed., *The Making of a Christian Mind* (Downers Grove, IL: InterVarsity Press, 1985); and Brian J. Walsh & J. Richard Middleton, *The Transforming Vision* (Downers Grove, IL: InterVarsity Press, 1984). The latter book contains an excellent bibliography of literature on faith-learning integration.

learner but rather argue that attempts to bring a Christian perspective to bear on the subject matter of scholarship in the various academic disciplines can indeed be termed "Christian learning." The purpose of this book is to promote careful scholarship informed by Christian presuppositions that is recognizable as appropriate by academicians within the disciplines, including those who bring different presuppositions to their own scholarship.

In selecting essays for this collection we strove to achieve a diversity of approaches to integration. We would have liked to solicit essays in most of the traditional disciplines. This might have been possible if we had settled on one essay for each discipline. However, we decided that our overall goal was best served by soliciting *two* essays in each chosen discipline: a principal essay followed by a respondent essay which provides an analysis of the integrative strategies used in the principal essay and suggests alternatives. It is our conviction that this approach will best contribute to an understanding of alternative integrative strategies, thereby providing the best springboard for further integrative work on the part of scholars and students who read these pages. In order to keep the length of this volume within reason we limited ourselves to seven areas, with representation from at least two disciplines within each of the three major areas of knowledge: the humanities, the social sciences, and the natural sciences and mathematics.

Principal essayists were given the following statement of assignment:

> The purpose of each principal essay is to treat a concrete issue which exemplifies the way(s) basic Christian concerns and your academic discipline interrelate. The intent of the essay is not to be devotional or apologetic (in any narrow sense), neither is it to be *simply* a systematic treatment of the structural interrelations of Christian thinking and your discipline, though your systematic thinking about these relations should inform the essay. For most disciplines we wish to exclude papers which are "a philosophy of . . . ," and present papers which are an exercise in doing your discipline as a Christian.

We tried to be flexible with respect to the above assignment, allowing for variations if the topic proposed by the principal essayist seemed promising in light of our search for a diversity of integrative strategies.

Respondent essayists were provided with the following statement of assignment:

> The purpose of each respondent essay is two-fold. First, to identify the integrative strategy that the principal author has pursued in dealing with the concrete issue under discussion and to analyze the strengths and limitations of this strategy. Second, the respondent should suggest at least one alternative integrative strategy in the context of the given concrete issue

and should contrast strengths and weaknesses of one of these alternative strategies with the strategy of the principal essayist.

Consistent with the nature of this assignment, the respondent essayist was generally chosen from the same discipline as the principal essayist. However, in two cases (biology and political science) we judged that the issues dealt with were sufficiently philosophical in nature to suggest responses from professional philosophers having particular interests in these issues. In the interests of preserving genuine pluralism we did not grant any principal essayist the opportunity to revise his proposal in light of the critical comments of the respondent.

We maintained as much consistency in the essayists' use of notes and bibliographies as was possible while still respecting differing conventions for such usage in various of the academic disciplines, most notably in the social sciences.

Although each of the fourteen disciplinary essays within this volume can be read with profit by thinking persons interested in these issues, the two essays in each area may be read with particular benefit by the practicing scholar, teacher, and student in that discipline. The essays sometimes presuppose a certain level of familiarity with the discipline's basic ideas.

With the above comments on audience in mind, we can suggest a number of routes for the reader to take through this book. The introductory and concluding chapters are fairly self-contained, with the fourteen disciplinary essays between serving as illustrations of the main ideas presented in these two chapters. Therefore, the reader who is exclusively interested in one academic discipline would be best served by reading the first and last chapters and then reading the two essays within that particular discipline. However, this volume is intended to be read in its entirety, since only such a reading will capture its coherence. One way to grasp this coherence would be to read in serial order the first chapter, the seven commentary sections, and the last chapter. The reader should then be prepared to read the entire volume with maximum benefit.

We extend a special word of appreciation to our wives, Pat and Jean, for their encouragement and patience throughout this writing project and for their steadfast love and support throughout our years of involvement with Christian learning. We express thanks to our contributors for their patience throughout what proved to be a long seven-year process and for the commitment to Christian learning exemplified in their essays. Many of them are personal friends whose dedication to the integrative task has been an inspiration to us. We also extend a special word of thanks to Beth De Leeuw for her many hours of typing and retyping of numerous drafts of these pages.

We have devoted our professional lives to Christian liberal arts education. It is our firm conviction that the major distinction of such education must be commitment to the development of integrative positions such as those exemplified in this volume. In spite of rhetoric to the contrary, all too often Christian college trustees and administrators have in practice placed integration low on their list of priorities, while Christian teachers often have been content to be simply good pedagogues or professionals. The uniqueness of Christian higher education requires that our priorities be revised and that integration of faith and learning become a genuine imperative, not in place of pedagogical or professional excellence, but as their necessary fulfillment. Our hope and prayer is that future integrative scholarship will be so extensive and profound that the present reality of Christian learning will seem but a small tributary to that stream.

HAROLD HEIE
DAVID WOLFE
Tunbridge, VT
June 1985

Notes on Contributors

HAROLD M. BEST is professor of music and dean of the Conservatory of Music at Wheaton College (IL), where he has taught since 1970. He holds a D.S.M. degree in organ and composition from Union Theological Seminary. He previously taught at Nyack College (NY).

RONALD J. BURWELL is professor of sociology at Messiah College (PA). He holds a Ph.D. in religion from New York University. He previously taught sociology and anthropology at The King's College (NY) and was a visiting professor at Wheaton College (IL).

GENE B. CHASE is professor of mathematics and computer science at Messiah College (PA), where he has taught since 1973. He holds a Ph.D. in mathematics from Cornell University. He previously taught at Houghton College (NY) and Wells College (NY).

ROBERT A. CLARK is associate professor of sociology at Gordon College (MA), where he has taught since 1977. He holds a Ph.D. in sociology from Washington State University. He previously taught at Whitworth College (WA).

MARK COPPENGER is pastor of the First Baptist Church in El Dorado, Arkansas. He holds a Ph.D. in philosophy from Vanderbilt University and a Masters of Divinity degree from Southwestern Baptist Theological Seminary. He previously taught philosophy at Wheaton College (IL).

C. STEPHEN EVANS is associate professor of philosophy and curator of the Howard and Edna Hong Kierkegaard Library at St. Olaf College (MN). He previously taught at Wheaton College (IL) and holds the Ph.D. in philosophy from Yale University.

S. D. GAEDE is professor of sociology at Gordon College (MA), where he has taught since 1974. He holds a Ph.D. in sociology from Vanderbilt University.

WILLIAM HASKER is professor of philosophy at Huntington College (IN), where he has taught since 1966. He holds a Ph.D. in philosophy from the University of Edinburgh. He previously taught at Frederick College (VA) and has been a visiting professor at Earlham College (IN).

HAROLD HEIE is vice president for academic affairs and professor of mathematics at Northwestern College (IA), a position he has held since 1980. He holds a Ph.D. in the aerospace and mechanical sciences from Princeton University. He previously taught mathematics at The King's College (NY) and Gordon College (MA).

BERT HODGES is professor of psychology at Gordon College (MA), where he has taught since 1972. He holds a Ph.D. in psychology from Vanderbilt University and has been a visiting professor at the University of California, Santa Barbara.

D. GARETH JONES is occupant of the Chair of Anatomy at the University of Otago (New Zealand), a position he has held since 1983. He holds a D.Sc. in anatomy from the University of Western Australia. He previously taught at University College in London and the University of Western Australia.

JAMES M. MARTIN is associate professor of psychology at the Pennsylvania State University, where he has taught since 1966. He holds a Ph.D. in psycholinguistics from the University of Illinois.

RICHARD J. MOUW is professor of Christian philosophy and ethics at Fuller Theological Seminary. He holds a Ph.D. in philosophy from the University of Chicago. He previously taught philosophy at Calvin College (MI) and has been a visiting professor at the Free University of Amsterdam and Juniata College (PA).

RONALD R. NELSON was professor of humanities and history at Northwestern College (IA) prior to his tragic and untimely death in March of 1985. He held a Ph.D. in history from the University of Michigan and previously taught at Eastern Michigan University and Michigan State University.

MALCOLM A. REID is professor of philosophy at Gordon College (MA), where he has taught since 1968. He holds a Ph.D. in philosophy and theology from the University of Edinburgh.

JAMES W. SKILLEN is executive director of the Association for Public Justice, a position he has held since 1981, and adjunct professor of political science at Dordt College (IA), where he has taught since 1978. He holds a Ph.D. in political science from Duke University. He previously taught political science at Messiah College (PA) and Gordon College (MA).

DAVID L. WOLFE is professor of philosophy at Gordon College (MA), where he has taught since 1974. He holds a Ph.D. in philosophy of education from New York University. He previously taught at The King's College (NY), Wheaton College (IL), and Trinity Evangelical Divinity School (IL).

PART I
Introduction

The Line of Demarcation between Integration and Pseudointegration

DAVID L. WOLFE

LINES OF DEMARCATION AS PERSUASIVE DEFINITIONS

How can we distinguish genuine efforts to integrate Christian concerns and the academic disciplines from efforts that superficially resemble such integration?

Always be suspicious of anyone who offers you an authoritative "line of demarcation" between one thing and another (especially between a "thing" and a "pseudothing"). The twentieth century has seen plenty of ink spilled trying to draw a line of demarcation between science and pseudoscience, between meaningful and meaningless discourse, even between language and nonlinguistic phenomena. In all of these areas several decades of debate and discussion have greatly softened all lines of demarcation. In retrospect these lines appear to be in fact proposals about how we should view the subjects being considered. Lines of demarcation are persuasive definitions, that is, attempts to convince us to use words in certain ways and to feel certain ways about the issues we discuss with those words.

What follows in this essay is an attempt to persuade you to use the word *integration* in a certain way and to draw you into thinking along certain lines about the integration of Christian faith with your scholarly concerns. Having warned you that lines of demarcation are not absolute, I should also point out that while all definitions are human conventions, some are profoundly more fruitful than others.

In this essay I will make a proposal about distinguishing genuine integration from apparent integration. This means that I will be proposing a definition of integration by specifying the features that characterize integration and are absent in cases of nonintegration. Admittedly there is a circularity here, for what counts as integration (or nonintegration) will be determined by the presence or absence of these features. Nevertheless, such circularity may still be fruitful provided that the resulting proposal articulates and clarifies our intuitions about integration, generates new insights, and serves us in additional ways (some of which we may not be able to specify in advance). One interesting test of a line of

3

demarcation such as I am proposing is to see how well it handles respected, already existing attempts to relate faith and learning.

PSEUDOINTEGRATION

Most Christian academicians sense intuitively that some apparent attempts at faith-learning integration really lie outside genuine integrative efforts. For example, a recent denominational periodical, in an article on Christian day schools, used the following example "to explain how teaching in the [Christian] day school differs from teaching in public schools": "Two and two is always four . . . and God is always the same; you can depend on Him" (deletion in original).

I once heard a biology teacher give a devotional talk at a fall faculty workshop. This quiet, eccentric bachelor gave a colorful, highly descriptive and unintentionally erotic account of how the female of a certain species of firefly lures the male of a different species by imitating the signal of an eligible female, then devouring the expectant male when he arrives. The incredulous and wildly amused faculty then heard the biologist, oblivious to the hilarity or embarrassment he was creating, go on to make a devotional point about the "true light" and the "false light."

A physicist was arguing for the intelligibility of the doctrine of the Trinity. He pointed out that water can be one substance but still exist in three very different physical states, in some cases with all three states coexisting in the same environment.

In these examples we have instances in which Christian beliefs are indeed related in some way to ideas in academic disciplines (mathematics, entomology, physics), but in a way that lacks an *integral* relation to those disciplines. The examples use the data from the disciplines for illustrative, devotional, or apologetic purposes. They *use* the disciplines, but are quite irrelevant to *doing* the disciplines. Nothing in these examples requires the person to be inside the assumptions, concerns, and methodologies of the disciplines mentioned. It is this wholly external setting of Christian and disciplinary ideas side by side that makes these into superficial or negative instances of integration.

THE NOTION OF INTEGRATION

Some would think that the foregoing examples illustrate objectionable practice but also object to the word *integration*, which I have been using so freely. Does it not presuppose a denial that truth is already one, though it may be found in different places and by different methods? There is a point to this objection. The unity of truth certainly must be affirmed. Nevertheless, integration is more about the *process of how truth is grasped* than it is about the ultimate unity of all God's truth. Unfortunately, though God may have a fully comprehensive and unified view of reality, we finite human beings do not. Even our hermeneutic and theological methodologies are subject to the distortions and limitations of human interpretation and construction.

To make matters even more complicated, the academic disciplines are human projects which are (1) abstractive in the sense that they are directed only to certain aspects of reality (and so demand completion by being brought together with complementary studies of other aspects) and (2) operate according to guiding ideals or goals which were formulated historically (in most cases) without any reference to Judaeo-Christian assumptions (except as those may have been generally influential in the culture). Christian academicians who have been carefully educated have been initiated into projects which are often troublesome in their interrelations (or lack of them) to the faith that is embodied in those same scholars.

So I will not flinch at the accusation that integration presupposes the bringing together of two or more recognizably separate components. For Christians these will always involve the relating of our admittedly human grasp of God's revelation in Jesus Christ through the Judaeo-Christian Scriptures as one component, and our respective areas of academic expertise as another. In some cases we will seek to relate the disciplines to each other as well as to Christian convictions and values. The very notion of integration, then, involves bringing these things together. The issue now becomes, "How can this enterprise be carried out in a legitimate fashion?" or "What distinguishes genuine integration from pseudointegration?" So we come to my proposal for recognizing genuine integration. *Genuine integration occurs when an assumption or concern can be shown to be internally shared by (integral to) both the Judaeo-Christian vision and an academic discipline.* The line of demarcation between integration and pseudointegration is therefore "integral sharing" or "integral commonality." Integration is the process by which two often very differing visions are related in an interesting and informative way on the basis of one or more shared presuppositions.

INTEGRATIVE STRATEGIES

What sort of presuppositions might the Christian way of seeing and a disciplinary way of seeing share? To answer this question completely would require us to analyze the structure of the various human cognitive and creative projects which we call "academic disciplines" in order to find points of contact or commonalities that could explain why a discipline is interesting or attractive from a Christian point of view. Let us content ourselves here with a merely suggestive analysis. Perhaps this cursory highlighting of disciplinary features will stimulate some reader to a more penetrating, refined, or fruitful analysis; mine is only provisional for the purposes at hand.

Substantive and Methodological Presuppositions

Disciplines make factual claims which can be expressed in statements about alleged states of affairs. These claims may be explicit for the practitioners or they may be made tacitly and so serve silently as a basis of activity in the discipline.

Disciplinary work requires making substantive assumptions about the nature of the subject matter, types of explanations appropriate to that subject matter, and methodologies effective in making the subject matter accessible for study. These assumptions give common ground to all practitioners who share them and, especially when made tacitly, preserve practitioners from endless philosophical debate, allowing them to get on with disciplinary business. When these assumptions are made explicitly, they are frequently thought of as empirically validated "facts" by those immersed in disciplinary activity.

To flesh out these ideas a bit, let us look at some examples of substantive (i.e., ontological) and methodological (i.e., epistemological) presuppositions in the sense I have been using these terms. These examples are drawn from the human sciences. They involve ideas about the nature of human persons, notions about the determinants of human behavior, and perspectives on how human beings are to be known and investigated.

One set of assumptions might hold that human beings are physical systems to be completely explained by physical-chemical laws or principles of behavioral conditioning and investigated by the same methods as other physical systems. On the other hand a different set of assumptions conceives human beings to be conscious, purposive agents who are explainable, at least in part, by purposes directed to anticipated future goals. The purposes of human agents are accessible to investigators by the fact that the investigators are also human beings who share the same socio-cultural milieu as the subject agents (a process sometimes called *Verstehen*).

Notice that assumptions about the nature of the subject matter (e.g., that human beings are nothing but physical systems) have a strong effect on the methodology of the investigator who accepts those assumptions. A physical system may be investigated by perceptual processes which produce reports in the physical-behavioral categories of physics or biology. It is this close connection between substantive and methodological presuppositions that led me to include them in the same broad set of disciplinary characteristics.

Notice also that in this example the Christian is offered a choice between an alternative that is reductionistic in its substantive and methodological assumptions and a very different alternative that distinguishes between human and nonhuman subject matter. Given such a choice, the Christian academician may very well find the second set of assumptions more appealing than the first.

How Christians relate their Christian beliefs to the assumptions of a discipline will depend in part on what assumptions they find in the discipline, whether those assumptions are considered obligatory, or whether there are optional disciplinary assumptions available (as in the illustration above). Christians may find that their assumptions are indeed shared by their discipline, as in the case of philosophy's commitment to truth and the demand for reasonable beliefs. Although certain ways in which these assumptions are carried out may be antithetical to Christian beliefs, a great many Christians find the discipline itself inherently *compatible* with the Judaeo-Christian tradition. This is manifestly so in the case of Evans's essay, "Could Divine Rewards Provide a Reason To Be Moral?" in which he attempts to show that the assumptions of a major tradition in philosophical ethics may be brought fruitfully into an integral relation with the biblical notion of divine rewards.

On the other hand Christians may find that the controlling assumptions in dominant disciplinary paradigms present problems for their Christian commitments. This is the case in Skillen's analysis, "Can There Be a Christian Approach to Political Science?" Skillen is critical of reductionistic approaches to political science that pretend to be value free. This does not entail a Christian rejection of political science, in his view. Rather, the Christian may engage in political studies proposing an alternative paradigm; one which has, nonetheless, the genuinely political category of "justice" as its central focus.

Skillen's approach raises an issue which must be faced squarely. If a Christian finds that his discipline's assumptions present very little shared ground with his Christian assumptions, he may wish to remake or *transform* his discipline into one with a Christian orientation. Such transformations may play a very important role in Christian scholarship. It is a valid and significant integrative strategy, but it is possible only because there was some legitimate insight in the disciplinary assumptions to begin with.

Any *reconstruction* of a new "Christian discipline" that has *no* common features with the received professional discipline collapses the two-sided nature of the integrative process into a one-sided collection of Christian insights without systematic relevance to an academic discipline. Such a move trespasses the line of demarcation, since there is no "integral commonality" possible.

Value Commitments

In its valuational aspects a discipline displays both explicit and tacit values. Genuinely to understand a discipline requires a grasp of both. For instance a discipline may set a high value on intellectual honesty in gathering and assessing empirical evidence. This value is not given the same priority in all disciplines. It is, for instance, not as prominent in mathematics and artistic creation. Each discipline tacitly assumes the values of understanding its chosen subject matter. Yet within a given discipline some traditions may value certain types of explanation over others, may value certain applications of its theories in practice and so promote certain forms of technological or social change. On the other hand the need for research may favor protecting a phenomenon from change. A discipline may even require of its adherents certain lifestyles (such as participant-observer in an alien social setting) or place unusual stresses on personal or family life. It has been suggested that professionally "inside" jokes reveal shared tacit values of a discipline.

These value dimensions provide for several sorts of commonality with Christian values. Commonality, of course, may be an occasion not only for integration, but also for tension. The Christian in any discipline must therefore explore the values of his discipline in order to uncover areas of common commitment as well as areas of tension.

Consider the value commitments and tensions experienced by a Christian anthropologist. Her work as an investigator may require the sacrifice of important family values while living in the culture she is investigating. The priorities of her investigation, moreover, may favor protecting the culture from external influences that contaminate her observations, while her Christian values suggest the importance of evangelistic work among the people of the culture. On the other hand the investigation of the culture might be seen as important as a preliminary stage in such evangelism. Of course such study may also be a source of tension for the Christian anthropologist because of the realization that her work may also be the first step in secularizing and introducing many of the baser western influences into the culture.

Two of the writers in this volume explore the relation of Judaeo-Christian value notions to the values imbedded in their disciplines. Interestingly both focus on the value of creation and creativity. In

"God's Creation and Human Creativity," Best explores some of the ways divine creativity is suggestive for human, Christian creativity in the arts. In "Mathematics: Freedom Within Bounds," Heie probes the value assumptions that underlie various types of mathematical activity to determine what legitimate satisfactions these might offer a Christian mathematician.

Systematic Schemata

Because academic disciplines are abstractive projects, their results demand supplementation from other perspectives to be rendered meaningful and to guard against reductionism. In addition to exploring commonalities and tensions in the assumptions of disciplines, a third strategy involves relating the *results* of disciplinary study to Christian beliefs within a broader framework that embraces both. This attempt to create a consistent, coherent, comprehensive way of seeing is sometimes referred to as constructing a world and life view.

Perhaps a simpler way of thinking about this process is that it involves placing the results of the discipline and the biblical vision into a single picture, or interpreting the various results from a Christian point of view. Putting it this way must not distract us from the way the various disciplines and theories within disciplines mold and abstract their facts. It is necessary to examine carefully the assumptions underlying "factual results" before a synthesis has integrity. In any case, disciplines *do* produce results that invite or require Christian interpretation, and that is the essence of this integrative strategy.

There are two basic approaches to forming systematic schemata. One I will call the *heterogeneous* type. In this type of schema the individual disciplines (or even different theoretical approaches within a single discipline) are regarded as separate perspectives on reality, but the results are not synthesized into a higher conceptual unity. Rather they are preserved as complementary accounts which resist "reduction" to each other or some other philosophical framework. Often this approach ranks the disciplines in some ascending order, so that the higher levels reveal more fully the meaning of the lower levels. Usually the theological level is regarded as the highest level in such a Christian system. The Dooyeweerdian view stresses the irreducibility of the various orders of creation to any alternative categories but sees them all as part of a system of distinct spheres which are nevertheless interdependent for their meaning and all dependent upon God. In MacKay's view each discipline tells a different but complementary "story" about reality, but there are higher and lower levels of meaning. Each of these is an example of heterogeneous schematizing.

The other sort of systematizing I will call the *homogeneous* type. In this type of schema the results of the various disciplines are synthesized into a single, unified conceptual framework. The categories employed in the specific disciplines are superseded by a more comprehensive set of categories that are taken to permeate and explain all disciplinary results, or of which all disciplinary activities are taken to be partial, special cases. The Aristotelian-Thomistic synthesis sees everything as instances of hylomorphic individuals progressing from potentiality to actuality under the influence of a prime mover. The Whitehead-Hartshorne synthesis sees everything as processes lured toward value by a bipolar God. The Bowne-Brightman-Bertocci synthesis sees all of reality, including nature, as ultimately reflecting personal categories. All of these are examples of homogeneous schematizing.

Among the essays in this book the articles by Hodges, Clark and Gaede, and Jones are examples of schematic systematizing. In "Perception Is Relative and Veridical," Hodges argues that an adequate psychology of knowing has a great deal in common with a biblical view of knowing. The paper by Clark and Gaede, entitled "Knowing Together," explores the implications for Christian belief of a condition that both Christians and sociologists must take seriously, the effects of social reality on the knowing process. Jones, in "The Human Brain and the Meaning of Humanness," speaks to a concern common to both Christians and many biologists, specifically how the narrowly biological categories of brain research relate to our broader concept of persons and their abilities.

INTEGRATIVE PLURALISM

This brief taxonomy of integrative strategies focusing on substantive and methodological presuppositions, value commitments, and systematic schemata suggests that there are a variety of legitimate approaches to the integration of faith and learning. Perhaps some disciplines lend themselves to one approach better than another. Perhaps the personality of the integrator is an important factor in the particular insights that are generated. In any case it must not be thought that one and only one approach is possible. Even the essays mentioned above may be seen in different ways. Perhaps the philosophy essay by Evans focuses more on the common value of rational inquiry than on common substantive or methodological presuppositions. Hodges's psychology essay and the sociology essay by Clark and Gaede may be seen as attempts to rethink and transform the substantive presuppositions of these disciplines as well as create a synthetic view. In the mathematics essay by Heie the analysis of value commitments is embedded in an integrative proposal that "freedom within bounds" is a concept that provides the proper framework for all of one's choices as a Christian, not just the choice to do mathematics. Sometimes the carrying out of one strategy demands one or more of the other strategies as a preliminary step.

Some of the advantages of drawing the line of demarcation where I have, using the criterion of integral commonality between the Christian faith and the historically diverse projects we call academic disciplines, are the following: (1) The commonalities between the Christian faith and a discipline give us and our students reasons as Christians for engaging in that discipline (in addition to whatever personal or social reasons may be operating). (2) In the integrative process a legitimate discipline may be enriched with Christian insights. (3) Alternately, our Christian vision may be enriched and enlarged by the insights of our discipline.

All integration is based on the notion of integral commonality, or the sharing of concepts and concerns by the areas to be placed within a single vision. To speak of the integration of faith and learning, of religion and science, of Christianity and the arts, of revelation and philosophy, is to postulate some common ground between the members of the pairs mentioned. The diversity of integrative strategies which Christian thinkers employ discloses the various sorts of commonality possible.

PART II
Disciplinary Essays

Political Science

COMMENTARY

Skillen begins his essay by calling into question the way political science has been conceived by one important contemporary practitioner, Karl Deutsch. Skillen rejects the substantive (ontological) assumptions underlying Deutsch's positivistic and behavioristic view that conceives political reality in natural scientific terms. Such a view fails as a foundation for value judgments (including the value commitments it assumes), nor does it deal adequately with the complexity of the political order.

In place of Deutsch's view Skillen proposes an ontological view that sees the political as one of the many dimensions of human life, each of which has been given its appropriate values in the structure of God's creation. This view requires that we distinguish the political (public legal relationships) from other areas of human life and see it as appropriately shaped by its special value, namely public justice.

Mouw points out that Skillen has made three substantive and value assumptions in his proposal. (1) God has created the variety in human cultural life, (2) God has ordained specific values for each aspect of that cultural life, and (3) public justice is the value appropriate to political communities. Mouw expresses some difficulty with each of these claims, suggesting that they "follow an order . . . of increasing challengeability from a Christian point of view." In contrast to Skillen, Mouw suggests that we take seriously John Yoder's proposal that human cultural life is so infected by sin that our only option is to create alternative communities governed by patterns of mutual servanthood. This further calls into question Skillen's assumption that justice is *the* central norm of political life.

Three distinct Christian approaches to the political are discussed in these essays. (1) The dualistic Lutheran-Niebuhr approach: There is a tension between the independent, nonreligious natural order (including the political sphere) and the spiritual order which is under submission to Christ. (2) The Reformed-Dooyeweerd approach: Reality is an integral whole ordered by God into interrelated spheres, each subject to God according to its appropriate norms. In the political sphere this norm is public justice. (3) The Anabaptist-Yoder approach: Sin is so radical that we neither know the original purposes of God in creation, nor does the cultural order reflect them. We must obey the gospel then by following

Christ, setting up counter-institutions informed by Jesus' principles without hoping for any widespread renewal of society.

In terms of the taxonomy of integrative strategies spelled out in the introduction, this pair of essays focuses on value commitments in political science, though especially in Skillen's essay this is closely wedded to substantive assumptions about the nature of human beings and political reality. Skillen's approach is to transform current political science along lines guided by the Christian philosophy of Herman Dooyeweerd. Mouw's view, while sympathetic to much of what Skillen has done, is much more pluralistic. Not only may various theories in political science be insightful (including Deutsch's), but Christians may legitimately take alternative approaches to the political arena. Mouw's essay reflects a greater tolerance for compatibility between existing ways of doing political science and the Christian faith.

Can There Be a Christian Approach to Political Science?

JAMES W. SKILLEN

An essay that attempts to display the meaningfulness of a Christian approach to political science should do more than pick out one particular method or one piece of the science in order to show some point of connection between it and Christian faith. At the same time, a single essay cannot encompass all of the issues and problems in the discipline in a comprehensive fashion. An important decision about the scope and aim of such an essay must be made at the start.

This essay will aim for a broad focus—trying to deal with questions and issues that touch or control the whole field of politics. It will do so by concentrating on the point of departure, the starting point, of a science of politics, the point where the most important controlling assumptions and convictions of the political scientist are uncovered. The reason for choosing this approach can perhaps best be explained by looking briefly at one of the most influential political scientists of our day, Karl W. Deutsch, of Harvard University. Even a brief consideration of Deutsch will show how the details of a science are selected, shaped, guided, and refined within a basic framework or fundamental view of both politics and science held by the scientist. The implications for a Christian approach to political study should become evident rather quickly.

Karl Deutsch is the kind of political scientist that wants to rationalize or systematize politics in an almost natural scientific fashion. His assumptions are clear and simple in their disregard of what Plato or Aristotle would have recognized as the integral complexity of human moral and political reality. Deutsch is not simply agnostic when it comes to considerations of justice and morality. His view of human nature and the world is that of a closed universe manifesting stimulus-response actions and reactions based on the struggle for satisfaction and survival against pain and death. True justice is not merely unknowable for a science of politics; it is an irrelevant matter when it comes to an examination of the "facts."

Repeatedly Deutsch makes use of physical, mathematical, and mechanical illustrations and concepts in order to render his analysis of political life. For example, with respect to international relations, Deutsch says:

> The making of foreign policy thus resembles a pinball machine game. Each interest group, each agency, each important official, legislator, or national opinion leader, is in the position of a pin, while the emerging decision resembles the end-point of the path of a steel ball bouncing down the board from pin to pin. Clearly, some pins will be placed more strategically than others, and on the average they will thus have a somewhat greater influence on the outcome of the game. But no one pin will determine the outcome. Only the distribution of all the relevant pins on the board—for some or many pins may be so far out on the periphery as to be negligible—will determine the distribution of outcomes. This distribution often can be predicted with fair confidence for large numbers of runs, but for the single run—as for the single decision—even at best only some probability can be stated.[1]

Deutsch's approach requires that his questions be confined arbitrarily to the "hows" that might yield empirical descriptions and measurements. He does not ask about the "whys" and "oughts" or about the conditioning assumptions which guide his investigation of the "hows." Such questions about politics are not "scientific" in Deutsch's view. Nevertheless, since he needs a general concept with which to integrate all the factual details related to politics, Deutsch readily accepts the term *system* for that purpose. The concept of *system* is a very abstract and general "tool" which is supposed to guide the scientist in selecting and collecting *political* facts. But Deutsch defines *politics* only after he has defined *system*, and by that time the full moral, juridical, human reality of political life can no longer be grasped or contained in his reduced concept of system. Deutsch's view of both science and politics is highly reductionistic at the very outset.

What does it mean to charge Deutsch with reductionism? In his writings Deutsch shows great dependence on the work of Norbert Wiener, the mathematician and cybernetic theorist, and Talcott Parsons, a sociological systems theorist.[2] From Parsons he obtains an idea of the social system that is not qualified in any specific way. Deutsch accepts Parson's conclusion that "there are certain fundamental things

---

1. Karl W. Deutsch, *The Analysis of International Relations*, 2d ed. (Englewood Cliffs, NJ: Prentice-Hall, 1978), pp. 89–90. Another example is Deutsch's comparison of the political system with a telephone switchboard. See *The Nerves of Government* (New York: Free Press, 1964), pp. 76–98.

2. See especially Deutsch's *Nerves of Government*. Also see Robert L. Pfaltzgraff, Jr., "Karl Deutsch and the Study of Political Science," *The Political Science Reviewer* 2 (Fall 1972):90–111, and Egbert Schurrman, *Technology and the Future: A Philosophical Challenge* (Toronto: Wedge Publishing, 1980), pp. 179–213.

that must be done in every social system, large or small (that is, in every group, every organization, every country) if it is to endure."[3] The things which must be done by a social system include (1) maintaining itself, (2) adapting itself to change, (3) attaining its goals, and (4) integrating its own internal and complex diversity. The scientific key to the functions of any social system, according to Deutsch, is to chart the "flow" of the system's communication network which functions as a cybernetic web (Wiener's concept) within the system and which also connects it with its external environment.

It should be clear to any social scientist that Deutsch, following Wiener and Parsons, has indeed abstracted certain universal dimensions or functions of every social entity. It is hard to object to Deutsch's conclusion that social entities generally seek to maintain their identities, adapt to change, maintain a flow of communication, and so forth. The fundamental problem is that the study of any particular function of a social system presupposes the system's identity as a whole. Deutsch does not indicate an awareness of this, and as a consequence he tends to reduce the political (or any other) system to its communication patterns or to its general functions without explaining *what* it is that is functioning in that way. Instead of first accounting for *what* is political and then carefully examining the abstracted communication flows, Deutsch works backward by first positing an abstract, general social or cybernetic system and then using that abstraction to identify political life and processes. The effect is to reduce the integral reality of political life to one or two of its functions.[4]

Furthermore, even though Deutsch is not claiming to say anything moral or normative, he nevertheless believes that a political system which suffers a communication breakdown or disappears or fails to adapt quickly to change or fails to attain its goals or remains disorganized is not living up to the universal necessity of survival and development which is incumbent upon all systems by definition. In other words, such a system is *not* doing what it *ought* to do if it wants to survive and grow. The conceptual tool of *system* thus enables the theorist to do more than simply describe facts; it also helps him make judgments about "successful" and "unsuccessful" systems based on the analyst's predisposition

3. Deutsch, *Analysis of International Relations*, p. 14.

4. When Deutsch, both in this book and elsewhere, defines a "people," he does so in a very abstract way: "A people, then, is a group with complementary communication habits whose members usually share the same language, and always share a similar culture so that all members of the group attach the same meanings to words. In that sense a people is a community of shared meanings." *Politics and Government: How People Decide Their Fate*, 2d ed. (Boston: Houghton Mifflin, 1974), p. 130.

to believe that things (including social things) *ought* to survive rather than perish.

Every social system is defined by the above abstraction, in Deutsch's view. What, then, is a "political system" as distinguished from a non-political system? Deutsch cannot be very helpful at this point. He assumes that by common sense we are all acquainted with "laws" and "forces" which characterize a "nation-state."[5] A state is a political system which, in turn, is nothing more than combined individual behavior patterns. "*Politics* consists in the more or less incomplete control of human behavior through voluntary habits of *compliance* in combination with threats of probable *enforcement*. In its essence, politics is based on the interplay of habits of cooperation as modified by threats."[6]

Deutsch does not ask whether the individual habits preceded and helped shape the particular contours of the political system or whether, to the contrary, they were created by the system. He does not ask why such systems came into existence in the variety of shapes and sizes in which we find them. He does not defend himself against the charge that the above definition no more defines a *political* system than it defines a family, a school, a business enterprise, or some other institution, since all social systems depend on voluntary compliance and the use of some kind of enforceable threats. Deutsch goes on to talk about "law," but he does not distinguish state (political) law from church law or school rules or business regulations. In other words, the very thing which needs to be accounted for, namely, the identity of the political system, is passed over rather quickly with some statements about behavior patterns. If this seems inadequate or peculiar, it is so only for the person who is looking for something more than measurements of and probability predictions about certain functions performed by existing domestic and international habits of political behavior.

Almost unrelated to his scientific study of communication flows and system functions, and certainly without adequate historical evidence or argument, Deutsch voices his hope at one point for the eventual attainment of world security and unity. His expression of hope seems to be rooted in nothing more than his belief that human beings, when forced up against the wall, will find a way to survive rather than perish. Deutsch believes that somehow a system will appear that can survive.

> An era of pluralism and, at best, of pluralistic security communities, may well characterize the near future. In the long term, however, the search for

5. The term *nation-state*, which Deutsch frequently uses, manifests one of the ways in which he has inadequately identified politics or the state. Note the criticism of Walker Connor, "Nation-Building or Nation Destroying," *World Politics* 24 (April 1972):319–55.

6. Deutsch, *Analysis of International Relations*, p. 19.

integrated political communities that command both peace and power, and that entail a good deal of amalgamation, is likely to continue until it succeeds. For such success, not only good will and sustained effort, but political creativity and inventiveness will be needed, together with a political culture of greater international openness, understanding, and compassion.

Without such a new political climate and new political efforts, humanity is unlikely to survive for long. But the fact that so many people in so many countries are becoming aware of the problem, and of the need for increasing efforts to deal with it, makes it likely that it will be solved.[7]

Unfortunately Deutsch contributes little or nothing to our understanding of how compassion, openness, understanding, inventiveness, and political creativity can be found or nurtured. He offers no explanation of why these ingredients will be or should be desired and sought by the same human beings who display behavior patterns that all too frequently lack such virtues.[8] He excludes these matters from his consideration as a political scientist.

The point of these remarks about Deutsch is to show that a political scientist's general disposition toward both science and politics will structure the outcome of all the particular investigations that scientist carries out. In Deutsch's case the key to the discipline is training in systems theory and measurement of behavior patterns. Historical, philosophical, moral, and legal reflection is minimized if not ignored altogether. One's views of science and politics mutually limit and reinforce each other; the historical, legal, and ethical dimensions of politics do not figure prominently in Deutsch's work.

What should this mean for a Christian approach to the study of politics? At the very least, a Christian approach to the discipline should

7. Ibid., p. 253.

8. Pfaltzgraff comments: "Deutsch calls for unprecedented breakthroughs in the social sciences toward an understanding of international conflict. His assumption is that, having gained such understanding, peoples would forego war for peace. He thus calls for a transformation in human behavior as remarkable as the advances which he proposes in the social sciences. The political transformation for which Deutsch calls at the international level far exceeds both in scope and in rapidity those which he describes in the development historically of political communities at the national level. If the prospects for their realization in the international system of the next generation are minimal, the question remains as to whether Deutsch's assessment of the future is accurate." "Karl Deutsch and the Study of Political Science," p. 107. For some background and criticism of the traditions in which Deutsch stands, see Floyd W. Matson, The Broken Image (Garden City, NY: Doubleday, Anchor Books, 1964), pp. 66–110; Alec Barbrook, Patterns of Political Behaviour (Itasca, IL: F. E. Peacock, 1975); Stanislav Andreski, Social Sciences as Sorcery (New York: St. Martin's Press, 1972); Gabriel Almond, "Political Theory and Political Science," American Political Science Review 60 (December 1966):869–79; Peter Nettl, "Concept of System in Political Science," Political Studies (October 1966):305–38.

include reflection on the roots and predispositions of different theorists' approaches. Deutsch's methods and assumptions are rooted in positivistic theory, with its peculiar bias toward the phenomena that can be measured. Those methods are not universally accepted, nor are they very old. A Christian approach ought to be more empirical, at least in the sense that it tries to account for all or most of the approaches being used in political science rather than being dogmatic in its own approach while ignoring those approaches which it finds incompatible with its own. Such an effort will necessitate considerable historical and philosophical study. Political philosophy (theory) will be an important dimension of the discipline as taught and studied by Christians.

Furthermore, a Christian approach ought to be fully self-conscious of its own starting point and basic convictions. Since every scientist has a starting point, it is not problematic that Christians have one also. The only unscientific mistake would be to act as if one's own biases are not influential or to be ignorant of one's own presuppositions. Political science, like every other discipline, is a constant effort to interpret reality in the light of one's experience, convictions, methods of analysis, and suppositions about what science and politics are all about.

A Christian interpretation of politics should begin self-consciously and without apology as part of the broader response of Christians to the only true God, revealed in Jesus Christ. It should not be embarrassed to reject the starting points of the dominant political ideologies and philosophies of the day—the religious myths of "popular sovereignty," "the withering away of the state," "nationalism," "economic progress," "pragmatism," "balance of power," "positivism," and so forth. A Christian science of politics is not mythical or religious in contrast to the supposedly secular-rational character of other sciences of politics. It is simply a self-conscious approach that does not seek to hide its deepest presuppositions under the myth of "neutrality."

In introductory political science courses it has been my habit to spend time encouraging students to reflect on their experiences at home, in school, and elsewhere through which they have gained their "perspective" on politics. I explain my own background quite personally, showing some of the difficulties of dealing with politics and political science as a Christian. The chief error to be avoided, in other words, is that of pretending that some "research methods" can be learned which will give the student "objective" entrance into political reality without having to become conscious of the biases and contradictions that already inhabit or control the student's life and perspective.

A Christian understanding of politics should have everything to do with the present world in its actual political configurations. It should be concerned with the power of justice in God's creation, nothing more, nothing less. But it recognizes that it has its roots in God's creation, normed by divine justice, and in the confession of Christ's lordship over that creation. It does not begin dogmatically with the reduction of politics to the maintenance of certain system functions or with the unaccounted for norm of "survivability."

Not every attempt by Christians to interpret or explain politics has led in the same direction, of course, and thus we cannot speak of a Christian approach to politics as if there has been only one. Our dialogue with other Christians, then, will be as important as the ongoing dialogue with non-Christians about their approaches and conclusions. As a brief illustration of this important ingredient in studying politics, let us consider the work of Reinhold Niebuhr, one of the most important twentieth-century Christian students of politics. Niebuhr's view of politics was certainly shaped by the biblical tradition, but it is clear that his appreciation of God's sovereignty, Christ's lordship, and the creation's meaningfulness was an ambiguous one, due to the influence of other streams of thought.

Human beings, according to Niebuhr, differ from the world of nature to the degree that reason directs their energy. "Man is the only creature which is fully self-conscious. His reason endows him with a capacity for self-transcendence."[9] Within this reasoning consciousness, however, humans also harbor a sense of the absolute, a sense which transcends the limits of reason. That sense is religion.[10] Religious experience is the special domain of the imagination. In higher religions the imagination tends toward an interpretation of the absolute as benevolent will with a consequent increase in its condemnation of all selfish actions and desires.

> In investing the heart of the cosmos with an ethical will, the religious imagination unites its awe before the infinitude and majesty of the physical world with its reverence for the ethical principle of the inner life. The inner world of conscience, which is in constant rebellion against the outer world of nature, is made supreme over the world of nature by the fiat of religion.[11]

For Niebuhr the creation is not a harmonious unity, subject in its totality to the ordinances of God. God is not the unambiguous author and norm-giver of all of life. According to Niebuhr, human beings are really the authors of their religion, and religion, by its very character (a

9. Reinhold Niebuhr, *Moral Man and Immoral Society* (New York: Scribner's, 1960), p. 25.

10. Ibid., p. 52

11. Ibid.

product of the inner spirit), stands in constant rebellion against the world of nature. The creation is inherently ambiguous, existing with an inner dualism between the free, human spirit and the world of nature. This is important for an understanding of Niebuhr's conception of political life because the religious consciousness with its ethical viewpoint also exists in tension with the social world and the political arena. Religion belongs to the individual person and is related to the social world only by way of irreconcilable conflict. "The social viewpoint stands in sharpest contrast to religious morality when it views the behavior of collective rather than individual man, and when it deals with the necessities of political life. Political morality, in other words, is in the most uncompromising antithesis to religious morality."[12]

With respect to the biblical revelation about human sinfulness, Niebuhr is emphatic but also ambiguous. He stresses the power and importance of sin—human rebellion against God. But that rebellion does not in itself explain the malformation of society and politics. In fact, according to Niebuhr, the emphasis placed on human sin against God may tend to obscure rather than illumine some "lesser sins."

> One interesting aspect of the religious yearning after the absolute is that, in the contrast between the divine and the human, all lesser contrasts between good and evil on the human and historic level are obscured. Sin finally becomes disobedience to God and nothing else. Only rebellion against God, and only the impertinence of self-will in the sight of God, are regarded as sinful. . . . The sin which the religious man feels himself committing against God is indeed the sin of self-will; but his recognition of that fact may, but need not, have special social significance.[13]

The meaning of religion, for Niebuhr, and consequently the significance of sin, is not interpreted in relation to a wholly dependent creation. Rebellion against God "need not" have special social significance. Human religion and human sin against God belong to that inner spirit of the individual; consequently, the malformation of society and of political life cannot be judged simply as disobedience to God through the failure to heed his creational norms. As Niebuhr explains: "If we contemplate the conflict between religious and political morality it may be well to recall that the religious ideal in its purest form has nothing to do with the problem of social justice. . . . Pure religious idealism does not concern itself with the social problem."[14]

---

12. Ibid., p. 259.

13. Ibid., p. 269. On Niebuhr at this point see John H. Hallowell, *Main Currents in Modern Political Thought* (New York: Holt, Rinehart & Winston, 1950), pp. 663ff., and Cecil L. Eubanks, "Reinhold Niebuhr: The Dialectics of Grace and Power," *The Political Science Reviewer* 8 (Fall 1978):115ff.

14. Niebuhr, *Moral Man and Immoral Society*, p. 263.

From Niebuhr's standpoint, those who enter politics actively should try to work for the best answers. There is a normativity that binds human beings somehow. Many if not most decisions, however, will involve choosing the lesser of two evils, and in democratic countries it can mean, at best, "finding proximate solutions for insoluble problems."[15] To whatever degree this may sound realistic, it raises at least one problem to which John H. Hallowell points: "Since Niebuhr rejects, however, any conception of absolute and universal justice it is difficult to understand what the solutions are to 'approximate' or how we are to determine or evaluate the degree of 'proximity' attained."[16]

Niebuhr does confess that the kingdom of God is "relevant to every problem of the world,"[17] but he does not show very clearly how that kingdom is related to the creation. The kingdom of God, though pertaining to every earthly problem, is not a kingdom which restores creational norms governing every sphere of human life. The judgment of sin is not something that gives us a clear guide to responsible action here and now in politics in relation to those principles which *do* belong to the coming kingdom of righteousness. Religious faith in Christ can at best envision an ideal situation that has only an ambiguous relationship to the real circumstances of present-day politics.

> Whenever religious idealism brings forth its purest fruits and places the strongest check upon selfish desire it results in policies which, from the political perspective, are quite impossible. There is, in other words, no possibility of harmonising the two strategists [sic] designed to bring the strongest inner and most effective social restraint upon egoistic impulse. It would therefore seem better to accept a frank dualism in morals than to attempt a harmony between the two methods which threatens the effectiveness of both.[18]

Thus, the idea that the religious vision of God's kingdom, held by individuals, could be effective in shaping both political life and a uniquely Christian science of politics is an illusion. Absolute principles of justice and love will hardly be glimpsed by the purest of religious individuals and will never be practiced perfectly by them. Societal discernment or action has no chance of displaying a principled character which could presume to identify itself with the cause or perspective of Christ's kingdom. The compelling judgment and redemption of Christ may not be thought of as embracing the historical world in such a fashion.

Niebuhr does not intend his "dualism in morals" to be a simple separa-

---

15. Quoted in Hallowell, *Main Currents*, p. 671.
16. Ibid.
17. Ibid., pp. 666–67.
18. Niebuhr, *Moral Man and Immoral Society*, pp. 270–71.

tion of the religious and the political realms.[19] In fact, people with religious illusions will always be necessary for the improvement of the social world. But the relation between these two spheres remains one of interacting ambiguity. If the kingdom of God is the fulfillment of human history, its meaning cannot be anticipated now in terms of any unambiguous, concrete action which would point toward and reveal a bit of that "heavenly light." A science of politics could hardly claim to take as its point of departure a biblical insight into the normative principles of justice which hold for earthly politics. Helmut Kuhn commented:

> [Niebuhr's] portrayal shows man as the sinner groping along a hazardous path between precipices of error rather than as the ardent lover who presses on, divinely guided, toward an exuberance of light; and the Deity to Whom this finite and erring creature raises his eyes is the righteous God "that trieth the hearts and reins" (Ps. 7, 9) rather than bounty without measure.[20]

In contrast to Niebuhr's ambiguity regarding the nature of politics, I believe that Christians should approach politics with a very clear and unambiguous assertion about God's sovereignty and the creation's meaningfulness. God's rule over all things in Christ is an integral, total, nondualistic, creational, redemptive lordship. (See, e.g., Gen. 1; Lev. 25; Job 38–42; Dan. 4:1–3, 6:25–27; Luke 1:30–33, 46–55, 4:16–30; John 1:1–5; Rom. 8:18–39; 1 Cor. 15:20–28; Col. 1:15–19; Heb. 1:1–

19. A frank and simple dualism uncharacteristic of Niebuhr is nonetheless characteristic of many Christians, whether political scientists or simply citizens. One clear illustration is the following by Manford G. Gutzke. Political events and systems, he argues, do not pertain "to faith and none of that is any part of the issues associated with the Gospel. God has a message for believers and He has given a commission to believers, but neither the message nor the commission pertain to human *politics!* . . . Some today conceive that the Lord Jesus Christ wants His people to play political games in the international and national arenas. Well, I can tell you that the Lord Jesus Christ had two things to say about politics. In His first statement He said, 'Render unto Caesar the things that are Caesar's and unto God the things that are God's.' In other words, a Christian's attitude towards practical politics is that he has an obligation as a citizen to pay his taxes, to obey the laws and to do everything that his country rightfully requires of him.

"The second saying of the Lord Jesus on the subject of politics was even more succinct. He said: 'My kingdom is not of this world. If my kingdom were of this world then would my servants fight.'

"The Lord Jesus, in other words, was saying He did not intend to convey the impression that it was His mission to become involved in 'political realities', nor was it His desire that His followers should go forth believing they had a mandate to become involved in political realities as an expression of their fundamental mission in the world." *The Presbyterian Journal* (14 June 1972):20.

20. Helmut Kuhn, "Charity and Contemplation: Comments on Reinhold Niebuhr's Gifford Lectures, Vol. Two," *Philosophy and Phenomenological Research* 4 (1944):432.

4; Rev. 1:4–8, 4:1–11, 20–22.) This view of God's rule would imply the rejection not only of Niebuhr's conflicting dualities (religion/nature; individual/social) but also of Deutsch's fact/value dichotomy. It would also require a critical reassessment of the traditional "Christian" positions which have borrowed so heavily from Greek and Roman traditions. A biblical approach to the study of politics cannot begin with the idea of an independent natural realm ruled by natural law or natural reason, existing alongside a supernatural realm ruled by Christ and the church.[21] Taking biblical revelation seriously will require criticism of Luther's understanding of two kingdoms—one of law and one of love, one of nature and one of grace, one ruled by the sword and another ruled by mercy and peace, one in which Christians serve the gospel inwardly and another in which all people serve the world outwardly.[22] Attempting to gain a Christian perspective on political life will require a reevaluation of the Augustinian and Anabaptist view that "the sword is ordained of God outside the perfection of Christ"—a viewpoint which grants that a political authority "serves as God's instrument" but cannot be "truly righteous."[23] A biblical view of politics would also appear to be incom-

21. For a discussion of the western idea of a natural/supernatural distinction in politics, see Ernst Cassirer, *The Myth of the State* (New Haven: Yale University Press, 1946), pp. 106–15, and Walter Ullman, *A History of Political Thought: The Middle Ages* (Baltimore: Penguin Books, 1965), pp. 174–85.

22. See William A. Mueller, *Church and State in Luther and Calvin* (Garden City, NY: Doubleday, Anchor Books, 1954), pp. 1–70, and Thomas G. Sanders, *Protestant Concepts of Church and State* (Garden City, NY: Doubleday, Anchor Books, 1964), pp. 29–39.

23. Sanders, *Protestant Concepts*, pp. 94–97, 108, and the Schleitheim Confession (1527), art. 6. In his book *The Politics of Jesus* (Grand Rapids: Eerdmans, 1972), John Howard Yoder continues the basic Anabaptist argument. He admits that the New Testament speaks of the whole creation being established in Christ (Col. 1), but, he argues, since the fall into sin we no longer have "access to the good creation of God." The fall is not total in the sense that the "powers" have now become "limitlessly evil," but they "have claimed the status of idols and have succeeded in making men serve them as if they were of absolute value" (pp. 143–44). Yoder's problem, it seems to me, comes in failing to distinguish between the actual sinful responses of humans and the normative goodness of the creation order. What he does not see is that the good creation order in its perfect normativity is not what falls into sin but is precisely that which exposes our sinful failure to fulfill its demands. The Scriptures certainly do not enjoin us to subject ourselves to idolatrous powers on their own terms. It is not *fallen* powers and structures claiming to be God that continue to give order to society; they are what bring the disorder. It is not *fallen* powers that are necessary to life, as Yoder claims; they are what lead to death. Whatever order is maintained on earth by the powers is due to God's gracious creational goodness and redemptive work in Christ in spite of sin, not by means of it. Indeed, by God's redeeming grace we *do* have access to the creation, for if we did not, there would be no way to understand sin and restoration.

The ambiguity in which Yoder is caught comes clearly to light when he discusses Romans 13. He argues that all governments exercise a sovereignty that includes violence

patible with the idea of the nonreligious character of the state as that idea functions in the dogma about separation of church and state.

The biblical proclamation of Christ's lordship is opposed to every notion that Christianity is primarily a personal, ecclesiastical, or super-natural force which Christians then must apply to the supposedly secular state.[24] It is an injustice to the Scriptures to begin with the supposition that politics can be understood by some neutral, empirical method which can bracket or ignore Christian "values." If a serious attempt is to be made to do political science from a Christian point of view, then the real meaning of the biblical claims about God's sovereignty, Christ's lordship, the creation's meaningfulness, sin's distorting power, and the authority of governmental offices must all be studied carefully.

In place of any dualistic or ambiguous conception, the biblical writings proclaim the single, all-embracing kingdom of God in Christ. The

---

and killing which can in no way be made a "channel of the will of God" (p. 204). A little later, however, Yoder contends that there is a norm for government whereby we can judge whether God's will is being accomplished by governmental ministers. Romans 13 teaches us, therefore, that the "ministers of God" are ministers "only to the extent to which they carry out their function. . . . We can judge and measure the extent to which a government is accomplishing its ministry, by asking namely whether it persistently (present participle) attends to rewarding of good and evil according to their merits; to be 'minister to you for good' is a criterion, not a description" (p. 208). "We are instructed," Yoder concludes, "to give government certain types of 'honor' or 'fear.' The place of government in the prov-idential designs of God is not such that our duty would be simply to do whatever it says" (p. 211).

What comes through in Yoder's argument at this point is a recognition of the God-ordained, God-revealed normativity to which we are truly subject as Christians. Indeed, then, we are not subject to fallen powers in their sinfulness come what may; we are not enjoined to obey evil commands of those powers. Much rather, we are subject to the Lord in all things and are subject to government by God's command in order to fulfill his justice. Likewise, governmental authorities are also subject to the norm which Yoder has enunci-ated, and insofar as they do not serve the Lord in rendering justice, they are not his true servants.

Such insight into Paul's letter to the Romans should be enough to drive Yoder back to a reexamination of his pacifist conviction that the use of the sword as such can in no way serve the Lord's call to obedient and loving servanthood "inside the perfection of Christ." Instead of insisting on the great disjunction between Rom. 12:19 and 13:4, we should recognize that God's establishment of the earthly office of government for the exercise of God's wrath against the evil doer is God's act and God's command. Precisely because Christians must leave vengeance and wrath to the Lord, they ought not to be unwilling to hold a divinely ordained office for the exercise of governmental justice. For the unique character of the governmental office is that it is normed by God. Killing, murder, and human vengeance are no more a legitimate part of that office than they are a legitimate part of an individual's office of loving servanthood. Earthly governments are commissioned to use the sword only in a way that is fully compatible with Christ's redemptive authority.

24. Sanders, Protestant Concepts, pp. 264–312.

very possibility for the existence of any political order (distinguishable from ecclesiastical, economic, scientific, educational, and familial orders) is due to God's gracious rule in Christ—the rule through which God also upholds marriage, family, business, education, and everything else. The fact that many states manifest so much injustice, or that so many marriages end in divorce, or that many families are warped by hatred, or that many businesses harm the environment or the labor force, or that many schools are not doing much educating—all of these are sinful distortions of God's gracious order of life which holds the legitimate diversity of creaturely life together for good. The meaning of such human malformation should be interpreted as distortion of the good creation order which God is renewing in Christ. That divine orderliness remains as the normative light which exposes disorder and maintains the identities of creaturely things and actions. Without that creation order upheld in Christ, there would be no ability for a political scientist even to distinguish what is political from what is nonpolitical.

Sin, therefore, does not wipe out the creation, nor does it completely dominate politics. God's grace in Christ restores all things and calls us to seek justice on earth as it exists in heaven. The political scientist cannot confine himself to a description of the so-called political facts as though war or peace, racism or racial harmony, instability or stability are without a meaning to be evaluated. Even the possibility of distinguishing political reality from that which is not political requires a preconception, a pre-identity of the order of politics. It is not simply an option, therefore, but an obligation for Christians to discover what the unique task of government is in society, and for political scientists to explain as much of political reality as possible in the light of that task. As creatures on earth we are obligated to practice justice among our neighbors as well as to do truthful science if we are given the intellectual talents for such work. This will require the ability to distinguish justice from injustice, good political order from bad political order. Making normative judgments and distinctions about politics is an integral part of political science for a Christian, who must reject the idea that political facts can be discerned or understood apart from their norm-bound character.

The starting point for a Christian science of politics, then, must be the denial of the typical humanistic confession that human beings are the completely autonomous creators of the diverse cultural components of their existence, including their political behavior. Christians should acknowledge that human life in all its diverse dimensions is structured normatively by divine ordinances. With respect to politics this means that the Christian student should take seriously the assumption that the divine norm of public justice holds for every type of political community.

This requires, of course, that one must distinguish the normative differences among marriages, families, schools, businesses, churches, voluntary associations, informal interpersonal relationships, and political communities, because the different character of each of these communities and relationships is not accidental or arbitrary. The church must not be made over into or confused with a political party; the state must not attempt to function as a universal church or as a totalitarian community within the territory of its dominion. The state ought to be limited to its divinely given task; and business, art, science, education, and worship ought to be free to unfold according to their own distinct, nonpolitical characters. All communities and institutions cannot be treated simply as large and small "social systems" with some common system functions. The political scientist should not simply look at conflicts between personal beliefs and social morality.

The conception of political, educational, ecclesiastical, economic, and cultural life that I am describing very briefly is that of *freedom in diversity*—a *diversity* of God-ordained offices of human responsibility on the one hand, and a *unity of creational life* under God's authority on the other hand. All of the diversity is embraced by and grounded in the religious unity of creaturely life, but each area of natural and human life is free to unfold and respond to the Creator in its own way, according to its own nature. The basis for a Christian conception of politics is not the relationship of the church to political life, nor is it the relationship of confessing Christians to politics. It is neither the ecclesiastical nor individual identities of persons as Christians that provides the entrée to a Christian view of politics. A Christian approach to a science of politics must be guided by the recognition of the normative authority of God's creative, redemptive word of justice as that is obeyed and disobeyed in the actual political formations and activities that human beings carry out. All governments and political activities are obedient or disobedient responses to God's word of justice—his normative commandment for human life. Moreover, the alternative to a Christian approach is not a "neutral" or "areligious" one, but one that is driven by other religious drives and persuasions that are not Christian.

This idea that the political arena of life ought to be shaped by its own norm of public justice, in distinction from churches, schools, business enterprises, families, etc., is not the same as the idea of the separation of church and state as articulated in the liberal-conservative tradition. According to Herman Dooyeweerd, from whom I have learned a great deal about Christian normative thinking in the political and legal realms, the liberal-conservative tradition tries to "effect a watertight division between state and church" and at the same time "introduce the 'religionless state,' where faith is completely excluded." Scriptural Christianity, Dooyeweerd argues, cannot take over this idea of separation of church and state "without spiritual suicide," because it believes in the "religious root-unity of the life-spheres."[25]

Religion, as we emphasized earlier, cannot be identified solely with church life. The fact that all of life is religious, however, does not obliterate important structural differences among God-ordained communities, institutions, and relationships. All of the spheres of earthly social life are closely interwoven because they are all part of one divine creation. At the same time the diversity is guaranteed by the Creator who holds all things together. Consequently we see neither the obliteration and amalgamation of the different spheres of life nor their isolation and total separation from one another. "The various social structures by which sphere-sovereignty is internally guaranteed," Dooyeweerd explains, "do not stand alongside each other in isolation."[26]

This structural condition of the creation is what makes political totalitarianism reprehensible yet possible. Totalitarianism is possible because all spheres of life are integrally connected. If governments begin to try to take the place of the transcendent God instead of remaining bound to their normative purpose, they can attempt to reduce all of life to the dictates of superior power. When we respond to the appearance of totalitarian claims and practices with disapproval, it is because we sense that the true purpose and meaning of politics is being violated. We realize that normative limits for the state are being overrun.

A proper, healthy, just expression of the intertwinement of social spheres might be expressed in the following description that Dooyeweerd provides:

> In temporal life they are intertwined and interwoven. All other societal relationships also have a function within the state, just as conversely the state functions in all other societal relationships. But all these structural interplays remain in the final analysis of an external character with respect to sphere-sovereignty. Members of a family, a congregation, or a business enterprise are at the same time citizens. And conversely, the state is always dealing with families, churches, and business enterprises. But the competence, the sphere of jurisdiction of the state can never be expanded into the

25. Herman Dooyeweerd, *The Christian Idea of the State*. trans. John Kraay (Nutley, NJ: Craig Press, 1968), p. 49. For detailed development of Dooyeweerd's political thought see his *A New Critique of Theoretical Thought*, vol. 3, trans. David H. Freeman and H. De Jongste (Philadelphia: Presbyterian & Reformed Publishing, 1957), pp. 379–508; see also James W. Skillen, *The Development of Calvinistic Political Theory in the Netherlands, with Special Reference to the Thought of Herman Dooyeweerd*, Diss. (Duke University, 1974).

26. Dooyeweerd, *Christian Idea of the State*, p. 49. See also Bob Goudzwaard's *A Christian Political Option* (Toronto: Wedge Publishing, 1972).

internal, structurally determined concerns that are proper to these societal relationships without thereby violating in a revolutionary way the cosmic constitution of sphere-sovereignty.[27]

At this point one might well ask about the difference between a church in which all the members confess Christ's lordship and a state in which many (perhaps most) citizens do not confess Christ's lordship. Does the Christian confession of Christ's lordship over the political sphere lead to the idea that Christians should (if possible) try to *transform* the state into a commonwealth of confessing Christians, even if that requires the expulsion or forced "conversion" of those who do not confess Christ's lordship? It is understandable that much confusion exists over this matter, since the western world has endured centuries of Constantinian and ecclesiastical efforts to make a certain territory "Christian" by various means that have not recognized either the importance of religious freedom or the proper relation between church and state. It is also understandable that many evangelical Christians distrust the idea of "political transformationalism" after the efforts of liberal social gospelers earlier in this century and conservative "moral majority" crusaders in recent years. In fact, it is not surprising that many Christians are the most ardent advocates of a neutral, "objective" science of politics because they are most conscious of the evils and distortions in life and thought that can be perpetrated by ideologically close-minded Christians. But one need not take the so-called neutralist approach to gain an understanding of politics that is clear, realistic, and enlightened by God's word.

Biblical revelation is quite clear that whereas God constituted Israel of the old covenant in a compact way that included a political territorial organization, God has, in the revelation of Jesus Christ, inaugurated the universal kingdom of peace and justice that cannot be embraced by or identified with any earthly political state as such. The commands of Christ did not include any directives that would have required Christians to rebuild the walls of Jerusalem, or to crusade in the old territory of Israel in the Middle Ages to destroy Islam, or to establish on some new continent in the seventeenth century a "true" nation of God's people separated from all other nations.

We can only interpret this fact (together with Christ's claim to possess all authority in heaven and on earth) as a further revelation of Christ's grace during the time until he returns. In other words, human responsibility to establish political communities of justice on earth does not include the task of compelling people within those communities to

27. Dooyeweerd, *Christian Idea of the State*, pp. 49–50.

confess a particular faith or of punishing people for idolatrous worship. Such judgment is now finally and fully in the hands of Christ, the risen one. He has chosen, for a time, to restrain the final judgment which will indeed separate the confessing members of the Father's kingdom from those rebellious ones who have no part in it.

From a Christian point of view, therefore, political communities should be viewed as explicitly limited by this measure of Christ's gracious restraint of judgment; they may not attempt to reconstruct the present earth by means which Christ has not delegated to them. The state is not to be a community guided by a uniform confession of faith on the part of all its citizens. Here we can appreciate the Anabaptist contribution, which has emphasized Christ's parable of the wheat and the tares. Balthasar Hubmaier argued in 1524 that "the slayers of heretics are the worst heretics of all, in that they, contrary to Christ's teaching and practice, condemn heretics to the fire. By pulling up the harvest prematurely they destroy the wheat along with the tares."[28]

God's grace as it expresses itself in the political sphere extends by implication not only to the protection of heretics from the death penalty but also to the evenhanded distribution of public care, protection, and welfare to all, no matter what their religious confession. A Christian view of politics, therefore, is not guided by the assumption that governments should give special privilege to Christian persons and institutions over against non-Christian persons and institutions. That would be the self-seeking deformation of public justice, not Christian responsibility. Rather, politics should be understood as the responsibility for implementing the divine norm of justice for every person and social community within the state, including non-Christian persons and communities, even where and when the Christian view of life is held by a majority of citizens within that political community.

Here we can begin to see the unique shape and character that the political sphere ought to have in this age of grace. Quite unlike a family, a school, an industry, a church, or a personal friendship, the state is an all-embracing *public* community which ought to integrate all of the nonpolitical communities, relationships, institutions, and persons into a *public legal* relationship of evenhanded justice for everyone and everything within its territory of jurisdiction. It is not personal friendship or familial love or economic purpose or ecclesiastical faith that can define the nature of citizenship in a state. Nor may a state seek to turn its "power for public justice" into a "power for totalitarian control." The fact is that an all-embracing public legal community—a state—does not

28. Sanders, *Protestant Concepts*, p. 104.

own or possess the families, churches, schools, businesses, and individuals within its borders. Its embrace is solely one of guaranteeing public justice. Its task is to see that justice rules all the relationships among these persons and diverse communities.

A Christian view of politics should certainly be concerned with the Christian transformation of earthly society ("Thy will be done on earth as it is in heaven"), but the kind of *political* transformation which should interest Christians is the transformation which comes by God's grace working through obedience to his norm of justice and mercy for every person. The norm of politics is not Christians transforming the state into a church for God by force. It is God transforming politics into true justice for all human creatures. Christ is the one who is redeeming and transforming the world by his power. No group of people, no earthly nation, may claim to be God's unique, transforming, political instrument since the only transforming instrument has already been revealed—Jesus Christ. Still, every group of Christians in every earthly state ought to be acting communally, in obedience to Christ's gracious, resurrection rule, to transform public injustice into public justice in those earthly political communities. This view of political life ought to be the structured framework within which a careful, exact, and empirical study of contemporary politics is carried out.

In the light of what has just been said, we can conclude by pointing out three important interconnected dimensions of a Christian understanding of politics: historical development, the relation of actual political structures to divine normativity, and human responsibility.

From the initial chapters of Genesis on through to Revelation, Scripture teaches clearly that God has given us *responsibilities* for which we are held accountable. That is, it is our stewardly job to form and shape life on earth. Among other things this has meant that with the unfolding of human culture, including agriculture, art, science, technology, architecture, trade, education, and so on, new social relations have grown apace. In this creational pattern of *historical development* or unfolding, God did not reveal some "ideal form" of human government (a monarchy or a democracy or whatever), which we were supposed to aim for and, after achieving, hold onto forever without change. The ideal of frozen cultural forms comes from those ancient civilizations which did not obey God's command to go forward and follow him into the promised land in a dynamic history.

The biblical picture of stewardship, of human historical responsibility, means that we have been called in Christ to a renewed service before the face of God on earth. We have been called to assume responsibility for the historical unfolding of human culture and society. We have not been given some frozen ideal form of political society such as David's monarchy or the original constitutional order of American federalism as our "Christian" norm. To the contrary, the gospel *norm* of love, including public justice, requires that we give responsible attention to the current social configurations and circumstances of the political communities in which we live and of the world political order (disorder) as a whole. Today in the United States we face social-historical realities such as nuclear weapons, complex industrial technologies, multinational corporations, severe natural resource depletion, pollution, organized crime, institutionalized racism, urban decay, and many others, which were unknown or less problematic to the organizers of our political system at the end of the eighteenth century. As Christians we must face this state of affairs and seek new ways to obey the Lord in our political responsibilities.

For political science this means emphasizing a historically dynamic, philosophically critical, and normatively sensitive study of contemporary political systems. It is a serious mistake to concentrate too heavily on the systematizing and measuring of regularities of behavior or on the classification of comparable data, especially when the data are small elements abstracted from the larger political system. This is not to say that there is nothing to be measured or quantified or classified in politics. Rather, it is to stress the importance of the dynamic, rapidly changing, historically complex character of political life in which all kinds of human beings are making decisions which can only be understood if one has a feel for the cultural and institutional framework within which people live. A Christian approach to political science cannot simply pick a few Scripture verses or moral ideals and then look at some politically relevant data to see if they "fit" the preconceived notions. Not only will such an approach miss the broader meaning of scriptural revelation, it will leave most of politics untouched and therefore open to other methods which will have little or nothing to do with one's "Christian" analysis. A Christian approach to political science will realize the historical responsibility of the scientists as well as of citizens and politicians. It will enter into all the details of different investigative approaches to see how adequate they are for getting at contemporary political life. And it will be highly critical of methods and assumptions (on the part of both Christians and non-Christians) that ignore biblical normativity or that predetermine what is political before examining all that goes on in politics or that attempt to reduce political science to the study of only one dimension or one element of political life.

With respect to the political life that the scientist studies, historical responsibility means that human beings should be responding to *divine norms* for life. The norms are not frozen ideal forms from past experience and reflection, but the normative Word of God as it illumines the actual circumstances of our time. Every actual political, economic, and social formation—including the U.S. Constitution, the two-party system, the laws about trade and business, education and health care, etc.—all these established laws and structures are subject to the judgment of God's normative Word. That Word calls human beings to change, to repent, to overthrow, to reform the existing order where it is unjust so that God's will might be done on earth in the political arena.

Christian political scientists, therefore, should spend time directly with the Bible in their study and teaching. Not that the study of political science can be limited to Bible study, but if the approach we have outlined has any merit, then it requires politically relevant biblical interpretation, just as the study of American politics requires some interpretation of the U.S. Constitution, or the study of contemporary world politics requires some interpretation of the United Nations Charter. I am not suggesting that the Bible is a constitution or a political charter, but rather that it is a light-giving lamp for human life, including political life, and its historical, political meaning is not a dead letter. Even in order to explain most of modern political life one needs to be able to understand the secularization process in the West whereby the amalgamated biblical, Roman, and Greek cultural forms have been changed. But the Christian looks to the Bible for much more than its past influence in social life. The Christian political scientist, just as any Christian citizen, should treat the Bible as the special book that it is— God's Word, Christ's evangel, the power of life growing out of the resurrection. It is not some abstract "truth" left up to us to do with what we want. As Bob Goudzwaard, the Dutch economist and statesman, says, the gospel of Christ grabs us; we don't make use of it:

> Those who believe that truly scriptural principles for the state can be obtained solely from explicit Bible texts, base their beliefs on a completely wrong view of Scripture. They merely see words, but forget that God's Word is Spirit and Power, and that this Word has to bear upon all of life. God's Word-revelation puts you to work. It wants to influence your whole existence, it wants to bring new life where death and spiritual laziness rule. You who'd like to take it easy hope the ripe fruits of God's Word-revelation will be given to you without any efforts on your part. But Christ Jesus tells you that you yourself have to bear fruit when the seed of God's Word has fallen in fertile soil.[29]

What this means for a Christian understanding of politics is that Christians must work together in the light of the gospel according to the principles and norms which the good news allows them to see and

---

29. Goudzwaard, *Christian Political Option*, p. 27.

articulate now. Their work together must be a humble, repenting, re-forming effort to gain clearer insight and to establish greater justice with each new day. The articulation of a principle like "sphere sovereignty" is not to be taken as a final frozen revelation from God or as some complete model for political scientists to use in evaluating all political systems. Rather, it should be seen as one way to express an understanding of and response to God's revelation—a revelation which continues to tran-scend and bring into judgment all human articulations and responses.

Many important aspects of the study of politics have not been consid-ered here. Historical, numerical, legal, economic, and countless other dimensions of political study need to be refined by teams of Christian political scientists. That job cannot be done in a Christian manner, however, unless biblical revelation is taken seriously from the start rather than merely accommodated at the conclusion of one's study. A Christian approach to political science is not first of all a matter of the details; it is a matter of fundamental perspective and point of departure. Christ is King; that kingship cannot be sidetracked onto a merely sym-bolic plane. This simple fact has everything to do with a truthful in-terpretation of political reality today.[30]

30. Some other efforts by Christians to reflect on a Christian perspective in political science include: Stephen V. Monsma, *The Unraveling of America* (Downers Grove, IL: InterVarsity Press, 1974); S. Richey Kamm, "The Social Sciences: A Christian Perspec-tive," in Hudson T. Armerding, ed., *Christianity and the World of Thought* (Chicago: Moody Press, 1968), pp. 11–30; John Hallowell, "Political Science," in Hoxie N. Fairchild, ed., *Religious Perspectives in College Teaching* (New York: Ronald Press, 1952), pp. 384–422; Eduard Heiman, "Christian Foundations of the Social Sciences," *Social Research* 26 (Au-tumn 1959):325–46.

Some of my own efforts to work on particular aspects of political study from the perspective developed in this essay can be found in: "Toward Just Representation: A Proposal for Revitalizing our System of Political Participation" (a pamphlet published by the Association for Public Justice, Box 56348, Washington, D.C. 20011); "God's Ordi-nances: Calvinism in Revival," *Pro Rege* (Faculty Publication of Dordt College, June 1980):24–33; "From Covenant of Grace to Tolerant Public Pluralism: The Dutch Cal-vinist Contribution" (soon to appear in a book growing out of the Workshop on Covenant and Politics of the Center for the Study of Federalism at Temple University); "Herman Dooyeweerd's Contribution to the Philosophy of the Social Sciences," *Journal of the American Scientific Affiliation* 31 (March 1979):20–24; "Augustine and Contemporary Evangelical Social Thought," *Reformed Journal* (January 1979):19–24; and *International Politics and the Demand for Global Justice* (Sioux Center, IA: Dordt College Press, 1981). On the practical side of politics is my *Christians Organizing for Political Service* (Washington, D.C.: APJ Education Fund, 1980).

Alternative Christian Approaches to Political Science: Toward a More Comprehensive Perspective

RICHARD J. MOUW

It is obvious to some of us that the integration of faith and learning is a matter of high priority. We believe that it is of the utmost importance to attempt to formulate a Christian perspective on this or that academic discipline. We are also confident that such a perspective is within our reach, if only we would devote sufficient energy to its pursuit. The tendency to view things in this light is especially strong among those of us who, as Christian scholars, are particularly interested in the philosophical and historical aspects of one or another of the academic disciplines. "Christian perspectives" are our bread and butter, and we pursue them eagerly and confidently.

Some of our Christian colleagues, however, especially those who are hardcore "practitioners" in the disciplines, do not always share either our enthusiasm or our confidence. They exhibit a certain wariness about our pursuit of Christian perspectives. This wariness is not directed toward a specific claim or thesis that we set forth. It is much more basic—a kind of free-floating wariness. They are suspicious of the very attempt to develop a Christian perspective on the discipline in which they work.

This wariness need not be totally unfounded. To be sure, indifference to the notion of a self-consciously Christian perspective on one's discipline can stem from intellectual laziness or an uncritical acceptance of a non-Christian approach—for example, the "positivism" which Skillen discusses—or personal insecurity. But the wariness may also be rooted in concerns which have some degree of plausibility.

It is not difficult to think of understandable concerns along these lines with reference to political science. For one thing, the social sciences in general and political science in particular have experienced spectacular growth in recent decades. In many liberal arts colleges the political science departments are less than twenty years old. In recent years the discipline has experienced much refinement and diversification, with the introduction of a variety of methodological emphases and proliferation of subdisciplines ("electoral behavior," "legislative behavior," international politics, comparative government, political sociology).

Twenty years ago in a moderate-sized liberal arts college, political science was an area of teaching assigned as an extra chore to some member of the history department. Today that same college may have four political scientists with differing specialities, who worry about the fact that their department still does not have enough breadth to offer a balanced program in their discipline. In this relatively new discipline it would not be surprising if many political scientists feel harassed in their efforts to keep up with the rapid extensive and intensive growth of their discipline. Nor is it surprising if they are somewhat wary regarding the insistence that they produce a "Christian perspective"—to say nothing of *the* Christian perspective—on their field of study.

Of course, there is something especially poignant about the insistence that this particular subject matter—regardless of the relative age of the departments which study it—be integrated with Christian beliefs. Long before there were Christian political science departments, popular wisdom had it that there were two subjects about which it was futile to argue: politics and religion. Putting the two together, then, seems to be a risky business.

Suppose, for example, that you are a political science teacher at a midwestern Christian liberal arts college. Not long ago you received a Ph.D. at a reputable university. You wrote your dissertation on a comparison of the voting habits of ethnic groups in a large city. Your discoveries were not startling, but they did produce results—through the examination of voting records and the like—which differed from hunches that were shaped only by "common sense." You are excited by the fact that an empirical study of statistics can expand your students' understanding of "electoral behavior." You are convinced that there is no substitute for a painstaking examination of public records, and you are eager to show your students that it is possible to subject political phenomena to something like a "scientific" approach.

Then you read Skillen's essay. You find it irritating—not because he has said anything that is specifically nasty or illogical or unintelligent—but because you get the clear impression that he wants to undercut the very thing that you have found exciting in your work as a political scientist. People, perhaps especially Christian people, deal with political issues almost exclusively in terms of hunches and biases and prejudices, but you have found a way of cutting through much or all of that, of putting the study of politics on a firmer footing. Now Skillen seems to be insisting that you betray that project by adopting a perspective that views politics, even the study of politics, as inevitably grounded upon a "faith-commitment." Isn't Skillen asking you to trade certainties for uncertainties? Isn't it better to get on with the business of allowing political science to unfold further as a discipline than to return to a highly "philosophical" orientation toward the study of political life?

These concerns ought to be taken seriously by those of us who push for a Christian perspective on political science. For one thing, we ought to be very grateful that political phenomena are being examined much more carefully today than they have been in the past. The study of politics has finally found its proper curricular place, and present-day students in colleges and universities have unprecedented opportunities for the scholarly investigation of a host of political topics.

Even if we thought that the study of politics as it is presently pursued were hopelessly and pervasively wrongheaded, we would still find much to be grateful for. If it were the case that a total reformation of political thought is necessary, there is still so much more to reform these days than there was in the past. The Christian political scientist must rejoice over the fact that political science departments have sprouted all over the map, and that professional organizations, along with think-tanks, funding sources, and publishing ventures, have come into being in recent years.

It would be foolhardy to suggest that everything about political science today is completely confused, however. Take the two examples of wrongheadedness which Skillen offers, Deutsch and Niebuhr. Karl Deutsch may be wrong in suggesting that the making of foreign policy is *just* like a pinball game. On the other hand, it is not totally *unlike* a pinball game either. In his "reductionism" Deutsch may still have shed some light on what is going on in this area of decision making. Indeed, since many foreign policy specialists have read Karl Deutsch, they try very hard to turn foreign policy making into a pinball game. The result is that the very things which Skillen says are *missed* by Deutsch's approach—"compassion, openness, understanding, inventiveness, and political creativity"—are actually *missing* from the processes of policy making. For a variety of reasons, then, it would be myopic to ignore Deutsch's pinball metaphor in studying political processes.

And even if Reinhold Niebuhr is the kind of "dualist" Skillen accuses him of being (and I think he is), there can be no doubt that he has offered many illuminating observations and analyses about political life. Certainly no Christian political thinker can ignore his work; nor may we treat his writings as nothing more than a catalogue of interesting errors.

Skillen might have done more to assure his readers that he is aware of the gains and benefits that are ours because of recent developments in political science, but it is likely that he too is grateful for these things. Indeed, he senses something of the attraction for some Christians of the kind of "positivist" approach which he himself rejects: "It is not surprising that many Christians are the most ardent advocates of a neutral, 'objective' science of politics because they are most conscious of the evils and distortions in life and thought that can be perpetrated by ideologically close-minded Christians." Skillen too wants a "framework within which a careful, exact, and empirical study of contemporary politics is carried out."

Skillen is not against the careful study of political phenomena. Nor does he want to turn the clock back to an era when political perspectives were shaped by ideology and prejudice. Indeed it is possible to discern in his discussion a conviction that we have been witnessing positive developments in political science in recent years—albeit developments which must be harnessed and reshaped in the light of divine norms for political life. We will attempt here to get a little clearer about this conviction.

There was a Christian consensus in the medieval period that all areas of human life had to be brought into harmony with the will of God. Divine revelation addressed all spheres of life: business, family relations, art, politics, education. Of course, it was also widely believed that Christians and non-Christians would not differ significantly in their understanding of how human beings ought to behave in these various spheres. Both participated in the realm of "nature," and both had some grasp of "natural law," which provided all with some sense of norms for living in these various areas of human interaction. "Special revelation"—the teachings of the Scriptures as interpreted by the church—provided Christians with guidance which could be "added on" to what they already knew by "nature." Thus the medieval slogan, "Grace fulfills nature."

There are many complexities and nuances which could be sorted out here. But, to make a long story short, there emerged in medieval times a picture of how the will of God ought to be related to the diverse spheres of human life. We can give the picture the label *ecclesiasticism*. According to the ecclesiasticist view, God's will was mediated through the church for the other areas of life. Thus it was the church's job to see that natural law, plus the additional guidance offered by special revelation, was respected in a variety of spheres. The church stipulated certain regulations for family life (rules for marital sexual relations) and economic practices (laws against usury). The church also established ecclesiastically controlled universities and sponsored the production of "church art" by artists.

In the political sphere, the assumption was that the state was in some sense "under" the church—even if the church understood itself as offering only "spiritual" guidance to the rulers. The picture, then, is one of the will of God being mediated to the political sphere through the church, just as the church mediated God's will for all areas of life.

In the modern period this ecclesiastical picture was rejected in favor of a very different one, which we can label (for lack of a better term) *secularism*. The secularists launched a project of liberating these various spheres of human interaction from the control of the church. And since in the medieval picture the authority of the church and the will of God were viewed as intimately intertwined, the secularist project viewed itself as liberating the other spheres from divine authority as well as from ecclesiastical control.

Many Christians in the modern period—especially many Protestants—have sensed that the choice between the ecclesiasticist and secularist pictures is not an easy one to make. They sense that ecclesiasticism was correct in insisting that God's authority extends to all spheres of life; but they are also uneasy about the medieval propensity for identifying divine authority too closely with ecclesiastical authority. On the other hand, they approve of the secularist impulse to free these many spheres from the rigid control of ecclesiastical power; but they still want to maintain the conviction that by moving these areas of life out from under the control of the church, they have not thereby moved them out from under the will of God.

Many Christians, therefore, have made uneasy compromises with the secularist picture; they have, we might say, adopted a kind of modified secularism. The church may not regulate the marriage bed, but families should do some "spiritual" things together. The world of business must be free of ecclesiastical control, but it is still important for Christian businesspeople to "witness on the job." The church has no business establishing schools, but it is good to have prayers in the public schools. Political life must proceed along largely secularist lines, but "we must never forget the convictions that made this nation great." In each case Christians are adding a "spiritual" gloss to an understanding of these spheres which is basically secularist.

There is a third picture available, however, and this is the one Skillen proposes. In doing so he draws heavily on the Dutch Calvinist tradition as developed by Abraham Kuyper and Herman Dooyeweerd, but we will concentrate here, for the time being, on the more ecumenical elements of the picture.

Once we understand the respective merits and demerits of ecclesiasticism and secularism, it is not difficult to discern the basic components of the alternative picture. Ecclesiasticism is correct in insisting that all spheres of human life function under the rule of God; it is wrong in thinking that God's will for these other spheres must be mediated by ecclesiastical authority. Secularism is correct in wanting to liberate these other spheres from ecclesiastical authority; it is wrong in thinking that in doing so it has freed them from the rule of God. The alternative picture, then, accepts the respective insights of ecclesiasticism and secularism, while eliminating their confusions. The resulting view: all spheres of life function under the rule of God; this rule is not to be mediated by ecclesiastical authority.

This alternative picture has implications for politics on two levels. First, it suggests certain guidelines for active *involvement* in the political sphere. We must apply biblical norms to political activity without thereby seeking to "establish religion." Christian political action must not be directed toward serving some ecclesiastically sponsored or ecclesiastically defined cause; rather Christians must—in the words of the message which the Lord gave to the exiled Israelites—"seek the welfare of the city where I have sent you into exile, and pray to the Lord on its behalf, for in its welfare you will find your welfare" (Jer. 29:7). In Skillen's account, the quest for political "welfare" is the attempt to establish justice—a sound suggestion.

Second, this picture has implications for the scholarly *study* of politics. Skillen insists that "a political scientist's general disposition toward both science and politics will structure the outcome of all the particular investigations that scientist carries out." Thus, if someone, for example, Deutsch, is disposed toward a positivist account of science and toward mechanistic explanations of political processes, then this disposition will shape the conclusions he arrives at.

Some Christian political scientists might want to challenge Skillen's way of viewing these matters. His case is not airtight. For example, even if Skillen could show that not only Deutsch but thousands of other political scientists operate with predispositions which affect their conclusions, it would not follow from this that things have to be this way. Someone could argue that while predispositions often color a political scientist's investigations, this is a regrettable fact. Scholars ought to try to eliminate these influences on their work. Even if the influences cannot be completely eradicated, we ought at least to try to minimize them.

It is notoriously difficult to put this kind of objection to rest and, as has already been noted, Skillen does not do so. In order to make the case convincing he would have to write, not an essay for a volume of this sort, but a book, or even a series of books.

Nonetheless, Skillen has already offered some helpful and provocative clues as to what a convincing case would look like. It is certainly not irrelevant to show that a professedly "neutral" political scientist of Karl Deutsch's ilk has in fact been influenced by his own predispositions regarding science and politics. Skillen has also suggested a number of ways in which a Christian faith-commitment might illuminate the study of politics, if we are willing to give that commitment free reign in our thinking.

This latter area of discussion deserves much attention on the part of Christian political scientists. Not all of us are skilled epistemologists or philosophers of science, but all Christian scholars are, as Christians, committed to obedience to the lordship of Jesus Christ. A crucial question, then, is: Does our fundamental Christian posture of obedience to the will of God provide us with important predispositions with regard to the study of politics?

Skillen's answer to this question is clearly an affirmative one, and rightly so. His case is both stimulating and helpful. I am inclined to agree with most of what he says, but there are a number of points in Skillen's discussion at which I experience some discomfort. I suspect that others might experience even greater discomfort than I do, so I will do some probing regarding these matters.

Skillen's discussion begins with a critique of the views of Deutsch and Niebuhr. Having pointed to some problems with their views, he turns—about halfway through his essay—to a more constructive and systematic treatment of the bearing of Christian commitment on political thought:

> The starting point for a Christian science of politics, then, must be the denial of the typical humanistic confession that human beings are the completely autonomous creators of the diverse cultural components of their existence, including their political behavior. Christians should acknowledge that human life in all its diverse dimensions is structured normatively by divine ordinances. With respect to politics this means that the Christian student should take seriously the assumption that the divine norm of public justice holds for every type of political community (p. 29).

These comments contain at least three pegs on which Skillen hangs the remainder of his discussion. Skillen is pointing here to (1) the fact of a divinely created, diverse cultural life; (2) God's normative structuring of those diverse cultural components; and (3) public justice as the specific divine norm for political communities.

We will examine these claims shortly. Before looking at them more closely, however, some general observations must be made about this set of claims as formulated by Skillen. For one thing, it will strike many readers that Skillen's formulations of these claims give the appearance of "theory-ladenness"—some might even say that they are quite heavily jargoned. We have already noted that Skillen draws heavily on the Dutch Calvinist tradition, as developed in the area of political thought by Abraham Kuyper and Herman Dooyeweerd. This influence is quite obvious in his use of terminology here: "humanistic confession," "structured normatively," "divine ordinances," a norm which "holds for" each political community. For many Christian scholars, these claims will have to be translated before they can be understood and evaluated.

These three claims also follow an order—or so it seems to me—of increasing challengeability from a Christian point of view. Thus, the first seems to lend itself to more general Christian acceptance than the second, and the second more than the third.

It is also noteworthy that Skillen offers very little by way of specific biblical defense of these claims. He seems to think that, once mentioned, they will be intuitively obvious to all Christian thinkers. It is unlikely that this is so. I should make it clear once again that I am generally sympathetic to the case which Skillen is making, but I am not as confident as he seems to be that others will find it convincing at its present stage of articulation. My critical probings here, then, should be taken as constructive rather than destructive.

Let us consider the first of Skillen's theses: that our diverse cultural life is created by God. What does it mean to say this? There is an important sense, of course, in which human beings are the shapers of the diversity of culture. God did not, in the beginning, create a Garden replete with schools and baseball teams and factories and legislatures. We find no explicit reference to such things in the first two chapters of Genesis. The patterns and institutions of cultural life were not called forth by God out of nothing in the original work of creation. They were developed gradually by human beings in the course of history. What can it mean to say that they are created by God?

Skillen gives us an important clue in the comments which we have already quoted. He rejects the notion "that human beings are the completely autonomous creators of the diverse cultural components of their existence." Cultural life does not have its origin in human beings viewed as "completely autonomous." "Autonomy" means "self-legislating." We human beings may in some sense "make" culture, but it would be wrong to think that in doing so we are the sources of the norms according to which culture gets shaped. These norms originate in the will of God, the only true and righteous Sovereign.

Many Calvinists have insisted that there is a reference to culture—an implicit one at least—in the biblical account of creation.[1] They have given the label "cultural mandate" to the instructions which God gave to the newly created human beings in Gen. 1:28: "Be fruitful and multi-

---

1. For a good exposition of various formulations of this theme, see Henry R. Van Til, *The Calvinist Concept of Culture* (Grand Rapids: Baker, 1959).

ply, and fill the earth and subdue it; and have dominion over the fish of the sea and over the birds of the air and over every living thing that moves upon the earth." The references here to subduing, filling, and exercising dominion over the earth are taken to be instructions to engage in the kinds of activities which we now think of as cultural formation. Human beings were not created to bask in a hedonistic paradise. They were placed on the earth to "fill" it, to impose a kind of rule on it. God wanted the earth—including the social dimensions of human existence—to be developed, and God assigned this task to human creatures.

This seems to be a very plausible way of reading the instructions given in Genesis 1, but even if someone were to challenge the specific exegesis of this particular passage, the Bible gives overwhelming evidence for the claim that God cares deeply about how human beings engage in cultural development. Because of human sin, people have become disobedient cultural agents, engaging in rebellious patterns of life in their economic, technological, sexual, and cultic behavior. In all of these areas the divine call is to cultural obedience; human beings must transform their economic, technological, sexual, and cultic activity into instruments of service to the will of the Creator. In the diversity of cultural activity, human beings must not pretend to be "autonomous creators," responsible to no higher authority than that which resides in their own wills. In making this case, then, Skillen seems to be on a solid biblical footing.

What of his second thesis, that the diverse components of our cultural life are "structured normatively" by God? The Calvinist perspective represented by Skillen places a heavy emphasis on law. This interest extends beyond a recognition of the continuing relevance of the moral law of the Old Testament for the Christian life. Law has a crucial role in God's relationship to the creation as such. Divine laws do not make their first appearance in Exodus or Deuteronomy. They are present in the very act of creation. God's will for the creation is a lawful will; God's creating purposes are mediated by law. Law stands at the crucial boundary between Creator and creature. Thus Skillen tells us that "human life in all its diverse dimensions is structured normatively by divine ordinances."

Why should anyone accept this way of viewing things? Suppose someone responded to Skillen by saying that she simply did not see the situation in this manner. How could Skillen convince her to adopt this point of view? Are there biblical texts that he would point to in making his case? Skillen does think that the Bible has supreme authority for political thought, and he urges Christian political scientists to "spend time directly with the Bible" in their teaching. But he also warns us that we cannot develop an adequate Christian perspective on politics if we "simply pick a few Scripture verses," trying to correlate them with our data. He quotes approvingly Bob Goudzwaard's insistence that "truly scriptural principles" cannot "be obtained solely from explicit Bible texts."

How then do we use the Bible in order to discover the "norms" or "laws" or "ordinances" according to which God has structured the diversity of cultural life? Skillen's answer is "that Christians must work together in the light of the gospel according to principles and norms which the good news allows them to see and articulate now." The Bible "is a light-giving lamp for human life"; as Goudzwaard puts it, it is not mere "words," it is "Spirit and Power" (see discussion on pp. 35–36).

Skillen and Goudzwaard seem to be warning against the expectation that we can discern the normative structure of creation merely by exegeting Bible verses. Rather the scriptural message grips us and transforms us in such a way that we will be empowered by it to see the normative structure of creation in the creation itself. The biblical Word, as a lamp, illumines the world which we study as scholars. Or, to use the metaphor of which John Calvin was fond, the Bible serves as the spectacles through which we can look at the world in obedient ways.

Needless to say, this view raises some problems. It is simply a fact that not every Christian who has carefully studied the biblical record does view the world in the way that these Calvinist writers prescribe. Not all who have been gripped by the inscripturated Word seem to be automatically empowered thereby to discern God's normative structuring of the cultural diversity of the creation.

It is possible to challenge Skillen's perspective at two different stages. First, one could question whether "laws" and "ordinances" and "norms" are that central a feature of God's relationship to the creation. What grounds does the Calvinist have for viewing law as having a primary mediating role in the relation of the Creator to the creaturely?

This seems to be a fruitful line of discussion to pursue, but for our purposes here it is more helpful to look at an objection which can be raised at a later stage. Let us grant Skillen and his fellow Calvinists their point regarding "creation ordinances." Let us, for the sake of the argument, concede the point that in the beginning God both created the world and at the same time normatively structured it, including its cultural dimensions. What reason do we have to think that we today have any kind of reliable cognitive access to that normative structure? After the glorious accounts of divine creation in Genesis 1 and 2, we are given the tragic story of the human fall into sin in Genesis 3. Calvinists, of all people, have paid much attention to this fallen condition, stressing the extensive damage which sin and rebellion have wrought in all areas of human life and action.

It is precisely this kind of emphasis on our sinful condition which provides John Howard Yoder with his point of departure in elaborating a Christian perspective on politics in his stimulating book, *The Politics of Jesus*. In a lengthy footnote (n. 23), Skillen discusses Yoder's views, especially with regard to the impact of sin on political life. For Yoder, this impact is manifested in at least two different ways. First, the fall into sin changed the general "metaphysical" situation with regard to political patterns. The good "powers" which in some sense organize our political activity became *fallen* powers. So, under sinful conditions, human political action is a response to a perverse political environment—in which the perversity is a more-than-human perversity.

Second, there is also now a perversity that resides in humankind itself. We have become sinners, living in rebellion against God's good intentions for creation. There is, then, a double problem, as Yoder views things. Our own rebellious wills cut us off from the "good creation." But it is also the case that the creation is no longer all that good. The structures themselves have become perverted.

The gospel, according to Yoder, is profoundly political. It repairs the perverse political situation which sin—both cosmic and human—has brought about in the creation. Jesus institutes and models a radically different political alternative to the kind of politics which is taken for granted in a sinful world. The politics of Jesus is noncoercive; it organizes groups and group decision making in terms of patterns of mutual servanthood. This is the structure of the kingdom of Christ. We cannot hope to institute this order in the contemporary world to any widespread extent. But the Christian community must live out this alternative model in anticipation of the new order that is yet to come.

Does Yoder think that the politics of Jesus is a reestablishing of the politics of the "good creation"? He doesn't know. This is, he thinks, useless speculation. The gospel does not necessarily restore some "original order." It empowers us to submit to the kingship of Jesus, so that we can live out an alternative political style in a politically fallen and broken world.

Skillen claims that this is an inadequate perspective. The normative structure of the good creation has not been cancelled out by sin. The relative political order achieved by sinful humankind is made possible by this creation order. The followers of Christ are given clear cognitive access to that original order of creation: "By God's redeeming grace we *do* have access to the creation, for if we did not, there would be no way to understand sin and restoration."

It is not difficult to imagine how Yoder would respond to this. We must understand "sin and restoration" with reference to the model and ministry and teachings of Jesus. Jesus may or may not be the restorer of some "original creation"—in any event, this is not our business. Our task is to focus on the clear teachings of the gospel, for this is the way in which we learn how we are to live in anticipation of the new age which is to come.

There are intriguing and important issues at stake in this debate. At the very least it seems at present that there are alternative ways available for organizing our thoughts with regard to a Christian political perspective on these matters. It is not at all obvious that either of these positions can claim, at its present stage of formulation, that it alone captures the central thrust of the biblical message regarding creation and sin.

I suggested earlier that Skillen's three theses are characterized by an increasing order of challengeability. The claim that the richness of cultural diversity comes from the hand of God will have wider currency than the insistence that this created diversity is "structured normatively" by God. And if there are problems with this second thesis, there surely will be even more problems with the third—that the divine norm for the political sphere is "justice." This claim, being in an important sense an application of the second thesis, will inherit many of the problems associated with it, but the claim also raises a few problems of its own.

Suppose—again for the sake of argument—that Skillen's second thesis were accepted. We would still have to decide how the political sphere in particular is "structured normatively." Skillen's proposal is that the central norm for political life is that of justice. In ordering his diverse creation God decided that human culture should include a political dimension. This dimension would differ significantly from other areas of cultural life, such as family, church, recreation, business, education. Each sphere has its own proper normative structuring and to discern this structure in a given case is to know something about how that sphere fits uniquely into the scheme of things.

Consider an example. Suppose that you are the dean of student life at a college which your daughter attends as a student. She lives in a dormitory on campus and flagrantly violates the rules which have been clearly formulated for dormitory living. Her behavior is so seriously delinquent that a disciplinary committee, of which you are a member, expels her from the college. She confronts you in anger with a charge of this sort: "You are an insensitive mother! You are supposed to care for me and promote my well-being. But now you have me expelled from college. How can you do this to me? I'm your *daughter!*"

It would be perfectly legitimate (although, in all likelihood, not an easy thing to do) to suggest to this young woman that she is plagued by sphere-confusion. She has failed to distinguish properly between a school and a family. As her mother you are indeed strongly committed to her welfare. You may be upset with her behavior as a student, but you should not evict her from the family on this account. You are still her mother, no matter what she has done as a dormitory resident. The family bond, while strained, is still intact. But you are no longer her dean. That bond has been broken.

Colleges are different from families. Families are different from churches. Churches are different from states. Each has its own institutional business with its own unique patterns of bonding. Colleges are organized around educational and scholarly pursuits, families around ties of kinship, churches around patterns of worship and confessional beliefs, states around the ordering of a larger public sphere.

That there are important differences among spheres of social interaction seems to be intuitively obvious. Still it is notoriously difficult to come up with a clear definitional account, with respect to a given sphere, of what uniquely characterizes that area of interaction. What is a family? What is a church? These are difficult questions to answer with any degree of precision.

However, political scientists have felt compelled to give some account of the domain of their own studies, so they have offered definitional statements regarding the nature of politics. Robert A. Dahl, for example, offers this kind of account of "political system": "A political system is any persistent pattern of human relationships that involves, to a significant extent, power, rule, or authority."[2]

Dahl's account is very broad. On his definition, all kinds of organizations and institutions are characterized by "political systems." Dahl himself admits this point. Families, baseball teams, insurance firms, and Sunday school classes all possess some patterns of "power, rule, or authority." Karl Deutsch's account is equally broad—as Skillen argues.

Skillen believes that the Christian political scientist must not settle for this kind of vagueness. It is important to clarify how political communities are to be distinguished from other spheres of social interaction; the political scientist must "distinguish what is political from what is nonpolitical." This can be done only by discerning the normative structures of the various spheres. With regard to politics, Skillen proposes that the political has to do with the area of "public legal" matters for which the proper norm is justice.

This is, I think, a very helpful suggestion, but it needs much more

2. Robert A. Dahl, *Modern Political Analysis* (Englewood Cliffs, NJ: Prentice-Hall, 1963), p. 6.

clarification and defense than Skillen has provided in his essay. I will demonstrate this need by raising a few questions concerning his proposal.

First, on what grounds does Skillen want to argue that justice ought to be viewed by Christian political scientists as *the* central norm for political life? Can this be established, for example, on biblical grounds? The Bible offers many examples of normative political guidance. Daniel witnesses to a pagan king in this manner: "Therefore, O king, let my counsel be acceptable to you; break off your sins by practicing righteousness, and your iniquities by showing mercy to the oppressed, that there may perhaps be a lengthening of your tranquillity" (Dan. 4:27). There is no word here translated as "justice"; is the concept of justice nonetheless the controlling motif in this advice?

Psalm 72 is a prayer for the king of Israel. Justice is mentioned here several times. But there are also other concepts applied to proper political rule: "righteousness," "prosperity," "defense," "deliverance," "peace," "pity." Is there good reason to think that justice is the central norm operating here? Or the only purely political norm? Or the overarching norm?

Second, can't Skillen's account be faulted on the same grounds that Deutsch's and Dahl's can be criticized? Isn't the norm of justice applicable to spheres other than the political? Shouldn't parents treat their children justly in the familial setting? Mustn't church discipline aim at, among other things, justice? Can't an office manager treat her employees unjustly? Doesn't injustice visit the locker room and the classroom?

Third, why is Skillen's account preferable to those of other Christians who also want to formulate a uniquely Christian approach to politics? Yoder, for example, manages to write a highly provocative book on "the politics of Jesus" without ever exhibiting the felt need to define politics in a careful manner. The closest he comes is in a footnote, where he tells us that the "nonviolence and non-nationalism" which characterize the message of Jesus "are relevant to the *polis*, i.e., to the structuring of relationships among men in groups, and therefore are political in their own proper way."[3] Like other accounts mentioned, Yoder's formulation here is very broad: "the structuring of relationships among men in groups." But this broadness serves certain heuristic purposes for Yoder. If he can allow both church and state to be political in a broad sense, then he can call the ecclesiastical community—in its

3. John Howard Yoder, *The Politics of Jesus* (Grand Rapids: Eerdmans, 1972), p. 50, n. 36.

own patterns of policy formation, decision making, and exercise of authority—to function as a "political model" for other institutions. Are there not important ways in which this is helpful and illuminating?

Skillen would perform a good service to all of us if he would wrestle with these and other questions and clarify his account. In this regard his regular references to the need for further "dialogue" among Christians, and between Christians and non-Christians, are encouraging. Skillen raises issues of immense importance, and many of the issues which can be raised by a critical reflection on his discussion are also of immense importance.

Peter Berger has written about his own discipline of sociology that it

> comes time and again on the fundamental question of what it means to be a man and what it means to be a man in a particular situation. This question may often be obscured by the paraphernalia of scientific research and by the bloodless vocabulary that sociology has developed in its desire to legitimate its own scientific status. But sociology's data are cut so close from the living marrow of human life that this question comes through again and again, at least for those sociologists who are sensitive to the human significance of what they are doing.[4]

Many of Berger's comments apply directly to political science as well. They can be seen to have a special poignancy when we view them from an explicitly Christian perspective. Political scientists, whether they realize it or not, and however thay may strive to disguise their inquiries in a "bloodless vocabulary," are cutting very close from the marrow of created human life. They are dealing with structures and authority patterns which—however perverted and distorted—are not the mere products of human scheming but are part and parcel of the fullness— the "filling"—of an earth that still belongs to the Lord. For those of us who are Christians committed to the study of politics, this means that our scholarly probings must always be viewed as the exploration of territory which belongs to our King.

---

4. Peter Berger, *Invitation to Sociology: A Humanistic Perspective* (Garden City, NY: Doubleday, Anchor Books, 1963), p. 167.

Sociology

COMMENTARY

Clark and Gaede review the effects of that sociological research which seems to show that everything we believe is socially determined. This research is often accompanied by the conclusion that our beliefs can never be known to be true because they are contaminated by social relativism. Clark and Gaede criticize these claims as self-annihilating. They trace the deterministic aspect of these claims to substantive (ontological) assumptions operating in the thinking of Marx and others and propose replacing these reductionistic assumptions with ones that are more compatible with Christian beliefs. Specifically they wish to be open to "the full range of possibilities surrounding the human condition" and to assume the possibility of truth which becomes accessible through social conditions.

Clark and Gaede's essay raises the problem of justifying knowledge claims in the face of the relativizing effects of sociology of knowledge. Burwell extends that exploration, making several constructive suggestions about testing, intersubjective confirmation, and cultural universals. (The reader may find it fruitful to compare Burwell's taxonomy of integrative strategies with Wolfe's taxonomy in the introduction and Nelson's in the conclusion.) Burwell describes Clark and Gaede's essay as beginning with a reactive (problem-solving) approach and ending with a dialectical or transformative approach (i.e., transforming or revising some of the assumptions of the discipline in light of their Christian commitments).

In terms of the introductory taxonomy, Clark and Gaede are occupied principally with ways in which the results of the sociology of knowledge can be made part of a coherent Christian worldview (systematic schema). At the very outset they find that the sociological results they wish to explore are flawed by inadequate assumptions and damaging implications. In order to better focus the results of sociology of knowledge they find it necessary to transform its materialist and reductionist assumptions. In this way they become concerned with the methodological and substantive (especially the latter) assumptions of their discipline. This is a clear example of the way in which schematic systematizing presupposes preliminary evaluation of the assumptions and commitments of a discipline in order to be sufficiently critical. Burwell extends and seeks to clarify and justify these emphases.

One aspect of these essays bears special mention. Burwell, in his taxonomy of integrative strategies, discusses the idea that integration may be achieved by viewing the various perspectives on a phenomenon as complementary. In this context he discusses the work of Donald MacKay. This approach is an example of the heterogeneous version of systematizing noted by Wolfe in the introduction. Clearly Clark and Gaede (and Burwell) seem to be moving toward the other alternative (homogeneous systematizing) in which Christian and disciplinary ideas are molded into a framework which uses a single set of concepts rather than preserving the separateness of the disciplinary perspectives. (Examples of the heterogeneous approach will be seen in Chase's responsive essay in mathematics and Jones's essay in biology.)

These sociology essays display a concern about the nature, possibility, and limitations of human knowing, which is a major issue for Christian scholars involved in integration. Further exploration of this theme will be found in this volume in the psychology and mathematics essays.

Knowing Together: Reflections on a Holistic Sociology of Knowledge

ROBERT A. CLARK
S. D. GAEDE

Conflict has long attended the relationship of Christianity and sociology (see Burwell, 1981; Lyon, 1976). Typical is the reaction of many Christians upon encountering the sociological literature on Christian conversion. In their "pre-enlightened" state, Christians often conceive of conversion as a spontaneous, random event, provoked and miraculously effected by the Holy Spirit in the life of the convert. In contradistinction to this view, the sociological literature demonstrates the social relativity of conversion experiences. It shows, for example, that most Christian conversions occur within Christian families; they are clearly not randomly distributed throughout the population. Moreover, these conversions are more likely to occur within certain socioeconomic classes, and the form of these conversion experiences will depend upon class, ethnicity, and educational factors. If that were not enough, the social psychological literature also indicates that the pre- and postconversion experiences of Christians are fairly predictable and that certain types of people are more susceptible to the experience than are others. In short, the "enlightened" Christian will discover that there is a clear, patterned, predictable social context for Christian conversion.

Similar conflicts are encountered when Christian documents are placed under the scrutiny of sociological analysis. The effort in higher criticism is a case in point. Here biblical revelation is contextualized and understood as a product of the same social influences which affect the writing of all other documents. As a result, any particular biblical book may be understood as the product of a specific historical period, the writer being subject to the effects of family, class, status, power, self-interest, personality, and so forth. While the nonsociologist may easily dismiss this as drivel, the Christian sociologist has no such license. Indeed, without strong evidence to the contrary, one must assume the Bible was affected by social influences. Once that is done, however, the Christian sociologist is confronted with the inevitable question: Can the biblical record be accepted as God's infallible Word if it is socially constructed?

While the circumstances of this conflict may vary from situation to situation, it seems to us that a common thread binds most of them together; this strand is provided by the sociology of knowledge and its weave is the notion that human knowledge is relative to its social location. Put another way, sociology appears to undermine Christian beliefs (concerning doctrine, morality, apologetics, etc.) and experiences (such as conversion) by placing them in a causal framework wherein they become dependent variables, the product of a whole host of social factors. Thus, knowledge which once was seen as ontologically given (revelation) may, under the scrutiny of the sociology of knowledge, be viewed as the consequence of a particular sociohistorical context, conveniently designed to legitimate the status quo and/or secure the interests of its carriers.

If the sociology of knowledge is the potential source of many Christian difficulties with sociology, then its understanding is crucial for Christian sociologists. At least that shall be our contention. Indeed, we believe that a Christian exploration of the sociology of knowledge not only will yield fruitful insights into the nature of perceived conflict between Christianity and sociology but can contribute as well to a more complete understanding of human thought and belief. Upon such a premise our paper was born, and to such an end it is now directed. Our first task is to highlight key themes and characters in the sociology of knowledge tradition. We will then examine critically the views of both sociologists and Christians regarding knowledge in social context in an attempt to overcome their inadequacies and proceed toward a holistic sociology of knowledge.

SOCIOLOGY OF KNOWLEDGE: AN OVERVIEW

The sociology of knowledge is an effort to understand the interrelationships of socially shared knowledge and the social conditions of existence in which people produce, accept, and use such knowledge. *Socially shared knowledge* may include political and economic ideologies, religious beliefs, science, worldviews and philosophies, as well as the humor, art, and categories of thought of a people. Moreover, some social group or category serves as a *carrier* for the unit of knowledge under investigation. This varies from economic classes, political parties, religious and ethnic groups to occupational groups or generations. This carrier is analyzed as producing, affirming, or applying the knowledge in question. Finally, the *social conditions of existence* (the social location) of the carrier of knowledge may include the resource base (wealth, power, time, space), occupational and organizational conditions, kinship structure, and the social centrality or marginality of the carrier group.

The relationship of these three components is of most significance. Ideas, groups of people, and social contexts are not randomly distributed across each other. There are, instead, patterned relationships between these factors. The central goal of the sociology of knowledge project, then, is to explain this relationship between knowledge, carriers, and social contexts. Why are they connected? Let us take as an example Mannheim's (1936) observation that utopian beliefs are commonly held by relatively weak minorities; their ideas radically challenge the status quo and locate hope in a glorious, if uncertain, future. Mannheim went on to observe, however, that if such a marginal revolutionary group should come to power, its thinking would tend to shift toward a defense of the established order. Why are these ideas and social contexts connected? The new social location of power and privilege presents the group with new problems to address, new interests to advance and defend, new opportunities and constraints. Rethought within the context of privilege and power, revolutionary ideas are given new meanings; radical notions are revised and supplemented by the new elite in ways that will legitimize the new status quo. Thus it is that changes in the social situation of a group are accompanied by changes in its thinking: Utopians with new power become ideologues who call for unity, order, and obedience.

The effort to explain the relationship between knowledge and social context has been the focus of debate between idealists and materialists. Idealists maintain that this relationship exists because social conditions are an expression of the "spirit" of an age or "Zeitgeist." History is the tangible outcome of the unfolding of great ideas; changes in ideas or *Weltanschauungen* (worldviews) produce changes in social conditions. Which ideas appear, prevail, or fade to oblivion is largely the result of their intrinsic character, their rational merits relative to alternative ideas.[1] Materialists argue, by contrast, that ideas are an expression of people's material and social conditions or interests. Changes in social conditions produce changes in ideas. What people hold to be true, good, and beautiful, therefore, is not simply a result of the intrinsic merits of their beliefs. It is, rather, a reflection of extrinsic factors, a construction expressing what people must or need to believe is true as determined by their social conditions and interests. A relativist theme follows from this, of course, in that people in different social contexts will of consequence possess different conceptions of truth, goodness, and beauty.

We can put some flesh on this skeleton of the sociology of knowledge (and pursue the crucial issues in the idealist-materialist debate) by exam-

1. These views are most common in the "history of ideas" tradition. In the sociology of knowledge, the closest approximations to an idealist approach are found in the contributions of Scheler (1980), Sorokin (Maquet, 1951), and Stark (1958a).

ining the work of three major contributors to the sociology of knowledge: Karl Marx, Max Scheler, and Karl Mannheim.

Karl Marx

For Marx, society rests on an economic or material base. The means and relations of production form the substructure of social life. Around this base develops a superstructure of social and cultural forms which express the relationships of conflict and domination found in the substructure. According to one interpretation of Marx, ideas and beliefs as part of the superstructure are not prime movers in society but, instead, are products of the material interests and conditions of existence characteristic of the substructure: "It is not the consciousness of men that determines their existence, but, on the contrary, their social existence determines their consciousness" (Marx, 1959:43). A second interpretation, relying on the later Marx, stresses the dialectical nature of the relationship of ideas and social structure, though it remains a relationship in which economic factors ultimately prevail. In either case, consciousness ultimately reflects people's conditions of existence.

As a consequence of these processes, the economic division of class conditions is paralleled by a division of consciousness. Here Marx and Engels introduce the concept of ideology. Since knowledge is a form of power, the ruling class uses ideas to justify its domination and maintain control of the proletariat. Ideologies are distortions of the truth, interest-bound ideas used to maintain power and privilege, to mystify and obscure the real workings of the capitalist system from its victims (Marx and Engels, 1956).[2]

There is, of course, a striking relativism in these materialistic ideas. Marx attacked absolutist epistemologies, arguing that ideas do not mirror the universe in a uniform truth. Rather, ideas express our varied material conditions and interests. Hence, as the economic substructure changes, so will "truth." If one were to change class location, one's ideas would change as well.

As Abercrombie (1980) has outlined it, Marx advanced two strategies

2. Note the apparent contradiction here. The division of economic conditions will naturally produce a division of consciousness among the people. It follows that the antagonistic material interests of the bourgeoise and proletariat should be expressed in an antagonism of ideas. Yet the ideas of the ruling class are the ruling ideas, accepted by the proletariat. How does Marx resolve this? The proletariat are deemed to be trapped in false consciousness, holding ideas that betray rather than express their own interests and conditions of life. Such false consciousness can occur because the ruling class controls the coercive power of the state (which can stifle dissent) as well as the production and distribution of ideas (schools, textbooks, media, intellectuals, etc.). The "natural" radicalism of the proletariat can thus be overridden by the power of the ruling class.

for handling the problem of relativism. First, Marx stressed the unique truth-bearing quality of the proletariat. While all belief systems are distorted by class interests, there will come a time when the working class no longer has class interests as such. Its interests will be for the society as a whole. With no privileged interests to defend, then, the working class and those associated with it (Marx) have closer access to "true consciousness," undistorted truth which avoids relativism.

Marx's second strategy involves the autonomy of science. The older Marx was less polemic about the dependence of all ideas upon material conditions and claimed that some autonomy was possible in the development of mathematics, logic, natural science, and some forms of political economy (scientific socialism). That is, these idea systems develop outside of the class structure, escaping the determination by material interests. As Mulkay (1979) notes, Marx believed that science was misused by the ruling class to exploit and control the proletariat; yet, in and of itself, science was nonideological. While more recent Marxists have modified or extended this work (see Abercrombie, 1980; Mulkay, 1979), these two strategies represent the heart of Marx's treatment of the relativistic implications of his thought.

In sum, Marx's sociology of knowledge stresses the dependence of ideas on social conditions and the distorting effects such conditions have on thought. His sociology of knowledge is largely a critical tool for unmasking ideologies and debunking political adversaries in the process of promoting revolutionary change.

Max Scheler

Max Scheler (1874–1928) was the German philosopher, phenomenologist, renegade Catholic, and cultural conservative who coined the term *Wissenssoziologie* (the sociology of knowledge). Scheler had an idealist vision of man as a spiritual being, and he developed a neo-Platonic metaphysical dualism as the grounding for his sociology of knowledge (Staude, 1967). Scheler believed that there existed an absolute order of "ideal factors," a hierarchy of values, ideals, and eternal essences, which transcend history and society. He also recognized a substructure of "real factors" consisting of the drives for food, sex, and power, and the institutions based on them.

Scheler's central thesis was that human action and history are always a necessary combination or interaction of ideal and real factors, of superstructure and substructure. Neither determines the other; both materialists and idealists are wrong, insisted Scheler (1980). Rather, the real factors determine which of the ideal factors will become actualized in history. In contrast to Marx, then, Scheler viewed material conditions as only a selective agent which "opens and closes the sluices of the spiritual stream" (1980:54); real factors determine the presence but not the content or truth value of knowledge and belief.

Scheler was concerned to overcome the relativism he saw as part of the intellectual and moral disunity of his time. How could he present an absolute system when he knew that different societies and historical eras had different ideas and values? His sociology of knowledge proposed an interesting, if flawed, solution. He compared the absolute truths to a mountain range which surrounds the valleys and plains in which we exist. For each people and age a particular constellation of real factors serve as windows to the mountain range; consequently, to each people or epoch is revealed, according to their perspective, a different view of the mountain (absolute truths). Each view is partially true, yet each differs from the others. What we are left with, according to Scheler, is not a relativism of ideas and values, but a relativism of perspectives on the truth. Only the Divine Logos is in a position to see the whole mountain range and know the truth in its entirety (Stark, 1968b). Scheler proposed that the aristocracy, the intellectual elite, using these insights could produce a creative synthesis of partial truths, working back from the particular truths to an approximation of the absolute. This synthesis could provide a base for creative leadership and unity in society.

This metaphysical effort to overcome relativism is not, however, ultimately satisfying.[3] We applaud his recognition of truth which is beyond human construction and the potent role he assigns to both ideal and real factors. Yet, his assumption that all peoples have equal and direct (though different) access to a fixed realm of ultimate truth does not account for human error, self-deception, or collective illusions. Are some human ideas true and others false? If so, which are the true ones? Moreover, a creative synthesis may only be a compounding of errors and lies rather than a combination of partial truths. Scheler was not alone in this problem, however; Mannheim fell prey to a similar error.

Karl Mannheim

Karl Mannheim (1893–1947), the Jewish Hungarian philosopher and sociologist, was very influential in establishing and using the sociology of knowledge, especially through his classic work, *Ideology and Utopia* (1936). Mannheim sought to explore the "existential determination of knowledge." This involved the ways in which the characteristics and

---

3. For critical evaluations of Scheler's effort, see Baum (1977), Mannheim (1971), and Staude (1967). Scheler has had little lasting influence on the sociology of knowledge; Catholic sociologist Werner Stark (1958a; 1958b) is one of the few who have followed themes in Scheler's work.

changes of social groups, their social milieu, concerns, and historical
circumstances, were related to the "knowledge" carried by that group.
Knowledge for Mannheim included not just the content of ideas, beliefs,
and ideologies, but the categories, form, scope, and level of abstraction
of thought as well.

Mannheim extended the scope of Marx's sociology of knowledge in
several important respects. Mannheim believed that while economic
classes and class interests were crucial, other important factors, such as
generations, must also be considered. But more significantly, while Marx
had in effect exempted his own thought from the sociology of knowledge
analysis, Mannheim took the more honest yet dangerous step of arguing
that *all* viewpoints, including one's own, must be seen in their relation to
social milieu. Mannheim said that it is one thing for the rural young man
who moves to the city to develop more sophisticated ideas and then see
his former way of thinking as tied to the rural way of life. It is quite
another thing for him to realize that his newly found sophistication is
itself a product of social milieu. No longer can he have an absolutist,
taken for granted attitude toward his thought-ways. He has developed
what Mannheim called the "detached attitude" (1936:281–82).

Mannheim sought to overcome both absolutism and relativism.
Mannheim suggested that the discovery of the multiplicity and contradictory nature of what are taken to be absolute truths denies the validity
of the absolutist position. It is a position held by people who need
certainty, who are "unable to look life in the face" (1936:87). But
Mannheim also rejected relativism, involving as it does a destructive
skepticism and nihilism wherein no shared knowledge of reality could be
obtained. He addressed this problem on two fronts. The first involved his
concept of relationism which he attempted to distinguish from relativism. All knowledge is related to one's social perspective of values,
interests, and opportunities. This means that knowledge is limited and
partial but not necessarily untrue. Relationism does not deny truth;
rather, it makes conditional the truth of an assertion by always relating it
to the context or perspective from which it is known.

Mannheim thus staked out an alternative to relativism and absolutism. To paraphrase him (1959:581; 1971:97), we humans can only
see a house from various limited perspectives. No one of the views is
absolutely the representation of the house. Yet, there is still "knowing"
of the house; each view has a real counterpart in the actual house; each is
a true rather than fictional picture of the house as it really is. Each view of
the house is true, but true *relational to* a given perspective. We are not
lost in a myriad of discrete, arbitrary, and unrelated perspectives of the
house; there is some unity and coherence among the partial perspectives.

Hence, to the relativist Mannheim says truth can be obtained; to the absolutist Mannheim says it is partial truth, limited by our socially grounded perspectives.

His second major strategy to deal with relativism involved the synthesis of diverse perspectives. Mannheim argued that only by recognizing the limitations of our thought could we transcend them. The search for truth must, then, be a communal, multiperspectival venture. Since the more perspectives of the house we draw from the more we approach a complete and accurate picture of the house, we should synthesize diverse perspectives. It is in the context of this concern that Mannheim made his oft-criticized proposal regarding the "socially unattached intellectuals" (1936:155). He felt that they were particularly suited for the task of synthesizing diverse perspectives by virtue of their social location. They were from a variety of backgrounds, had comparatively fewer vested interests, and were trained to see a variety of perspectives.

Needless to say, scholars differ as to whether or not Mannheim succeeded in avoiding relativism. Some, like Merton (1968), say he failed, that there is little to distinguish relationism from relativism. Critics also argue that his notions of cultural synthesis and unattached intellectuals hardly pass muster. Why should intellectuals be less socially influenced in their cognition than are others? With what criteria do they determine what is true and false in each of the perspectives included in the synthesis? As Abercrombie (1980:46) suggests, only if one has the whole truth (and nothing but the truth) in hand can one recognize whether a particular viewpoint is a part of it or if a synthesis approximates the whole truth. The synthesis of perspectives is, in fact, merely another perspective, one which may be a combination of errors and illusions. More generally, critics point out that Mannheim's relationism must apply to itself; if all perspectives are partial, then so is the sociology of knowledge. Can there then be any general validity to the sociology of knowledge?

The more appreciative reading of Mannheim sees him as hermeneutic or interpretive in purpose (Baum, 1977; Simonds, 1980). In this view, Mannheim's sociology of knowledge is not a deterministic, relativistic, debunking enterprise but an attempt to *understand* the diverse groups and viewpoints in society by contextualizing them. To locate an idea in a social context is not thereby to scorn it as illusion but better to understand what the idea means to those who carry it, a process with both scientific and political benefits.[4] Mannheim claimed that in pluralistic

4. Mannheim was involved in the debate among German scholars regarding the need for special methods in the social sciences: One explains nature but one understands (*verstehen*) culture. He argued for a balance of historicism and positivism in which human meanings *can* be studied scientifically; they are not irretrievably subjective and particular.

societies, groups that must live and work together tend to "talk past each other" (1936:280–81), misunderstanding each other's goals, ideas, and statements. For groups and nations to communicate and cooperate effectively, they must better understand each other. This, Mannheim contended, could only be done by interpreting statements in terms of the sociohistorical milieu in which they exist and by learning to translate the contents of one frame of reference into that of another.

CONTEMPORARY TWISTS IN THE SOCIOLOGY OF KNOWLEDGE

In the American context, the classic European tradition in the sociology of knowledge became rather isolated as a small and esoteric specialty within sociology.[5] This rich tradition has, however, had a wider influence in sociology as a form of argument used in textbooks, teaching, professional battles, and popular sociology writing. Unfortunately, while the classic tradition involved a range of positions with very different philosophical and theological implications, the less nuanced "pop" sociology of knowledge seems to represent the most relativistic, materialistic, and reductionist elements of the classic tradition. It tends to be used as a tool for debunking traditions and unmasking illusions (McGehee, 1982). The following excerpt from an introductory text illustrates this naturalistic framework taken to its Nietzschean limits:

> Fundamental to our view is the assumption that the universe has no intrinsic meaning—it is, at bottom, absurd—and that the task of the sociologist is to discover the various imputed or fabricated meanings constructed by people in society. Or, to put it another way, the sociologist's job is to find out by what illusions people live. Without these artifacts, these delicately poised fantasies, most of us would not survive. Society, as we know it, could not exist. Meaninglessness produces terror. And terror must be dissipated by participating in, and believing in, collective fictions. They constitute society's "noble lie," the lie that there is some sort of inherent significance in the universe. It is the job of sociology to understand how people impute meaning to the various aspects of life (Farberman and Goode, 1973:2).

Practitioners of this "art of mistrust" explain away their opponents, reducing their ideas to nothing but fronts for base interests. Apparent truth in scholarship is really only ideology, a thin veneer over the quest

---

Yet, cultural items are not objectlike things with fixed meanings which can be determined using natural science methods. The way to understand meaning scientifically is to ground it in its social and historical context (Simonds, 1980).

5. The interested reader can consult Barth (1976), Curtis and Petras (1970), Merton (1968), Remmling (1967; 1973), and Stark (1958a) for discussions of the historical development of the sociology of knowledge and the differences between the European philosophical, epistemological approach and the American empirical approach.

for money, power, professional fame, or maintenance of the status quo. Ideas connected with social interests are false; indeed, to show this connection is to discredit an idea. Such an exaggerated sociology of knowledge is particularly evident in the sociology of sociology, radical sociology, and in the battles between rival theoretical and philosophical factions within the discipline.

This strong version of the sociology of knowledge undermines our confidence that we can know and believe in rational ways. As Remmling (1967) claims, the sociology of knowledge has moved us down the "road to suspicion" into a state of "mental entropy." Just as it erodes commitments to traditional institutions by debunking them, it also undermines hope, social criticism, and efforts at constructive social change (McGehee, 1982). How can one critique and work for change if one cannot firmly believe in some vision of human betterment? We are left, then, with a very low view of ourselves as materially bound fools who believe our own propaganda. Our rationality is nothing more than the froth on an irrational cauldron, the front for vulgar interests. We are reduced to socially determined receptacles of illusions which satisfy.[6]

Nowhere are these themes more evident than in the sociological analysis of religious beliefs. The sociology of knowledge is commonly used to debunk and discredit religious belief. Religion, from this perspective, is a mere human projection, present in all societies, serving the same functions and interests; only the content of the myth varies. It legitimates oppression and serves as an apologia for the status quo. Fictional theodicies help people endure structurally induced suffering and divert their discontent away from the real oppressors. Sociology of knowledge explains the social sources and functions of religion and explains how and why we come to believe in it.

In *The Sacred Canopy* (1967), for example, Peter Berger attempts to bracket his own religious commitments while developing a sociology of knowledge analysis of religion based on naturalistic premises. According to Berger, humans must build and maintain their social worlds of meaning and institutions. Religion, as with all other institutions, is a socially constructed reality. It is basic to the world-building process. Religion serves as an agent of social control and solidarity, providing a *nomos* (coherent set of meanings) which legitimates and preserves the institutional order. In the same way that one becomes a delinquent or a Republican (or both), natural processes of socialization move one to accept certain forms of religiosity. Whether Methodism, Mormonism, or

6. For additional analysis of the debilitating effects of the sociology of knowledge, see Barth's *Truth and Ideology* (1976) and C. S. Lewis's *The Abolition of Man* (1947) as well as his essay on "Bulverism" (1970).

"Moonism," whether "true" religion or a "fraud," the conversion process and its consequences ("inner peace") are the same. The content
varies, but becoming a believer is predictable, natural, and scientifically
explainable. Berger concludes his work with the troubling question:

> And if all religious plausibility is susceptible to "social engineering," how
> can one be sure that those religious propositions (or for that matter "re-
> ligious experiences") that are plausible to oneself are not just that—prod-
> ucts of "social engineering"—and nothing else? (1967:184)

One begins to wonder: Do I believe only because of group dynamics,
role models, socialization, and plausibility structures? If I *must* believe it
by virtue of the determining effects of my social location, can it really be
authentic?

It should come as no surprise, then, that many Christians become
disenchanted with the sociology of knowledge and the discipline with
which it is associated. The version they encounter is cynical, iconoclastic, relativistic, reductionistic, naturalistic, and materialistic. It
seems to discredit and explain away faith. It may then confront the
believer with some very difficult choices. One can sacrifice one's integrity as a scholar by rejecting or ignoring the sociology of knowledge (and
sociology) in order to save one's faith. Or, one can sacrifice confidence in
the faith by affirming a vigorous sociology of knowledge. Or one can try
to live with both—which seems to create impulses to jump out the
window.

A little sociology of knowledge is a dangerous thing.

THE SOCIOLOGY OF KNOWLEDGE: A CRITIQUE

When materialistic, reductionist assumptions are used to guide sociological inquiry which then "scientifically" asserts that human affirmations are nothing but ideological distortions or force-fed fictions, then
we are led to suspect that the game has been rigged. Foul play. Such
assertions may be true, but they may in fact be false or seriously incomplete; we dare not foreclose such a possibility.

We contend that the truncated view of humanity produced by such a
sociology of knowledge is in part the result of the metasociology, the
particular philosophical commitments which guide and inform it.[7]

7. The term "metasociology," introduced by Catholic sociologist Paul Furfey (1963),
refers to reflections about sociology, philosophical considerations which direct and constrain sociological work, including beliefs regarding the scope and goals of the discipline,
epistemological and methodological issues, and assumptions about the nature of the subject
matter (human nature, society, social history). For discussions of the bearing of such
philosophical presuppositions on sociological work, see Alexander (1982), Friedrichs
(1970), Gouldner (1970), and Wolterstorff (1976).

While philosophical commitments are necessary (even if unrecognized) preconditions for sociological work, these *particular* commitments are not; indeed, as Christian scholars we are convinced that an alternative set of presuppositions is more justifiable. It is our thesis that by beginning with biblical understandings of the human situation we can construct the metasociological basis for a holistic sociology of knowledge that is more true to the world, more open to the full range of possibilities surrounding the human condition than is the orthodox sociology of knowledge, based as it is on materialistic, reductionist assumptions.

We will critique the established sociology of knowledge from the position that the sociology of knowledge must always remain open to the possibility of truth beyond relativism and social construction. An honest sociology of knowledge cannot be constructed such that it must by nature deny the truth of various human affirmations, whether religious or otherwise. However, because of our Christian assumptions, we are also obliged to critique the reductionist thinking of many Christians who deny or overlook the social influences on human knowing and belief. A holistic sociology of knowledge must vigorously explore the socially situated nature of human beliefs.

Our project is thus informed by and in critical dialogue with both sociology and Christian thought. We seek to go beyond the false polarities of secular materialism versus Christian idealism, natural versus supernatural explanation, freely chosen versus socially determined beliefs. We take strong exception to the reductionism at either pole which distorts humanity into a one-dimensional caricature of its rich complexity: Humans are viewed as either oversocialized captives of their material interests and environment or as disembodied spirits floating above and immune to the social landscape.

In our multidimensional view, humans are religious beings who aspire to understand their existence, to know that which is true, good, and beautiful. Moreover, these beings seek to realize their understandings of truth and goodness in life experience; hence, their understandings have historical import. Yet, as beings-in-the-world, humans pursue and apply their notions of truth and goodness within the grandeur and messiness of human history. Consequently, their notions are subject to the constraints and opportunities of their historical situation.

Working from this holistic metasociology, we intend to show that rather than being a source of alienation for Christians, a sociology of knowledge can be an enterprise of great, if at times painful, benefit to Christian thought and practice. Our task begins, however, with a critique of the established sociology of knowledge.

The Self-Referential Fallacy

As numerous critics have shown, if the sociology of knowledge is to have any credibility at all it must avoid the self-referential fallacy. Sociologists must grant that any statements they make about the social bases of knowledge apply to their own statements as well. To say that all perspectives are relative, ideological, or covers for base interests requires us to apply this claim to itself, thereby relieving us of the obligation to believe it. Gordon Allport related the story of Archbishop William Temple who, after giving an address at Oxford, was challenged by an undergraduate: "You only believe what you believe because of your early upbringing." To which the archbishop replied: "You only believe that I believe what I believe because of my early upbringing, because of *your* early upbringing" (1950:124). The sociology of knowledge is thus a two-edged sword. When sociologists state that all ideas are illusions or fictional fabrications, we have reason to suspect that they have been hoisted with their own petard.

To avoid the self-referential fallacy while carrying on the debunking enterprise, sociologists usually claim special immunity for their own position. Marx granted himself such cognitive privilege with the doctrine of "proletarian infallibility" and the claim that science and political economy were immune from distortions of ideology. But this epistemological double standard simply will not wash. Why should Marx and other sociologists of knowledge be immune to the effects of debunking?

Berger argues, then, that if we take the sociology of knowledge far enough we see that "relativizing analysis, in being pushed to its final consequence, bends back upon itself. The relativizers are relativized, the debunkers are debunked—indeed, relativization is somehow liquidated" (1969:42). In other words, we come to see the sociology of knowledge as more modest and tentative, providing a partial perspective rather than an invulnerable place to stand.

It seems that C. S. Lewis is correct in arguing that "a theory cannot be accepted if it does not allow our thinking to be a genuine insight, nor if the fact of our knowledge is not explicable in terms of that theory" (1970:275). For humans to construct rational theories and explanations of their own behavior (as in the sociology of knowledge) it must be presupposed that the human mind and senses, operating within a community of scholars, have the possibility of making claims which bear some approximation to reality. To argue otherwise is to make the exercise a nihilistic absurdity.

By including it within the hermeneutical circle we have thus tempered the epistemological arrogance of the sociology of knowledge. We are then allowed to be rightfully suspicious of the wholesale debunking of religion in the name of social science.

The Genetic Fallacy

A second important criticism of the sociology of knowledge involves the genetic fallacy. In simple terms, to explain the origin and presence of an idea system in a culture or to explain why someone comes to believe in it tells us nothing about the veracity of the idea itself. Many Christians believe that if their Christian idea system is "explained" by sociologists in terms of social functions, psychological projections, class interests, etc., *then it must be false*. It has been reduced to "nothing but" an ideology. Further, they believe that if their personal acceptance of that idea system is explained in terms of peer pressure, role models, personality needs, etc., then the belief itself is not authentic. Who could have confidence in a faith that is "merely" a product of socialization and social support?

We must argue, however, that the question of why we believe in an idea is quite different from, and perhaps less important than, the question of whether or not we are justified in believing it. As C. S. Lewis notes,

In other words, you must show *that* a man is wrong before you start explaining *why* he is wrong. The modern method is to assume without discussion *that* he is wrong and then distract his attention from this (the only real issue) by busily explaining how he became so silly (1970:273).

Hence, David Myers can rightly argue that "God either exists or he doesn't. That is not affeced by the causes of our belief or disbelief. If the athiest's disbelief and the Christian's belief were completely explained psychologically, this would tell us nothing about the truth of their beliefs" (1978:204).

An important corollary error to the genetic fallacy is the assumption that the social, extrinsic influences on thought must produce error. Conversely, truth can be obtained only by removing all these distorting influences, transcending any "social location." In effect, the sociology of knowledge becomes a theory of the *social bases of error*.

We would contend that the sociology of knowledge is not just a debunking enterprise, revealing socially based distortion and error. Rather, our social location, the interests, values, opportunities, and incentives of our social context may be the social basis for obtaining truth as well as error (Stark, 1958a). As the Catholic theologian and social thinker Gregory Baum (1979) points out, the sociology of knowledge allows us to see how error and cultural blindness are profoundly rooted in our social histories as nations and churches. But we can also see that truth, intellectual freedom, and creativity have a social foundation; the sociology of knowledge displays the historicity of truth as well as error.

Berger applies these ideas to the theological situation with great insight. He observes that many have attempted to discredit theological beliefs by showing that they are grounded in a social plausibility structure. But he argues that mathematics and modern science are also rooted in specific social structures: "So far nobody has suggested that *therefore* modern science is to be regarded as a great illusion" (1967:181–82). As with mathematics, theology can be correctly viewed as a socially grounded human projection while simultaneously viewing it as a reflection of reality (see Berger, 1969; 1979).

We need not choose between socially conditioned ideas and true ideas. Socially conditioned ideas can reflect the truth. The sociology of knowledge must always be an analysis of the social bases of both error and truth.

The final dimension of the genetic fallacy involves the "ideological" label applied to ideas which serve social or individual interests. Motivated ideas, self-serving beliefs, or ideas which legitimate an institution are seen as necessarily distorted or false; such ideas reflect the interests of the carrier *rather than* the truth.

Religious belief is often debunked in just such terms. Because religion is a "crutch," serving psychic and social needs, it is a representation of these needs rather than the nature of reality. Theodicies, for example, are self-serving. They are religious beliefs which help one endure and understand life's injustices, suffering, and death. Religious beliefs are thus "functional."

Theodicies may be true or false, but does the fact that they are self-serving say anything about their truth or falsity? We would argue that *all* ideas can be shown to have benefits of one sort or another for their carriers. That is a constant; it does nothing to distinguish true from false ideas. We must not, then, reject an idea solely because it is comforting, nor seek truth by the criterion of its painfulness.

The Fallacy of Relativistic Inferences

The relativism that is associated with the sociology of knowledge (and sociology generally) largely derives from the process of observing the diversity of socially bound idea systems. The fact that ideas, religions, and ethical systems vary in history and across cultures is used to undermine the belief in any absolute truth. The situation of multiple and contradictory "realities" becomes the basis for the inference that all beliefs are arbitrary constructions. There is no absolute truth, only conventional truth. Each society naively assumes that its ideas, religion, and ethics are ultimately true, yet when we observe all societies doing this we come to recognize that their ideas, religions, and ethical systems are merely social constructions whose truth is relative to time and place.

So it is that the fact of cultural diversity led to the doctrine of moral and ethical relativism which denies the existence of universal and absolute values, religious beliefs, or standards of right and wrong. These are always relative to a given viewpoint. Christians have been plagued by such relativism and have become justifiably suspicious of sociology and its "relativizing motif." Yet, as Moberg (1962) has indicated, this ethical relativism is based on a logical error: One cannot legitimately infer from the fact of cultural diversity that there are or can be no universal values and beliefs. A difference of opinion among different peoples as to what is true "in no way proves that the object toward which the opinion refers does not exist" (1962:39). Cultural variety only demonstrates a difference in judgment regarding what is true, sacred, or moral. In effect, a relativism of judgments of truth can coexist with a truth that transcends relativism and social construction.

The Fallacy of Sociological Materialism

The sociological tradition has long contained elements of idealism and materialism in an uneasy tension. The sociology of knowledge, however, has largely reflected a sociological materialism, stressing the role of extrinsic factors in the origin, use, and change of ideas. It is presupposed that ideas, beliefs, and values are little more than flimsy tissues over the real forces of history, impotent derivatives of social, economic, and political conditions. Religious beliefs are then viewed as epiphenomena which can be reduced to the material forces which produce and change them; they have no force of their own in social history.

These materialist assumptions are not mandatory as a starting point for the sociology of knowledge. Given our reading of history and our Christian worldview, we reject the reductionist claims of those who would confine reality to either its material or ideational forms. We choose to ground the sociology of knowledge in the kind of multi-dimensional theoretical logic recently advanced by Alexander which transcends the dilemma of sociological materialism versus idealism:

> A multidimensional perspective encompasses the voluntary striving for ideals without which human society would be bankrupt indeed, and does

this without emphasizing individualization to the point of foregoing the communality and mutual identification without which such striving becomes a hollow shell. But multidimensionality preserves also the reality of the external conditions that impinge on action. It recognizes in them both the barriers that so often prevent the realization of human ideals and also the concrete opportunities for their actualization. (1982:124)

Ideas have intellectual and social consequences; the origin, use, and change of idea systems is due to the *intrinsic* character of ideas as well as to the extrinsic, nonideational conditions of existence.[8] Our multidimensional alternative thus assumes the reciprocal relationship of human thought and social context: History is a process in which human thought and social forms act back upon each other in manifold ways (Berger and Luckmann, 1966).

In sum, our critique points to shortcomings of the "strong program" in the sociology of knowledge with its reductionist, materialist, and relativist commitments. The sociology of knowledge cannot be an immune place to stand from which "scientifically" to debunk and discredit all other knowledge claims, including religious belief. Moreover, if the goal of the sociology of knowledge is to understand and explain the rich complexities of knowledge in social context, then we are convinced that a holistic, multidimensional sociology of knowledge is more adequate to the task.

DUALISM AND IDEALISM IN CHRISTIAN THOUGHT: A CRITIQUE

It would be a mistake if our project of working toward a holistic sociology of knowledge were understood as a mere apologetic effort to defend the faith by annihilating the sociology of knowledge. Indeed, our critical appreciation of the sociology of knowledge and our Christian assumptions require that we challenge what we deem to be errors in Christian thought. Christians have difficulty with the sociology of knowledge not only because it has sometimes operated outside the parameters of a Christian worldview. Periodically, the problem rests squarely with the assumptions that are presumed to be Christian.

8. Sociologists in the Weberian, symbolic interactionist, and phenomenological traditions have long stressed the sociological significance of human meanings, beliefs, ideas, and "definitions of the situation." In addition to Alexander (1982), see for example Bell (1976), Bendix (1970), Berger and Luckmann (1966), Dixon (1980), Rabinow and Sullivan (1979), and Shils (1981).

The Problem of Dualism

Many Christians think in terms of an ontological dualism which assumes a strict dichotomy between a natural realm of human events and a supernatural realm. The dualist stresses a transcendent God who is above and apart from creation. Most of nature operates in a natural system of cause and effect sequences which scientists can discover and explain. Some aspects of human behavior may be allowed into the natural realm, most commonly our "lower order" physical and mundane psychological and social characteristics.

By contrast, other events and aspects of human life are not viewed as products of the natural causal order but are instead results of supernatural spiritual forces. Some events or "territories" of the person (Evans, 1977) are subjects of the initiative of God. These events or territories are inaccessible to science and can be properly understood only by faith. God *intervenes* or tinkers with the natural realm, producing a miracle; the Holy Spririt accomplishes a conversion, a healing, an answer to prayer, or opens a door of opportunity.

In this dualistic view, God's action is assumed to exist in the mysterious, the unusual, the nonempirical, and scientifically unexplained events (which are given great emphasis). In effect, the "God-of-the-gaps" (MacKay, 1974) operates only in the realms of our scientific ignorance, the gaps in our knowledge. In the effort to explain a human social pattern, such as conversions, it will be granted that "natural" factors can explain some, but not all, of the variance observed. However, as Myers (1978) notes, the action of the Holy Spirit is seen as having distinct effects which need to be added into the equation to provide a complete explanation.

Historically, this stance has put many Christians on the defensive, attempting to maintain the mysterious, supernatural, unexplained realm against the onslaughts of naturalistic science. Unfortunately, those pesky scientists have continually penetrated the alleged boundary of the supernatural territory, reducing the mysterious and spiritual to the explained and mundane. As the natural realm thus grows, shrinking the gaps in our scientific knowledge, the supernatural realm and its "God-of-the-gaps" must also shrink. Christians then retreat and defend a new boundary of the supernatural, perhaps the mind, the soul, love, or religious experiences. Science has become the enemy of the faith to be guarded against and attacked.

It is evident that Christians holding such dualistic views will be troubled by sociological research and theory. They will feel as if they must choose between a sociological explanation and a supernatural one. If sociologists explain conversion using social variables, then either one believes them (and views one's faith as a fantasy), or one rejects the sociological view and affirms instead that the Holy Spirit produced one's faith (which is thereby authentic). Either it is an act of God or it is nothing but a natural process. Needless to say, that cynical, materialistic demon known as the sociology of knowledge is a source of great torment for these dualistic Christians.

We would suggest that the problem here lies less in the demon than in the theology which defines it as such. We reject the strict dichotomy between natural and supernatural realms and events. Alternatively, we propose that in biblical perspective God both transcends creation and is *immanent* within it. God dwells within, sustains, and participates in the creation. Nature cannot function apart from God's action. Rather than being limited to occasional mysterious interventions in and disruptions of nature, God is the continuing author of nature, its regularities and irregularities. God may at times choose to act in historically unusual ways (e.g., the Incarnation) which we call "miracles," but we dare not limit God to such actions nor consider them to be any more miraculous than the continuing and orderly sustenance of creation.

Similarly, we ought not to restrict God's actions to the mysterious (and shrinking) gaps in our naturalistic scientific accounts. If, instead, God is seen as acting through and behind "natural" processes to accomplish his purposes, then we need not fight science in order to have room for God.[9] We do not necessarily need to pose sociologically explainable natural social processes against the action of the Holy Spirit. We are not required to choose either a sociological account *or* a supernatural explanation of our faith. We must avoid thinking that our conversion or the growth of evangelicalism are necessarily inauthentic fictions if they can be shown to flow from natural processes. Rather, it is through natural processes (such as family socialization, anomic social structures, etc.) that one may be led by God to see truth. Indeed, even a casual acquaintance with Sunday-night testimonies will provide a rich list of natural factors along the pathway to faith, from saintly mothers to burnt out ventures in drunken debauchery. God does not just work around natural

9. This argument must not be interpreted as a Christian blessing on the empiricist approach in science and the naturalistic interpretation of reality associated with it. We disagree, at this point, with those Christian scholars, such as MacKay (1974) and Myers (1978), who use the proviso that God is behind the events and processes of the natural world as a theological blank check, allowing them to practice orthodox science with few constraints by their Christian assumptions. Our more limited argument is that God's action and natural social processes are not mutually exclusive categories; in a sociological account of conversion patterns or the religious reawakening of a nation one *may* be seeing the immediate processes through which God is acting to realize his agenda.

processes but honors such factors as families, friends, and peer groups by working through them.[10] Hence, one cannot determine whether actions or beliefs are of God on the basis of whether or not they involve mundane social processes.

The Problem of Christian Idealism

A related problem involves Christian thought regarding the nature of social influence. Some Christian traditions participate in a philosophical idealism that resembles Platonic or gnostic dualism (Macaulay and Barrs, 1978; Myers, 1978). Human nature is viewed as a dualism of mind versus body, spirit versus matter, and God's heavenly kingdom versus this fallen world. This dualism is also a spiritual hierarchy: While God and the spiritual are good, matter, the body, and this world are evil, the source of temptation. The life of the Christian is consequently ascetic; though we (spirits) are temporarily "imprisoned" in bodies and this world, we continually seek release from the mundane. To be "one with God," to "dwell in the Spirit," is to deny the body, to become impervious to the influences of this world. Moreover, in a "mind over matter" logic, the human spirit is free to determine what a person will do with minimal influence of social structure; one *chooses* the environmental influences to which one will submit. Attitudes produce behavior, and the worldview of a people determines its social patterns, but not the reverse. In this form of Christian idealism, then, the person is reduced to a disembodied mind-spirit which seeks to achieve immunity to the influences of the material, social world.

It is clear that these idealist and "free will" elements in Christian thought militate against the materialistic sociological views that our beliefs reflect our social conditions, that our attitudes are influenced by our behavior, and that in general our lives are shaped by the social environment we inhabit.

We assert, however, that the Bible presents a holistic view of the human condition which challenges idealist reductionism. Rather than viewing social influences on our attitudes and behavior as evil and to be avoided, the Bible portrays social influence as a normal part of our created and God-ordained nature as social beings. Interpersonal influence appears throughout the Bible, from Eve's attempts to persuade Adam to share in the fruit to the directive that we "train up a child in the way he should go" (Prov. 22:6), to Paul's numerous efforts to change the

10. Admittedly this view of God as both transcendent and immanent brings up the problems of evil and suffering and the relation of God's sovereignty to human freedom. These weighty issues cannot be settled here. Suffice it to say that these matters are equally problematic for the dualists who stress God's transcendence.

minds and behavior of the early Christians ("Join with others in follow-ing my example, brothers, and take note of those who live according to the pattern we gave you"; Phil. 3:17, NIV).

God's people are instructed to create social conditions that will teach and sustain Godly ways, as manifested in laws, rituals, customs, punish-ments for nonconformity, and an emphasis on community among be-lievers. Like good sociological consultants, Paul and other writers encouraged Christians to bind themselves together in communities to provide support in the faith (a plausibility structure) as they functioned in the world (see Heb. 10:24–25). Christians are also admonished to be a positive influence on the world around them, to evangelize, be witness-es to God's truth, a "fragrance" of Christ's presence, "salt," and "light." Finally, God's people are repeatedly cautioned not to be "conformed to this world," warned to guard against evil influences around us. The early Christians were entreated not to "be carried away by all kinds of strange teachings" (Heb. 13:9, NIV), to persevere by withstanding temptation, deception, and false teaching (see James 1:2–18; Titus; Jude). Even Christ pointed to the positive and negative influences of social condi-tions on faith, as in the parable of the sower (Luke 8) and in the encounter with the rich young ruler (Luke 18).

These instances amply demonstrate that though we are created as responsible moral agents, it is part of our created nature as social beings both to influence and to be influenced by other persons and conditions. To become Christian is not to become immune to social influences. In effect, by creating us as influential and influenced social beings, God has bestowed on us the great responsibility to be careful stewards of our influence and guardians over the influences the world has upon us. It would seem both appropriate and helpful, then, to study the interaction of faith and social context.

FINITE AND FALLEN: A CHRISTIAN CORRECTIVE

As Christians working toward a holistic sociology of knowledge, we must counter the philosophical idealism in Christian thought by emphasizing the biblical notions of human finitude and fallenness. Christians need to be reminded that in the biblical view we were created as meaning-seeking and meaning-producing creatures, but these capacities are lim-ited and warped by our finite and fallen condition.

Christians begin by affirming that truth exists and that God is its author. This truth is absolute and universal in scope. It is not a social construction determined by social context; it comes to us from outside of our human system, revealed through Scriptures, creation, and God's action in history. Christians further believe that God created us as rational beings who are capable of some understanding of truth. We are not just behaving animals but creatures who seek to find meaning, purpose, value, and understanding of our existence. We have a desire to comprehend, to obtain truth.

Given these premises regarding God's absolute and revealed truth, many Christians feel justified in denouncing relativism and the sociology of knowledge, especially as applied to Christian beliefs. We contend, however, that this is a mistaken judgment. While God is the source of all truth, and this truth is absolute, our understanding of that truth is relative, incomplete, selective, and distorted by our human condition. In this sense, then, Christians are limited relativists. Our knowledge of God's infinite truth is conditioned and contextualized by our nature as finite and fallen creatures. We shall explore these concepts in turn.

First of all, the absolute, infinite truth must be discovered, interpreted, understood, transmitted, and institutionalized by *finite* humans. We are creatures of God, created out of the dust of the earth. Apart from the Fall, then, humans are subject to the limitations of being perfect but finite creatures of the infinite God, not equal in capacities with our Creator. We are not omniscient; as individuals we have finite brains, limited memories, limited sensory and perceptual processes. We are limited to existence in one place at a time; we cannot know the future.

Humans are also constrained by social finitude. Societies have limited technology, social organization, and language for acquiring, storing, distributing, communicating, and applying cultural elements (e.g., information, beliefs, wisdom, poetry), and for transmitting it effectively across generations. Further, each culture's experience is both limited and different from that of other civilizations or stages of history. Within a society different segments of the population have different pools of experience. Consequently, each people's knowledge will be partial and selective. Moreover, each people will approach the quest for truth within the confines of their distinctive knowledge base, concerns, opportunities, and experiences. These differences brought to the knowing process will influence what comes to be known. As Mannheim might put it, our knowledge of the mountain of God's truth is relational to our perspective or vantage point.

These characteristics of our finitude condition not only our knowledge of nature, but our religious understandings as well. Theologies, as efforts to systematize our human understandings of God, are human constructions. Biblical interpretations are human constructions, as are church doctrines, customs, and traditions. These idea systems are human understandings of God's truth, discovered, interpreted, transmitted, built into systems, and institutionalized by finite humans in varying social circumstances.

The clearest case of this process involves the variety of biblical interpretations and theological traditions throughout history and across cultures. The sources of such diversity (and perhaps error) are numerous, but among them would be the varied social and cultural conditions of the people constructing such interpretations (see Kraft, 1979). Christians bring particular socially induced concerns, problems, and interpretive frameworks to the Bible and thereby give a passage one reading rather than another or emphasize some portions of God's rich Word to the neglect of others (e.g., grace versus judgment, faith versus works, piety versus social action).

Thus, apart from sin, we as finite beings are limited knowers, possessing a selective, incomplete, and at times mistaken knowledge of God's infinite truth: "For now we see in a mirror dimly, but then face to face. Now I know in part; then I shall understand fully, even as I have been fully understood" (1 Cor. 13:12).

Our grasp of God's truth is also conditioned by our status as *fallen* beings. Though we are rational, meaning-producing, and truth-seeking beings, we often use and distort these capacities in our sinful rebellion against God and our fellows. Though church traditions differ regarding the extent to which sin distorts human reason, there is general agreement that our ability to discover and understand God's truth is influenced to some degree by sin.

Many Christians have accepted variants of the Enlightenment myth of autonomous reason which glorifies the creative and salvific qualities of the human mind. On its own, unencumbered by "irrational" religious and metaphysical commitments, the human mind through "neutral" reason and science can discover and control the workings of our world. The problems we face result from ignorance and the lack of sufficient rationality. Progress will be forthcoming if we but extend our knowledge, educate people, communicate more, use reason and science to guide our efforts in politics, the marketplace, family, and community. Reason, it is claimed, is the dependable tool which can save us, serving as the basis for creating material abundance, health, justice, and social harmony.

This view is expressed in the church in more specific forms as well. These range from efforts to construct natural theologies, the notion that salvation comes from having right doctrine, to the idea that people will become Christians if we simply *tell* them the good news, communicating in a rational, persuasive form.

While acknowledging the magnificence of the minds God gave us, the

Bible assigns human reasoning a more modest and vulnerable role (Myers, 1981). Rather than being the independent director of the person, in the biblical view the reasoning mind is an interdependent part of the whole person. As such it is directed by the self; human rationality is a servant of the ultimate concerns, loyalties, and commitments—the "gods"—of the self. Indeed, idolatry is a biblical theme regarding the human mind and the beliefs we construct and cling to. The Bible reveals humanity rejecting the meaning and truth that God provides; we declare ourselves to be the arbiters of truth, goodness, and beauty. Autonomous humans together search for and create their own meaning systems to make sense out of existence, to justify the way of life they have constructed, and to defend the gods they have chosen to serve (Walter, 1979). We use our reason and culture-building capacities for our individual and collective self-interests. The sinful concerns of biblical characters, groups, and nations led them, for example, to distort the truth through self-deception, lies, rationalizations, and legitimations of evil systems (Berger, 1961).

Jesus speaks to this idolatrous use of the human mind in words resembling those of Marx: "For where your treasure is, there will your heart be also" (Luke 12:34). Our most compelling loyalties, commitments, and concerns, whether to God or human substitutes, direct our consciousness. Sinful, idolatrous loyalties distort our consciousness and culture building away from God's truth. Jesus pursued this rather materialistic theme in speaking to the rich young ruler whose treasure (and heart) was in his wealth: "How hard it is for those who have riches to enter the kingdom of God!" (Luke 18:24). Because he would not let go of his treasure, the rich young ruler walked away—from the truth.

Jesus confronted the Pharisees in similar terms. He attacked them as vain hypocrites who promoted a religion because it served their interests in prestige and wealth. Their love for their own traditions diverted them from the truth: "You have a fine way of setting aside the commands of God in order to observe your own traditions! . . . Thus you nullify the word of God by your tradition that you have handed down" (Mark 7:9, 13, NIV). Their idolatrous "treasures" distorted their thinking and teaching; they became preoccupied with their self-serving traditions, rules, rituals, and appearances while neglecting "justice and the love of God" (Luke 11:42).

Christ also claimed that because of our sinful ways we often do not want to know the truth: "Light has come into the world, but men loved darkness instead of light because their deeds were evil. Everyone who does evil hates the light, and will not come into the light for fear that his deeds will be exposed" (John 3:19–20, NIV). As with the Pharisees and the rich young ruler, we resist the truth when it comes at the cost of our "treasures." We prefer to continue in false consciousness, denying and hiding from the truth of our spiritual condition. We cling to ideological opiates which numb us from the pain of our condition and divert us from facing our doubts about the gods we serve.

In the biblical view, then, our ability to know the truth and be rational is rather fragile, subject to the warpings of our sinful nature. We practice "cheap rationality," if you will, being rational and open to the truth only so long as it serves our interests. As Langdon Gilkey (1966) notes in his theological reflections on life in a prisoner of war camp, rationality and fairmindedness often come at a price, requiring some sacrifice of our worldly "treasures." When these sources of our security are threatened, Gilkey observed, our self-love overrides rationality. We become inclined to use our reasoning in self-protective and partisan ways, being careful, perhaps, to disguise our con with appearances of reasonableness and morality. Few of us will pay the price of a "costly rationality" that is fairminded and open to the truth even when it will be our own ox that is gored.

Given these beliefs in human sinfulness, Christians should expect to find social classes, nations, races, and religious groups using ideologies as instruments of social control; as means of justifying oppression and injustice; and as instruments for securing power, privilege, and comfort. We should not be surprised at the human appetite for hateful fictions which deflect blame (and guilt) onto weak scapegoats, nor at the readiness with which autonomous humans embrace fantasies that claim to provide hope.

By no means, then, can human reason serve as the dependable basis for social harmony and well-being. Our ability to reason soundly is fragile, and our problems are not merely the result of ignorance; the issue goes deeper, to the "treasures" which have captured our allegiance. As Gilkey's work suggests, only when we "store up treasures in heaven" will our well-being be ultimately secure and our minds freed from the distortive tyranny of self-advancement and protection.

These biblical considerations thus counter Christian dualism and idealist reductionism with themes consonant with a holistic sociology of knowledge. Human knowing is indeed influenced by our conditions of existence; both error and truth are discovered through and acted on in socially situated activity. While God's absolute truth is available to us, our finitude limits, contextualizes, and diversifies our understandings of it; our fallenness leads us to resist, distort, and misuse the truth in self-serving ways.

CONCLUSIONS FOR THE COMFORTABLE SAINT AND THE DOUBTING THOMAS

Our project is grounded in the assumption that there need not be an irreducible conflict between sociology and Christian faith which requires one to affirm either faith or a relativistic, reductionist sociology. We have used biblical assumptions to critique and renew both the sociology of knowledge and Christian thought, building a metasociological basis for a holistic sociology of knowledge. This multidimensional approach seeks to overcome sociological and Christian reductionism, working toward a holistic sociology of knowledge which neither rules out the transcendent God nor ignores the social construction and conditioning of human knowledge. It is our intent that such a holistic sociology of knowledge will be recognizably sociological, productive of research and conversation within the sociological community, while simultaneously being consistent with, expressive of, and broadly constrained by our Christian worldview. Given that we seek to enter the dialogue on both fronts, our conclusions speak to Christians in both audiences.

For the Comfortable Saint

It would be quite erroneous (and most unfortunate) to conclude from our analysis that a Christian perspective on the sociology of knowledge eliminates its sting for Christians. Indeed, for the Comfortable Saint a holistic sociology of knowledge remains a vexation, an appropriate "thorn in the flesh."

Because of their dualistic and idealistic thinking, some Christians ignore the social influences on thought, the contextual nature of our understanding. For them, religious belief is not problematic; God has spoken and it is all very clear. Dogmatic in the certainty that they have the truth, Comfortable Saints rest on "now we see," conveniently neglecting the qualifier "in a mirror dimly."[11]

We contend that Comfortable Saints have much to learn from a holistic sociology of knowledge. The awareness of our limitations as finite, fallen creatures directs us to the need for humility. We see ourselves as gullible creatures who can be seduced readily into accepting social fictions, self-deceptions, and distortions of the truth. We must recognize that in faith as in science we have at best an incomplete grasp of God's truth, that we cling to illusions and operate from partial perspectives. Though we affirm the reality of God's absolute truth, we confess that our understanding of these absolutes is relative, conditioned

11. We thank Dr. Arthur Forrester for suggesting this reading of 1 Cor. 13:12.

by social context. Our theologies and biblical interpretations are human constructions, subject to the misunderstandings and misuses of finite and fallen beings.[12] Comfortable Saints are counseled, then, to hold their beliefs more self-critically, always open to the possibility that they have embraced error.

We further claim that if Comfortable Saints are to understand and effectively deal with theological and ecclesiastical movements within the church, they must consider the material social currents and interests which motivate and constrain segments of the Christian community and the population at large. Many efforts to explain theological and church history are presented as if such history were a centuries-long seminar in which "this tradition reacted against that tradition" and "this doctrine influenced that one." Christian idealists (e.g., Francis Schaeffer) often act as if only the intrinsic character and logic of theological ideas influences their history and as if the actions of the church simply emanate from its worldview. Yet, theology as a human construct is socially contextualized. Only with this realization could we understand such historical movements as the Reformation; the church's changing views of marriage, women, and sexuality; or the rise of dispensationalism and fundamentalism (Marsden, 1980). Similarly, contemporary issues, whether the controversy over scriptural authority, the moral majority, evangelical feminism, liberation theology, or the growth of cults, can best be understood, nourished, or resisted if we link them to their social contexts.[13] Moreover, we need a sociology of knowledge to aid us as Christians in reading the signs of the times, in establishing a point of contact with peoples in diverse social circumstances.

Finally, Comfortable Saints need to be cautioned by the sociology of knowledge, warned of the conditions which can lead them into errors of belief and conduct. We Christians have shown our vulnerability, for example, to the "treasures" of wealth, prestige, and power, which can capture our hearts and divert us from faith and obedience. Prosperity and power can distort our thinking, lead us to trust in our own power, to forget God, and to become indifferent to the poor and weak among us (see Deut. 8:11–18; Sider, 1977). We can (and have) become seduced

12. Here we tread again on the dangerous ground of the recent debate over scriptural inerrancy. Two comments are warranted here. First, while the biblical text can be viewed as sacred and infallible, our interpretations of the text are neither sacred nor infallible. Second, the sociology of knowledge can be a useful (though complicating) tool in helping us obtain more adequate understandings of Scripture.

13. Thoughtful efforts to relate contemporary religious developments to social conditions would include work by Baum (1975; 1979), Berger (1967; 1969; 1979; 1981), Gill (1975; 1977), and Hunter (1983).

into all manner of evil, whether slavery, apartheid, militaristic nationalism, or gluttony, which we justify with clever biblical rationalizations. Baum (1975; 1979) maintains that by becoming comfortable in and identified with the major institutions and powers of modern society, the church has been lured into legitimating the status quo and producing self-serving and oppressive theodicies. Christianity has become, in Baum's view, an ideological rather than utopian religion. But just as social conditions have led the church into error and disobedience, other social conditions can help us see and obey God's truth. Both Baum and Sider (1977) suggest, for example, that a life of economic marginality and work among the poor will help us to remain aware of our dependence upon God, to identify with the "least of these" rather than with the powers that be.

A holistic sociology of knowledge thus retains its sting, not because the game has been rigged to produce cynical, reductionist conclusions, but because the truth can be painful. At times the sociology of knowledge will justly be the bearer of bad news. It confronts us with our weakness in the face of social pressure: To believe what is easy to believe and to perform on cue from our environment. As long as human beings are attracted (or seduced) by social circumstances that pamper their pocketbooks, comfort their souls, and confirm their prejudices and preconceived notions, then the sociology of knowledge will remain an agent of woe to those who wish it were otherwise.

For the Doubting Thomas

Other Christians are haunted by a strikingly different concern. Having come to appreciate the orthodox sociology of knowledge, they become skeptical regarding the validity of their faith. They have "seen through" their beliefs, recognized them as dependent variables, the result of mundane social forces and irrational needs. After their beliefs have thereby been debunked and explained away, Doubting Thomases may wonder how they can believe in anything, lapsing into a Christian agnosticism. How can they be committed to anything, be confident enough in their beliefs to critique their world and attempt to change it? Immobilized by doubt, such Thomases focus on "in a mirror dimly" to the exclusion of "now we see."

Doubting Thomases have much to reconsider. Our sociology of knowledge affirms that beliefs are human constructions; yet, they may not be *just* that. A holistic sociology of knowledge remains open to the possibility of truth beyond relativism and social construction. In our critique of the orthodox position, we saw that when the sociology of knowledge avoids the self-referential fallacy it becomes a limited, partial view of our situation which cannot rule out the possibility of knowing truth, whether religious or otherwise. We recognized the genetic fallacy as well, indicating that the truth or falsity of an idea is unrelated to the causes of our belief in it. To explain our beliefs sociologically is not to explain them away. We stressed also that social conditions can lead us to truth as well as to error, that motivated and interest-serving ideas are not necessarily fictions. And we saw that the diversity of cultural beliefs, religions, and ethical systems cannot imply that all of them are culturally relative fictions without any absolute reference point. Instead, diversity represents different judgments about truth and tells us nothing about the existence and form of absolute truth.

In effect, Thomas's affirmation of transcendent truths remains consistent with a vigorous sociological examination of the social influences on human thought. The central questions for our Doubting Thomas, then, are not those of the sociology of knowledge—why he came to believe as he does or what shaped his thinking. Instead, the real issue is whether his conditions of existence have brought him to truth rather than error. Are his beliefs *justified,* more justified than all the rival alternatives? There is no certainty here; our commitment to any framework of thought must be made by our best critical judgment of its merits compared to those of alternatives (Wolfe, 1983). We are convinced that there is "reason enough" (Pinnock, 1980) to warrant belief in the God of Abraham and that we are more justified in trusting the Christian worldview than any other.

Still, Thomases may remain concerned that because they are finite and fallen humans, subject to varied social influences, they will be unable to see God's truth adequately or to avoid being lured into myriad heresies. Admittedly, our judgments do involve risks and uncertainties which must be taken seriously. Mysteries and the possibility of error will remain, but we are convinced that one can gain a *sufficient* grasp of God's truth. Indeed, a more substantial problem is acting on the truth we do have!

The sociology of knowledge can be helpful at this point in suggesting how we finite, fallen folk can best obtain truth and minimize error. As Baum (1977) contends, following Mannheim, the recognition of our limited perspectives and understandings points to the need for a more communal, multiperspectival effort to apprehend truth. By listening to and testing the views of those with different experiences and interests (including the oppressed and marginal), we are more likely to discover errors and omissions in our viewpoint. Thus, by reaching beyond our contextual perspectives and their limits we may better approach the truth which transcends relativism.

We conclude that there can be a vigorous, theoretically and empirically fruitful sociology of knowledge within a Christian worldview. Moreover, we propose that this holistic sociology of knowledge can be used to the glory of God, from cross-cultural ministries to biblical hermeneutics. In examining our churches, communities, and society, the sociology of knowledge can equip us to recognize and expose ideas being used to legitimate evil social structures. The sociology of knowledge can help us discover and cling to those life conditions which best enable us to see and walk in the light, ever vigilant against the power of finite treasures to lure us into darkness. Fated as we are to the social construction of our institutions, faiths, and worldviews, our quest should be to produce social constructions that conform to rather than depart from God's truth—and to have the wisdom to know the difference.

BIBLIOGRAPHY

Abercrombie, N. *Class, Structure and Knowledge*. New York: New York University Press, 1980.

Alexander, J. *Theoretical Logic in Sociology*, vol. 1. Berkeley: University of California Press, 1982.

Allport, G. *The Individual and His Religion*. New York: Macmillan, 1950.

Barth, H. *Truth and Ideology*. Berkeley: University of California Press, 1976.

Baum, G. *Religion and Alienation: A Theological Reading of Sociology*. New York: Paulist Press, 1975.

_____. *Truth Beyond Relativism*. Milwaukee: Marquette University Press, 1977.

_____. *The Social Imperative*. New York: Paulist Press, 1979.

Bell, D. *The Cultural Contradictions of Capitalism*. New York: Basic Books, 1976.

Bendix, R. *Embattled Reason: Essays on Social Knowledge*. New York: Oxford, 1970.

Berger, P. *The Precarious Vision*. New York: Doubleday, 1961.

_____. *The Sacred Canopy*. New York: Doubleday, 1967.

_____. *Rumor of Angels*. New York: Doubleday, 1969.

_____. *The Heretical Imperative*. New York: Doubleday, 1979.

_____. "The Class Struggle in American Religion." *Christian Century*, 25 February 1981, pp. 194–99.

Berger, P., and T. Luckmann. *The Social Construction of Reality*. New York: Doubleday, 1966.

Burwell, R. "Sleeping With an Elephant: The Uneasy Alliance Between Christian Faith and Sociology." *Christian Scholar's Review* 10 (1981):195–203.

Curtis, J., and J. Petras, eds. *The Sociology of Knowledge*. New York: Praeger, 1970.

Dixon, K. *The Sociology of Belief: Fallacy and Foundation*. London: Routledge & Kegan Paul, 1980.

Evans, C. S. *Preserving the Person: A Look at the Human Sciences*. Downers Grove, IL: InterVarsity Press, 1977.

Farberman, H., and E. Goode. *Social Reality*. Englewood Cliffs, NJ: Prentice-Hall, 1973.

Friedrichs, R. *A Sociology of Sociology*. New York: Macmillan, 1970.

Furfey, P. H. *The Scope and Method of Sociology: A Metasociological Treatise*. New York: Harper & Row, 1983.

Gilkey, L. *Shantung Compound*. New York: Harper & Row, 1966.

Gill, R. *The Social Context of Theology*. Oxford: Mowbrays, 1975.

———. *Theology and Social Structure*. Oxford: Mowbrays, 1977.

Gouldner, A. *The Coming Crisis of Western Sociology*. New York: Avon Books, 1970.

Hunter, J. *American Evangelicalism: Conservative Religion and the Quandary of Modernity*. New Brunswick: Rutgers University Press, 1983.

Kraft, C. *Christianity in Culture*. Maryknoll, NY: Orbis Books, 1979.

Lewis, C. S. *Abolition of Man*. New York: Macmillan, 1947.

———. *God in the Dock: Essays on Theology and Ethics*. Ed. W. Hooper. Grand Rapids: Eerdmans, 1970.

Lyon, D. *Christians and Sociology*. Downers Grove, IL: InterVarsity Press, 1976.

Macaulay, R., and J. Barrs. *Being Human: The Nature of Spiritual Experience*. Downers Grove, IL: InterVarsity Press, 1978.

MacKay, D. *The Clockwork Image*. Downers Grove, IL: InterVarsity Press, 1974.

Mannheim, K. *Ideology and Utopia*. Trans. L. Wirth and E. Shils. New York: Harcourt, Brace & World, 1936.

———. "Letter to Kurt Wolff" in K. Wolff, "The Sociology of Knowledge and Sociological Theory." In L. Gross, ed., *Symposium on Sociological Theory*. New York: Harper & Row, 1959.

———. "The Problem of a Sociology of Knowledge." In K. Wolff, ed., *From Karl Mannheim*. New York: Oxford, 1971.

Marsden, G. *Fundamentalism and American Culture: The Shaping of Twentieth Century Evangelicalism, 1870–1925*. New York: Oxford, 1980.

Maquet, J. *The Sociology of Knowledge: A Critical Analysis of the Systems of Karl Mannheim and Pitirim A. Sorokin*. Translated by J. Locke. Boston: Beacon Press, 1951.

Marx, K. "Preface to a Contribution to the Critique of Political Economy." In *Marx and Engels: Basic Writings on Politics and Philosophy*. Edited by L. Feuer. New York: Doubleday, 1959.

Marx, K., and F. Engels. "German Ideology" in *Karl Marx: Selected Writings in Sociology and Social Philosophy*. Edited by T. B. Bottomore and M. Rubel. Translated by T. B. Bottomore. New York: McGraw-Hill, 1956.

McGehee, C. "Spiritual Values and Sociology: When We Have Debunked Everything, What Then." *The American Sociologist* 17 (1982):40–46.

Merton, R. *Social Theory and Social Structure*. New York: Free Press, 1968.

Moberg, D. "Cultural Relativity and Christian Faith." *Journal of the American Scientific Affiliation* 6 (1962):34–48.

Mulkay, M. *Science and the Sociology of Knowledge*. London: George Allen & Unwin, 1979.

Myers, D. *The Human Puzzle: Psychological Research and Christian Belief*. New York: Harper & Row, 1978.

———. *The Inflated Self: Human Illusions and the Biblical Call to Hope*. New York: Seabury Press, 1981.

Pinnock, C. *Reason Enough: A Case for the Christian Faith*. Downers Grove, IL: InterVarsity Press, 1980.

Rabinow, P., and W. Sullivan, eds. *Interpretive Social Science: A Reader*. Berkeley: University of California Press, 1979.

Remmling, G. *Road to Suspicion: A Study of Modern Mentality and the Sociology of Knowledge.* Englewood Cliffs, NJ: Prentice-Hall, 1967.

Remmling, G., ed. *Towards the Sociology of Knowledge.* New York: Humanities Press, 1973.

Scheler, M. *Problems of a Sociology of Knowledge.* Edited by K. Stikkers. Translated by M. Frings. London: Routledge & Kegan Paul, 1980.

Shils, E. *Tradition.* Chicago: University of Chicago Press, 1981.

Sider, R. *Rich Christians in an Age of Hunger: A Biblical Study.* Downers Grove, IL: InterVarsity Press, 1977.

Simonds, A. *Karl Mannheim's Sociology of Knowledge.* New York: Oxford, 1980.

Stark, W. *The Sociology of Knowledge.* London: Routledge & Kegan Paul, 1958a.

———. *Social Theory and Christian Thought.* London: Routledge & Kegan Paul, 1958b.

Staude, J. *Max Scheler: An Intellectual Portrait.* New York: Free Press, 1967.

Walter, J. *Sacred Cows: Exploring Contemporary Idolatry.* Grand Rapids: Zondervan, 1979.

Wolfe, D. *Epistemology.* Downers Grove, IL: InterVarsity Press, 1983.

Wolterstorff, N. *Reason Within the Bounds of Religion.* Grand Rapids: Eerdmans, 1976.

Epistemic Justification, Cultural Universals, and Revelation: Further Reflections on the Sociology of Knowledge

RONALD BURWELL

> We see the puppets dancing on their miniature stage, moving up and down as the strings pull them around, following the prescribed course of their various little parts. We learn to understand the logic of this theater and we find ourselves in its motions. We locate ourselves in society and thus recognize our own position as we hang from its subtle strings. For a moment we see ourselves as puppets indeed.
>
> Peter Berger[1]

One of the exhilarating aspects of teaching sociology to undergraduates is the experience of seeing them become conscious of the mechanisms of society as it swirls about all of us. As they come through our classes we profess to them the sociological perspective and they begin to see the power that society exerts over them—even to the extent of shaping their thoughts. Such an experience is fraught with dangers, too, as they come to realize that the "OK World" is perhaps not what they thought it was.[2] Particularly troubling is the relativization of knowledge that seems inherent in the sociological perspective. Because this is so, the choice of Clark and Gaede to address the issue of the sociology of knowledge and to interact with the topic as sociologists and Christians is to be applauded. The sociology of knowledge raises questions both for Christians and for non-Christians; because of their commitment to knowing truth about God and humanity's relationship to God, however, Christians may find the topic particularly unsettling.

In my response to "Knowing Together: Reflections on a Holistic Sociology of Knowledge," I will proceed along the following lines: First, I will give a brief synopsis of the argument of the paper. This will serve to indicate how I understand their position and it will also indicate those things that I find of most significance in what they have written. Second,

1. Peter Berger, *Invitation to Sociology: A Humanistic Perspective* (New York: Doubleday, 1963), p. 176.
2. For more on the "O.K. World" see Peter Berger, *The Noise of Solemn Assemblies* (New York: Doubleday, 1961), pp. 117–20.

I will discuss some possible approaches to integration and attempt to identify what strategy Clark and Gaede have taken in their work. Third, I will offer some comments and criticisms of their proposals. Finally, I will try to show some alternative approaches to what they have done.

SYNOPSIS

Clark and Gaede begin their paper by noting that Christians frequently confront the sociology of knowledge indirectly when they discover that social settings seem to influence the ideas, beliefs, and knowledge of the people involved in those settings. Such an insight raises troubling questions about the truthworthiness of knowledge. This problem demands some response from the Christian sociologist who takes seriously the sociological ideas that are foundational to the sociology of knowledge.

Given this concern, the authors set forth an overview of the sociology of knowledge with particular attention to three prominent European thinkers who contributed heavily to the sociology of knowledge: Karl Marx, Max Scheler, and Karl Mannheim. Each of these men recognized the fact that ideas (ideology) are intrinsically linked to the social context. Marx stressed the class-based nature of human knowledge. The underlying motif in much of this thought was the larger philosophical debate regarding materialism and idealism.

However, these three shared a common concern. While recognizing the social relatedness of human thought, they all foresaw the self-stultifying implications of their arguments. If ideas are to some extent dependent and determined by one's social location, will not that observation extend to the ideas of Karl Marx and Max Scheler themselves? Indeed, Marx, Scheler, and Mannheim tried to find ways to avoid this relativization of their own thought. Each, in his own way, drew back from the brink of complete cognitive relativism by offering a basis for security. For Marx, security might be found in the potential of the proletariat or the sciences to avoid ideological thinking. Scheler hoped that the aristocracy, the intellectual elite, might be able to piece together competing perspectives on the truth and come up with an approximation of ultimate truth. Finally, Mannheim, borrowing from both Marx and Scheler, looked to a category of people who could synthesize the relative viewpoints into something worth trusting. He referred to this group as the "free-floating intelligentsia."[3]

Clark and Gaede show how each of these three great theorists contrib-

---

3. Karl Mannheim, *Ideology and Utopia* (New York: Harcourt, Brace & World, 1936), pp. 153–64.

uted to the growth of the sociology of knowledge but still left the need to solve the problem of relativism. They rightly point out that when the sociology of knowledge is presented in American sociological thought it is usually less integrated into larger theory and more often than not used as a tool in iconoclastic debates. As a result it becomes merely an exaggerated debunking of all knowledge.

Having presented an overview of the sociology of knowledge, the authors turned to a critique of the sociology of knowledge in its various forms. Their assumption is that the sociology of knowledge can have validity if it is linked to a holistic metasociology ultimately based in a commitment to certain assumptions. Included in these assumptions is that one can know truth beyond relativism and social construction; that certain false dichotomies must be avoided (e.g., natural vs. supernatural); and that human beings are indeed constrained by social context but can also transcend that context.

In developing their critique of the sociology of knowledge Clark and Gaede suggest four fallacies: the self-referential fallacy, the genetic fallacy, the fallacy of relativistic inferences, and the fallacy of sociological materialism. The self-referential fallacy has already been alluded to under the notion that the sociology of knowledge, if it is true, must apply to statements sociologists themselves make. Although this does not do away with the sociology of knowledge, it tempers the tendency of some who, from that vantage point, would debunk the knowledge of others without realizing that they are undercutting their own arguments. The genetic fallacy rightfully cautions against rejecting an idea as necessarily false just because we understand its genesis or source. It might well be the case that an idea is socially constructed but still true or justified. The fallacy of relativistic inferences is the mistaken conclusion that because there is a multiplicity of ideas all ideas are therefore arbitrary and unwarranted. Finally, the fallacy of sociological materialism is to accept materialism uncritically as necessarily part of sociology and proceed to reject the possibility that ideas can be in any way independent from material factors. It is possible, on the contrary, to construct a sociology that accommodates a measure of idealism.

Having tempered the demon of the sociology of knowledge, Clark and Gaede turn to a more explicitly Christian reflection on the issue. In a section titled "Dualism and Idealism in Christian Thought: A Critique," they attempt to rectify the tendency they see for Christians to develop a dualistic approach to life. They identify this with certain strategies whereby the Christian sets up mutually exclusive territories in order to solve problems of conflict between faith and knowledge. Instead they argue for a unity so that one does not choose, for example, for supernaturalism and against naturalism in trying to explain a given phenomenon.

Furthermore, they identify another problem for Christians under the heading "The Problem of Christian Idealism." According to the authors the dualism already noted tends to make Christians look to the realm of idea (mind) as the place where certain essential factors operate (e.g., freedom). What seems to be at issue here is that some Christians have opted for certain philosophical positions (dualism, idealism) that complicate the problem of dealing with the sociology of knowledge.

Finally, after arguing for a certain view of human existence, Clark and Gaede draw some applications of the sociology of knowledge for two kinds of Christians. For them man is finite and fallen. Translated into the terms of the debate this means that social forces operate to affect, influence, control, and at times create our thoughts. What this means is a partial acceptance of the message of the sociology of knowledge. This is an important corrective to the tendency among Christians (and others) toward an idolatrous elevation of the human mind and thought to the level of being ". . . the dependable tool which can save us, serving as the basis for creating material abundance, health, justice, and social harmony." Given this sobering acceptance of much of the validity of the sociology of knowledge, how can Christians respond?

The "comfortable saints" need to become a bit less comfortable. They need to see that their knowledge is affected by social factors and they must come to terms with that fact by confessing their limitations in seeking certitude. On the other hand the "doubting Thomases" are Christians who are deeply troubled by the sociology of knowledge. They may even despair at the possibility of being justified in believing anything. They need to see that the sociology of knowledge does not inevitably rob us of knowing the truth. They need to be encouraged to seek ways of overcoming the relativity of knowledge—perhaps through the operation of a principle like intersubjectivity. For the "doubting Thomas," the need is to see the limits of the sociology of knowledge.

INTEGRATIVE STRATEGIES

Before looking more closely at the integrative strategy employed by Clark and Gaede, I shall review some of the options available. In the past fifteen years the number of books and articles published on the integration of the Christian faith and various academic disciplines has grown appreciably. Now the discussion of "faith and learning" has become commonplace for student orientation and faculty development in the Christian college and to a lesser extent for Christians in a variety of secular academic settings. Although actual substantive examples of integration are still relatively rare, the discussion has served to do several things. For one it has convinced the doubtful that an enterprise such as integration is both feasible and legitimate for Christian scholars. Further, reflection on this topic has produced a number of proposals of how integration ideally should be carried on. Books like Harry Blamires, *The Christian Mind*; Arthur Holmes, *All Truth is God's Truth*; Nicholas Wolterstorff, *Reason Within the Bounds of Religion*; and Frank Gaebelein, *The Pattern of God's Truth*, have shown us how we might think about integration.[4]

At the risk of oversimplification it is possible to see the various ideas on integration reduced to three or four basic strategies.[5] Setting aside the outright rejection of integration (which some might still argue for), perhaps the most popular approach is to argue for some type of accumulation of complementary perspectives. Perhaps the most widely read proposals of this nature are associated with Donald MacKay. MacKay is a highly respected British brain physiologist who has written widely about the interface of Christianity and science.[6] His thinking has been adopted by many Christian scholars, even those outside the natural sciences. MacKay's general approach is to argue that there are several different perspectives or "stories" that, while complete in their own terms, may be used conjointly to provide the most comprehensive understanding possible. The beauty of this approach is that it reduces potential conflicts between perspectives and accepts them as complementary. Hence, a mechanistic, deterministic brain physiology account of human behavior is compatible with a personalistic, indeterministic discussion of human action. Problems, according to MacKay, come when one perspective claims sole authority or legitimacy for itself. While some Christian thinkers have noted difficulties with MacKay's approach, it has been extremely persuasive for many others.[7]

Another general approach to integration may be referred to as dialec-

---

4. Harry Blamires, *The Christian Mind* (New York: Seabury Press, 1963); Arthur Holmes, *All Truth is God's Truth* (Grand Rapids: Eerdmans, 1977); Nicholas Wolterstorff, *Reason Within the Bounds of Religion* (Grand Rapids: Eerdmans, 1976); Frank Gaebelein, *The Pattern of God's Truth* (Chicago: Moody Press, 1968).

5. For a more elaborate categorization of the possible types of integrative strategies see Ronald J. Burwell, "Integrative Strategies in a Secular Age," *Journal of the American Scientific Affiliation* (December 1979):198–201.

6. Donald MacKay, *Brains, Machines and Persons* (Grand Rapids: Eerdmans, 1980).

7. For criticisms of MacKay see John Cramer, "The Clockwork Image Controversy," *Journal of the American Scientific Affiliation* (September 1976):123–27; William Hasker, "MacKay on Being a Responsible Mechanism: Freedom in a Clockwork Universe," *Christian Scholar's Review*, 8:2:130–40.

tical or transformative depending on how it is presented. Nicholas Wolterstorff has given one expression of this general orientation. Essentially, Wolterstorff argues that one's authentic Christian commitment should function as a set of control beliefs in the weighing and devising of theories.[8] In other words, as scholars in a given discipline survey various theoretical options, their Christian faith should be a factor in sorting out which theories are feasible and which are not feasible for a Christian to hold. Ideally, Christian scholars will also be creating theories which are framed with explicit consideration of their Christian commitments.

Wolterstorff presents the process as an active one whereby one overtly uses Christian commitment in the doing of one's discipline. What makes the process dialectic is that a Christian scholar will also allow data and theories from his discipline to introduce revisions in what he takes to be his authentic Christian commitment.[9] Integration, then, is not merely working passively within the terrain set forth by the mostly non-Christian scholars in a discipline, it is an attempt to do sociology or anything else "Christianly."

A final kind of integration worth mentioning is one that is perhaps the oldest type of integration practiced by Christian scholars. The basic approach is reactive. In the course of working in a given discipline, certain problems arise for the Christian scholar. They present challenges to the Christian views accepted by the scholar. So, the scholar stops to solve the problem and to defuse the threat to Christian faith. This "problem-solving" approach is modest. It does not seek to construct a Christian perspective, theory, model, etc. Instead, it is content to solve whatever problems are generated by the given data or theories of a discipline. It is understandable that this may be the earliest and simplest type of integration (if one can even use that word for it). Often one does not perceive philosophical or worldview differences until one is confronted with a specific tangible instance of a conflict between a given discipline and traditional Christian teaching. Yet, the problem may only be the tip of the iceberg of larger, more significant issues that will confront the Christian scholar in a discipline.

8. Wolterstorff, *Reason Within the Bounds of Religion*, p. 72. "The Christian scholar ought to allow the belief-content of his authentic Christian commitment to function as control within his devising and weighing of theories."

9. Wolterstorff, p. 90. "So far I have been pressing the point that the Christian in the practice of scholarship ought to let the belief content of his authentic commitment function as control over his theory-weighing. My emphasis here is almost the opposite. Sometimes he should allow scientific developments to induce revision in *what he views as* his authentic Christian commitment."

CLARK AND GAEDE'S INTEGRATIVE STRATEGY

It appears that Clark and Gaede employ not one but at least two different kinds of integrative strategies. In one sense they move into their discussion of the sociology of knowledge because it is "problematic." In other words, ideas clustering around the general topic of the sociology of knowledge have been troublesome for Christians. How can we solve the problem? Their approach is to criticize formulations of the sociology of knowledge (the "strong" version) which are based upon fallacious extensions of certain concepts. Further, they try to turn what had been a problem into something that can aid the Christian.

Nevertheless, their integrative strategy is more elaborate and sophisticated than just solving a problem. I would interpret what they are doing as, in some ways, fitting into the dialectical or transformative mode as well. Beginning with certain control beliefs (e.g., metasociology) that they believe are of central importance, they weigh existing theories regarding the sociology of knowledge. They conclude that the formulations of Marx, Scheler, Mannheim, and contemporary pop sociologists are all defective in light of their metasociology. It is necessary, therefore, for them to create an alternative view of the sociology of knowledge that is consonant with their control beliefs. At this point it is less clear what has been accomplished. They do not offer the formal, developed theory of the sociology of knowledge that one might expect. Instead, they argue that while ideas are socially formed, influenced, and determined, this does not lead to materialism or the inability to know the truth.

To their credit Clark and Gaede attempt to allow their authentic Christian commitment to operate as control beliefs in their weighing of theories in sociology. Further, the process is dialectical. In other words, they are not content just to let their authentic Christian commitment operate upon their understanding of the sociology of knowledge. Indeed, they show effectively how the sociology of knowledge as they understand it can and has reformed their understanding of authentic Christian commitment. Their strong (and I believe essentially correct) comments on the tendency of Christians to overlook the influence of social factors on the human mind leads to a consideration of the possibility of idolizing the rational constructions of the human mind (whether such constructions be theology, biblical interpretation, or scientific theory).

CRITICISMS/ALTERNATIVE STRATEGY

I find that I am generally in sympathy with the approach that Clark and Gaede have taken on the issue of the sociology of knowledge. The ideal would be to take the skeleton of their approach and flesh it out in greater detail. Obviously such a project is beyond the scope of this particular essay. What I will proceed to do, therefore, is to offer some comments, observations that are extensions and elaborations of the basic strategy Clark and Gaede have followed. As has been mentioned, I construe their integrative strategy to be patterned loosely after that outlined by Nicholas Wolterstorff in *Reason Within the Bounds of Religion*—an approach I earlier labeled "dialectical."

I am committed to the view that integration of the Christian faith by its very nature must transcend traditional academic discipline boundaries. Although they do not state this explicitly it is clear that Clark and Gaede, in struggling with the issue of the sociology of knowledge, were compelled to go outside of the narrow boundaries of sociology. To begin with, they stated a series of assumptions of a metasociological nature. These were in effect a set of control beliefs that were applied to the traditional classic formulations of theories in the sociology of knowledge. At that point they had stepped back from sociology to a different level. Later on in their essay materials from theology and philosophy were introduced to further support their points. My first general comment, then, is that Clark and Gaede could have strengthened their integrative endeavors by explicitly relating the specialized case of the sociology of knowledge to the more fundamental issue of establishing a basis of justifiable knowledge or belief. A perennial human question has been, "How can I have assurance that what I believe or know is warranted?" Since we can come at this question from many different directions, the sociology of knowledge is only one concrete instance of human beings questioning the trustworthiness of human ideas.

In recent years a number of writers in differing academic disciplines have probed in new ways the issue of the nature of human knowledge. A book like Thomas Kuhn's *The Structure of Scientific Revolutions* has stimulated a variety of controversies about scientific knowledge that also have implications for other kinds of knowledge.[10] Although writing as a historian of science, Kuhn presents some ideas that are strikingly similar to those raised in the sociology of knowledge. For example, what is the impact on scientific research and theory of the scientist's membership in a particular scientific community at a particular point in history? Are there social forces that weigh upon the conduct of the scientist's science? In the philosophy of social science a book like Peter Winch's *The Idea of a Social Science* presses the issues of human thought even to the point of

10. Thomas Kuhn, *The Structure of Scientific Revolutions* (Chicago: University of Chicago Press, 1962); for an example of some of the debate stimulated by Kuhn see: Imre Lakatos and Alan Musgrove, eds., *Criticism and the Growth of Knowledge* (London: Cambridge University Press, 1970).

asking about the social bases of rationality.[11] Are systems of logic and thought culturally relative? How can we understand another culture unless we adopt the patterns of thought of that culture? Can we translate observations of one culture into the language of another culture? What has come to be referred to as the philosophical debate about rationality has great affinities with the central concerns of the sociology of knowledge.[12] The result of all of this is that the resources of thinkers from a variety of disciplines continue to be brought to bear on the fundamental issues of the nature of human knowledge.

Once the sociology of knowledge is linked with this more general discussion of human knowledge, it is possible to search for answers through a variety of means. If sociology of knowledge leads to cognitive relativism, what are some possible solutions to such relativism suggested by philosophers, theologians, sociologists, and others? Clark and Gaede recognize that this search to overcome cognitive relativism can be problematic for Christians. They note the need to ask how our beliefs are justified. Without devoting a great deal of time to answering this question the authors do offer some brief comments. At this point their efforts can be enhanced by showing how we can join forces with others who have been and are struggling with similar problems (even if not under the rubric of the sociology of knowledge). In a recent book, for example, David Wolfe has offered some clues about how one might establish beliefs in the face of uncertainty. He writes:

> The strategy for providing warrant, then, is to start where you are. Extend your most important beliefs into a broader interpretive scheme. This may involve a certain amount of self-examination in order to see what your unstated assumptions and their implications are. It may also involve some intellectual house cleaning as you discover inconsistencies and other difficulties in your beliefs. When this is done, you may begin the indefinite procedure of criticism and refinement that is the warranting process. If your scheme is inadequate, the only honest thing to do is to dump it or overhaul it drastically. The discovery of error is a genuine advance, not a loss of face, for the person who is concerned with truth.[13]

Here a philosopher who is a Christian gives some guidance that could be useful to someone trying to develop a foundation for knowledge in the face of the sociology of knowledge. This is a good example of the benefits of Christian thinkers extending their views beyond just one or two disciplines.

11. Peter Winch, *The Idea of a Social Science* (London: Routledge & Kegan Paul, 1958).

12. For examples of the thinking done in this area see Bryan R. Wilson, ed., *Rationality* (New York: Harper & Row, 1971).

13. David L. Wolfe, *Epistemology: The Justification of Belief* (Downers Grove, IL: Inter-Varsity Press, 1982), pp. 65–66.

The other aspect of the attempt to solve the problem of relativism that Clark and Gaede allude to is the ". . . need for a more communal, multiperspectival effort to apprehend truth." This is an important observation but receives little elaboration. This is particularly unfortunate since there is a rich tradition in sociology that emphasizes the value of intersubjectivity as an antidote to error and deception. The Christian who is a sociologist would seem to be able to help "doubting Thomases" through a careful consideration of the role of intersubjectivity. Here one set of insights from sociology could well help to rectify difficulties in another area of sociology. Actually, Clark and Gaede could have shown that Scheler's stress on the convergence of interpretations is analogous to what they are proposing as a hopeful direction in solving the problem. One sociologist who has helped a great deal in understanding intersubjectivity is Alfred Schutz. Note how he applies this concept to our gaining knowledge (both sociologically and personally):

> My experience of the world justifies and corrects itself by the experience of others with whom I am interrelated by common knowledge, common work, and common suffering. The world, interpreted as the possible field of action for us all: that is the first and most primitive principle of organization of my knowledge of the exterior world in general.[14]

The search for valid knowledge can be enhanced by attentiveness to those, like Schutz, who have pondered these questions and have shared their ideas with us.

A second general observation arises out of Clark and Gaede's reference to the fallacy of relativistic inferences. They rightly caution against inferring from a variety of conflicting beliefs that all the beliefs are in error. Frequently sociologists and anthropologists participate in this fallacy as they introduce people to the data on cultural relativity. However, the argument can be stood on its head. Instead of looking for variations, one can look for universals cross-culturally. Granted, to be consistent we must note that if a belief or idea existed in all cultures (i.e., was universal) its truth might still be questioned. Nevertheless, such universals might suggest the possibility of gaining knowledge that transcends social factors. In other words, it makes sense to ask, "Do universal beliefs provide an antidote to the relativizing effects of the sociology of knowledge?" Readers familiar with C. S. Lewis's *The Abolition of Man* will recognize that that is exactly the approach that Lewis took to the prob-

---

14. Alfred Schutz, "The Social World and the Theory of Social Action," in David Braybrooke, ed., *Philosophical Problems of the Social Sciences* (New York: Macmillan, 1965), p. 59.

lem of moral (and cognitive?) relativism.[15] By isolating the existence of a core of universal moral beliefs (the TAO) Lewis was attempting to overcome the relativizing current in modern thought. Certainly, social scientists such as sociologists and anthropologists would be in a good position to reflect on the existence of universal beliefs or knowledge.

A third observation comes from reflection on the way those who traditionally thought about the sociology of knowledge dealt with the issue of justification of belief. There is a common thread that runs from Marx and Scheler through Mannheim. They speculated that those persons who were detached from the social setting had the best chance of rising above societal determination of their thinking, whether it be the disadvantaged proletarian, the disenfranchised revolutionary, or the disinterested intellectual. This observation, which is certainly open to criticism, does, however, raise an interesting question. Do Christians, who belong to a different kingdom from that of this world, have potential for rising above the ideological, self-serving thought of a given social stratum? At least hypothetically I would like to propose that they do. After all, although God's Word comes to the Christian in relative, culturally laden form, it is at least initially constructed outside the social world (providing one believes in some doctrine of special revelation). Obviously, Christians still have to overcome the problem of the sociology of knowledge as it applies to the construction of their interpretations of revelation. Furthermore, to the extent that one sees Christianity as providing a counter-cultural critique, it may be that the Christian has access to resources for rising above ideological thinking. The major difficulty, however, is that the Christian (whether an "intellectual" or not) is typically more likely to be conforming to the culture than attempting to transform the culture. The potential, though, does raise some interesting possibilities.

In offering a critique of dualism and idealism in Christian thought Clark and Gaede are actually doing two things. First, they are manifesting the dialectical nature of their integrative strategy by allowing the data of sociology (e.g., the sociology of knowledge) to act back upon what they wish to hold as authentic Christian commitment. This is entirely appropriate and necessary. Certainly this approach aides in the revision and refinement of what one believes Christianity to be all about. Second, they are obliquely criticizing an integrative strategy that is frequently adopted by Christians. By focusing on the twin issues of idealism and dualism they wish to demonstrate the inadequacy of the

15. C. S. Lewis, *The Abolition of Man* (New York: Macmillan, 1947).

approach that Stephen Evans has labeled "territorialism." Evans identifies the position as follows:

> Territorialists conceive the limits of science in terms of regions of reality—types of entities that science is incapable of dealing with.[16]

The classic example is Cartesian dualism regarding the mind and body. This approach is attractive because it seems to allow one to accept contradictory propositions. If adopted, territorialism would allow one to affirm the sociology of knowledge as valid and accurate for a variety of things but would exempt Christianity from its purview. Instead, Christianity would be relegated to a different realm (territory)—the supernatural—where the principles of the sociology of knowledge do not apply. Clark and Gaede show that one then faces a dilemma of choosing for or against a sociological explanation of a given phenomenon. Unfortunately, territorialism is not a very helpful solution in the case of the sociology of knowledge.

In making their point, however, Clark and Gaede might well have pointed out the opposite strategy, which can likewise be disastrous. The opposite approach would be to identify the Christian position with materialism and monism. No doubt they felt that the dangers of idealism and dualism were greater. It is my perception, though, that Christians who are trained in the social sciences are more likely to make the mistake of opting uncritically for materialism and monism. In actuality, the Christian may need to seek to transcend the polarities of idealism/materialism and dualism/monism in order to achieve a more comprehensive and satisfying view of the world.

Another observation that could be made has to do with a general approach to any issue that is linked with the general topic of relativism. Whether the specific case is that of the sociology of knowledge, cultural relativism, aesthetic evaluation, and so on, a fundamental flaw in any relativizing argument is its self-stultifying potential. Nevertheless, those proposing some variant on the relativizing motif usually try to carve out for themselves some Archimedean point on which to stand—immune from the significance of the argument they are presenting.[17] In their survey of Marx, Scheler, and Mannheim, Clark and Gaede note how each of these three tried to preserve the possibility of dependable, accurate knowledge while creating doubt about the integrity of ideas held by other groups and individuals. Yet, as they further observe, these at-

---

16. C. Stephen Evans, *Preserving the Person* (Downers Grove, IL: InterVarsity Press, 1977), p. 102.

17. For an interesting application of this point to theology see Peter Berger, *The Sacred Canopy* (New York: Doubleday, 1969), p. 163.

tempts to stave off the wolf of relativism lurking at the door may not have been particularly successful.

What this suggests is the necessity of pushing anyone who argues for the sociology of knowledge to the logical extension of that basic approach. What one finds when this is done is that there are very few who can accept complete cognitive and moral relativism. As Steven Lukes points out, "It is . . . striking that few relativists seem able in the end to take the theory-dependence of their worlds, and the pluralistic solipsism it entails, really seriously. A familiar pattern of retreat is discernible. . . ."[18] It would seem then that anyone who wishes to argue at all (since that presupposes some nonsolipsistic grounds for persuasion) has concluded against complete cognitive relativism. The problem of the sociology of knowledge exists for all reasonable people—whether Christian or not. Hence, those using the sociology of knowledge to debunk Christian beliefs must realize that they are ultimately using a saw that can cut the limb of the tree on which they sit. This would suggest that the search for solutions to the problems created by the sociology of knowledge is a challenge to which a variety of thinkers need to respond. Clark and Gaede can use this fact to assure the "doubting Thomas" that he has a diversity of allies to help solve his problem.

A final observation may be made about the sociology of knowledge. Let me make this observation in the form of a proposition: Understanding the sociology of knowledge leads to a realization of the need to integrate one's Christian faith with sociology. A word of explanation is needed here. In the past decade there has been a growing discussion/debate among Christians who are sociologists about the necessity, propriety, and possibility of integrating Christian faith with sociology. In the contexts in which I have participated in these discussions, there have been a number of common recurring themes. One of these is a concern that the integrity of sociology is threatened by integration.[19] As I have explored this concern with those who mention it, I have found that usually there is an image of sociology as a type of knowledge that is unusually protected from bias, distortion, or ideological thought through strict adherence to the scientific method. Granting that science is a

18. Steven Lukes and W. G. Runciman, "Relativism: Cognitive and Moral," *Proceedings of the Aristotelian Society* 48 (1974):168–69.

19. Although not operating in an evangelical context, Peter Berger voices this concern: "I continue to believe that Weber's position on the value-free character of the social sciences is as valid today as it was in his time, and if anything, more urgently necessary. Science ceases to be science when it becomes the expression of personal faith or faith commitments, no matter whether these are political or religious." Peter Berger, "Review Symposium: Peter Berger's *The Heretical Imperative,*" in *Journal for the Scientific Study of Religion* 20 (June 1981):2:195.

powerful means of gaining knowledge, as a sociologist I find great irony here. For what has happened is that the person arguing for the special role of sociology has either consciously or unconsciously exempted sociology from the impact of the sociology of knowledge. I believe that the implications of the sociology of knowledge extend to *all* kinds of human knowledge.[20] Whether they realize it or not, even the knowledge generated by sociologists is subject to social forces, personal subjectivity, and the possibility of distortion. Such factors as worldview do enter into the process of doing sociology. The implication of all of this is that conscious attention to how one's social location, worldview, and value commitments link up with one's sociology is preferable to an unreal denial of the connection between these factors.

A further implication, however, once one accepts the validity of integration, is the realization of the need to probe for ways to insure that what one has come to believe (either regarding Christianity or sociology) has merit and is warranted. We are then back at the need for a way of justifying our beliefs.

Years ago John Dewey captured a universal human yearning in the title of one of his books—*The Quest for Certainty.*[21] In the light of the sociology of knowledge such a quest has profound limitations. Yet Christians, if they have begun to understand how God helps them grow through a process of faith, will have discovered already that certitude does not rest upon some epistemological magic. We *can* know, but our knowing always will be conditioned upon our finitude and fallenness, as Clark and Gaede have persuasively argued. Our response to this is not despair but a greater awareness of the need to balance faith and reason. As Wolfe has written: "Faith is the courage to commit oneself to belief in the face of human finitude . . . only by doing so can reason operate."[22]

20. A book that has been most persuasive in bringing me to this conclusion is Michael Mulkay, *Science and the Sociology of Knowledge* (London: George Allen & Unwin, 1979). See especially the summary and concluding remarks, pp. 118–22.

21. John Dewey, *The Quest for Certainty* (London: Kegan Paul, 1930).

22. Wolfe, *Epistemology*, p. 71.

Psychology

COMMENTARY

Hodges argues that a biblical perspective on knowing and doing the truth has much in common with an adequate psychological perspective. Hodges rejects a passive approach to truth in both areas, proposing that knowing requires active exploration, involving reciprocity or interaction between the knower and the known (termed an ecological perspective). Therefore, commitment is required to discover the truth in all areas. (This theme will be further elaborated in the concluding essay by Nelson.)

Hodges argues that the results of psychological research and an adequate biblical perspective on knowing and doing have the following commonalities: (1) the value of multiple perspectives in detecting truth; (2) the progressive nature of perception and revelation (we perceive God's redemptive purposes more adequately as the history of the world unfolds for us); (3) the inadequacy of foundationalist theories of knowledge that view all knowledge as "built upon" an observational level of "indubitable facts" (such views fail to recognize that all observation is "theory-laden"); and (4) the value of community in knowing the truth.

An important aspect of Hodges's proposal is his emphasis on the limits of human knowledge. The quest for certainty is not appropriate for human beings because of our finitude. The "humility of comprehensive criticism" is a more appropriate stance, wherein we do not absolutize our current level of understanding but subject our tentative conclusions to careful criticism.

Martin argues that Hodges has attempted unsuccessfully to combine incompatible elements (direct perception and the conceptual relativity of facts). Nevertheless, Hodges is on the right track in sensing that any adequate theory of knowledge must understand the world to be both "not-other" (hence knowable, as in direct perception) and "other" (hence error is possible, as in a representational view of knowledge). Martin undertakes to develop a view of knowing that adequately accounts for these divergent aspects and at the same time deals with what he thinks is "*the* central epistemological issue for psychology." This central issue is, "How do we know other persons?" Martin believes the pivotal concept that applies to knowing persons, whether human or divine, is personal self-disclosure (revelation) that preserves the otherness of the known and yet makes it available to us.

In terms of the introductory taxonomy, Hodges's essay is dominantly concerned with creating a systematic schema of the homogeneous type, i.e., placing the results of disciplinary research into a synthetic framework using overarching unifying concepts. To do this, he has carefully evaluated alternative methodological and substantive assumptions in psychology (as Clark and Gaede have done in sociology) and (unlike Clark and Gaede) has adopted an existing but by no means majority approach, that of J. Gibson. In this sense there is a moderate attempt to transform the way the discipline is widely conceived. Martin's approach attempts to transform the discipline much more radically. This stems in part from Martin's concern to question the exclusion of personal knowledge from much of existing psychology (calling for a transformation of both methodological and substantive assumptions).

Implicit in both Hodges's and Martin's papers is a theme that was evident in several of the earlier papers, specifically a resistance to reductionism, i.e., to view human beings as merely material systems responding to physical stimuli. Skillen opposes Deutsch's view that the world is "a closed universe manifesting stimulus-response actions and reactions based on the struggle for satisfaction and survival against pain and death." Clark and Gaede object to the "materialistic, reductionistic assumptions . . . used to guide sociological inquiry." Hodges affirms that "the various disciplines are mutually constraining and cannot be done comprehensively and clearly without reference to each other. . . . There is no final grain of analysis to which all other disciplinary perspectives can be reduced." This issue of reductionism will be examined systematically in the biology essays by Jones and Hasker.

Clearly Hodges and Martin share the sociologists' concerns about the problems for knowing raised by relativism. Clark and Gaede, Burwell, and Hodges are all concerned about specifying conditions under which one can discriminate between truth and error, at least provisionally. Martin attempts to account for how truth and error are possible but does not address the issue of how rival truth claims can be judged.

Perception Is Relative and Veridical: Ecological and Biblical Perspectives on Knowing and Doing the Truth

BERT H. HODGES

THE PROBLEM OF RELATIVITY

Perception as Fiction

Most of us grow up as "naive realists." Naive realism assumes that experience faithfully mirrors reality, that my mental representation of the world is true to the world in all important aspects. It asserts, "I have the truth, the whole truth, and nothing but the truth." Why is it that this view has been labeled "naive"?

The view is naive, first of all, because the world is complex; consequently the information available to an observer may be ambiguous. When I was in the first grade we were asked to color a picture of a robin, the harbinger of spring. When I colored the breast of my robin orange, I was informed by my teacher that robins were "red-breasted." We argued. I don't recall who won the argument, but if I had been older one of us could have retreated gracefully muttering something about "artistic license." The point is that we disagreed about where orange stops and red starts (or vice versa, depending on your side of the argument). Unfortunately for us, there is no clear boundary between red and orange, only a fuzzy one. A good case can be made that most of the categories we use to refer to objects and events in the world have fuzzy boundaries (Labov, 1973; Rosch & Mervis, 1975; Wittgenstein, 1953).

A second reason this view of the world is naive is that it overlooks the finite character of organisms and their perceptual processes. Several years ago at the Boston Museum of Fine Arts, I looked into a special display room through the designated peephole. I saw a stepladder, a chair with a jacket on it, etc. When I walked around the room and viewed it from other peepholes, however, the stepladder had "vanished" into an odd collection of boards nailed together in ways that only vaguely resembled an ordinary stepladder and the chair was mostly painted on the floor and had no seat.

A second example of the effects of limited perspective is less dramatic but more characteristic of daily life. Shelley Taylor and Susan Fiske

(1975) had two persons carry on a simple conversation with observers sitting in chairs around them as shown in figure 1. The conversation was a prearranged one designed so that X and Y contributed equally to the conversation in almost every imaginable way (e.g., the number of topics initiated). Observers A and B thought that conversant Y dominated the conversation (i.e., the extent to which the person had caused her partner's comments), while observers E and F thought that conversant X dominated the conversation. Only observers C and D perceived the conversation reasonably accurately as equal. Why? Taylor and Fiske argue convincingly that the focus of attention for subjects A and B is Y (they can see her face), while the focus of E and F is X, and that we are biased in our perceptions of causality toward the focus of our attention. In short, what we attend to affects our perception more than what we do not attend to. Humans, by virtue of being finite, are forced to be choosers. We must notice some aspects of reality and miss others. We cannot eat our perceptual cake and have it too.

A third reason this realism is naive is that perception is constrained by prior experience. Lack of prior experience may make the pick-up of available information difficult or impossible. If someone had never tasted wine he would no doubt be quite poor at tasting the difference between a claret and chianti. On the other hand prior experience may often set up "expectancies" that cause us to "see" what is not there, as the following true story illustrates. A woman shopping for groceries hears a young child scream, "Stop, stop, you're killing my father." She turns the corner to see a very large man on top of another man choking him, with blood all around the victim's head. She runs for help thinking she

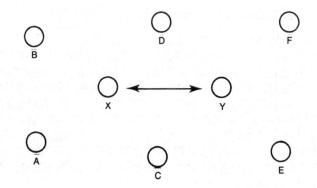

Fig. 1. The seating arrangement in the Taylor & Fiske study (1975).

has witnessed a murderous assault. When she returns several minutes later she discovers that the "murder" she would have sworn in court she saw was not a murder at all. A man had an epileptic seizure and fell, hitting and cutting his head. A second man had tried to prevent further injury to the first man by loosening the man's tie and holding his head up. The woman realized on her second look that there was only a small amount of blood from the quite minor cut, and even more amazing was her realization that the vicious, huge "man on top" was a neighbor of hers, actually small of stature (Coon, 1977, p. 127).

The evidence sampled above suggests that perception is neither simple nor exhaustive nor inerrant. Realism may not have to go, but naiveté will. It can be said more starkly. Perception is *relative*: it depends on our *point of view*, what we *selectively attend* to, the *ambiguity* and *complexity* of the available information, and our *prior knowledge* and *expectations* about the situation. If we admit perceptual relativity, should we conclude that one may see or hear whatever one wishes? Do we all live in our own make-believe worlds, perceptually created and different from the perceptual worlds created by everyone else? Richard Gregory suggests something like that when he says:

> . . . normal everyday perceptions are not selections of reality but are rather imaginative constructions—fictions—based . . . more on the stored past than on the present. On this view all perceptions are essentially fictions. . . (1972).

Although it is beyond the scope of this chapter, an examination of memory and social perception, as well as linguistic and artistic perception, only enlarges the problem of relativity (Hodges, 1981). But perhaps science can rescue objectivity and realism.

Science: Its Unjustified Justificationism

Science can be viewed as the perceptions, inferences, and memories of a community examining reality from a particular point of view. Traditionally, science has been thought to be based on a firm foundation of indisputable facts that accumulate over time as the result of the application of "the scientific method," a set of logical, rational steps that, used correctly, are free of bias.

This traditional view of science, referred to as "foundationalism" (Wolterstorff, 1976) or "justificationism" (Weimer, 1979), assumes facts and theory are separable, that facts can be identified, described, and tested independently of theory. But theory is needed just to get data collection off the ground, as the following example illustrates. Which of the following data are relevant to the question, "What causes nosebleeds"? The astrological sign the person was born under? The current phase of the moon? The color of the person's eyes? The temperature of the room? I would have been unlikely to pick phases of the moon as relevant data, but I once read an article in a psychiatric journal (obviously, a crackpot source) that proposed that the phases of the moon and nosebleeds were causally related (nasal tides?!). Lots of other theories that sound sensible now once sounded like the fantasies of lunatics: a round earth, attraction of bodies at a distance (gravitation), a moving earth, etc. What will they think of next, black holes? Facts exist only in theories; in fact, facts are theories (Popper, 1959, p. 95).[1]

A second problem for justificationism is that experiments cannot actually prove or disprove the validity of a theory. Imagine you are a detective sent to examine a body lying in the entrance hall of a great mansion. Your phenomenon of interest is the corpse, your question is "who dunnit?" and your theory is "the butler did it." Based on your theory you hypothesize that if the butler did it, the bloody footprints next to the corpse should be those of a man. You measure the footprints and decide they are those of a man. (Note that your methodology involved some theory of footprints and how certain measurements were related to the gender of the wearer.) Can you conclude the butler did it since the evidence supports your theory? Obviously not (although I find it surprising how many students will make this mistake if the example is a scientific one further removed from their everyday experience). On the other hand, suppose you decided the bloody footprints were those of a woman in high heels. Would your "butler did it" theory be falsified? Perhaps not. Maybe the butler is a transvestite! Or maybe he is cunning and wore the high heels to make you think Dame Edith or the scullery maid is the culprit. In any event it is unlikely that you would easily relinquish your theory. If and when you did give it up, it would probably be in favor of a "better" theory, not simply because of inconsistent facts. At least this is what Kuhn (1962) argues is historically true of scientists. Theory testing is always a choice among competing theoretical statements:

> No theory forbids some state of affairs specifiable in advance: it is not that we propose a theory and Nature may shout NO. Rather, we propose a maze of theories, and Nature may shout INCONSISTENT (Lakatos, 1968, p. 162).

Science proceeds by relating theories to each other, and scientists working contemporaneously may disagree about data theory, meth-

---

1. Facts might be viewed as one end of a continuum of theories with worldviews at the other end. Methodologies, models, paradigms, etc., could be viewed as various types of intermediate theories.

odological theory, or explanatory theory. A scientific community as a whole may reject earlier theoretical decisions by the community, i.e., Kuhn's "revolutions." Since one theory choice biases another, scientific theories appear to be like personal theories, subjective "fictions," always open to revision.

THE VALUE OF RELATIVITY

I shall argue that (1) relativity is here to stay; (2) relativity is necessary to perceive the world accurately; (3) invariants ("absolutes") do exist but only as relationships; (4) we can truly know the world and our place in it; and (5) this knowledge is largely tacit and action oriented rather than explicit and justifiable. To substantiate the above assertions I shall elaborate three themes: (1) the world and the perceiving organisms in it are structured in nonarbitrary ways; (2) perception is the pick-up of information (invariant relationships) that is meaningful to the organisms; and (3) this pick-up requires and intends action and is generally veridical, direct, and tacit.

Structure, Invariants, and Ambiguity

Are there limits to the ambiguity, relativity, and subjectivity of perception? What if the world is structured and perceivers are structured so that the two shape each other perceptually and behaviorally in nonarbitrary ways? What if there are "universals," relationships that constrain the perception of everyone, or at least all members of a given species?

Categorization. Early anthropological research on the use of color terms seemed to support the arbitrary divisions of the color space. For example, while English has eleven basic color terms (black, white, gray, red, orange, yellow, brown, green, blue, purple, and pink), other languages have as few as two (e.g., the Dani of West Irian). Even for languages with similar basic color terms, the boundaries drawn by native speakers between terms (e.g., the red and orange of my earlier example) vary considerably. However, Berlin & Kay (1969) and Rosch (Heider, 1972; Rosch, 1973, 1975) have shown that certain colors are universally perceived as salient and that some aspects of color naming are universal as well. For example, when asked to identify the best example of a specific color there was high agreement among speakers within and across languages (Berlin & Kay, 1969). Thus, while two people may disagree about the precise boundary between red and orange, they show high agreement on the "best orange" and the "best red." Further, Rosch showed that the Dani (a two-color-term language) learned and remembered focal colors (the "best red," "best orange," etc.) better than nonfocal colors (borderline reds, oranges, etc.), even though their language had no terms for those colors. Put simply, it seems much of color perception is universal and invariant, although some aspects (boundary lines) are not.

Direct Perception. James J. Gibson (1966, 1979) has articulated an ecological approach to perception that assumes that "the nature of humans is inextricably intertwined with the nature of a world in which they live, move, and have their being" (Shaw & Bransford, 1977). Organisms adapt to their environments both individually (perceptual learning) and as a species (evolution). If one looks at the perceptually guided actions of organisms, for example, a human walking through a cluttered room without barking her shins, or threading a needle, or recognizing an old friend's voice or face after two decade's interim, it appears that they are enormously successful in that adaptation. A theory of perception should account for this knowing of the environment; it should account for the fact that perception is generally veridical. [2]

Virtually all theories (e.g., Berkeley, 1709/1910; Gregory, 1978) besides Gibson's have assumed that the information available to the senses is too impoverished or ambiguous to specify adequately the nature of the environment. For example, the tiny, upside-down image on the retina of an eye does not contain information sufficient for the perceiver to know unambiguously the three-dimensional layout of his environment. The insufficient information of the environment is assumed to be supplemented in some way by cognitive operations (e.g., inference, memory, imagination), so that the true character of the world can be discovered. Thus, traditional theories of perception are *indirect*: something(s) (e.g., a retinal image, the state of our nerves) comes between us and the objects and events of the world we wish to know so that vital information is either lost or distorted.

Gibson argues perception is *direct*: the information available in light, sound, etc., is sufficient to specify the ecologically significant properties of the world to a properly tuned perceiver. The media in which the

2. Information-processing theories (e.g., Lindsay & Norman, 1977) have often investigated what a perceptual system *can do*, instead of what it ordinarily does do, and other theorists (e.g., Gregory, 1978) have focused on illusions as the appropriate means for discovering the nature of perceptual systems. Gibson thinks both approaches ask the wrong questions, and no matter how clever the "answers" provided to these questions the results will be sterile for a theory of perception.

My extensive use of the ecological perceptual theory of Gibson, Shaw, Turvey, and others is primarily *heuristic*: it is used as a strategic frame of reference to explore significant psychological themes about knowledge, meaning, and truth. While I prefer Gibsonian perceptual theory to alternative theories, I am not convinced it is always right in its differences with those alternatives. This chapter includes several criticisms of ecological theory in the text and footnotes that follow.

information is embodied (e.g., light, the nervous system) are transparent to the information; that is, the media are not perceived, only the structure of the environment. Perceivers need not infer or construct what the world is like; they are in direct contact with it whether they are touching, looking, or listening.

"To argue that sensory input need not be embellished is to argue that, at some level, the light to an eye, the pressure waves to an ear, or the pattern of pressures on the skin are uniquely and invariantly tied to their sources in the environment" (Michaels & Carello, 1981, p. 19). Thus, for Gibson perceptual systems are attuned to invariants, unchanging patterns of energy (e.g., light, sound) within the general flux of energy. Several simple examples of invariants in vision are given to illustrate what it is that visual systems might "zero in" on.

The horizon is a reference line "perpendicular to the pull of gravity" by which a person judges when something is upright or tilted, including herself (Gibson, 1979, p. 164). The invariant horizon can also specify sizes of objects. As figure 2 illustrates, the horizon "cuts" objects of the same size (the telephone poles) into the same ratio (two-thirds of each pole is above the horizon and one-third below). Any two objects divided into these ratios, no matter how close or far from the observer, are the same height. (Of course, objects of different heights are divided into different ratios.) Furthermore, the horizon "cuts" an object at the height of the observer's eyes; thus, the tree in figure 2 is twice the observer's eye height, and the telephone poles are three times taller than eye height. It is interesting to note that this "horizon ratio relation" is neither subjective nor objective (i.e., it is not "in the observer" or "out there"). It is

Fig. 2. An illustration of the invariant information made available by the horizon ratio relation (from Gibson, 1979).

ecological: it reveals the *reciprocity* of observer and environment (Gibson, 1979).

The previous example involved object perception. Are there invariants in *event* perception? A couple of simple but important examples will suggest that there are universal, fixed reference points (or relations) for moving objects and observers. If a portion of your visual field expands symmetrically and rapidly—duck! An optical expansion pattern of this sort specifies unambiguously that an object is on a collision course with you. Humans, monkeys, kittens, chicks, frogs, and fiddler crabs all show avoidance behavior when such a "looming" sequence is optically presented (a real object was not approaching the animals) (Schiff, 1965; Schiff, Caviness, & Gibson, 1962). If the *entire* visual field were to expand, it would create optical flow similar to that illustrated in figure 3. Such a flow pattern invariantly specifies movement of the perceiver through a stable environment. Thus, vision alone can specify movement without muscle-joint kinesthesis. Even more significantly, the point toward which the perceiver is moving is invariantly specified by the point (unmoving) from which the optical outflow occurs. This center of optical expansion is "formless" and absolute; it is the same for any structure approached, whether a brick wall or the face of a spouse (Gibson, 1979). It is a reference point by which we may control our locomotion. (See Regan & Beverly, 1979, for neurophysiological evidence in support of Gibson's theory and Regan & Beverly, 1982, for complications regarding direction of gaze.)

Perceptual invariants demonstrate that the world is structured in nonarbitrary ways that allow us to know what is true about the world as we

Fig. 3. An optical expansion pattern that specifies movement of the observer (if it occurs over the whole visual field) toward the point at the center.

relate to it. Vertical perception is made possible by such "absolute" reference points (lines, relations) and many of these invariants appear to hold universally for all humans and other terrestrial animals. While much is variable in the world, some things do not change.

Some of the examples of ambiguity in the first part of the paper seem less severe when reexamined in this light. For example, we may disagree about robins being red- or orange-breasted, but no teacher would have told me that robins were green-breasted! Even the woman who saw the "murder" was not wrong about much of what she saw: she did see two men, one on top of the other, blood, etc. Her errors were about sizes and amounts and the inference of "intent to kill." The errors and disagreements about the world are real and sometimes serious, but they do not occur in an amorphous, undifferentiated world. The world may not be the black and white of naive realism, but it is not a dull, undifferentiated gray either.

Perception Is Absolutely Relative

Gibson's ecological theory says that *what* organisms perceive is "information," invariants detected over temporal and spatial transformations. Information is something specific to an object or an event that differentiates it from other objects and events. The punchline is: something can be known only *in relation to* something else. Knowledge is relative.

Even the invariants illustrated in the previous section are relative; all involve relationships. The "horizon ratio relation" was relative to the perceiver's eye height and also was a ratio, the mathematical term for a relationship. Events are temporally extended spatial movements by one or more objects. Temporal extension and movement are inherently relative. For example, a melody is an invariant set of temporal and pitch relations. Since invariants are relative, the "absolute" values of the members of the relationship are irrelevant.[3] Thus, we can transpose a melody across keys and instruments: the melody of the opening line of Beethoven's Fifth Symphony is the same when played by a violin or trumpet, sung by a soprano or a bass, performed in the key of C or E-flat. All of these are different embodiments of the same structure and differ in numerous ways irrelevant to the melody.

If the "absolute" value of an element in a relationship remains unchanged but the relationship it is in changes, we perceive a change. A simple example is "color contrast": if an orange of a certain wavelength

3. "Absolutes" in the sense used here are arbitrary, more or less, as in "standard" measurements of time (e.g., one minute, one year, although this latter is ecologically based).

is put on a black background it appears to be a different shade from the same orange on a white background. We perceive relationships, not objects in isolation.

What an organism perceives and *how* it perceives it cannot be described unless we know *who* is doing the perceiving (Shaw & McIntyre, 1974). What can be detected by one animal cannot be detected by another. Heat patterns identify warm-blooded prey for rattlesnakes (temperature changes of .002°C can be detected), and ultraviolet radiation patterns locate nectar for honeybees. What is information for rattlesnakes and bees is not information for humans. Even when two animals can both detect the same thing, it may be perceived differently. For my cat a windowsill "affords" (a favorite Gibsonian term) sleeping. It does not for me. Even for two animals of the same species, "affordances" attended to may differ depending on their ecological habitat and their behavioral purposes. A fire or a stove affords cooking food, depending on where I am, and a frying pan affords frying fish or flinging at an irritating spouse (which I notice depends on whether I am hungry or angry).

"The *affordances* of the environment are what it *offers* the animal, what it *provides* or *furnishes*, either for good or ill" (Gibson, 1979, p. 127). Thus, an affordance of an object or event is the *meaning* it has for a given animal. Meaning is neither subjective nor objective but relative to both the animal and its environment. When an animal perceives the meaning (affordance) of an object it is detecting what behaviors it could enter into with respect to the object. "Objects become meaningful by virtue of their interrelations with other objects (including the knowing organism); and objects are not always identified as mere objects. Instead they are understood relative to their roles in events" (Bransford & McCarrell, 1974). This does not mean perception necessarily involves conscious categorization; humans can perceive that an object affords sitting without "recognizing" it as a member of the category "chair" (Michaels & Carello, 1981, p. 42; Neisser, 1976, pp. 74–75).

An object can have multiple meanings because it can enter multiple relationships. As noted earlier, a frying pan can be used for (can mean) quite different things. Objects afford much more than we notice, but there are constraints on the meanings an object can have. Some constraints are relative to the organism (I cannot sleep on a windowsill), while others are relative to environmental relations (household scissors do not afford cutting sheet metal).

Burke (1969) has noted that the very words we use to designate the meaning of the thing itself, such as "substance" and "definition," are themselves contextual.

Literally, a person's or a thing's sub-stance would be something that stands beneath or supports the person or thing. . . . The word "substance" used to designate what a thing is, derives from a word designating something that a thing is not. . . . To define, or determine a thing, is to mark its boundaries, hence to use terms that possess, implicitly at least, contextual reference (pp. 21–24).

Meaning is relational, multiple, and does not necessarily involve conscious categorization.

Since meaning is related both to the environment and the animal perceiving it, the meaning of an object cannot be said to reside either in the environment or in the organism. Meaning is the specification of the animal-environment relation. Gibson's perceptual theory undermines the usual dichotomy of objective-subjective by its insistence that the who, how, and what questions of information detection are mutually constraining.

What we usually call subjective and objective are only differing "poles of attention" (Gibson, 1979). First, it can be noted that the boundary between subjective and objective is a shifting one. Our use of tools, which are separate from us when not in use, become part of us when in use. For example, we can *feel* the cutting action of the blades of scissors though our fingers are placed in rounded holes. A blind person using a white-tipped cane feels the sidewalk or grass he taps with his stick. What is ordinarily perceived (noticed) in both of these instances is information about events (cutting) or objects (sidewalk). One can, however, shift attention to the hand and its sensations as it cuts or taps; such a shift is from objective to subjective.

An even better example of subjectivity being the reciprocal of objectivity is the visual information that specifies *self*. Shut one eye and notice the field of view of the open eye. It is somewhat like a window on the world, but the boundaries (e.g., I can see some cheek, a bit of mustache, my nose, etc.) that hide my surroundings specify *me*. I (and all egos) am unique, since no other person sees me as I do. If my head or body moves, visual information alone specifies "me moving." Thus, vision co-perceives "internal" and "external," "here" and "there."

To perceive is to know both the world and the self. An organism cannot be separated from its environment without loss of self. To detect affordances is to detect how something relates to self, and knowledge of the self is found in its perceptual-behavioral interaction with its ecological niche. Thus, meaning is neither phenomenal ("in my head") nor impersonal (out there, unrelated to me). Knowing is ecological, both personal and true to the world.

The Necessity of Activity

Meaningful knowing of the world requires action. This action is two-edged: action is required to perceive accurately, and the reason for perceiving is to control action, to make behavior effective. As Gibson (1979, p. 223) puts it: "The theory of affordances implies that to see things is to see how to get about among them and what to do or not to do with them. If this is true, visual perception serves behavior, and behavior is controlled by perception."

The necessity of movement. Traditional perceptual theory has assumed that movement makes perception more difficult. No doubt this was related to the comparison of eyes to cameras; if the camera or the object being photographed moved, blur occurred. However, Gibson's theory suggests that the invariant structure of objects is best revealed in events. Johannsson (1973) has provided an elegant and important demonstration of the role of temporal transformations in visual perception. Imagine that you are looking at a film that shows you the random arrangement of light spots diagrammed in figure 4. Suddenly the lights move, and instantly you see not a random collection of lights but a person, a person walking! There is such a film and its effect is as fully dramatic as I have attempted to describe (Maas, 1971). As figure 5 reveals, the film is created by attaching lights to the major joints of a human body dressed in black and photographing in the dark. If other actions are taken, hopping, sit-ups, or in the cutest demonstration, two

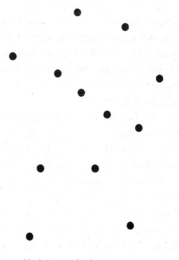

Fig. 4. "Random" pattern of lights attached to a nonmoving person (from Michaels & Carello, 1981.

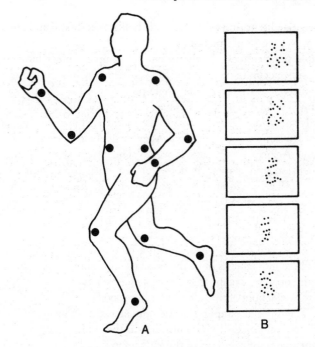

Fig. 5. An example of the type of displays used by investigators to study patterns of humans in motion. (A) Positions of lights affixed to individuals. (B) A sequence of movement positions made by a dancing couple. (From S. Coren, C. Porac, & L. Ward, *Sensation and Perception*, 2d ed. [New York: Academic Press, 1984].)

persons dancing a polka (see Fig. 5), the nature of the event and the participants in the event are immediately seen. If the movement stops, the random light spots reappear. More recent research indicates that the distinctive gait of a friend or the gender of the walking individual can even be detected by watching the moving lights (Cutting & Koslowski, 1977; Koslowski & Cutting, 1977).

A fascinating set of experiments by Pritchard (1961) reveals that motion is a necessity for vision, not just a convenient way of resolving ambiguity. Due to the antagonistic muscle sets holding the eye in place, there is a constant small movement of the eyes. The light reflected from an unmoving object does not, therefore, project onto exactly the same receptors. Pritchard, however, attached a tiny camera to a contact lens that when placed on the cornea stabilized an image onto the same receptors since the contact lens moved with the eye. The result was intriguing: subjects reported seeing the image (the letter "A") for a few seconds, then it broke up and disappeared. Thus, it appears that the visual system quite literally responds only to relationships, some temporal or spatial discontinuity. If the world held perfectly still and our eyes did not move, we would be blind.

Multiple perspectives. In the previous examples object movement made possible accurate perception. But sometimes things do not move. Is the perceiver restricted to the single perspective (or "sample of the optic array") available at the perceiver's current location? Usually not. Ordinarily the visual system is free to explore, to get as many angles as necessary (to sample the optic array as extensively as necessary) to see accurately. Again Gibson says it well: "The visual system *hunts* for comprehension and clarity. It does not rest until the invariants are extracted" (1979, p. 219). The visual system can begin to do this by opening *two* eyes, instead of only one. Two eyes provide two overlapping samples of the optic array and enhance our perception of the three-dimensional layout of the world (e.g., stereoscopes).[4] Of course the eyes can move, as well as the head, and the body within which they are nested. These movements have the same effect on object perception as moving the objects, except that the co-perceived event is not a movement of the object but of the self—eyes, head, body, or any combination thereof. The ordered sampling of the optical structure available in the light reflected off objects (what Gibson calls the "ambient optic array") reveals the invariant geometry of the surfaces in the place observed. Any ambiguity of geometry in a single perspective on the environment dissolves with the "overall perspective" provided by locomotion (e.g., multiple perspectives reveal the "distorted" room to be just that). In fact, perspective ("this view from here") vanishes with movement; only the extracted invariants of the motion and the place remain.

Perception takes time. It is obvious from the preceding paragraphs that accurate perception takes time, sufficient time for an event to run its "cycle," or for the perceiver to walk around, look, touch, sniff, or whatever is necessary to detect the object's affordances. Thus, the "perceptual moment" is no fixed unit of "absolute" Newtonian time but is relative to "who" and "what" as much as to "how." For example, Shaw and his colleagues (Shaw & Pittenger, 1977; Todd, Mark, Shaw, & Pittenger, 1980) have studied how we perceive growth and aging of faces. The research suggests that some version of a cardioidal strain transformation may be the geometric invariant we perceive when we

---

4. Having two views (eyes) is problematical in traditional perceptual theories since they assume that two images would be transmitted to the brain that would have to be integrated into a single perception. Ecological theory treats two eyes as two samples of the same ambient optic array; thus, seeing one object with two eyes should be no more difficult than feeling one object with two hands or hearing one sound with two ears (cf. Gibson, 1979, pp. 213–14; Michaels & Carello, 1981, pp. 116ff.).

recognize someone as aged. The important point for present purposes is that this invariant emerges over a long period of years, while Johansson's walking sequence can be perceived as such within a fraction of a second. Traditional theory assumes time and motion are enemies of perceptual clarity; ecological theory assumes temporally and spatially extended events are the coin of the perceptual realm.[5]

Truth in perspective. That the truth of the world is best apprehended by activity, events involving movements of objects and/or observers, suggests that there is no correct or absolute perspective from which to view the world. Rather, the best perspective is *no* perspective. To discover the absolutes of the world, its invariants, we must *relativize* our perspective on it. Again Gibson sees and writes clearly:

> It is not so obvious but it is true that an observer who is moving about sees the world at no point of observation and thus, strictly speaking, cannot notice the perspectives of things. The implications are radical. Seeing the world at a traveling point of observation, over a long enough time for a sufficiently extended set of paths, begins to be perceiving the world at all points of observation, as if one could be everywhere at once. To be everywhere at once with nothing hidden is to be all-seeing, like God (1979, p. 197).

A given perspective specifies not so much the environment as it does the perceiver, the subjective "seen now from here" rather than a comprehensive view of the environment.

The truth of the world can be known by any observer who moves through it and extracts the invariants. Although two people cannot be in the same place simultaneously, they can both share the same path of locomotion and thus have available to them the same invariants (at least for those objects or events that are stable over time). Public knowledge is possible: we can all know the same world, although incompletely, as well as be aware of our own place in it.

Gibson suggests that "the most decisive test for reality is whether you can discover new features and details by the act of scrutiny" (1979, p. 257). If further exploration does not allow previously unnoticed or unavailable information to be detected, one is probably not examining reality. If we already "know it all" about some object or event, the object or event is probably imaginary.

Knowing takes time and active exploration. Commitment is required to discover truth.

Perception as tacit restructuring. Traditional theories assume that

---

5. Michaels & Carello, 1981, chap. 6, gives a clear, concise comparison of traditional and ecological accounts of long-term perception.

organisms detect very simple properties of the energy available to them and then modify (add to) this simple information by processing it through a hierarchy of cognitive operations. This bottom-to-top approach is characteristic of many theoretical models in science, but both its assumptions of atomism (some low-level basic units exist) and reductionism (complex phenomena can be reduced to basic units) can be questioned (Anderson, 1974; Jenkins, 1974; Koestler & Smythies, 1971; Michaels & Carello, 1981). Ecological theory assumes no "final units" into which the perceptual world must be decomposed (Gibson, 1979, p. 9). Organisms are assumed to be able to detect higher-order invariants directly. Processing may be top-to-bottom, from complex wholes to constituent parts, as well as the reverse. For example, Klapp (1971) has found that the number of syllables needed to pronounce a number (eight-y, sev-en-ty) affects the amount of time it takes to identify visually the number (80, 70). When presented with "80-80" subjects pressed a key as quickly as possible to denote they were the same; numbers with three syllable pronunciations took longer to identify than pairs with shorter pronunciations. One would assume visual identification of a number would need to take place *before* its pronunciation could be known. Turvey (1974) describes numerous other experiments which apparently show that "higher-order" properties (e.g., meaningfulness, coherence, symmetry) affect the identification of lower-order properties of which the higher-order properties "should be" composed. How can this be?

The primary purpose of perception is effective action, not passive contemplation. An organism's purpose (value) is inextricably linked to its knowing and doing; according to Lewis (1946):

> The primary and pervasive significance of knowledge lies in its guidance of action: knowing is for the sake of doing. And action, obviously, is rooted in evaluation. For a being which did not assign comparative values, deliberate action would be pointless; and for one which did not know, it would be impossible (p. 3).

Weimer (1979, p. 79) provides the punchline: ". . . knowing, doing and valuing can and must be reunited." Gibson's (1966, 1979) concept of "affordance" is his theoretical attempt to carry out Weimer's "mandate." Regardless of whether Gibson's theory is adequate or not, the theory's motivation cannot be faulted.

Not only does the theory of affordances attempt to bring together perception, behavior, and meaning, the "subjective" and "objective," but it tries to mend the mind-body break as well. Perception is an activity, not an experience in consciousness. According to Gibson (1979):

Perceiving is an achievement of the individual, not an appearance in the theater of his consciousness. It is a keeping-in-touch with the world, an experiencing of things rather than a having of experiences. It involves awareness-of instead of just awareness. It may be awareness of something in the environment or something in the observer or both at once, but there is no content of awareness independent of that of which one is aware. This is close to the act psychology of the nineteenth century except that perception is not a mental act. Neither is it a bodily act. Perceiving is a psychosomatic act, not of the mind or of the body but of a living observer (pp. 239–40).

Perceptual knowledge of the world, then, is "tacit," to use Polanyi's (1966) term. We need not be able to experience consciously or describe our knowledge to have it. Knowledge is more a matter of *knowing how* to do something (e.g., locomote in a cluttered environment) than *knowing about* the doing. For example, a typist's knowledge is "in her fingers," and consequently answering a verbal question about the keyboard (e.g., where is the colon?) is harder than typing it.

The typist example suggests a more general principle. Knowledge is embodied and dispersed. Knowing is a skilled interaction with the world and is dispersed throughout the body of the knower. Thus, knowing involves a restructuring (a constraining) of a body, its muscles, nervous system, etc., not just an appearance in consciousness. In fact, if a typist thinks too much about what she is doing, speed and accuracy decrease. To learn about the world and act effectively in it generally requires that we be unself-conscious.

Having observed that knowledge may be tacit, embodied, and unself-conscious, we are in a position to see why not all perceptual processing must be bottom-to-top, "basic" properties to "higher-order" properties. Much of what we know we are not conscious of; as Turvey (1974) puts it, we can know "about things we do not know we know about" (p. 171). Tacit knowledge of invariants affording action may precede conscious identification or categorization (cf. pp. 171–72). Most of our perceptual skills are tacit: neither the invariant relationships that make perception possible nor our perceptual activities in detecting those relationships is something of which we are ordinarily aware.

When someone learns a new perceptual skill (attends to previously undetected invariants and their affordances), the new information *restructures* the perceiver into a new person. "The consequence of personal experience is not that the old animal has new knowledge, but that it is a new animal that knows better" (Michaels & Carello, 1981, p. 78). Perceptual learning involves what Gibson calls "the education of attention." This education of attention requires doing. Only in the activity of doing the skill we wish to learn, however unskilled our first attempts, will we be able to extract the invariants that will make possible the control necessary to do the skill effectively. And verbalization (explicit knowledge) is of minimal help in perceptual learning. Reading about having a baby, riding a bicycle, doing a scientific experiment, will never substitute for the doing of those activities. Only as a body actively interacts with the world will it be tacitly constrained and restructured in ways similar to those bodies already "in the know."

Knowing is tacit because it is embodied in a finite organism that must move to relate to the world. The body exists to make ethical choices, life-affirming actions both for its own sake and its world's. To be too self-conscious gets in the way of accurate perception and effective behavior. Knowing and doing demand the humility of tacit knowledge.

Normative criteria for perception. An ecological approach to perception does not rule out all ambiguity in the world or the possibility of illusion. There seem to be two general categories of perceptual errors. First, there may be inadequate or conflicting information available to the perceiver. For example, optical texture may be masked by fog, or too little light, or too much light. Further, the perceiver may be too close or too far from the objects or events to register their invariant structure. The second reason for perceptual errors is the reciprocal of inadequate information: errors may occur because of inadequacies of the perceiver. Cones in the retina may be defective, leading to red-green color blindness, or LSD or other chemicals may afford hallucinations rather than perceptions. More commonly, perceiver inadequacies occur because of voluntary or involuntary restrictions on the sampling activities of the perceiver. A perceiver who chooses not to open two eyes, or move eyes, head, and body to make new samples of information available will consequently see the world less clearly. Of course, many demonstrations of illusion involuntarily restrict the observer in just this way. The distorted room described earlier appears as it does only because the peephole allows looking with one immobile eye. Similarly, the time a perceptual system has to explore its subject may be too restricted to reveal the invariants affording effective action. This is Gibson's complaint against much of the information-processing research.

Sometimes in everyday life perceptual activity is spatially or temporally restricted. Certainly the observers of Taylor and Fiske's (1975) conversation experiment described earlier would have discerned what happened better if they had not been required by politeness to remain in their seats. And the woman who saw the "murder" would have seen the event more accurately if she had only taken a bit longer to sample the optic and acoustic information available to her. But sometimes we cannot move or do not have the time we would like. In such cases we would expect focus of attention, prior expectations, etc., to have maximal effect. Gibson (1979) may well underestimate the extent to which accuracy of perception is limited by time and place. Many important events we perceive are irreversible and of sufficiently short duration that we may be unsure of the accuracy of our perceptions.[6] I suspect that these sorts of events are the ones that we are most likely to disagree about.

Errors may be minimized by temporally extended perceptual activity, but by what standard do we judge truth or error in perception? Although we routinely judge others or ourselves to have made errors, perceptual norms are problematic. First, errors can only be identified by comparing them to what a more sufficient sample of the available information has revealed to be true.

Second, the standard used to evaluate the effectiveness of an animal's action cannot be chosen without regard to the animal and its purposes. In this sense, what is true is relative, relative to a particular occasion. A prosaic example is provided by my daughter, who when she was two struggled to understand why I called her a "big girl" one day and a "little girl" the next. Of course, it all depended on whether I was comparing her to a baby or a ten-year-old. What is big depends on the animal deciding. The appropriateness of this sort of relativity is easily seen, but that other physical measurements must be ecological, not animal-neutral, is less well appreciated. An ecological approach to the phenomenon of color contrast suggests that wavelength reflectance, the classical and animal-neutral description of color by physicists, is an inappropriate standard for human perception of color. Other physical descriptions, too complex to describe here but which take into account the relationships of all wavelengths presented (Land, 1977), seem better for describing the invariants that afford color vision in humans. Thus, a spectrometer which reads out that two oranges, one on black and one on white, are identical is no truer a description of the world than is a human's perception of the oranges as different. Spectrometers detect one invariant relationship; the human visual system detects another.

Finally, what is often called an error in perception implicitly restricts the perceiver to his initial sampling of information. Truth detection is restricted to one perceptual system "here-and-now" ("now" being of very short duration). All this has been argued to be unecological and inappropriate. An assumption that lies behind this implicit restriction is that perceiving is a process that has a conscious *percept* as an end-point.

6. See Gibson, 1979, pp. 190, 208–9, and 257 for a discussion of reversible and irreversible events. A ball rolling to the left is the reverse of a ball rolling to the right; but an apple being eaten is irreversible.

Thus, if I am in a desert and I become aware of a shimmering oasis in the distance which is really a mirage, my percept is illusory. If, however, perceptual knowing is ecologically controlled action that involves activity by all perceptual systems over extended periods of time, then it is less clear that it is erroneous to walk toward what my perceptual systems will come to detect as "more sand affording walking but not drinking." As Michaels and Carello (1981, p. 95) point out: "The mistake would be to take no action" (on the assumption that I wanted to find water).

Since perceiving is a temporally extended activity rather than a matter of having discrete percepts, it is not easy to decide when a perceiver has made a mistake. Given that it takes time and activity to gain clear and comprehensive knowledge, a cessation of activity by the perceiver would seem the fairest point at which to assess her knowledge. Since further activity may educate the perceiver's attention to previously unnoticed invariants affording new, more effective behavior, perception may always be said to be erroneous because it is incompletely comprehensive and clear.[7] Our knowledge does not conform to the ontological standard of an all-knowing God. In this sense all human beings fall short of the (epistemic) glory of God (Rom. 3:23).

The epistemological character of finitude can be stated more positively, however. Since our knowing is finite, truth for us and other animals is always relative and pragmatic rather than absolute and ontological. Only a foundationalist approach to knowing requires atemporal certainty and a stress on the "erroneous character" of perception. An ecological approach to knowing suggests that we never stop learning, growing in knowledge; if we do, we have ultimately erred—we die. Finite perceiving requires learning and development. Action that "hunts for comprehension and clarity" in the interest of living is what is demanded by

7. In their most recent and philosophically sophisticated description of ecological perceptual theory, Shaw, Turvey, and Mace (1982) argue quite the reverse of what I have said. They argue perception is *never* erroneous by arguing that (1) perception impresses its truth upon you by force of existence rather than by force of argument (e.g., a skeptic dies if he steps off a cliff even though he may refuse to believe there is a cliff); (2) perceptions are nonpropositional states of affairs which provide "necessary *a posteriori* knowledge about the world" (p. 194); and (3) "perception, unlike judgment, is *of* the actual (necessarily true) world rather than *about* possible (only contingently true) worlds" (p. 194). But the practical effect of this provocative argument is not unlike what I have said. To let Shaw et al. speak for themselves: "Of course, not all objects of experience at every moment get disambiguated by right action; sometimes the actions are wrong or irrelevant. Thus, we must recognize that since experience is broader than perception, the world we truly experience—and to some extent know—is never fully specified nor completely disambiguated from other 'possible-worlds'" (p. 202).

God and the world, not passive, contemplative certitude. Animals and humans must *work* to know and live.[8]

KNOWING TO LIVE: THE CALL TO CRITICISM AND COMMITMENT

What are the implications of an ecological approach to perception for knowing and doing the truth as a scientist and as a Christian? How does the psychological perspective taken in this paper constrain other levels of analysis—the biological, the theological, etc.—and how is it mutually constrained by them? In this final section the nature of postfoundationalist science will be briefly explored and then a biblical perspective on knowing and doing the truth will be related to the psychological perspective taken so far. The similarity of the characteristics of scientific communities and Christian communities will emerge repeatedly.

Science and the Humility of Comprehensive Criticism

An ecological approach suggests scientific knowledge is (1) limited and relative, (2) social, (3) tacit and dispersed, and (4) contextually constrained and value laden. First, science is no different from ordinary perception in being finite and relative. Scientific theories are not absolutely comprehensive and clear; they do not capture all of the details and relationships of the world even as known at the time of the theory. Because of this, Bartley (1962) and Weimer (1979) have argued that the rationality of science is found in "comprehensive criticism." Weimer describes what he means as follows:

> Knowledge claims, whether scientific or otherwise, are always *fallible;* anything in both common sense and the "body of science" is subject to criticism and consequent revision or rejection, *at all times and for all time.* . . . Nothing in science is immune to criticism or justified fideistically, by appeal to authority. . . . The only way to defend fallible knowledge claims is by marshaling other fallible knowledge claims. . . (1979, pp. 40–41).

Even the claim that rationality is embodied in comprehensive criticism cannot avoid critical scrutiny. It too is a fallible knowledge claim. "Comprehensively critical rationalism" does *not* mean "anything goes" and does not rule out commitment; as articulated by Weimer (1979):

---

8. Rest will come only in the *shalom* of God's sabbath; and even in the new heaven and earth I suspect we will be active. Hell, I suspect, will be enforced passivity or the "activity" of self-focused attention, endlessly subjective and unchanging. Contrary to Sartre (1954), one does not need other people to be in hell: one only needs oneself.

But is [a comprehensively critical] rationality "nothing but" the idea of being constantly critical? The answer is emphatically "no" . . . [for] *what counts* as criticism, in a nonjustificational point of view, *is far from obvious*. . . . In a broad, vague sense, to criticize a position or theory (scientific or otherwise) is to work within it, to explore and articulate it and examine its consequences (pp. 48–49).

. . . Criticism, far from being an intuitively clear and unproblematic notion, is a matter for intensive study. What constitutes (adequate) criticism may vary from case to case. . . . Indeed there are times when being *committed* to a position (even dogmatically) may be an effective means of being critical. . . (p. 41).

Comprehensive critical relationalism does not rule out faith commitment, only "blind faith." It suggests that scientific truth can be pursued in the context of a commitment to a particular research paradigm (Kuhn, 1962, calls this "normal science") as well as in the critical evaluation of alternative paradigms in times of "revolutionary science." Comprehensive criticism indicates that the rationality of science resides in humility. Only individuals and communities that know their limits, that admit to errors and the need to learn more can learn more.

Second, science is intrinsically social; it can only be done within a community. The communal character of science is necessary for at least two reasons. First, the sheer enormity and complexity of the subject which any discipline attempts to describe demands multiple perspectives. The phenomena that physicists or psychologists seek to perceive is "larger" and "takes longer" than most objects and events of everyday perception. Second, scientists must communicate with each other to share their perspectives and to engage in comprehensive criticism.[9] To be a scientist is to open one's theorizing and research to critical scrutiny.

Third, scientific knowledge is tacit and dispersed. Scientists know more than they can tell (explicitly to the scientific novice), and the community as a whole knows more than any of its members. The rationality of science may reside *implicitly* in its communal activity rather than in any explicit, logical reconstruction. If scientific knowledge is tacit and dispersed, it defies "conscious planning and explicit control" (Weimer, 1979, p. 91).

---

9. The fact that science can get fewer perspectives on its "object-event" than ordinary perception usually can, and that much of its perception is indirect because of inferential methodology and its dependency on social communication, lead to scientific "truth" being more ambiguous than is usually true of ordinary perception. It should be noted in passing that a direct theory of perception such as Gibson's does not constrain one to be a foundationalist. In fact, the contextual character of the ecological approach (e.g., information cannot be defined in an animal-neutral way) seems to fit the "comprehensive criticism" view of science just described.

Finally, an ecological approach to science suggests that various disciplines are mutually constraining and cannot be done comprehensively and clearly without reference to each other. As noted earlier, ecological constraints are contextual, top-to-bottom as well as the reverse. This means for example that physics needs psychology (e.g., concept of the observer) as much as psychologists need an ecologized physics (cf. Shaw & McKintyre, 1974, pp. 320ff.). Just as there are no "final units" in perception there is no final grain of analysis to which all other disciplinary perspectives can be reduced. Physics is not more "basic" or "real" than is psychology, which is no more so than theology.

Science involves choices which require values. Unless these choices (of research questions and methodological and explanatory theories) are to be capriciously random, and thus irrational, they must be made in a valuational context. The valuational context is formed by everything from economic structures, as Marxists are quick to point out (Brown, 1974), to religious worldview structures, as Christians have noted (Wolterstorff, 1976, 1980).[10] Most of these values are implicit, but scientists and philosophers need not cringe when these hidden values are discovered. Only comprehensive criticism is required.[11]

Knowing and Doing in Biblical Perspective

A theological or worldview analysis of truth, knowledge, and meaning contextually constrains a psychological analysis and vice versa. This is just a specific case of the general principle that all disciplinary perspectives mutually constrain each other, that our knowing is ecological and not based on some foundational discipline. For the most part the theology embodied in the discussion of perception has been tacit; now parts of it will be made more explicit. Perhaps the view afforded by two

10. Some postjustificationist philosophers of science (e.g., Lakatos, 1970; Laudan, 1977) see philosophy as describing the rational development of scientific knowledge and sociopsychological theories as describing the nonrational (valuational) aspects of scientific development. Weimer (1979, pp. 86–92) argues that relegating psychology and sociology to explaining aberrations and gaps in "the logic of scientific discovery" is ill advised. In support of Weimer, ecological theory suggests that the subjective and objective poles of scientific theorizing are inseparable and reciprocal. Scientific theories *co-specify* relational structures in the world and in the communal "self" that holds the theories. Behaviorist psychology and Newtonian physics tell us not only about the subject of scientific observation, but about the sociology, aesthetics, theology, etc. of the scientists who believe those theories.

11. Everything I have said about the nature of science in this section is applicable to the descriptions of psychological research and theory made in this paper. Neither the psychological assertions made earlier nor the theological assertions made in the following section are beyond criticism. Foundationalism, scientific or theological, is disavowed.

perspectives on perception and truth will enhance the depth of our understanding.[12]

Finiteness: its psychological and theological consequences. All perceivers, human and animal, are finite, creatures of the infinite God who brought them forth from the dust and water of the earth (Gen. 1:20, 24; 2:7, 19). As creatures all animals are constrained, subject to God and God's purposes, and constrained by their place in the earth environment. As a consequence, knowing and doing are limited; omniscience and omnipotence do not characterize creatures.

The finiteness of perception forces a cognitive economy on organisms: they must be selective—and choices always mean trade-offs. For example, looking at a pointillist painting at close range causes the cathedral facade to "disappear," but choosing to view the painting from across the gallery causes the pigment dots to "vanish." Both are true views of the painting, but they are different. Clarity of the dots must be sacrificed if one is to have a more comprehensive view of the painting. The need of organisms for clarity, definition, and precision is constrained by the competing need for comprehensiveness, extension, and flexibility. What organisms need is truth, clarity that is comprehensive. Alas, organisms are finite; neither clarity nor comprehensiveness can be fully realized. The truth available to organisms is limited. Finite creatures cannot avoid being economical.

A recurrent problem within Judaism and Christianity has been the tension between freedom and responsibility in moral conduct. "Legalists" have great clarity in their moral conduct, but Jesus condemned them for their lack of comprehension ("the Sabbath was made for man and not man for the Sabbath") and comprehensiveness ("you tithe mint and dill and cummin, and have neglected the weightier matters of the law, justice, mercy, and faith"). There can be multiple embodiments of the same truth, but legalism restricts the biblical flexibility (Rom. 14). On the other hand, "libertines" are so adapted to the hedonism of the culture that they have lost their definition (clarity) as Christians. Such Christians are salt which has lost its taste (Matt. 5:15).

Since truth can be multiply embodied and is constrained by comprehensiveness as well as clarity, it is relative. Only a God that is omnipresent (comprehensiveness) and holy (clarity) will be ultimately True ("in

12. This is what I take to be the task of what is sometimes called "faith-learning integration." This paper does most of its looking from the psychological perspective, since that is where I as a psychologist stand. Theologians can speak better for their perspective than I, just as physicists can speak better for their discipline than I. This suggests "faith-learning integration" requires more expertise and more communal, interdisciplinary scholarship than is often supposed.

him all things hold together"; Col. 1:17). For finite humans, being true means knowing and doing with sufficient clarity and comprehensiveness to fulfill our God-given and environmentally constrained mandates. Compared to the perfection of God's perceiving and doing, human perceptual efforts are incomplete, always in need of growth. God calls humans to learn. What is sufficient knowing and doing for a child is not for an adult, and what was adequate perceiving and acting for previous generations is inadequate for current ones. The biblical evidence suggests that humans will be judged by relative standards (e.g., "to whom much is given, of him will much be required"; Luke 12:48). But the biblical evidence also suggests all humans have fallen short of an absolute, minimum standard (Rom. 3:23); this "fall" presents a major complication for knowing and doing the truth.

Rejection of limits and the search for certainty. The crux of the biblical story is that humans rejected their creaturely status as beneath their dignity. They were not content to be finite perceivers: they wanted to know "like God" (Gen. 3:5). Rejecting their God-given task and the perceptual constraints it entailed, humans "fell short of the glory of God" ethically, not just ontologically. This rejection of the finiteness of their perception was a moral rebellion with profound, puzzling consequences. The first one noted in the Genesis account is that humans became painfully self-conscious (3:7). Then they became afraid (3:8–9). Then social cohesion and trust were ruptured (3:12). Finally, humans became divorced from their own environment (3:17–19). Ironically, humans' attempt to know more led to a diminution of their ability to know and do. The subjectivity of self-consciousness hinders rapid, accurate perception and action. Fear produces inactivity that minimizes the information afforded by multiple perspectives. The loss of communal trust among humans likewise reduces each human to his or her own perspectives with consequent loss of comprehensiveness. And the environmental dislocation of humans has led them to think of the environment as something "out there" that cannot be trusted. [13]

One of the distressing consequences of humans rejecting their creational constraints (e.g., obeying God, taking care of the earth, loving each other) is that humans "lost their identity." The identity, the meaning, of any given human is the relationships he or she has (through knowing and doing) with environmental objects and events, other persons, and the Creator. Since "the fall" distorted those relationships,

---

13. Some perceptual theories (e.g., Gregory, 1972) treat perceptual systems as if they were spies on an external enemy, gathering sensory snippets here and there that are pieced together by inferential agents into an intelligence report.

identity was distorted and needs to be recreated (redemption) and re-discovered (conversion).

The biblical account suggests inadequacies in psychological theories of perception; similarly, perceptual theories clarify the biblical data suggesting the inadequacy of most theological and philosophical epistemologies. Perceptual theorizing and research, including Gibson's ecological approach, insufficiently articulate the effects of human evil. Gibson seems not to consider the possibility that perceivers do not always "hunt without rest" for comprehension and clarity. A perceiver may choose to be passive rather than multiplying perspectives, etc., and even if the perceiver is motivated to seek the truth, other humans may deliberately (as well as inadvertently) restrict the perceiver's perspectives or divert his attention. Gibson is right to argue that perceptual errors usually can be avoided by sufficiently sampling the available information, but perceivers can engage in inadequate sampling. Both direct and indirect theories of perception locate sin (error) in finiteness.[14] The biblical promise to "seek and you will find" does not imply that everyone seeks. Numerous other biblical passages reveal that humans "stifle" the truth (e.g., Rom. 1) and deceive themselves and others (e.g., Jer. 17:9).

Epistemologies, Christian and otherwise, often seem to ignore the finiteness of perception in a search for absolutely certain knowledge. Despite enormous differences, each theory proposes some knowledge (e.g., biblical revelation, empirical "givens," "self-evident" analytic axioms) that escapes the relativity of finiteness. If I have not misread Genesis 3, this search for absolute certainty that has characterized evangelical Christians and analytic philosophers alike is a modernized recapitulation of original sin. Scientists in their theories and Christians in their theologies have wanted to be like God. Not only ecological perceptual theory, but also recent philosophical work (e.g., Williams, 1977; Weimer, 1979) and the biblical data suggest that the humility of comprehensive criticism might be more appropriate. The biblical call to knowledge and wisdom (e.g., Proverbs) requires faith, not certainty.

In discussing the constraints of finiteness on *who* humans are and *what* and *how* they perceive, I have implicitly assumed a theory of *why* humans perceive and behave. The purpose of perception and action both from

14. The clearest statement of finiteness rather than fallenness being the problem of knowledge is found in Shaw et al. (1982): "One cannot know the good (veridical) and do the evil (nonfelicitous)" (p. 224). One of the major tasks facing Christian psychologists is the articulation of a theory of evil, in psychological categories rather than theological ones, and its relation to finiteness. Christians (e.g., Plantinga, 1982, p. 17) sometimes treat all epistemic shortcomings as the result of sin. See Myers (1980, chap. 3) for a brief discussion of this issue.

biological and theological perspectives *is to live by knowing and doing the truth.*[15] The specifics of that knowing and doing are constrained by the animal-environment relationship and also by the creature-Creator relationship.[16] The biblical data make it clear that biological survival alone is not sufficient to answer the "why" of knowing and doing: man shall not live by bread alone but by all the words of God (Matt. 4:4). As the earlier quote from Lewis noted, knowing and doing require *valuing.* The value of what humans know and do is measured not just by whether it furthers the survival of the individual or the species, but by whether it allows the enjoyment of (knowing) God, persons, and the creation, and loving ("caring for" action) them.[17] Enjoyment is "subjective" and loving is "objective," but they are as inseparable as all forms of knowing and doing.

Psychology has been inadequately ecological by ignoring the "why" question as well as the "who" question.[18] It needs to take account of the constraints of who is perceiving and acting and why, which are suggested by other disciplines from biology to theology.

Embodied action: the call to growth and humility. Bodies that are spatially and temporally finite preclude the possibility of all knowledge being explicit (conscious and propositionally verbalizable). A body that is busy knowing and doing the truth does not have the time and space to

15. An adequate answer to any "why" question must be answered outside the discipline under question. Other disciplines besides biology and theology would be needed to give a complete answer to the "why" of perception, but they serve to illustrate how a "near-by" and "far-away" discipline, respectively, provide the constraints of "why."

16. Biologically, the answer to "why" we perceive is given in evolutionary terms; adaptation to the physical environment is necessary to survive. Theologically, we perceive so we can "listen to," "taste," and "see" God, the "ultimate environment." If we ignore the biological environment, we die. Similarly, if we ignore other real world structures we can die psychologically, historically, aesthetically, theologically, etc., as well. Psychologists usually implicitly answer the "why" question only in biological terms (cf. n. 17).

17. Ecological perceptual theory as developed by Gibson and extended by Shaw et al. is insufficiently ecological since "it construes psychological problems as instances of biological adaptation" (Shaw et al., 1982, p. 162). Psychological problems also can be instances of chemical, sociological, political, ethical, theological, etc., adaptation. Paradoxically, ecological perceptual theory which is so explicitly and eloquently antireductionist inadvertently slips into a biological reductionism.

Given that humans must adapt to the "Environment" as well as the environment, the estrangement of Creator-creation at the Fall poses grave problems for knowing and doing the truth (cf. n. 14). To adapt to a fallen, abnormal creation will not be redemptive in the way necessary to adapt to the Creator.

18. Actually, the "who" and "why" questions have not really been ignored. No explicit recognition or examination of these questions usually occurs in psychological theories. But, of course, hidden assumptions about what is true biologically, historically, theologically, etc., do set the stage for psychological theorizing.

provide a "running commentary," a conscious verbal description, of what it is up to. Sartre (1959) has argued that life can either be "told as a story" or "lived," but not both. I am not sure the choice is all or none, but available research (e.g., Nisbett & Wilson, 1977; Turvey, 1974) indicates that relatively little of what a human knows, does, and feels is available to introspection or verbalization.[19]

Many theologies (evangelical Protestant ones in particular) seem to have restricted the content of God's revelation and the obedience required of humans to a set of explicit, verbal propositions. These theologies seem to depend on a foundationalist conception of truth and knowledge, and they overemphasize the role of explicit knowledge. The biblical and psychological data suggest the importance of explicit *and* tacit knowing and doing. The psychological data suggest the precedence and greater extensiveness of tacit knowledge. The biblical description of the human task also seems more concerned with unself-conscious control of action, embodied tacit knowledge, than with conscious doctrinal description of that action. Micah (6:8) summarizes God's requirement for humans: "to do justice, and to love kindness, and to walk humbly with your God."

Knowledge that is tacit—embodied in action—is unself-conscious. Scientists and Christians explicitly urge humility on themselves. With good reason: knowledge of the world and God is intoxicating stuff and it is easy to become drunkenly arrogant. As Proverbs reminds us: "knowledge will be pleasant" . . . but the "scoffer seeks wisdom in vain . . ." (2:10; 14:6). F. A. Hayek (1967) has argued that the rationality of science and its applications lies in the recognition of the limits of knowing and doing:

> . . . this desire to make everything subject to rational control, far from achieving the maximal use of reason, is rather an abuse of reason based upon a misconception of its powers. . . . True rational insight seems indeed to indicate that one of the most important uses is the recognition of the proper limits of rational control (p. 93).

The intent of Hayek's remark is our inability to control *centrally* and *consciously* realities as complex as an economy, but the argument applies

---

19. Although feeling (emotion) is discussed explicitly very little in this paper, recent theorizing and research suggest it too cannot be separated from action (the famous James-Lange theory is the earliest version of this argument) or thought (Schachter's theory is an excellent recent example). Zajonc (1980) has argued that feeling (affect) may precede cognition and may be relatively independent of it. I suspect affect usually precedes and is independent of *conscious* cognition. (We often "feel" before we "think.") One of my research interests has been to examine why a person's affective impression of another may not always be consistent with his specific memories of that person.

to individual organisms as well. A conscious brain cannot *explicitly* control all that a body knows and does (cf. Turvey, 1977). Nor can a body consciously decide its destiny, its development, and its end.

Social bodies like scientific or Christian communities are also unable to prescribe the progress of data and doctrine. Scientific and Christian faith both demand activity, sweaty seeking of truth. Both require getting our hands dirty in the data of existence; neither vocation allows theorizing unsullied by "messy" data.[20] Christians and scientists often forget that knowing is a humble, physical business that demands patience. "Perseverance of the saints" is a tiresome but crucial business. Humans have an indefatigable urge to escape the fatigue of patience by jumping to conclusions. Research on human inferences (e.g., Anderson, Lepper, & Ross, 1980) reveals that people are content to go with the first reasonable hypothesis they can think of rather than gathering more data or exploring other theoretical perspectives. This cognitive laziness leads to the "problem of obviousness." Numerous persons (e.g., Chomsky, 1968; Jones & Gerard, 1967) have pointed out that the results of psychological research often seem obvious. The standard way psychologists have tried to debunk this appealing myth is to present the "obvious" findings of studies to an audience, but with the results reversed from what actually was observed. Audiences invariably fall heavily into the trap. Hindsight explanation encourages pride; prediction enforces humility. Waiting for data to accumulate or theory to progress tries the patience of the scientist. Waiting on God to reveal himself tried the patience of Job: Job's friends were quick to prescribe how he should act, but they proscribed God in their arrogant haste. Reality—the Creator and the creation—will not be restricted by the narrow confines of human consciousness, theological or otherwise. True rationality and spirituality begin with intellectual and moral humility. "The fear of the Lord is the beginning of knowledge" (Prov. 1:7). We live only if we start by recognizing our dependence on the creation and Creator.

The humility necessary to be a good scientist or Christian is simultaneously conservative and risky. Scientists and Christians have paradigmatic commitments: both conserve and honor the past by incorporating previous experience into present practice (doing) and belief (know-

20. I have often been asked, "Why do research?" after I have argued against a foundationalist conception of science. My answer has always been a précis of this section: it keeps me humble and forces me to look at the phenomenon under investigation from other perspectives (because my "data theory" and "explanatory theory" do not cohere sufficiently to suit me). Nevertheless, one of the hardest lessons I have had to learn as a scientist is the humility to accept results that "came out wrong" and learn from them. Comments of many colleagues suggest my difficulty is common.

ing). Both are living communities that tacitly embody their past; they may even explicitly recognize this dependence on the past. The comprehensive criticism that Weimer (1979) urges on science and all enterprises wishing to be rational does not preclude commitment to a "paradigm." In fact, he argues that sometimes the most effective way of being critical is to work to articulate and extend the "paradigm." Commitment to the Christian paradigm (although it no doubt entails a more metatheoretical commitment than does a specific scientific paradigm) need not be an irrational, *a priori* leap of faith. Christians can be and have been self-critical in the way that comprehensive criticism suggests. Christians, individually and corporately, reevaluate and revise what Wolterstorff (1976) calls their "authentic commitment" to Christianity from time to time. Thus, Christianity is not an unquestioned *a priori* foundation, but a "core" commitment (cf. Lakatos, 1970).

To make a commitment to a scientific paradigm, a worldview, a spouse, etc., is not to shut one's eyes to reality; it requires risk. It is not an unchanging commitment in the following sense: any commitment that is *true* must change and grow; else it is a dead faith. Knowledge grows or it dies. In this sense truth is not so much something one *has* as something one *does*. If I still loved the woman I promised to love seventeen years ago, I would not still be married to her. She is in important ways a different woman from the wife of my youth. We each have had to change so that the relationship remains invariant. Since knowledge grows, commitment is a continuing process. There may even be revolutionary episodes in that commitment. Certainty is not required for these commitments; only the humility and hope of faith to persevere.

A skill crucial to increased knowledge and increased commitment is what Gibson calls the "education of attention," the "tuning" of bodily activities to environmental information. This educational process is humbling because it requires the organism to "admit" that it could be a better organism. Further, the attempt to learn involves the humility of practice, clumsy initial attempts and repeated "stupid" errors. In the end, of course, it is the person too proud to learn who is truly embarrassed. As the New Testament letter to the Hebrews puts it:

> Though by this time you ought to be teachers, you need someone to teach you the ABC of God's oracles again; it has come to this, that you need milk instead of solid food. . . . But grown men can take solid food; their *perceptions are trained by long use to discriminate between good and evil* (5:12, 14, NEB, italics mine).

Being a good Christian, a good scientist, a good perceiver of any kind requires training to discriminate good from evil. The simple black and white world of the naive realist, the fundamentalist, the scientific novice does not exist. The biblical metaphors for evil (e.g., the confusion of the wheat and weeds, the leaven of the Pharisees) suggest that evil is dispersed and subtle. Discrimination born of practice is necessary to perceive the little evils in ourselves and the large evils of economic and social structures in which we participate.[21] The grace and beauty of goodness in individuals or institutions is equally difficult to detect. Comprehensive criticism of ourselves, individually and institutionally, whether as Christians, scientists, Americans, etc., is continually necessary if we are to "grow in grace and knowledge" (2 Pet. 3:18).

Christians as well as non-Christians have difficulty embodying humility. What differentiates Christians from their contemporaries is the education of their attention to the "ultimate" environment as well as the created environment. First, Christians must humbly confess that it is in God that "we live and move and have our being" (Acts 17:28). Second, we must recognize that as humans we live in a fundamentally abnormal ("fallen") world where humans pretend omniscience, goodness, and unchangingness. Third, we must dissociate ourselves from these human pretenses not only by admitting our finiteness and moral rebellion, but by changing and growing ("repentence" and "redemption" in theological terms). Non-Christians attend to the "distorted" data of the local ecology (the fallen world) often better than Christians. In this sense Christians have no corner on truth. What Christians can offer to their non-Christian colleagues are perspectives on a larger ecology that may add to the clarity or comprehensiveness of the local context. Put differently, Christians may provide helpful hints about the context-dependent, relative nature of human knowledge and about the normative (value) context within which knowing and doing occur. The biblical perspective helps answer the "why" and "who" of "what" and "how" knowing occurs.

The contextual nature of truth, knowing, and meaning. The earlier discussions of Gibson's perceptual theory, factual relativity in science, and the dispersed and tacit nature of knowledge all illustrate that truth and meaning emerge only in context. Knowing is relative. This does not mean that anything goes, but the reverse, that knowing is constrained.[22]

---

21. Because of the subtlety of sin and the limits of explicit knowledge, the *Book of Common Prayer* wisely recommends we pray for the forgiveness of our sins, "known" and "unknown."

22. The literature on biological constraints on learning (e.g., Seligman, 1970; Bolles, 1979) is relevant here as well as in earlier sections on world structure (pp. 107ff.) and information-animal relativity (pp. 112ff.). It is interesting to note that these constraints allow us to perceive, to know the truth, and the truth makes us free (Neisser, 1976, p. 185).

Knowing is ecological: it depends on the creature, creation, and Creator. Because knowing depends on relationships between who, what, and why, it opens up the use of invariants to control behavior. Knowledge then is *true to* creature, creation, and Creator.

The contextual nature of knowledge has important implications for the practical and theoretical lives of Christians: (1) the value of multiple perspectives in detecting Truth; (2) the progressive nature of perception and revelation; (3) the inadequacy of foundationalist theories of knowledge; and (4) the value of community in knowing the truth.

God has given humans multiple perspectives on the creation-Creator relationship. The structure and complexity of creation; the Jewish and Christian Scriptures written by patriarchs, prophets, poets, and apostles; and Jesus the Messiah are all the revelatory Word of God. The various embodiments of the Word are context dependent; each functions with greatest clarity and comprehensiveness only in the light of the other two. We cannot comprehend the Scriptures apart from knowing something about the world, language, and culture; we cannot know who Jesus is apart from the Scriptures; etc. Even within a single embodiment of God's Word such as the Scriptures, there are multiple authors, literary genres, historical contexts, etc. The multiplicity of perspectives on God's activity allows humans to discover his invariance (his covenanting faithfulness). Only a variety of perspectives would begin to do justice to the complexity and invariance of the one God. Not only is revelation like physical perception in valuing multiple perspectives, but revelation is progressive. Just as events must unfold for us to perceive structural and transformational invariants (e.g., an aging face), so must the history of the world unfold for us to perceive God's redemptive purposes. Who God is and what God is up to is something of which the church today has more comprehensive knowledge than did God's people in earlier eras. Not only does the environment unfold, but the perceivers in it may mature and become more attentive to its structure over time.

Our knowledge of God, the world, and ourselves must progress if we are to be "in the truth." Scientific activity and Christian living are events that unfold slowly. Perception, science, and Christian living require risk. Continuing reinterpretation of knowing and doing is necessary to remain in (to conserve) the truth. Human action is always in need of recalibration to current information, and the "theory" of our knowing always needs the corrective of the "data" of current activity. Neither

---

Thus, constraints afford freedom, a point often made by writers and Christians (e.g., L'Engle, 1972; Howard, 1969; *Book of Common Prayer*: ". . . whose service is perfect freedom").

data nor theory, action nor knowledge, can exist in the absence of the other. Thus, for Christians, the Scriptures reinterpret the cosmos, but those same Scriptures are reinterpreted by our knowing and doing in the world.

The contextualism of multiple perspectives and progressive revelation militates against a foundationalism of any sort. A foundation of factual indubitables or biblical absolutes or inerrant methods does not exist for the finite, fallen, perceiving Christian and scientist (cf. Wolterstorff, 1976). There is a "sure foundation" for perception, science, and Christian living—God—but our knowing is not his knowing (Is. 55:8). Foundationalism may be true in the sense that all of creation is dependent on the Creator, but it is a top-to-bottom foundationalism. The parts are dependent upon the whole, rather than the reverse, as western science, philosophy, and theology have assumed. Every theoretical truth has a foundation, but it is a foundation of the whole. Knowledge, truth, and meaning exist only in the total context of creation and Creator. That is the only "foundation" for a finite perceiver-doer.[23] This kind of foundation is far from unproblematical. It suggests humans must know the whole to know the part (Allport, 1978, pp. 85–87; Weimer, 1973) and that what is finite and fallen must comprehend what is infinite and perfectly good. Neither science nor the Scriptures provide an unproblematical description of reality. Hope is warranted, but living is a faith-activity that is not without problems.

Since any individual's time and energy is in short supply, how can the multiple perspectives and extended observation necessary to effective knowing and doing be had? The answer is obvious but profound: knowing is enhanced by social interaction. Perception, science, and Christian living are possible really only in community. Knowledge is embodied more in community than in any single perceiver. A scientific community and a church are more likely to know the truth than any individual scientist or Christian. Not only do communities embody more perspec-

23. In an elegant and important chapter, Martin (1982) attempts the grounding of the epistemological task in the absolute presuppositions necessary to rational judgments, including scientific theorizing. As I have suggested here, he indicates that such a grounding is top-to-bottom, whole-to-part. "We are in search of a kind of absolute—an absolute perspective that truly apprehends the whole of which it is a part. We will inquire into the assumptions underlying the possibility of criticism. We will, therefore, attempt to do no more than make explicit what we universally assume when we doubt. To the extent that we succeed, the adduced propositions will be beyond doubting. To doubt the objective truth of these presuppositions will be impossible, since the very act of doubting them requires utilizing them. . . . This is not to say that the account of the absolute I subsequently present is beyond further elucidation. It is only to say that in the future, psychology must explicitly concern itself with the problem of absolute knowledge" (p. 89).

tives than an individual, but the commitment of the discipline (of psychology, physics, or Christianity) of community life increases the possibility of the knowledge being dispersed throughout the entire community. The prophetic insight of a saint or scientific genius can become the common sense of the community, but only if the discipline of the usual priestly function of religious or scientific practice have been attended to. Without common commitment of a community *and* diversity of viewpoint within the community, growth of knowledge will be greatly retarded.[24]

Conclusion

The meaning of humans is found in their knowing and doing. That knowing and doing is contextually constrained by Creator, creation, and other creatures, and is for them. Knowing would be impossible apart from the self-revealing nature of God, the biological environment, and the community of other knower-doers. Individual and communal action is grounded in the ethical obligation to serve God, take care of the environment, and love neighbor as self. These epistemological and ethical constraints free humans to discover their identity as servants-caretakers-neighbors. To find our life we must lose it in knowing and doing the truth.

BIBLIOGRAPHY

Allport, G. *Waiting for the Lord: 33 Meditations on God and Man.* Edited by P. Bertocci. New York: Macmillan, 1978.

Anderson, C., Lepper, M., and Ross, L. "Perseverance of Social Theories: the Role of Explanation in the Persistence of Discredited Information." *Journal of Personality and Social Psychology* 39 (1980):1037–49.

Anderson, R., Jr. "Wholistic and Particulate Approaches in Neuropsychology." In *Cognition and the Symbolic Processes.* Edited by W. Wiemer and D. Palermo. Hillsdale, NJ: Lawrence Erlbaum, 1974.

Bartley, W., III. *The Retreat to Commitment.* New York: Alfred A. Knopf, 1962.

Berkeley, G. *A New Theory of Vision,* 1709. London: J. M. Dent & Sons, 1910.

Berlin, B., and Kay, P. *Basic Color Terms: Their Universality and Evolution.* Berkeley: University of California Press, 1969.

24. The fundamentally social character of meaning and truth seems inadequately specified in ecological perceptual theory. As noted earlier (n. 17) the Gibsonian approach is too biological. Furthermore, the theory is unnecessarily individualistic even in its biological account since it focuses on adaptation of individual organisms rather than species or other biological-ecological structures. Humans are contextually embedded in a social environment that is itself to be perceived ("object") and is a necessary ground to perception, physical and social. A fine exploration of the social-communicative character of knowing and its implications for psychology is the previously mentioned article by Martin (1982).

The Book of Common Prayer. New York: The Church Hymnal Corp. of the Protestant Episcopal Church and Seabury Press, 1979.

Bolles, R. *Learning Theory,* 2d ed. New York: Holt, Rinehart & Winston, 1979.

Bransford, J., and McCarrell, N. "A Sketch of a Cognitive Approach to Comprehension: Some Thoughts about Understanding What It Means to Comprehend." In *Cognition and the Symbolic Processes.* Edited by W. Weimer and D. Palermo. Hillsdale, NJ: Lawrence Erlbaum, 1974.

Brown, P. *Toward a Marxist Psychology.* New York: Harper & Row, 1974.

Burke, K. *A Grammar of Motives.* Berkeley: University of California Press, 1969.

Chomsky, N. *Language and Mind.* New York: Harcourt Brace Jovanovich, 1968.

Coon, D. *Introduction to Psychology: Exploration and Application.* St. Paul: West Publishing, 1977.

Cutting, J., and Koslowski, L. "Recognizing Friends by Their Walk: Gait Perception without Familiarity Cues." *Bulletin of the Psychonomic Society* 9 (1977):353–56.

Gibson, J. *The Ecological Approach to Visual Perception.* Boston: Houghton Mifflin, 1979.

———. *The Senses Considered as Perceptual Systems.* Boston: Houghton Mifflin, 1966.

Gregory, R. *Eye and Brain: The Psychology of Seeing,* 3d ed. New York: McGraw-Hill, 1978.

———. "Seeing as Thinking: An Active Theory of Perception." *London Times Literary Supplement,* 23 June 1972, pp. 707–8.

Heider, E. "Universals in Color Meaning and Memory." *Journal of Experimental Psychology* 93 (1972):10–20.

Hodges, B. "Perception is Relative and Veridical: Notes of a Psychologist on the Nature of Truth, Knowledge, and Meaning." Mimeographed. Wenham, MA: Gordon College, 1981.

Howard, T. *Chance or the Dance? A Critique of Modern Secularism.* Wheaton, IL: Harold Shaw, 1969.

Jenkins, J. "Remember That Old Theory of Memory? Well, Forget It!" *American Psychologist* 79 (1974):785–95.

Johansson, G. "Visual Perception of Biological Motion and a Model for Its Analysis." *Perception and Psychophysics* 14 (1973):201–11.

Jones, E., and Gerard, H. *Foundations of Social Psychology.* New York: John Wiley & Sons, 1967.

Klapp, S. "Implicit Speech Inferred from Response Latencies in Same-Different Decisions." *Journal of Experimental Psychology* 91 (1971):262–67.

Koestler, A., and Smythies, J. *Beyond Reductionism: New Perspectives in the Life Sciences.* New York: Macmillan, 1969.

Koslowski, L., and Cutting, J. "Recognizing the Sex of a Walker from a Dynamic Point-Light Display." *Perception and Psychophysics* 21 (1977):575–80.

Kuhn, T. "Reflections on My Critics." In *Criticism and the Growth of Knowledge.* Edited by I. Lakatos and A. Musgrave. Cambridge: Cambridge University Press, 1970.

———. *The Structure of Scientific Revolutions.* Chicago: University of Chicago Press, 1962. 2d ed. 1970.

Labov, W. "The Boundaries of Words and Their Meaning." In *New Ways of Analyzing Variation in English.* Edited by C. J. Bailey and R. Shuy. Washington, DC: Georgetown University Press, 1973.

Lakatos, I. "II—Criticism and the Methodology of Scientific Research Programmes."
    Proceedings of the Aristotelian Society 69 (1968):149–86 (cited in Weimer, 1979).
————. "Falsification and the Methodology of Scientific Research Programmes." In
    Criticism and the Growth of Knowledge. Edited by I. Lakatos and A. Musgrave.
    Cambridge: Cambridge University Press, 1970.
Land, E. "The Retinex Theory of Color Vision." *Scientific American* 237 (1977):108–
    28.
Laudan, L. *Progress and Its Problems.* Berkeley: University of California Press, 1977.
L'Engle, M. *A Circle of Quiet.* New York: Seabury Press, 1972.
Lewis, C. *An Analysis of Knowledge and Valuation.* LaSalle, IL: Open Court, 1946.
Lindsay, P., and Norman, D. *Human Information Processing: An Introduction to Psy-
    chology,* 2d ed. New York: Academic Press, 1977.
Maas, J. *Motion Perception I and II.* Syracuse: Syracuse University Films, 1971.
Martin, J. "Presentationalism: Toward a Self-Reflexive Psychological Theory." In
    Cognition and the Symbolic Processes, vol. 2. Edited by W. Weimer and D.
    Palermo. Hillsdale, NJ: Lawrence Erlbaum, 1982.
Michaels, C., and Carello, C. *Direct Perception.* Englewood Cliffs, NJ: Prentice-Hall,
    1981.
Myers, D. *The Inflated Self: Human Illusions and the Biblical Call to Hope.* New York:
    Seabury Press, 1980.
Neisser, U. *Cognition and Reality.* San Francisco: W. H. Freeman & Co., 1976.
Nisbett, R., and Wilson, T. "Telling More Than We Know: Verbal Reports on
    Mental Processes." *Psychological Review* 84 (1977):231–59.
Plantinga, A. "On Reformed Epistemology." *Reformed Journal* 32 (1982):13–17.
Pritchard, R. "Stabilized Images on the Retina." *Scientific American* 204 (1961):72–
    78.
Regan, D., and Beverley, K. "Visually Guided Locomotion: Psychophysical Evi-
    dence for a Neural Mechanism Sensitive to Flow Patterns." *Science* 205
    (1979):311–13.
————. "How Do We Avoid Confounding the Direction We Are Looking and the
    Direction We Are Moving?" *Science* 215 (1982):194–96.
Rosch, E. "Natural Categories." *Cognitive Psychology* 4 (1973):328–50.
————. "Universals and Cultural Specifics in Human Categorization." In *Cross-
    Cultural Perspectives on Learning.* Edited by R. Brislin, S. Bachner, and W.
    Lonner. New York: Halsted Press, 1975.
Rosch, E., and Mervis, C. "Family Resemblances: Studies in Internal Structure of
    Categories." *Cognitive Psychology* 7 (1975):573–605.
Satre, J. *Nausea.* New York: New Directions, 1959.
————. "No Exit." *No Exit and The Flies.* New York: Alfred A. Knopf, 1954.
Schiff, W. "Perception of Impending Collision." *Psychological Monographs* 79 (1965),
    no. 604.
Schiff, W., Caviness, J., and Gibson, J. "Persistent Fear Responses in Rhesus
    Monkeys to the Optical Stimulus of 'Looming.'" *Science* 136 (1962):982–83.
Seligman, M. "On the Generality of Laws of Learning." *Psychological Review* 77
    (1970):406–18.
Shaw, R., and Bransford, J. "Introduction: Psychological Approaches to the Problem
    of Knowledge." In *Perceiving, Acting, and Knowing.* Edited by R. Shaw and J.
    Bransford. Hillsdale, NJ: Lawrence Erlbaum, 1977.
Shaw, R., and McIntyre, M. "Algoristic Foundations to Cognitive Psychology." In
    Cognition and the Symbolic Processes. Edited by W. Weimer and D. Palermo.
    Hillsdale, NJ: Lawrence Erlbaum, 1974.

Shaw, R., and Pittenger, J. "Perceiving the Face of Change in Changing Faces: Implications for a Theory of Object Perception." In *Perceiving, Acting, and Knowing*. Edited by R. Shaw and J. Bransford. Hillsdale, NJ: Lawrence Erlbaum, 1977.

Shaw, R., M. Turvey, and W. Mace. "Ecological Psychology: The Consequence of a Commitment to Realism." In *Cognition and the Symbolic Processes*, vol. 2. Edited by W. Weimer and D. Palermo. Hillsdale, NJ: Lawrence Erlbaum, 1982.

Taylor, S., and Fiske, S. "Point of View and Perception of Causality." *Journal of Personality and Social Psychology* 32 (1975):439–45.

Todd, J., Mark, L., Shaw, R., and Pittenger, J. "The Perception of Human Growth." *Scientific American* 242 (1980):132–44.

Turvey, M. "Constructive Theory, Perceptual Systems, and Tacit Knowledge." In *Cognition and the Symbolic Processes*. Edited by W. Weimer and D. Palermo. Hillsdale, NJ: Lawrence Erlbaum, 1974.

———. "Preliminaries to a Theory of Action with Reference to Vision." In *Perceiving, Acting, and Knowing*. Edited by R. Shaw and J. Bransford. Hillsdale, NJ: Lawrence Erlbaum, 1977.

Weimer, W. *Notes on the Methodology of Scientific Research*. Hillsdale, NJ: Lawrence Erlbaum, 1979.

———. "Psycholinguistics and Plato's Paradoxes of the *Meno*." *American Psychologist* 28 (1973):15–33.

Williams, M. *Groundless Belief*. New Haven: Yale University Press, 1977.

Wittgenstein, L. *Philosophical Investigations*. Oxford: Basil Blackwell, 1953.

Wolterstorff, N. *Reason Within the Bounds of Religion*. Grand Rapids: Eerdmans, 1976.

———. "Theory and Praxis." *Christian Scholar's Review* 9 (1980):317–34.

Zajonc, R. "Feeling and Thinking: Preferences Need No Inferences." *American Psychologist* 35 (1980):151–75.

Toward an Epistemology of Revelation

JAMES E. MARTIN

> Nearly all the wisdom we possess, that is to say true and sound wisdom, consists of two parts: The knowledge of God and of ourselves. But while joined with many bonds, which one precedes and brings forth the other is not easy to discern.
>
> Calvin, *Institutes*, Book I, Chapter 1

Hodges has given us a provocative and complex essay. It contains an unquestionably competent account of the epistemological perspectives of the Gibsonian direct realists and the postempiricist philosophers of science. However, I am ambivalent toward Hodges's proposals. In this response I hope to bring out some points of agreement and disagreement between Hodges and me, as well as to make a few suggestions concerning the crucial issues he raises. I will also address the problem of the knowledge of persons. Curiously, this problem has been largely overlooked by Hodges and the authors he cites. Nevertheless, it is *the* central epistemological issue for psychology. An epistemology sufficient for psychology must be appropriate for the knowledge of persons as well as physical objects.

Before beginning, let me remind the reader that this paper is not intended to be a definitive statement and defense of my own epistemological position. My first responsibility has been to comment on Hodges's paper. This fact, combined with limitations of space, required that I present only the briefest sketch of my positive suggestions. I believe, however, that enough has been given for the reader to form a relatively clear idea of the direction of my thought. A fuller exposition and defense of the thesis will, I hope, be forthcoming.

POSTEMPIRICISM AND DIRECT REALISM

I begin with a brief characterization of some of the strengths and weaknesses of the two epistemologies (direct realism and postempiricism) which Hodges favors. Next, I move to a consideration of a few alternatives to either of the above views.

Postempiricist philosophy of science developed in response to positivism. On the positivist account, science grows through the accumulation of facts whose objectivity is ensured by their systematic relationship to repeatable observations. Such facts are held to be independent of, and prior to, theorizing. They constitute an objective foundation in terms of which theories are to be justified.

A primary claim of the postempiricists has involved an argument about what is referred to as the conceptual relativity of facts. In this view, facts never emerge except in relation to the conceptual frameworks within which they are interpreted. Accordingly, the facts appear to be different for persons (scientists) who hold different conceptual orientations toward a domain of inquiry. Thus, attempts to settle scientific disputes by referring to empirical observations are limited by the degree to which investigators hold the same conceptual perspective. The conceptual relativity of facts entails a kind of incommensurability of scientific discourse. Scientists who hold different conceptual positions (who work in different paradigms) can't agree about the world because they don't see the same world. Important scientific changes do *not* always result from the steady accumulation of facts. Rather those changes are sometimes better described as revolutions, radical shifts in perspective in which what were previously taken to be facts may no longer be so recognized. Conversely, a new set of previously unrecognized facts will have emerged.

Unfortunately, postempiricist philosophers of science, insofar as they have rejected foundationalist or justificationist epistemologies, have been unable to ground a scientific consensus in other than the social psychology of scientific communities (cf. Weimer, 1979). In Weimer's view, objectivity means consensus. Scientific argument, on this account, is ultimately persuasion. The natural implication of postempiricism is skepticism. To be sure, Weimer (1973) suggested that the skepticism implicit in the postempirical epistemology might be overcome by referring to the evolutionary constraints which have informed human minds such that those minds are somehow compatible with the to-be-known universe. However, this kind of attempt to save postempiricism from skepticism involves a circular argument. It is an example of the sort of argument that Hume has forever discredited in his *Enquiry Concerning Human Understanding*. We cannot justify the validity of the epistemic process through a scientific hypothesis, because all such hypotheses are formulated in the context of the presupposition of the validity of thought. Postempiricists have found no adequate way to overcome the skepticism entailed by their position. For reasons enumerated below, this indicates that the postempiricist epistemology is insufficient for the purposes of psychologists.

Let us now turn to Gibsonian direct realism. As Hodges stated,

Gibsonian realists assert that persons are never in error about what they perceive. Inadequacy in appreciating the world stems not from a *mis*-representation, *mis*understanding, or *mis*perception of reality, but simply in not yet having all the facts. A more adequate apprehension may be expected to emerge through the accumulation of more facts (more complete sampling of the stimulus energies available).

This view has been proposed in contrast to the representational realism which is the currently received position in psychology. Representational realists hold that we *construct* representations of reality on the basis of generally incomplete and imperfect data (sensory and otherwise). Representational realists tend to describe the process as analogous to the activity of scientists constructing theories. As the scientist constructs theories in terms of scientific observation and previous theorizing, so the psychological subject is said to construct a conception of reality grounded in the report of his senses plus what he already thinks he knows about the world.

However, it is manifest that such a constructivist account of knowing leads rather directly (via the doctrine of the conceptual relativity of facts) to skepticism with respect to the possibility that organisms might possess veridical knowledge of their worlds. If all we possess are representations of reality, how are we to evaluate their validity? This skepticism is certainly one reason for the attractiveness of alternatives to representational realism. Ultimately, most psychologists would reject such skepticism for three sorts of reasons. First, to take a fully general skeptical position is to engage in an act of self-refutation. We cannot consistently claim to know that knowledge is impossible. Second, insofar as psychologists endeavor to understand the development of competence, they assume that organisms can develop, to a degree, an appropriate understanding of reality (i.e., that competence is possible). Thoroughgoing skepticism would leave many psychologists little to study, and no reason for doing so. Third, if we assume that organisms are required to perceive the world veridically if they are to survive in their ecological niches, and if we take the representational view to be correct, then it will be difficult for us to explain how organisms more or less regularly and reliably survive. Direct realists are not blind to the skepticism inherent in representational realism. Accordingly, they opt for direct realism because they see it as the only viable alternative to representational realism.

Nevertheless, whatever its virtues, I find it impossible to understand how direct realism can be elevated to a general epistemology. For example, consider the psychologist who claims to be a direct realist. Now, as a direct realist, she would be obliged to say that we are never mistaken about reality. But someone else might want to say that it is possible to be profoundly mistaken about reality in precisely the sense that the direct realist denies. I take it that the former (the direct realist) would hold the latter to be mistaken, since the latter would have defined his position as the negation of the direct realist's. If the direct realist did this, however, she would have admitted the possibility of real error. To admit this, of course, would be to refute herself. On the other hand, the direct realist might, on her own principles, admit that her adversary sees reality as it is. In this case, the direct realist's view would be, by her own admission, incorrect.

Finally, it seems to me that the argument that we are never really wrong, just uninformed, is a misreading of the *meaning* of experience. Illusions and other forms of deception are of interest because when they occur we really do see the world in a way contrary to the way that we might know it to be from a broader perspective. Furthermore, from an ecological point of view direct realists forget that organisms are regularly deceived by their environment, and, as a function of the struggle for survival, by other organisms within it. Any ecologically valid account of behavior must include an account of the ways in which organisms deceive and are deceived by other organisms (cf. Martin, 1982). I do not deny that the world is the sort of place in which by moving around and picking up more information we might reduce the possibility of error, but this does not mean that we cannot be mistaken about the world. What it means is that the world is in some sense knowable, and to say that the world is knowable is definitely *not* to say that error is impossible.

In this context, it seems rather clear that Hodges's attempt to harmonize the direct realist and postempiricist epistemologies must fail. They are radically incompatible systems. In some respects, Gibsonian direct realism is a version of foundationalism. On the other hand, the postempiricist thesis of the *conceptual* relativity of facts is an explicit denial of the direct perceptual process, unmediated by judgment, which the Gibsonians propose. Postempiricism is nothing less than an extreme version of the representational realism which Gibson tried to avoid.

Nevertheless, it is interesting to observe the complementary advantages and disadvantages of direct and representative realism. The former is an attempt to explicate the presupposition that the world is "not-other" in relation to the knower and that, therefore, knowledge is possible; the latter, that the world is "other" in relation to the knower and that, therefore, error is possible. In fact, it is arguable that representational realism was invented to explain the fact of error which is unaccountable in terms of a primitive naive realism. Direct realism, on the other hand, while certainly not naive realism, is an attempt to avoid the difficulties inherent in representational realism through a partial return

to the immediacy of naive realism. However, as we have seen, consideration of the conceptual relativity of facts indicates that the return in
question has been rather more complete than can be justified. Direct
realism, however sophisticated, is still too naive to account for the
mistaking, deception, and even self-deception which sometimes characterizes the epistemic process.

In any case, it seems that both views are somehow necessary. More
accurately, the motive behind direct realism—to explicate the possibility of knowledge—and the motive behind representational realism—to explicate the possibility of error—must be realized in any
adequate epistemology. Hodges's simultaneous fascination with these
antithetical epistemological systems is understandable in this light. It
was precisely Hodges's sensitivity to the real character of the epistemological constraints in question which led him to the position he
took. It is impossible to accept Hodges's epistemology because the two
perspectives he utilizes, Gibsonian direct realism and Kuhnian post-
empiricism, are mutually contradictory. On the other hand, the complementary and antithetical values which guided his theorizing are undoubtedly those which must be taken up and realized in any adequate
epistemology.

BEYOND REALISM

What the foregoing antithesis suggests to me is not that we ought to
attempt to refine or revise either direct or representational realism, but
that we might look beyond the narrow confines of the current realist
orthodoxy for a more adequate epistemological perspective. Epistemologically, what we appear to presuppose is that we possess some sort
of access to reality (contrary to representational realism) and that no
aspect of our present vision of things is beyond revision (contrary to
direct realism). How can these two aspects of our epistemological presuppositions be articulated?

In Martin (1982) I proposed to resolve this difficulty by introducing an
epistemology which contained elements of idealism. Once it has been
awakened from the dogmatic slumber of naive realism, the natural epistemology of the modern mind is representational realism. The consequent epistemic nihilism of indirect realism constitutes one of the
classical and recurring problems of epistemology. There are two characteristic responses to this dilemma. The first is direct realism. For reasons
given above, this response represents a regression to an all-too-naive
realism. A second response, which has been shown historically to be
capable of much richer development, is idealism.

The strength of representational realism lies in its recognition of the radical otherness of the to-be-known. In this way it makes possible an account of error. However, because of the conceptual relativity of facts, representational realism tends toward skepticism insofar as the knower is conceived as cut off from the to-be-known. In the extreme case, the knower is seen as having no access to reality. And, for the same reason that the knower is conceived as having no access to truth, he also must be conceived as having no capacity to recognize error. Accordingly, representational realism tends to suggest the impossibility of valid critical activity as well as the impossibility of providing support for positive claims. Idealism, on the other hand, explicates the possibilities both of partial knowledge *and* of the recognition of error by positing that the knower has a *tacit* access to the inner principle of the to-be-known.

Like direct realism, idealism conceives the knower to have access to the to-be-known. In the case of idealism, however, that access is conceived to be not only tacit but axiological as well. In recent versions of idealism (cf. Blanshard, 1964; Urban, 1949) reality is construed to be the manifestation or realization of certain values (e.g., rational coherence)—the same values which guide the critical process of coming to know. It is the knower's tacit access to the values that constrain reality which is said to make the development and criticism of knowledge a real possibility. Thus the relationship between the knower and the to-be-known is much more abstractly conceived in idealism than in direct realism. Because of this, idealism is compatible with the insights of post-empiricism while avoiding the skepticism inherent in that movement.

In the view I am discussing (Blanshard, 1939), the truth is assumed to be that which would satisfy our epistemic valuing. That is, what we seek when we seek to know is simply the truth. We assume, therefore, that the values which guide and direct our coming to know are satisfied by and realized in the object of knowledge, the truth. In Blanshard's terms, the immanent and transcendent ends of thought are one. Accordingly, the relation between the idea and its object is not assumed to be that of mere similarity. Instead, it is a relation defined in terms of the epistemological values that constitute the learning process. Ideas are said to be the partial realization of those values which are fully realized in their objects. Thus, error is conceived to be possible because the epistemic values are not fully realized in the present idea of reality. On the other hand, because truth is taken to be defined in terms of the same epistemic values, criticism of putative ideas attains the possibility of validity. In this context, we may plausibly consider ordering a set of proposed theories in terms of the degree to which they do or do not satisfy our epistemological valuing. In this way we come to see how the possibility of relative incompetence and competence, with respect to the epistemic ideal, may be simultaneously achieved. Blanshard's idealism explicates the possibility of knowing without the dogmatism entailed by direct realism, and the possibility of error without the skepticism entailed by postempiricist representationalism.

It seems to me that, apart from its purely epistemological superiority, idealism is in many ways more consistent with the biblical view of humanity and nature than either direct or representational realism. For example, in Stoic epistemology the possibility of knowledge was conceived as being grounded in the fact that the knower and the to-be-known world both participated in a common reason or *logos*. This set of concepts was taken up and adapted by John in the first chapter of his gospel, where he speaks of the second person of the Trinity as the *logos* which both constitutes the world and is also "the true light which enlightens every man" (v. 9).

Certainly, John refers to an enlightenment that extends well beyond the epistemic. Nevertheless, there is no reason to believe that epistemic considerations are excluded. On the contrary, it would seem appropriate to include such considerations in light of the corresponding creation passages of Genesis. In that account, the world is described as being created for humans to govern and to describe (e.g., God presents the animals to Adam so that Adam may name them).

From the biblical perspective, part of humanity's intended destiny to rule and name the world is that we should approach a true understanding of the world because we have access to the *logos* which constitutes and upholds the world. Humanity, as the image of God (the image of the *logos* of John), would be constituted in terms of the values which are fully realized in the *logos* himself. This, perhaps, is what it means to be created in the image of God. In this view, God is humankind's good, our only good, because God alone fully realizes and satisfies the values which constitute human nature. Accordingly, the relation between humans as knowers and the truth might be taken to be an example of the relation between humans as developing persons and God. Humanity is becoming toward God in the sense that God and God alone could satisfy our notion of what it would be good to be. Therefore, only through union with God (participation in the divine nature) can the human desire for becoming be satisfied.

Let us reflect upon what we have seen thus far. First, the direct realists' thesis that we have an immediate and conscious access to reality makes it impossible to explicate properly the facts concerning error. Second, the view of the postempiricists and most psychologists that knowledge is only indirect entails an unacceptable epistemic nihilism. Third, a proper assessment of the phenomenon of criticism leads to the conclusion that the critic assumes an access (undoubtedly tacit) to the reality about which the criticized judgments are being made. Such an access may be thought of as an identity between the values which guide the epistemic process, which are partially realized by our imperfect ideas, and those epistemic values which would be fully realized in the object of knowledge itself. Consequently, following the idealism of Blanshard (1939), we can conceive the possibility of the critical development of knowledge without requiring the epistemological nihilism of representationalism or the dogmatism of direct realism.

BEYOND IDEALISM

Elegant as the foregoing solution is, it has to my mind a fundamental defect. As with most idealisms, the idealism I have described attains to intelligibility at the expense of opacity. This view accounts for error by understanding it as a kind of "missing the mark." There is no Kantian "thing in itself" which is, in principle, beyond the categories of the knower. From a biblical perspective, idealism seems incapable of handling the fact of unintelligibility as found, for example, in freedom, evil, and the arbitrariness of God's choosing. Beyond these we have the absolute unsearchability of God himself, "who . . . dwells in unapproachable light, whom no man has ever seen or can see" (1 Tim. 6:16) and whose ways are "inscrutable" (Rom. 11:33). Paradoxical as it may seem, if one holds a biblical view of reality, one can never be satisfied with a vision of reality in which all is intelligibility, or even approaches intelligibility. Accordingly, Blanshardian idealism in which the goal of thought is construed as pure intelligibility is still onesided and therefore only half right.

Let us then push on to a fourth epistemological position. This position I will call axiological-imaginative. In this view the epistemic process is grounded in the antagonistic values which we have already seen at work in our evaluation of the epistemologies of direct realism, representational realism, and idealism. These two values point toward, on the one hand, the direct knowability of reality (the absolute not-otherness of reality), and, on the other hand, the ultimate opacity of reality (the absolute otherness of reality). In this context, it appears that what is desired is a vision of reality in which reality is seen as simultaneously other and not-other. The only vision of reality which would satisfy the epistemic values which guide thought would be one that would express itself in terms of an ambiguity.

The difficulty with the idealism we have been considering is that it was thrown off balance by the fact that it was a response to the epistemic nihilism entailed by representationalism in its various forms. In that context, the issue became "How can I know, and know that I know?" In this way, the awareness of ignorance which was a product of criticism was seen only as a kind of privation, but this misconstrued the epistemological motives behind the development of thought. The historical development of thought, taken as a whole, has *not* resulted in our achieving a more coherent view of the whole of reality than our ancestors possessed. There is no doubt that a kind of progress has been made toward the solution of some particular problems. It is equally true that such progress has itself resulted in the discovery of much deeper obscurities than either we or our ancestors ever imagined. Blanshard began *The Nature of Thought* with the claim that "thought is that activity of mind which aims directly at the truth." Taken alone, this claim is false. We seek not only a vision of reality as fully intelligible but also a vision of reality as fully opaque and unintelligible. We have not been, nor can we ever be, satisfied with either alone.

The activity of criticism is grounded in a positive desire for separation or distinction of the developing idea from the object of knowledge. It is, of course, possible to claim that the critical activity is only a means to knowing, and therefore subordinate to, the valuing of knowledge. But this would be to see only what the valuing of knowledge makes of the results of the critical activity. It would not see the valuing of opacity to be what it is, a value in its own right. On the present view, we may see the permutations of thought as the interplay of these two motives. Each, as it is to some degree realized, provides grist for the other. The motive to know results in proposals which are open to criticism. The motive to doubt results in criticisms which, if explicated, reveal truths at least as valid as the explicated doubts.

In making this move I am following, to some extent, W. M. Urban in his *Beyond Realism and Idealism*. Urban's claim was that the foundational motive of (representational) realism is to acknowledge the "otherness" of reality. On the other hand, the fundamental motive of idealism is to acknowledge that reality is fundamentally "not-other." Urban proposed that these motives be held as antagonistic and complementary values in an ideal epistemology. I am claiming that these *same* motives direct the epistemic process. In developing an epistemology which is beyond realism and idealism, Urban saw these two motives as being held in a complementary dialectical opposition, as constraining our choice of an epistemology. I am arguing that these same motives operate in the development of our ideas about reality. In this context, what we seek is a vision of reality in which reality is seen to be simultaneously immanent and transcendent, that is at once immediately intelligibly present and forever absolutely other.

In some respects the same distinction was made by Kant (1970) when he opposed the phenomenal world of empirical experience and natural science to the noumenal world of things in themselves. The phenomenal world is a domain which is defined in relation to the categories of the mind which knows it. It is a world which is determined *a priori* in relation to the mind, and which, therefore, is not free. For Kant, this *a priori* determination of the phenomenal world in relation to the knower was the ground of the possibility of theoretical natural science. Because of this Kant held that any empirical psychology would be required to see the object of its inquiry as subject to the causal necessity of natural science in general. There could be no free agents in an empirical psychology for Kant for the reason that such entities, by definition, would not be determined in relation to the causal categories of phenomenal experience. A free agent would not, in its freedom, be an object of empirical knowledge because that which is empirically knowable is subject to the constraint of causality.

According to Kant, freedom resides outside the phenomenal realm, in the noumenal world of things in themselves. While the phenomenal world is a realm which is fundamentally not-other (a determined world), the noumenal world is radically other, not empirically knowable, and therefore provides for the possibility of freedom. In making the distinction between the phenomenal and noumenal realms Kant was giving articulation to the two goals of thought, a world of determined intelligibility and a world of opacity and freedom.

How, if at all, are these two ends realized in one vision? Clearly, they cannot be realized as a concept. The conception of a fully intelligible and fully unintelligible reality is a manifest contradiction. Because his discussion remains in the realm of the concept, the noumenal and phenomenal domains remain completely separate in Kant. On the other hand, I propose that these oppositions can be united in the imagination. In this way we come to see reality as a *mystery,* in the original sense of that term. A mystery in the original (biblical) sense is a truth or reality which, although it had been hidden, has been revealed. What is both presupposed and sought in the activity of knowing is the absolute and free *self-* revelation of an absolute opacity. The autonomous self-revelation of the to-be-known constitutes the satisfaction of the two epistemic motives considered here. In the freedom of that act, the knower's desire for opacity is satisfied. In the revelation of that act, the knower's desire for intelligibility is satisfied.

In what imaginative form are these antithetical motives united? I suggest that it is in the notion of the person that this happens. For example, reality might be apprehended as a personal and free self-revelation, in which it would be seen to be that which is simultaneously "other" (because free) and "non-other" (because revealed)—unintelligible and intelligible. My suggestion is, then, that a full explication of the values which we seek to realize in knowing reveals that what we seek is a mystery which is in turn a self-revelation. A personal world is precisely such a mystery, or self-revelation. Thus, the personal is a *coincidentia oppositorium* held together, not through the concept, but through the power of the imagination.

If I am correct, psychology cannot, insofar as it deals with persons, be construed only as a science. I take it as a distinctive characteristic of science that it involves a comprehension of a determined world through concepts. On my account, it is not through the determinate concept alone, but through the imagination that we apprehend persons. Knowledge of the personal world is a knowledge which must begin by acknowledging the radical opacity and freedom of the other. It follows that knowledge of persons is grounded first in the autonomous act of self-disclosure on the part of the persons who may be known. At this point, it becomes clear not only that we cannot provide a justification of or foundation for our knowledge of reality, but that we do not *need* to. That responsibility is not ours; it belongs to the self-revealing reality whose presence and activity we must await. Our responsibility is to be prepared to receive whatever is revealed.

It is also worth noting that our discussion of the object of psychology, the person, has direct relevance to theological questions. The ultimate ground of being, from the point of view developed here, could never be grasped with the concept. Thus philosophical versions of the Absolute, such as Hegel's, would be rejected. On the contrary, the goal which thought seeks and presupposes, the ground of the whole, is a mystery, hidden and revealed, free and determined, forever beyond the grasp of the concept.

Of course, that is just what the biblical revelation says about God. God is absolutely free and has freely chosen to reveal himself in Jesus Christ. "No one has ever seen God; the only Son, who is in the bosom of the Father, he has made him known" (John 1:18). In the confrontation with Moses at the burning bush (Ex. 3:14), God declares, "I will be what I will be," or "I am who I am." In God's self-revelation, he never permits us to forget his freedom in choosing to reveal himself to us. "So it depends not upon man's will or exertion, but upon God's mercy" (Rom. 9:16). The ground of being, the ultimate reality is, as such a *coincidentia oppositorium,* a personal being.

Accordingly, the one-sided view of nature articulated by the natural sciences, when taken alone, is an essentially false vision. The world cannot be appreciated properly in terms of the Kantian categories of the understanding alone. Only by seeing nature in the context of the ambiguity of which I have been speaking can it take on its truly contingent character and emerge as what it really is—the result of a freely chosen act of creation. This contingency in creation does not by itself proscribe the possibility in the knower of the sort of *a priori* access to phenomenal reality which Kant pointed out. On the contrary, insofar as nature is understood as a revelation to ourselves as knowers—as a mystery—we would *expect* that it would be constrained by the categories of our experience.

The ambiguity between freedom and necessity is also evident in the nonepistemic, or practical, aspects of personal community. For example, it provides the context for the possibility of biblical love. When it exists, such love is a freely chosen act of self-enslavement, or self-determination, for the good of the beloved. Love is an example in the practical sphere of the sort of ambiguity that self-revelation is in the theoretical.

In fact, is it not evident that love has an epistemic aspect? Does not the lover seek to know and to be known by the beloved? This affinity between loving and knowing is often alluded to by the biblical writers in connection with the love between men and women as well as that between God and humanity.

Finally, in understanding the person to be the point of union between the not-other and the radical other, I am of course in the center of the historical Christian tradition. What can be clearer than that the union of the two natures in the person of Christ is precisely of this sort? From the perspective of the New Testament authors, the Incarnation, the personal union of the divine (radically other) nature of Christ with his human (absolutely not-other) nature, is the central event in the history of the world. It is understood as a freely chosen act of self-enslavement in service of the self-revelation of God to humanity. "Though he was in the form of God, did not count equality with God a thing to be grasped, but emptied himself, taking the form of a servant, being born in the likeness of men. And being found in human form he humbled himself and became obedient unto death, even death on a cross" (Phil. 2:6–8). The self-revelation of God throughout the Scriptures is seen as being grounded in the Incarnation of Jesus Christ. All his works, especially his death and resurrection, derive their significance from the fact of the Incarnation. The distinction between the two natures is the distinction between created (not-other) and uncreated (other) being. In the person of the Son of God these are united without confusion and without separation.

An epistemology which makes room for persons—for self-revelation and love—is long overdue. Without such a positive foundation, the future of psychological investigation will be a continuation of the past—a series of retreats from a series of increasingly barbaric and sophisticated renderings of the thesis that a human is a piece of meat. Clearly, we need another metaphor. The Bible gives us one. Humanity is the image of God—God who both hides and reveals himself.

BIBLIOGRAPHY

Blanshard, B. *The Nature of Thought*. New York: Humanities Press, 1964.
Kant, I. *The Critique of Pure Reason*. New York: St. Martin's Press, 1970.
Martin, J. E. "Presentationalism: Toward a Self-Reflexive Psychological Theory." In *Cognition and the Symbolic Processes*, vol. 2. Edited by W. Wiemer and D. Palermo. Hillsdale, NJ: Lawrence Erlbaum, 1982.
Urban, W. M. *Beyond Realism and Idealism*. London: George Allen & Unwin, 1949.
Weimer, W. B. "Psycholinguistics and Plato's Paradoxes of the *Meno*." *American Psychologist* 28 (1973):15–33.
———. *Notes on the Methodology of Scientific Research*. Hillsdale, NJ: Lawrence Erlbaum, 1979.

Biology

COMMENTARY

Several essays in this book have reflected discomfort with materialist or reductionist views of human nature. Martin specifically laments the loss of the person in psychology. Jones's essay attempts to uncover ontological commonalities in a biological description of personhood and a description informed by the Christian faith. He argues that humanness in biological terms includes an awareness of one's self as an individual, an understanding of one's self and one's goals, an ability to judge one's self and others, self-reflection, creativity, and an awareness of one's own transience. He then proposes that perhaps the supreme characteristic of humanness beyond the narrowly biological is the potential for responding to the overtures of God. This might seem to lead to compartmentalization of humans into biological and spiritual beings, a form of body-soul (material-immaterial) dualism. Jones rejects such dualism, however, contending for a holistic view of the human person. His claim for holism is supported by proposing a complementary relationship between a mechanistic description of the functioning of a person's brain (neuroscience) and a personalistic description of behavior in terms of such notions as intentionality, freedom of choice, and responsibility.

Hasker agrees that an assumption of complementarity between mechanistic and personalistic descriptions of a person's behavior is a good "working [methodological] strategy" for the Christian scientist doing brain research, since the most productive brain research is presently being guided by mechanistic models and assumptions, but he rejects such complementarity as an ontological position. In fact, Hasker argues that in certain areas of human behavior (e.g., accepting a belief as the conclusion of a rational inference), mechanistic and personalistic explanations are *not* complementary, but are rather incompatible.

In contrast to Jones's complementarist position, Hasker proposes a unification of mechanistic and personalistic descriptions that he labels "emergentism." According to this view, the mental emerges from the physical when matter is organized and functioning in suitably complex organic systems, analogous somewhat to the theory of "fields" (electrical, magnetic, gravitational) in physical science.

In terms of the introductory taxonomy, Jones and Hasker are both concerned with ontological assumptions about human nature that are common to biology and the Christian faith. This concern develops into differing attempts to systematize the results of brain science and Christian belief into a unified view.

These essays are the clearest examples of divergent approaches to systematic schemata in this book. Jones's approach to systematic unity takes the form of a heterogeneous schema. That is, following MacKay, he sees the insights of neuroscience as distinct from but complementary to Christian belief. Hasker's essay is an example of a homogeneous schema. He moves to the overarching notion of emergentism as a unifying concept by which neuroscientific and personalistic descriptions of human beings may be synthesized.

Both of these essays take brain science, its methodology and results in their present forms, as compatible with Christian belief, though in differing ways. Neither proposes a transformation of biological theory or method (as Clark and Gaede did in sociology or Martin did in psychology), though Hasker hints that acceptance of current methodologies should be only provisional. It would seem that a complementarist like Jones (using a heterogeneous schema) would be less likely to feel a need for transforming his discipline.

The Human Brain and the Meaning of Humanness[1]

D. GARETH JONES

A little thought should convince even the most skeptical of us that our brains are essential for making us the sort of people we are. This is not the statement of a materialist but of a neuroscientist who is also a Christian. Furthermore, it is one of the bases from which we have to work for a realistic assessment of what human beings are as creatures made in the image of God. It may be one of the most contentious bases from which to work, and yet I hope to demonstrate in this essay that it is also one of the most profitable.

Let me first illustrate some of the facets of brain function from my present activities. As I write these words, I am also listening to music—two of my perennial activities. I am, therefore, engaged in two intellectual tasks simultaneously, and my ability to switch almost imperceptibly from the one to the other simply reflects the way in which a particular part of my brain operates. Any damage to this part of my brain may well prevent me from carrying out these tasks in this particular manner.

The music I am listening to and enjoying is also significant. Over the past hour or so I have heard Dvorak's Ninth Symphony and am currently reveling in Schubert's Ninth Symphony. The reasons why I enjoy this type of music are undoubtedly legion, and yet whatever they may be, my recognition of the music and subsequent response to it must be encoded in certain regions of my brain. Once again, damage to these regions—which are perhaps in the right cerebral hemisphere—will have profound repercussions upon my appreciation of this, and perhaps of any, type of music.

In between these symphonies I heard a number of Negro spirituals, which called forth in me not just musical appreciation but also an awareness of profound spiritual longings. In some ways they opened a door into a different facet of my being, and yet this was only possible because my brain provided this link by encoding and translating the feelings and the sound. The tragedy of brain damage is that it could

---

1. The issues discussed in this article are dealt with more fully in my book *Our Fragile Brains* (Downers Grove, IL: InterVarsity Press, 1981).

obliterate this response and render me oblivious to the significance of spiritual realities.

Together, these experiences tell us something about what it means to be human, and integral to these experiences is their dependence upon the integrity of our brains. Implicit then, in our humanness, is the fragile nature of our personhood. What we are is made possible by the potentiality of our brains, and yet this very potentiality is also the source of our weakness. Destroy a part of our brains, and many of the vistas of personhood may disappear.

It is important to start from this point because it reminds us that human beings have, on the one hand, a grandeur deriving from their creation in the image and after the likeness of God. On the other hand, they are created beings subject to the demands and constraints of finiteness and fallenness. Their vistas can be those of God; and yet they are also subject to disease, estrangement, and death. It is difficult for us to hold these seemingly opposing considerations in perspective, and yet this is the only basis which will help us gain a Christian understanding of the human brain.

Even this cursory glimpse at the issues confronting us in brain research demonstrates that a study of the brain must raise philosophical, ethical, and theological issues besides the more specific neuroscientific ones. Its implications for Christian thinking are many but probably center on the question of human responsibility, in that we have to consider how our understanding of brain function affects our concept of responsibility and also how we exercise responsibility in deciding how an understanding of brain function and brain control is to be applied.

This is a dual responsibility, underlining as it does a willingness to tackle difficult philosophical issues and a perceptiveness to see the need for an ethical superstructure to scientific research. Both aspects of this question are relevant to Christians, who should be thinking through the relationship between the brain and the mind (or soul) and who should also be discussing the possibilities of brain control and its social consequences. Rigorous thinking is required if these vistas opened up by brain research are to be grasped, and for Christians they should constitute the call to a search for relevant, biblically based principles.

The theoretical and practical issues raised by contemporary brain research usher in a more fundamental issue, and this is one's view of the nature of humanity. Study of the human brain forces us to consider our relationship to God, our sinfulness and finiteness, the importance of individuals over and against the demands of society, the nature of personal identity and its dependence upon the structural integrity of the brain, and the relationship between present existence with its reliance upon an adequately functioning brain and a future existence lacking any such reliance.

Study of the brain, therefore, brings us face-to-face with ourselves. While the major advances in our recent understanding of the brain have resulted from the application of the relatively objective approach of science and scientists, we can only arrive at a view of our place in the world by the use of our brains. It is impossible to separate our knowledge of the brain as a subject of interest and study from what we are as people. We use brains to study brains. Not only this, we are what we are because we possess the brains we do.

We cannot with impunity isolate brains from persons. Study of the brain precipitates us into a study of people. It repeatedly raises the question of humankind, of the value we place upon human life, and of the aspirations of individuals. All these are religious issues and are of deep concern to Christians. Moreover, the sort of control we endeavor to exert over people and their brains will depend in large measure on our beliefs about humanity. This introduces us to the realm of presuppositions which play a vital part in the attitudes of everyone, even when the presuppositions are not acknowledged.

Those who believe that humans are machines will treat them as pieces of machinery, to be modified at the whim of all and sundry. In such a scenario the most mechanistic and vulnerable part of a human is the brain, which consequently lends itself to manipulation. Any guidelines for manipulation, however, must be imposed from outside, as machines do not incorporate guidelines. This is an immense problem and an embarrassment for this school of thought. Fortunately, an alternative is available.

Humans may not be machines. Indeed, the Christian says that a human being is anything but a machine. A human is a person who finds himself in a meaningful universe. Admittedly, there are many ways in which humans can be *compared to* machines, and, for some scientific purposes, this is a useful procedure. In the end, though, this approach tells us little about humanity's nature and aspirations. It leaves the question about *who* we are unanswered.

It is imperative that humanity be seen in the context of a universe incorporating values and one based upon values. In other words, we are looking for a view of humans which sees them as beings of value because they are an integral part of a value-based world. Such is the Christian view because, according to this, human beings live in a world designed and upheld by a personal God to whom humanity has meaning. Humanity, therefore, fits into a God-centered system and achieves meaning and individuality within this framework.

With this as our base, we can appreciate that not only does humanity *in toto* have meaning, but every aspect of a human's make-up and life also achieves significance. It is not possible, therefore, to isolate the brain or personality from someone's existence as a person. It is tantalizingly easy to confuse a person's brain, and its array of psychological manifestations, with the person herself. Whenever this happens, we have fallen into the trap of confusing claims about brains with claims about people. We need to remember that *people* think and make decisions, not brains.

Discussions about the brain cannot be isolated from discussions about the people who possess those brains, and about the society in which these people live, and about their relationship to each other as well as to God. Whatever contributes to humanity's being must be seen in the context of our relationship to God as well as to our fellow creatures. The communal aspect of human existence is important because all people are created by one and the same God, to live out their lives in harmony and responsible community. Just as it is short-sighted to isolate brains from persons, it is dangerous to think that society has no responsibility for the way in which one human treats the brain of another human. We are responsible for each other, including each other's integrity as human persons, in a very profound way.

Christians are vitally involved in the whole realm of brain control, because they are deeply concerned about the integrity of human beings as people. It is a principle which needs to be worked out in some detail in relation to specific issues; hence the topics dealt with in the subsequent sections. Above all, what I trust will emerge is the intimate relationship between the state of people's brains and the quality of their lives.

SOME GUIDELINES TO THE BRAIN[2]

The brain is undoubtedly the most complex organ of the human body, and an appreciation of at least some basic terminology is essential if the arguments of the following sections are to be grasped. The present section, therefore, is an attempt to sketch a few of the fundamental features of brain organization.

Together with the spinal cord, the brain forms the central nervous system, which is kept in functional contact with the rest of the body and the external environment via the nerves of the peripheral nervous sys-

2. For further reading see C. Blakemore, *Mechanics of the Mind* (Cambridge, MA: Cambridge University Press, 1977); J. C. Eccles, *The Understanding of the Brain* (New York: McGraw-Hill, 1973); S. Rose, *The Conscious Brain* (New York: Penguin Books, 1976); M. C. Wittrock et al., *The Human Brain* (Englewood Cliffs, NJ: Prentice-Hall, 1977).

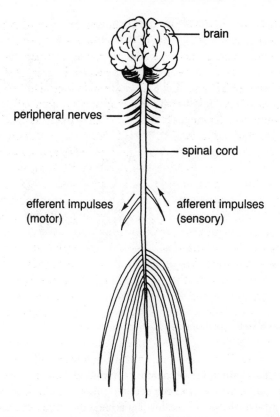

Fig. 1. The brain and spinal cord, which together make up the central nervous system. Also depicted are a few of the nerves constituting the peripheral nervous system.

tem (Fig. 1). These nerves either run toward the cord (afferent) or away from it (efferent); the former convey information about sensations at the surface of the body into the spinal cord, while the latter bring about the movement of muscles.

In this way the brain is kept in touch with events in its environment and is able to respond in terms of the information stores it has built up over the individual's lifetime. This enables the brain to remember and also to learn, because whenever the brain's response is inappropriate for a given situation, the response is modified on a subsequent occasion. In this way the individual is able to exercise control over his environment. In other words, this is the basis of all our learning experiences.

The human brain can be subdivided into three principal regions:

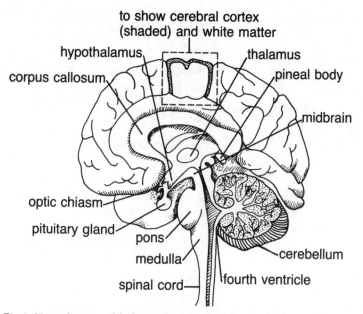

Fig. 2. Vertical section of the human brain in the midline to display medial views of a number of brain regions.

forebrain, midbrain, and hindbrain. Of these, my interest is in the forebrain and in particular in the cerebral hemispheres—one on either side and joined across the midline by a bundle of fibers known as the corpus callosum (Fig. 2). Each hemisphere consists of a core of white matter and a thin enveloping rind of grey matter, 3-4mm thick, and termed the cerebral cortex. This cerebral cortex contains many millions of nerve cells, which are densely packed together, while the underlying white matter is largely constructed from the long fibers of nerve cells. It is this part of the brain that is concerned with conscious behavior and with such higher activities as learning, memory, and the coding of the experiences of the individual.

From the side, each of the cerebral hemispheres can be seen to consist of a number of well-defined lobes (Fig. 3). These are the frontal, occipital, parietal, and temporal, each one of which can be subdivided into functionally distinct regions. Some of the major regions are depicted in figure 4, from which it can be seen that these relate to motor and sensory functions, vision, hearing, and speech. Other functions are similarly localized, although these are not in readily identifiable regions on the surface of the cerebral hemispheres.

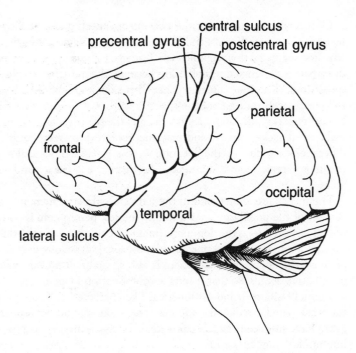

Fig. 3. Left cerebral hemisphere of the human brain to show the major lobes into which it is subdivided.

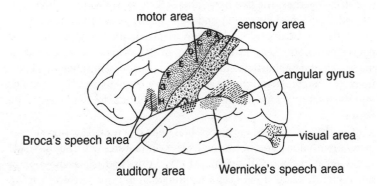

Fig. 4. Localization of functionally distinct areas in the left cerebral hemisphere. The letters within the motor area represent muscle groups from different parts of the body, e.g., A represents toes-knee, and F represents face-lips.

Of special importance are the two major speech areas, as shown in figure 4. These are Broca's and Wernicke's areas, named after the men who first suggested their significance. Damage to Broca's area results in a disturbance of language (aphasia), because the muscles involved in speech production are affected. Speech is slow and labored, although the patient can understand the speech of others. Wernicke's aphasia, by contrast, is quite different. Superficially the speech sounds quite normal, but it lacks content and may incorporate incorrect words. The differences are due to the location of the areas—Broca's alongside the motor region, and Wernicke's between the auditory and visual areas.

The speech areas are found in the left cerebral hemisphere in 96–98 percent of the population. As a result, the left hemisphere is conventionally referred to as the dominant (major) hemisphere and the right as the nondominant (minor) one. Besides the localization of speech in this manner, the dominant hemisphere is also specialized to deal with fine imaginative details, so that it sorts out information in an analytical and sequential fashion. It has arithmetical-like characteristics and is sometimes compared to a digital computer. The nondominant hemisphere is, as we have just seen, largely nonverbal. Its assets are that it processes information simultaneously; it is something like an analog computer building up whole pictures and discerning patterns rather than details. It is superior to the left hemisphere in all kinds of geometrical and perspective drawings, its goal being the synthesis of information. These ideas are strengthened by its involvement in musical appreciation, and perhaps even in poetry.

Taken together, the two hemispheres form an integrated whole. Although some functions are better developed in one hemisphere than the other, there is no opposition between them. Should the appearance of a particular function be delayed during an individual's development, it may be able to establish itself later in the opposite hemisphere. Accordingly, the cerebral hemispheres in human beings work together to maintain the integrity of mental functioning, and hence the wholeness of the person.

Even this description of the cerebral hemispheres fails to account for many essential features of human existence, features which must reside in the organization of the brain. At least, this is a basic assumption of neuroscientists and, I believe, a legitimate one. Among these features are attributes such as motivation, the determination to get things done, and the maintenance of a high level of interest in events, issues, and activities in the world around us. While these may appear to be rather

vague ideas, remove them from a human being and much that is characteristic of ordinary human living disappears; the person's humanness may
be tragically decimated.

The part of the cerebral hemispheres especially implicated in these
functions is the frontal lobe, damage to which may have catastrophic
repercussions for a person's humanness. For instance, the operation of
frontal lobotomy, which in its classical form was in vogue in the 1940s
and 1950s, consisted of cutting the nerve fibers connecting the frontal
lobes to the remainder of the brain. While the reasons for the operation,
principally severe depression and excruciating pain, were frequently
alleviated, far too many patients ended up disinterested vegetables.
What is significant is that this did not occur due to any loss of muscular or
sensory functions but simply because the patients had lost all interest in
themselves and their surroundings. The frontal lobes, therefore, constitute the apparatus so essential for the regulation of the state of activity
of the brain. They have the function of forming stable plans and intentions capable of controlling a person's conscious behavior. In short, they
are intimately concerned with the general regulation of a person's behavior, in that they are responsible for the orientation of behavior to the
future as well as to the present.

Before leaving this brief account of the cerebral hemispheres, a further
interesting feature of the temporal lobes should be mentioned (Fig. 2).
In the 1930s Wilder Penfield, a Canadian neurosurgeon, carried out
numerous stimulation studies of the brains of patients during brain operations. Since these operations are performed using local anaesthetics,
the patients can experience sensations or move certain muscles when
particular regions of the cerebral hemispheres are electrically stimulated.
Penfield noted that when the nonspeech parts of the temporal lobes were
stimulated, the patients experienced flashbacks in which they relived an
experience of an earlier period of their lives. One such example was of a
mother who, on cortical stimulation, was aware of being in her kitchen
listening to the voice of her little boy playing outside in the yard. She was
aware of the neighborhood noises, such as passing cars, that might mean
danger to him. What is intriguing is that stimulation of the same spot of
the temporal cortex in a particular individual may elicit exactly the same
memory time and time again.

In the light of these data, there should be no need to provide sophisticated arguments to prove the intimate interrelationship between the
brain and personhood of an individual. The significance of this interrelationship will be taken up in the final section; for the present, it is
sufficient to acknowledge its existence.

BRAIN DAMAGE AND PERSONALITY DISORDERS[3]

In order to investigate further the interrelationship between brain and personality, it behooves us to consider what happens to people when their brains are damaged. This will highlight the extent to which personality is dependent upon the brain, as well as the nature of the personality loss following brain injury. These two aspects of brain damage are important for an understanding of personal responsibility in a brain-damaged individual, and this itself forces us to consider our own finiteness as created beings.

As illustrations of what major brain damage may mean for an adult, I shall recount two classic examples from the medical literature. The damaged regions of the cerebral hemispheres vary in these two instances, and so highlight quite different aspects of personality deterioration.

For the first of these illustrations we go back to September 13, 1848, when a twenty-five-year-old construction foreman, Phineas P. Gage, was working on the new line of the Rutland and Burlington Railroad near Cavendish, Vermont. He was in charge of a gang of men about to blast away a rock by pouring gunpowder into a hole drilled in it. Unfortunately, the powder accidentally exploded and propelled an iron tamping rod, 3.5 feet long and 1.25 inches in diameter, through Gage's skull. The rod shot through his left cheek and emerged from a hole on the right side of his skull and then landed several yards away on the rocks.

Unbelievably, Phineas P. Gage was not killed. Within a few minutes of this incident, Gage was conscious and was asking his stunned workmates about the whereabouts of his rod. The local physician, John M. Harlow, could hardly believe his eyes, especially when he found he could insert his fingers into the holes in Gage's skull.

Although seriously ill for a few days from his infected wounds and loss of blood, Phineas Gage eventually recovered. By mid-November he was wandering around Cavendish, ready for the new life before him. Dramatic as his recovery had been, it was not more dramatic than his new life because Gage was, in many respects, a *new* person. Prior to the accident, he had been soft-spoken, purposeful, capable, and efficient; after the accident, he became bombastic, with little evidence of purpose in his existence, and with a violent temper. In a paper published in 1868, John Harlow, commenting on these personality changes, wrote: "He is

3. These matters are dealt with in more detail in C. W. Ellison, ed., *Modifying Man: Implications and Ethics* (Washington, D.C.: University Press of America, 1977); H. Gardner, *The Shattered Mind* (New York: Vintage Books, 1976); A. R. Luria, *The Working Brain* (New York: Penguin Books, 1973); A. R. Luria, *The Man with a Shattered World* (New York: Penguin Books, 1975).

fitful, irreverent, indulging at times in the grossest profanity (which was not previously his custom), manifesting but little deference for his fellows . . . at times pertinaciously obstinate, yet capricious and vacillating, devising many plans of future operation, which are no sooner arranged than they are abandoned." Harlow went as far as to quote Gage's friends to the effect that he is "no longer Gage."

Rejected by the railroad company and characterized by an aimless wanderlust, Gage became a fairground attraction, drifting around North and South America exhibiting himself and the by-now-infamous tamping bar. He eventually ended up in San Francisco, where he died in 1860.

This was a sad end for such an important, although mercifully unintentional, scientific experiment. Phineas Gage was a living monument to the fact that personality can be transformed dramatically by destroying a part of the brain, in his case the frontal lobes (Fig. 3) and their connections with the remainder of the brain. Indeed, he was a forerunner of the intentionally applied destruction of equivalent frontal lobe tissue in the classical frontal lobotomy operations of the 1940s and 1950s, as described in the last section.

The second illustration of brain damage is a more recent one, concerning twenty-three-year-old Sublieutenant Zasetsky of the Russian Army. On March 2, 1943, Zasetsky was involved in the Russian offensive against the Germans in the Battle of Smolensk when he was hit by a bullet in his head. From that day onward he became a different person. In many respects he had been killed, because his existence thereafter became a kind of half-sleep. In his own words: "Again and again I tell people I've become a totally different person since my injury, that I was killed on 2nd March, 1943, but because of some vital power of my organism, I miraculously remained alive. . . . I always feel as if I'm living out a hideous, fiendish nightmare—that I'm not a man but a shadow, some creature that's fit for nothing. . . ."

The head injury which led to this feeling of despair and helplessness affected the left temporo-parieto-occipital region of the brain (Fig. 3). For Zasetsky, the clinical consequences of this lesion were manifold, affecting his vision, body image, perception of space, and his reading ability. However, because his frontal lobes escaped damage, he was (and still is) trenchantly aware of his fate. Initially he was unable to perceive anything, as his world had collapsed into fragments. His brain was incapable of constructing complete pictures, and, to complicate matters even further, the right side of everything was nonexistent. He was left, therefore, with the unenviable task of attempting to assemble the fragments that he saw and guess the objects to which they belonged. Allied with the loss of the right side of his world was the loss of the right side of his own body. He simply could not see it.

To make matters worse his sense of his own body had also changed. Not only was he unable to *see* the right side of his body, he was *unaware that it even existed.* Sometimes he would have the terrifying feeling that his head had become inordinately large or his torso extremely small, and he would even forget where parts of his body were or what the function was of some of his organs. Accompanying these bodily aberrations were spatial aberrations, in that he had forgotten how to shake hands or what to do with a needle and thread. On top of this, he found he had forgotten the names of common objects, and of course he got lost repeatedly even in rooms and towns with which he had previously been familiar. The difficulty lay in his having lost any sense of space, so that he was unable to judge relationships between objects. Perhaps even worse than these tragedies for Zasetsky was the realization that he was now illiterate. Although prior to his head injury he had been a fourth-year student at a polytechnic institute, afterward he could read nothing. In his diary he put it like this: "When I look at a letter, it seems unfamiliar and foreign to me. But if I strain my memory and recite the alphabet out loud, I definitely can remember what the letter is."

Zasetsky is far from unique. Many others have suffered the sort of injury he endured—in the form of an external injury, the growth of a tumor, or some cerebrovascular accident. What is remarkable about Zasetsky, however, is his immense determination to transform his inordinately restricted existence into a meaningful life. To do this, he set out on the painful task of learning to read and write, all within the compass of his major visual and orientation limitations. Letter by letter, word by word, he very gradually progressed, forgetting as he went along, reading and rereading and finally writing in an automatic fashion. To give point to this immense effort, he devoted his time to writing a journal of his "terrible brain injury." For twenty-five years he toiled day after day, sometimes devoting an entire day to complete just half a page. Sometimes he would ponder over a page for a week or two. The writing was agonizingly slow, and yet after twenty-five years he had put together a three-thousand-page document which he could not even read without enormous toil and perseverance.

Living in a world of undeciphered images, without a past, and with no understanding of anything scientific or abstract, Zasetsky's determination to live—as he put it—without a brain was only possible through the writing of his journal. In this he revived the past in an attempt to ensure a future. It was his reason for living because he hoped to overcome his illness as he wrote his story and perhaps "become a man like other men." Writing became his only way of thinking.

As we contemplate these two illustrations it would be a gross understatement to conclude that brain damage may alter a person in profound and far-reaching ways. That is undoubtedly true; indeed, the person's outlook on life and even his ethical standards may appear to be modified by some lesions. By and large, brain lesions change a person's character for the worse and not for the better.

Some major brain lesions bring about such a radical disintegration of an individual's personality that it may be legitimate to speak about the virtual death of the personality. What I mean by this is that the impoverished personality is so unlike the original one as to lack essential human and spiritual continuity with it. In this sense, the original person may be more or less dead, despite a more or less intact body.

It may not be inappropriate to suggest that brain lesions may to some degree depersonalize a human being. This implies that a brain-damaged person ceases to be a person in some areas of conduct, the areas concerned depending upon the brain regions damaged. This argument, in turn, has repercussions for our concept of human responsibility, as a depersonalized individual should not be held responsible for those actions governed by the damaged brain regions. Before rushing in this direction, however, we should consider the consequences of treating an individual as less than a person. Zasetsky, with his extensive lesions, would probably have fallen into this category, and yet his response to his condition bears all the hallmarks of human personhood. Despite grave limitations, his determination to make life meaningful for himself and others epitomizes the human longing to achieve significance. It is unwise, therefore, to discard an individual as a person, even in the face of major brain damage. True, the personality of a brain-damaged individual may be but a dim reflection of what it previously was, and the choices open to such an individual may be tragically limited. Nevertheless, as long as some power to choose remains, that individual has not ceased to be a responsible personal agent. The framework of choice may have shifted, and it may be quite unlike the framework employed when dealing with a brain-intact person, but it still exists in most instances. The brain-damaged individual may have far less freedom, because her injuries may prevent her from attaining the results she intends. As long as some freedom remains, however, the power to choose also remains. If this is so, the brain-damaged person retains her status as a person, even though the range of alternatives open to her may be greatly narrowed.

For Christian thinking a central position is occupied by the individual and her personhood. A difficulty with assessing the consequences of brain damage for an individual is that the extent of responsibility is itself called into question due to limitations implicit within the damaged brain. Nevertheless, personhood remains a crucial issue, and a Christian should wish to maximize the use of whatever personhood remains, rather than to dismiss it as of little value. The significance of the individual person remains a hallmark of Christian concern, even though the task in brain damage becomes one of maintaining and perhaps enlarging whatever individual consciousness remains as much as defending it from external onslaughts.

The Christian is also concerned with the wholeness of an individual's experience and existence, as opposed to isolated segments of his being. An individual, therefore, is more than a brain, even though the expression of what he is owes so much to the adequate functioning of his brain. Damage to a person's brain may well inhibit the expression of what he is at present and, perhaps, will be in the future. If we are dealing with an adult, however, it cannot touch the past; that is, his history still has significance. His personhood owes far more to the past than is the case in a brain-intact individual, and as the years progress dependence upon his past may come to assume ever-increasing importance. The relationships begun while the individual was capable of them, the achievements, accomplishments, and perspectives of the individual at that time, must be regarded as the major contributions of that person, representing all he once stood for and, no doubt, would continue to stand for were he still in a position to do so.

In dealing with the brain-damaged individual, compassion in the face of suffering assumes a major role. Important as an understanding of the theoretical basis for the personality defects is, this alone is quite inadequate. After all, it is a person who is in peril, not simply a damaged brain. Individuals with damaged brains are people in jeopardy, not nuisances to be quietly disposed of or politely forgotten. They are people like us, except that their brains have been partially destroyed. They have suffered one of the consequences of a world in conflict—a conflict which has its roots in our alienation from God, whether it be expressed politically, socially, or biologically. We, too, may one day be victims of this conflict. We, like they, will be no less human than we are today and just as much in need of the concerned compassion of God and our fellow human beings. Brain-damaged individuals are still persons; they are beings with whom others must contend. Hence the manifold repercussions of brain damage for those not afflicted as well as for those afflicted, because it forces us to decide how to deal with those unable to think and act for themselves. This is the profound realm of grace and mercy.

LANGUAGE AND HUMANNESS[4]

It would probably be a misleading oversimplification to suggest that any one facet of the human brain was alone responsible for bestowing indelibly human features upon human beings. Nevertheless, it can be argued that language has immense significance for humans in that it forms the basis of a very adaptable means of communication between individuals. By providing a means whereby a very large number of signals can be combined to produce new words and combinations of words, language is essential for the elaboration of abstract concepts, the invention of new ideas, and humanity's attempts to understand ourselves and the world.

Not surprisingly, therefore, language has long been viewed as the dominant distinguishing feature of human beings. Descartes, in the seventeenth century, argued that the use of language was the critical factor distinguishing *Homo sapiens* from the "beasts," while John Locke in the same century contended that nonhuman animals are incapable of thinking in abstract terms. Can we now be so sure about this, in view of the immense strides made in teaching chimpanzees the use of language? Or is it that humans are not as distinct from the higher primates as once thought, and humanness is as much a trait of chimpanzees as of humans?

By employing American sign language, Beatrice and Robert Gardner have succeeded in teaching chimpanzees the signs for as many as two-hundred words. With this vocabulary, some of the chimpanzees are able to construct new words and phrases and also to utilize certain grammatical rules and syntaxes.

Numerous examples have been given of the linguistic capabilities of the two most famous of these chimpanzees, Washoe and Lucy. Washoe, for example, on first seeing a duck landing in a pond, made the gesture for "water bird." This piece of linguistic inventiveness was matched by another first occasion, when an orange was described as an "orange apple." Not previously having seen an orange, but recognizing an apple and colors, this proved a creative way of describing an orange. When a small doll was placed on Washoe's cup, the response was "baby in my drink." Lucy, after practice, was able to distinguish between the phrases "Roger tickle Lucy" and "Lucy tickle Roger."

---

4. For additional treatment of these issues see N. Geschwind, "Language and the Brain," *Scientific American* 226 (1972):76–83; J. Limber, "Language in Child and Chimp?" *American Psychologist* 32 (1977):280–95; D. Premack, "Language and Intelligence in Ape and Man," *American Scientist* 64 (1976):674–83; K. H. Pribram, *Languages of the Brain* (Englewood Cliffs, NJ: Prentice-Hall, 1971); E. S. Savage-Rumbaugh, D. M. Rumbaugh, and S. Boysen, "Do Apes Use Language?" *American Scientist* 68 (1980):49–61; H. S. Terrance, L. A. Petitto, R. J. Sanders, and T. G. Bever, "Can an Ape Create a Sentence?" *Science* 206 (1979):891–902.

Another chimpanzee celebrity is Sarah, who has been trained by University of Pennsylvania psychologist David Premack. Sarah communicates by means of plastic symbols, and not only can she produce simple sentences such as the well-known "gimme tickle gimme," but she has learned to understand complex sentences. An example of such a sentence is, "If red or green then Sarah take red." This is a double-barreled sentence; it is also a highly specific one. She also can understand compound sentences such as "Sarah insert banana in pail, apple in dish."

Particularly impressive was Sarah's accomplishment in actually elaborating for herself the rule for using plurals. Having been taught that "is + pl = are," Premack and his colleagues found that not only could she carry this out, but she could also recognize the subject as plural.

It is when we go beyond this point that complexities and differences in interpretation arise. Some research workers make far greater claims than others about the similarities between human and chimpanzee languages, while many claims made on behalf of this choice group of linguistic chimpanzees in the popular media far exceed the evidence.

David Premack contends that while apes do not compose sentences of human complexity, neither do they merely memorize words and sentences. Instead, he argues, they display linguistic creativity, in that they compose sentences they have never previously used. In so doing they are inducing a *syntax*. In spite of this linguistic creativity, however, they do not show linguistic novelty, because they cannot change the structure of sentences. In this their speech shows many similarities to that of the young child. Even here, though, a major difference exists—whereas a child is on its way toward adult syntax, the chimpanzee appears to be going no further.

This analysis in no way underestimates the extent of what some chimpanzees are capable of in the linguistic sphere. They have achieved a considerable degree of proficiency in using arbitrary symbols to communicate and are capable of some degree of structural analysis. They can also learn a fairly sophisticated substitution technique and can use words to describe new types of objects. A point of contention arises, however, over their ability to generate new words.

Besides this, it has to be admitted that there are many dissimilarities between the language of an ape and that of a normal three-year-old child. Possible explanations include differences between the vocal tracts, brains, and perhaps genetic dispositions for language of chimpanzees and humans.

To a limited and unsatisfactory extent these differences are of help in discovering why apes don't use human language. More interesting, however, is the further question: Why are apes and humans different? What is it about their respective brains that bestows humanness upon human beings and apeness upon chimpanzees? This is the inevitable point to which a discussion of the linguistic potential and limitations of chimpanzees has brought us.

Humans, in their thinking, can make and use abstract concepts which in turn open the way to the invention of new ideas and to the interplay of ideas. This latter attribute calls forth imagination, from which arise poetic language and scientific concepts. Before concept formation can be utilized adequately, however, another trait is essential, namely, generalization. It is generalization which lies at the heart of all human systems of explanation and forecasting. Being capable of thinking in abstract and general terms, humans are in a position to attempt to understand themselves and the world. In doing this, humans look at themselves as people and as individuals; this is where self-knowledge and self-consciousness begin to manifest themselves.

Because she possesses a degree of self-knowledge, each individual is confronted continually by a demand that she not only know but also understand herself as a human being. Integral to this is an awareness of other people and thus a comparison of how she—as an individual— matches up to those alongside her. The results of those encounters with other people and their images is a growing awareness of who she is as a person. It is this awareness that constitutes self-consciousness, which carries with it the implication that creatures characterized by it *know that they know*. Self-knowledge of this order has been regarded traditionally as a uniquely human capacity, although some commentators on chimpanzees' efforts at mastery of language claim that they, too, demonstrate this ability. The humility of this claim is matched only by its wishful thinking. Self-consciousness ensures that human beings are continually asking questions about themselves, their existence, their destiny, and any and every aspect of their world, surely the sort of questions chimpanzees have never begun to formulate, let alone think through.

Moreover, individual human beings are characterized by a desire to know and to be known. Each individual has a sense of his personal uniqueness and transience, so that one day he knows he will cease to be. In this, we are confronted by the *death awareness* of human beings, and by their concern with things beyond those of this present life. Implicit within this concern is a quest for meaning in life—for a philosophy that makes sense of the profundities of daily existence.

Not surprisingly, therefore, human life is dominated by the search for truth and is characterized by a concern for moral values. However much individuals may profess no interest in these pursuits, the human race has been unable to escape from their shadow. These pursuits in turn remind us that the dimensions of humanity are not only biological. Humans are aware of nonbiological obligations, rooted as these are in relationship to, and awareness of, God. Humanity's religious dimensions appear integral to our biological make-up, our yearning for that which is beyond us reflecting a deeply felt biological and human need.

In order to understand human dimensions, therefore, we must consider a number of pertinent facets. Human beings are rooted in nature, but we are also formed in the image of God. Humans have to contend with the vagaries of the physical cosmos; we also have to meet the standards of God. We come face to face with biological and social forces, but we also will come face to face with the One who is superior and to whom we will ultimately be subject. Humans are capable of a level of religious experience and spiritual existence quite different from all other living things, and we are made with the intention of responding to God's gracious Word in personal love and trust. Indeed, only in this response can we fulfill the potential of *being* complete human beings.

In the light of this discussion, it becomes possible to analyze humanness and its implications. What does it mean to *be* human and to *act* in a human fashion? Humanness includes an awareness of oneself as an individual, something which chimpanzees may be capable of as they recognize their images in a mirror. Beyond this, it includes an understanding of oneself and of one's goals, implicit within which is the ability to judge oneself, one's description of the world, and one's goals. Humans, therefore, make moral and aesthetic judgments. They are self-reflective beings, a feature of human existence basic to human life and which begins to manifest itself early in childhood when judgments are made about, for instance, the correctness of the sentences that are being used. It is impossible to know what aspects, if any, of these self-reflective features are present in apes, but they demand far more than the mere ability of apes to ask questions, describe states of affairs, and make truth claims.

Humanness demands creativity, the ability to think and act in totally new ways; to imagine new solutions and to see things in novel forms. It means that we can change ourselves and our environment to meet new demands. We can transform almost everything we touch. Creativity of this order is unknown among nonhumans, because it is dependent upon a level of intelligence found only within the genus *Homo*.

Also implicit within humanness is the *potential* for responding to the overtures of God. Individuals may or may not do this, and their response may vary from one of warm anticipation to outright hostility. Nevertheless, all these responses signify an involvement with God, something uniquely human. This is an essential feature of the framework of humanness and should not be overshadowed by considerations of brain organization, basic as these undoubtedly are.

What then does it mean to be human? On the one hand, it implies a brain capable of integrating the signals it receives from the outside world, learning from them, and communicating with others of its kind so that together a whole community can increase in wisdom. Such a brain must have a large cerebral cortex, well-developed and intimately interrelated sensory areas, and, therefore, greatly expanded parietal and temporal lobes (Figs. 3 and 4). It also requires specialized language centers closely integrated with the special sensory systems (Fig. 4). On the other hand, humanness implies beings stemming from the purposes of God and achieving both significance and freedom within the designs of God. Such beings are free to go their own way, but the only freedom that will enhance human status is one grounded within and developed according to the precepts of the Creator.

Perhaps supremely, humanness implies a knowledge of death, with all that flows from such knowledge. Would it be possible to impart to an ape the knowledge that it will die and, if so, would an ape appreciate the significance of this knowledge for its present existence? In other words, would this knowledge modify the way in which it now lives? Far-fetched as these questions may appear, they touch on a fundamental element in the gap separating apes and human beings. Critical as language is to humanness, it is a vehicle for even profounder elements of what *being human* means. Until it can be shown that the linguistic capabilities of chimpanzees also serve as harbingers of an awareness of transience, the distinction between human and nonhuman primates will not have been obliterated.

THE BRAIN-MIND DILEMMA[5]

In discussing some of the diverse facets of a contemporary view of the brain, I have taken a great deal for granted about the brain and the ways in which we approach it. In this section, therefore, I shall examine the relationship between a person's brain and what makes that person the

---

5. Readers seeking to explore this issue more fully should consult J. C. Eccles, *The Human Mystery* (Berlin: Springer International, 1979); J. C. Eccles, *The Human Psyche* (Berlin: Springer International, 1980); C. S. Evans, *Preserving the Person* (Downers Grove, IL: InterVarsity Press, 1977); G. G. Globus et al., eds., *Consciousness and the Brain* (New York: Plenum Press, 1976); D. M. MacKay, *The Clockwork Image* (Downers Grove, IL: InterVarsity Press, 1974); D. M. MacKay, *Human Science and Human Dignity* (London: Hodder and Stoughton, 1979); K. R. Popper and J. C. Eccles, *The Self and Its Brain* (Berlin: Springer International, 1977).

sort of being she is. If a person is no more than her brain, there is no place for mind or perhaps even for personhood. On the other hand, it is no easy task to accommodate mind within a contemporary neurobiological view of the brain.

The complexity of the brain daunts many people and sometimes proves almost too much even for leading neuroscientists. Nevertheless, piece by piece, the brain is being described in rudimentary, material terms. True, we have a very long way to go before we can say realistically that we *understand* the brain scientifically. Yet research fervor in the neurosciences continues, and without doubt the reductionism of this approach is paying dividends.

This reductionism unfortunately has a debit side, and this is the demise of the person. An increasing amount of human behavior can be accounted for without recourse to any explanation involving the conscious decisions of persons. A result of this trend is that it has become increasingly difficult to view persons as responsible agents. Actions and beliefs appear to be explainable by neurobiological concepts. When taken to logical extremes, no room is left for the person or freedom or responsibility; everything is related directly to a person's brain. The person becomes subordinated to the brain and contemporary understanding of it, using the limited and physical categories of scientific causality.

A mechanistic description of humans and their brains may herald the demise of the person and of the mind. In principle, a mechanist approach appears capable of explaining the whole of brain structure and function, and consequently of behavior, without any reference to the mind. A thoroughgoing mechanist might hold that mind as a discernible separate entity does not exist or that, if it does exist, it has to be viewed in radical ways. Perhaps the all-encompassing nature of this mechanistic description should be called into question.

The mind-body problem is a particularly pressing one for neuroscientists because it forces them to consider not only their philosophical positions on this question but also the nature of their science. Inevitably neuroscientists start from their knowledge of the brain as a physical entity or of the individual as a piece of observable behavior patterns. Once confronted by the possible existence of an immaterial mind, neuroscientists must assess the adequacy of their physical/observable base of physical phenomena. They must ask whether it alone provides an all-embracing framework for a complete view of the individual person as a human being like themselves. By the very nature of the scientific endeavor, neuroscientists may find themselves drawn toward some form of materialist answer without analyzing the philosophical implications of such an answer.

We must commence, therefore, with a brief review of the major positions that have developed in this debate, the inevitable starting point for which is with René Descartes and *dualism*. Living at a time when the natural sciences were being overturned by the success of mechanistic thinking, Descartes likened the universe to a vast machine capable of being explained by purely mechanical laws. Everything, including humanity, was encompassed by these all-powerful explanatory principles. In arguing thus, Descartes was being true to his rationalism, and yet unable to follow rationalism to its logical conclusion, he allowed an exception to his mechanical worldview—the human mind.

Descartes, intent on doubting the evidence of the senses and calling into question even the validity of his perceptions of the world, felt able to fall back on the trustworthiness of his own consciousness. Hence the fundamental divide within dualism between the *physical body* and the *nonphysical mind* or consciousness, the former a prisoner of the mechanical world-order and the latter the author of uniquely human characteristics such as rational thought and free choice. For Descartes it was the nonphysical mind which rendered a human being unique and which carried the marks of personhood. This nonphysical side to humans—the mind, soul, or consciousness—was the critical one and constituted, alongside the body, one of the two basic *substances* of the world.

This is the essence of classic dualism, with the body and mind as distinct substances. Nevertheless, the body and mind do interact, and they were regarded by Descartes as totally interdependent aspects of a living being. If this is the case, however, the way in which they interact must be faced. According to Descartes, the mind takes up no space but acts on the body through the brain's pineal gland. This, in turn, must entail that the nonmaterial mind can influence physical happenings in the material brain. This is the hallmark of *interactionism*, with its implicit suggestion that two different types of reality can affect one another.

From Descartes's time in the seventeenth century until the late nineteenth century, Cartesian dualism presented problems. The inherent difficulty of two different substances acting on each other led some dualists to adopt an aberrant version of it, *parallelism*: the mind and body are still distinct but run along parallel tracks. To declare them independent proved a convenient way out of the interactionist dilemma but opened the window to an influx of weird speculation. The difficulties associated with dualism have led, over the years, to the elaboration of an array of alternative positions. Of these, I shall allude to epiphenomenalism, behaviorism, and central-state materialism.

According to *epiphenomenalism*, a nonmaterial mind does exist but is an epiphenomenon or by-product of physical events. Consequently, the conscious events of the mind are unable to influence the physical brain and its processes. A major difficulty with this viewpoint is its contention that consciousness has no effect on the way in which the brain operates, thereby making a mockery both of human beliefs, actions, and conscious choices and also of the critical role played by the brain in human existence.

A far more rigorous alternative to dualism is *behaviorism*, with its attempt to eliminate nonphysical mental states altogether by reducing them to patterns of behavior. This is the form of behaviorism sometimes referred to as *negative* behaviorism, signifying that it is essentially a metaphysical doctrine as opposed to a straightforward psychological technique.

For the behaviorist, any talk about a "mind" is simply an inaccurate way of talking about human behavior. It is a form of linguistic confusion because the mind is neither a "thing" nor a "substance," in the way in which the brain is a thing. Only the brain can be referred to in these terms; such terminology is inappropriate when referring to actions, thoughts, feelings, and desires. These are expressions of brain states and are best described and analyzed using behavioral concepts.

By denigrating the consciousness of an individual, behaviorism is driven to seek for forces controlling individual behavior either in the physiological make-up of the individual or in that person's environment; hence the significance of conditioning as a technology of behavior. Since individuals are merely the sum of their behavior patterns, behaviorism has dispensed not only with consciousness and internal mental states but also with human freedom, human dignity, and human responsibility.

On the surface, behaviorism, with its simple reduction of mental states to actual or potential behavior, seems a welcome contrast to the tantalizing complexities of dualism. Its pitfalls, however, are immense. The attempt to resolve mental states into behavioral terms begs as many questions as it answers. That mental states can, to some extent, be analyzed in terms of behavior is not open to question; that they can be *completely* analyzed in this manner is. And if they cannot be completely analyzed in behavioral terms, the issue of the nature of mental states remains. Apart from this dilemma, however, behaviorism can be faulted for its loss of the wholeness and grandeur of the human person.

The third alternative to dualism is based on the presupposition that mental states are identical with brain states. This is the mind-brain identity theory or *central-state materialism*. In its simplest expression it asserts that the goings-on in the mind are manifestations of physical happenings within the brain. Unlike behaviorism, there is no attempt to deny the existence of consciousness or mental events; they are realities, albeit of the material brain rather than of an immaterial mind.

This equation of the mind with the brain by-passes certain difficulties experienced by epiphenomenalism and behaviorism. The self-evident phenomenon of consciousness is retained, while the problem of explaining how mind and brain interact does not arise. Materialism has many allurements as we become increasingly aware of the dependence of conscious states on brain function.

Nevertheless, materialism too has its drawbacks. Easy as it is to assert the oneness of the mind and brain, it is much more difficult to demonstrate what this identity amounts to in specific terms. Given the assumption that they are identical, and this is an assumption, the discussion then shifts to the implications this may have for our view of human nature. Does it threaten the concept of human freedom by necessitating a belief in determinism? In other words, acceptance of the validity of materialism precipitates a new discussion—that of determinism.

Dualism and its alternatives provide no panacea for those in search of a ready solution to the brain-mind controversy. Each illustrates some truth about the human person and human brain, and yet each also fails to hold the available data and insights in a manageable form. Attractive as it may be to dismiss all philosophical speculation and adopt a slick if unsatisfactory solution, the stakes are too high. The dignity and worth of humanity are in the balance, and a way forward must be found.

From the preceding discussion it would be easy to conclude that dualism has long since been in disrepute and that no respectable philosopher—certainly no respectable neurobiologist—would give it serious consideration as anything other than an important historical doctrine. This, at least, would apply to dualism in anything even remotely resembling its classic form. Such, however, is not the case. Dualism has been propounded in its classic form for at least twenty years by the much-respected and notable neurophysiologist Sir John Eccles.

While the details of Eccles's dualism do not concern us here, it is important to realize that it is based on the primacy of consciousness and is a worldview incorporating the mystery of our existence and the fact that we are part of some great design. He, therefore, views human beings as ends in themselves, with meaning, values, purpose, and responsibility. From a Christian angle, these ideas are exemplary, and yet in order to achieve them Eccles postulates an explicit dualism between the self and the brain, with the mind and brain as independent entities. More specifically, he proposes that the self-conscious mind influences neural events in special areas of the cerebral cortex, termed the *liaison brain*. In order to accommodate this interaction, he further proposes that there must be loopholes in the brain enabling it to be modified by the self-conscious mind.

There are numerous difficulties with this view, including the debatable nature of his neurophysiological interpretations. More fundamentally, this is a "God-of-the-gaps" position, with the interface between the mind/self/soul and the brain having to shift from one brain region or set of nerve cells to another as the scientific evidence shifts. Furthermore, it fails to side-step the perennial problem of dualism, namely, the feasibility of one sort of substance acting on another sort of substance. A final difficulty with this type of radical dualism is that it is in danger of overlooking the human person. It may be that Eccles's emphasis on the separation of the brain and the mind, the body and the soul, misses the crucial and very intimate relationship we, as people, have to our bodies.

A well-known evangelical contribution to this debate is that of Donald MacKay, who again starts from our immediate experience of what it is like to be persons. He, however, diverges from Eccles by stressing not brain-mind dualism but the complementarity of descriptions about people and their brains. This, in turn, leads him into the problem of determinism and to the principle of *logical indeterminacy*. A crucial point in his argument is that an individual's own experience ("I-story" or "mind-story") and a scientific description of his brain ("brain-story") are correlates of one another. As a result, the "I-story" can be indeterministic and the "brain-story" deterministic without mutual contradiction. The reason for this is that the two statements are descriptions of different aspects of an event, the one referring to people and the other to brains. With respect to the question of freedom, it is important to distinguish between people and brains, because it is people—not brains—who are free. Conversely, it is brains—not people—which may be machines.

From this it follows that the brain-mind debate should be viewed within the context of human personhood. The traditionally narrow perspective is a relatively unhelpful one, because of the inherent difficulties of formulating answerable philosophical questions. Even neurobiological approaches are shrouded in apparently intransigent perplexities.

To start with a man as a being aware of his own and other people's consciousness may appear to circumvent some of the traditional difficulties simply by ignoring them. There is some truth in this charge; yet, as reflected in MacKay's stance, the approach can explore new dimensions of insight which may prove valuable. An additional reason for taking the human person seriously is that so many of the challenges arising from the application of brain research are challenges to the nature of humanity. These can only be met by a clear appreciation of human nature, by the meaning of personhood, and by seeing the brain in the context of the value of the human person.

As we have already seen, humanness in biological terms includes an awareness of oneself as an individual, an understanding of oneself and one's goals, an ability to judge oneself and others, self-reflection, creativity, and an awareness of one's own transience. Perhaps the supreme characteristic of humanness beyond the narrowly biological is the potential for responding to the overtures of God. This, in turn, implies a being stemming from the purposes of God and achieving significance and freedom within the designs of God.

The danger even in a description such as this one is the incipient tendency toward compartmentalization. Human beings are both biological and spiritual. My disagreement is not with the two designations but with the all-too-frequently-encountered suggestion that one part of a human being is biological and another part spiritual. Once this idea surfaces, we are back at the interactionism of some exponents of brain-mind dualism. Of course, at the whole-person level, the parallel of brain-mind dualism is body-soul dualism. Using the latter concept, compartmentalization gives us human beings made up of a body plus a soul, a material entity plus an immaterial entity.

In place of this type of dualism we must contend for the holism of the human person. Each person is a unity, describable as a biological-spiritual being, as a body-soul, or as a material-immaterial entity. For certain purposes a human being can be compared usefully to a machine. But a human is simultaneously and equally a person created by God, not one more than the other. The fact that persons are one of these reflects the fact that they are also the other; they cannot be simply one without the other. Both facets of their being are necessary for them to be human. Consequently, the two complementary descriptions are intimately interwoven aspects of what being human is all about.

The wholeness of the human person I am advocating allows no sharp distinction between brain and mind, the brain being the *basis* of all that we know of the personality in this life. To understand human beings as persons is to accept them for what they are, to encourage the development of interrelationships with other people and with God, and to provide opportunities for them to exercise choices and make decisions. Human beings are characterized by what they are and can do as conscious agents. For this their brains are essential, and yet an understanding of their brains as neural machines is not the way to a complete understanding of human beings as persons. This level of explanation is inappropriate because human beings are not simply neural machines clothed with bodies. They are living creatures, with goals, purposes, aspirations, hopes, fears, and self-awareness, who have been created to respond to and delight in God and God's purposes and aspirations.

Although mind is a term traditionally employed to cover the mental abilities of human beings, it is not always a helpful concept. Instead, one can emphasize personhood, with its overtones of wholeness. This, I believe, is consistent with the holism of the biblical writers and ensures that we value *every* aspect of human existence rather than just the bodily/material or the mental/spiritual aspects—depending on our predilection. Insofar as God values every dimension of human existence, our perspective must be equally broad. It must take account of the needs of the body as much as the demands of the "soul"; it must be concerned with the manual aspects of life as much as the mental; it must respect the whole person.

The hallmark of a Christian approach to human nature is that it accepts as the fundamental reality about individuals their existence and significance as ends in themselves. Our biological make-up, genetic inheritance, brain organization, early childhood experiences, interpersonal relationships, family responsibilities, spiritual awareness or lack of it, are all integral aspects of our activity and meaning as human persons. The total activity of individuals—particularly the activity of the brain—expresses what they are as persons.

It may appear that I have deviated some distance from the brain. In fact, I have been faithful to my topic because, within a framework which views humans as indivisible, the brain has to be seen within the context of the human being as a whole. It is only within this context that it can be finally understood, and its significance for human existence appreciated. Christianity affirms the significance of human beings and the meaning of human existence; in so doing, it affirms the value of the human brain.

Brains and Persons

WILLIAM HASKER

PERSONHOOD AS HOLISTIC AND BRAIN DEPENDENT

What happens when we listen to music, the linguistic achievements of chimpanzees, the effects of lobotomy, epiphenomenalism, the moral responsibility of brain-damaged persons—the range of topics in Jones's essay is large, diverse, and perhaps at first appearance somewhat disconnected. Yet I believe a careful reading will show that the various things he has to say are unified around two central themes or theses concerning the nature of human personhood. According to Jones, personhood is *holistic* and it is also *brain dependent.* I will briefly explain each of these themes and then show how they are developed throughout his essay.

To say that personhood is brain dependent is to say that all of the aspects of our functioning as personal beings are intimately related to and crucially dependent on the functioning of various parts of our cerebral mechanism. This is not a very surprising claim, yet I think Jones is quite right to emphasize it as he does, for this is a truth which is rather consistently underestimated, lost sight of, or simply ignored by those who would stress the more transcendent or "spiritual" aspects of personhood.

To say that personhood is holistic is to stress the large variety of distinctively human activities which go to make up human personhood, and it involves the claim that the various aspects or dimensions of personhood must be seen together in an interpenetrating unity. Here Jones is protesting against the tendency, a powerful one both in scientific and in philosophical circles, to focus one's attention on a few of these aspects, give them a narrowly mechanistic or biological interpretation, and then either ignore or deny the significance of the rest of what makes human beings human.

It is already apparent that there is a certain tension between these major themes, at least to the extent that each represents an emphasis which tends to be ignored, denied, or minimized by those who espouse the other. Jones, on the other hand, wishes (quite properly, I think) to draw them together in a harmonious unity.

The introduction to Jones's paper develops both themes as it describes various activities and discusses the corresponding brain functions. After imparting some basic information about brain structure and function, he moves to a discussion of brain damage and its results. The main force of this discussion, I think, is to make us more keenly aware of the pervasive way in which our personal characteristics depend on the integrity of our brain function. Somehow it is more disturbing to realize that my personality and character could be drastically changed by a brain injury—that I could "become a different person," as we say—than to know that I could be killed by such an injury.

It is, I think, worth pointing out that this is the last section of Jones's paper in which he makes any significant use of the detailed results of brain science. In particular, the final section on the brain-mind dilemma makes no use of such results. This is not a criticism; what I have pointed out about Jones's paper is also true of the vast majority of discussions of this problem, whether by scientists or by philosophers.[1] The reason, no doubt, is that the presently available results of brain science are of limited value in deciding between the various solutions to the mind-body problem. Even when these solutions embody different hypotheses about brain functioning, and so in principle might be scientifically decidable, our current knowledge of brain function is generally insufficient to ground the decision. The significance of this observation in the present context is to point out that the problems Jones is concerned with are essentially *philosophical* problems, problems to which scientific data may well be relevant, but which must in the final analysis be answered, and the answers justified, by philosophical arguments. (There is of course the alternative of simply brushing aside all such problems as "unscientific." Jones, happily, has not taken this easy way out.)

Returning from this digression to our survey of Jones's paper, we come to the section on language and humanness, dealing with the use of language by apes. The upshot of this discussion is to underscore the holistic nature of personhood by bringing out the rich variety of human experiences which apparently are not shared even by the highest non-human animals. In making these points, Jones scores heavily against the current tendency to assume that if apes are capable of constructing grammatical sentences then there can't be any very important differences between them and human beings. (There is of course no earthly reason to suppose that Christians have a stake in denying the linguistic capabilities of apes.)

---

1. There are exceptions: see, e.g., Patricia Smith Churchland, "A Perspective on Mind-Brain Research," *Journal of Philosophy* 77 (1980):455–70; Thomas Nagel, "Brain Bisection and the Unity of Consciousness," in *Mortal Questions* (London: Cambridge University Press, 1979), pp. 147–64; and my "Brains, Persons, and Eternal Life," *Christian Scholar's Review* 12 (1983):294–309. But for the literature as a whole, the remarks in the text hold good.

In his concluding section on the brain-mind dilemma, Jones confronts head-on the tension we have noted between his two major themes. How are we to interpret the brain dependence of personhood so that it is compatible with its holistic nature, and vice versa? Since this section contains the philosophical "meat" of Jones's paper, it demands a more detailed, and more critical, discussion.

JONES ON THE BRAIN-MIND DILEMMA

Jones's procedure in this section is to review and reject several of the most influential theories on the mind-body problem, in order to prepare the way for his own constructive remarks. I shall have nothing to say about epiphenomenalism and behaviorism; I agree with Jones that these views are patently inadequate. Both dualistic interactionism and central-state materialism, on the other hand, require further discussion. I shall be concerned here mainly with Jones's reasons for rejecting these theories, and I may as well say at the outset that his reasons, as he states them, do not seem to me to be adequate.

Probably most readers of this volume will agree with Jones in his rejection of central-state materialism. Still, it is relevant to ask what his *reasons* for rejecting it are. The only reason explicitly given is that materialism may necessitate a belief in determinism and thus threaten the concept of human freedom. "In other words, acceptance of the validity of materialism precipitates a new discussion—that of determinism." Well, what then? Let the discussion begin! Does Jones suppose that he will be able to clarify the nature of human personhood *without* confronting the issue of determinism? This question is all the more pertinent in that the solution favored by Jones—that of D. M. MacKay—is itself arguably committed to determinism.[2]

One can, I think, read Jones as giving other reasons for rejecting materialism in other parts of his paper. The introduction, in particular, raises broad questions about the compatibility of mechanistic views of human life (presumably including central-state materialism) with the various aspects of holistic personhood. Accepting materialism may lead us to deny the significance of the moral, aesthetic, and religious dimensions of human life, and it may even cause us to treat humans as machines. These are real issues, but it remains to be shown just how

2. It is very questionable whether for MacKay "the 'I-story' can be indeterministic," as Jones states (p. 178), in view of MacKay's assumption that for a sufficiently well-informed observer all of the agent's actions and thoughts would be fully predictable. For a discussion of MacKay's theory of "logical indeterminacy," see my "MacKay on Being a Responsible Mechanism: Freedom in a Clockwork Universe," with a response by D. M. MacKay and reply, *Christian Scholar's Review* 8 (1978):130–52.

materialism has all these damaging consequences. For all Jones shows us, there may be perfectly good answers for all of his worries about materialism. Such vaguely focused perplexities may supply material for further reflection, but they can never constitute good grounds for dismissing a philosophical position.

What about dualism? It is certainly true that dualism asserts (not merely suggests) that two quite different types of reality—mind and body—can affect one another. But in spite of many claims to the contrary, this rather tired objection in no way constitutes a refutation of dualism. The most that can reasonably be said is that the dualist cannot provide a convincing and satisfying explanation of *how* this interaction is possible. The wise dualist will acknowledge this and maintain that the interaction of mind and body, like the fundamental laws of nature, is a basic fact about the universe which neither admits nor requires further explanation. Like other basic facts, it must simply be accepted because we find it to be so. I might add that a Christian, of all people, ought not to regard this as a conclusive objection to dualism, for God is presumably a very "different type of reality" from you, me, and the lamppost; and if God is capable of "affecting" such realities as these through creation, miracle, and providence it ill behooves us to proclaim that such interaction between diverse substances is impossible!

Nor is it obviously true that dualism "misses the crucial and very intimate relationship *we*, as people, have to our bodies." As H. D. Lewis has convincingly shown, it is entirely possible for the dualist to acknowledge all of the well-known facts about the importance of bodily life to our existence as human beings[3]—and while dualism *allows* for metaphysical and religious doctrines which denigrate the body and deny its value, it in no way *necessitates* these doctrines.

Jones directs some of his criticisms specifically at the contemporary version of dualism propounded by Sir John Eccles (pp. 177–78). I am afraid, however, that some of his comments in this connection are unfair and unjust. It is true that Eccles proposes to regard a specific area of the cerebral cortex as the "liaison brain"—the area in which mind-brain interaction takes place. It is also true that Eccles's neurophysiological interpretations are "debatable" (as whose, may I ask, are not?). But to characterize this as a "'God-of-the-gaps' position, with the interface between the mind/self/soul and the brain having to shift from one brain region or set of nerve cells to another as the scientific evidence shifts" is both demeaning and logically wide of the mark. What Eccles has done, I submit, is to propose a version of dualism which can be regarded, at least

3. Hywel D. Lewis, *The Self and Immortality* (New York: Seabury Press, 1973), chap. 7.

in part, as a scientific hypothesis in that it is *capable of being falsified.* As Karl Popper has long argued, falsifiability is of the essence of science.[4] As long as the dualist merely says that somewhere, somehow, mind and body act upon each other, he gives the scientist little to go on. But when, as Eccles has done, he proposes a specific region of the brain as the locus in which certain things happen, not as a result of previous physical events within the brain but as a result of the direct action of the conscious mind, then the scientist (e.g., Eccles himself as brain researcher) has his work cut out for him. If he can show that the area specified by Eccles is *not* the liaison brain, then Eccles's version of dualism will have been falsified. (This might be done, for instance, by providing a complete *and verified* account of the events which according to Eccles are the result of the mind's action on the brain, in which those events are completely explained in terms of previous physical events within the brain itself.) If there *is* no liaison brain, dualism as a whole is false.[5] Whether Eccles's theory will withstand such empirical testing is something which remains to be seen. (And, given the state of brain science, it may well remain so for quite some time.) From a methodological standpoint, however, Eccles is to be commended rather than criticized for presenting a version of dualism which is capable of scientific testing.

Perhaps I should say here that I do not particularly wish to play the role of an apologist for dualism—or, for that matter, for materialism. If these theories are to be dismissed, however, it must be on the basis of explicit and thoroughly considered reasons. Otherwise, we shall be abandoning prematurely some of the possibilities for solving a problem which on any account is bafflingly difficult.

Jones's own way of dealing with the mind-brain issue is derived from the ideas of Donald M. MacKay[6] (pp. 178–79). The key notion here is

4. See Karl R. Popper, *The Logic of Scientific Discovery* (London: Hutchinson Publishing Group, 1959); *Conjectures and Refutations* (London: Routledge & Kegan Paul, 1963). Jones's strictures on Eccles appear somewhat ironic in view of Popper's and Eccles's association as co-authors of *The Self and Its Brain* (New York: Springer, 1977), in which they support essentially the same dualistic position. Is it Jones's view that the most distinguished philosopher of science of our time has adopted a "God-of-the-gaps position"?

5. Jones's scenario, in which the dualistic neuroscientist repeatedly shifts the locus of the "liaison brain" as he retreats before the (inevitable?!) advance of scientific knowledge, is quite gratuitous. It is, I should think, very unlikely that neuroscience will demonstrate conclusively that the area indicated by Eccles *cannot* be the liaison brain, while leaving this question open for other areas which are likely candidates.

6. The comments and criticisms in this section are directed to MacKay's position *as Jones presents it in his essay;* thus they will fail to do full justice to MacKay. This is regrettable but unavoidable: a full discussion of MacKay's views would demand far more space than is available here. For more on MacKay, see the article referred to in n. 2; also C. Stephen Evans, *Preserving the Person* (Downers Grove, IL: InterVarsity Press, 1977), pp. 105–17.

complementarity—the "I-story" (the account of a person's experience in human and personal terms) and the "brain-story" (the scientific account of this experience in neurophysiological terms) are *complementary* to each other in that they both describe different aspects of one and the same series of events. (MacKay compares this complementarity to that of wave and particle descriptions in modern physics and discusses it extensively in his various writings.) Because of this complementarity, apparently contradictory things can be said about human beings without this involving any real inconsistency. "With respect to the question of freedom, it is important to distinguish between people and brains, because it is people—not brains—who are free. Conversely, it is brains—not people—which may be machines."

The main result of this view of humanity, as Jones develops it, is to reject dualism and every other kind of bifurcation or segmentation of human personality and to insist on the "holism of the human person."

> Each person is a unity, describable as a biological-spiritual being, as a body-soul, or as a material-immaterial entity. For certain purposes a human being can be compared usefully to a machine. But a human is simultaneously and equally a person created by God, not one more than the other (p. 179).

Surely any Christian thinker must applaud some of the things that are being said here, but as a way of resolving the mind-body problem, this view is remarkable chiefly for the many questions it does not answer. Consider the following piece of reasoning, based on the quotation given earlier concerning freedom: People are free, brains are not free, therefore people are not brains. Brains may be machines, people cannot be machines, therefore brains are not people. So we ask, What then *is* a person? Is it something which is *different* from an (embodied) brain? Or a brain *plus* something else? Both these answers are suggestive of dualism. Or is a person a brain *functioning* in a certain way, or perhaps the function itself? This smacks of materialism or behaviorism. Or is a person an *aspect* of an embodied brain, or a way of describing it? This again is suggestive of materialism. If all these answers are rejected, what else is there? Jones does not tell us.

Perhaps the talk of complementarity is meant to keep us from having to ask questions like these—though I must confess I cannot see how it does. But let us leave these questions aside and ask about complementarity itself. The key question is this: how are we to tell when two apparently contradictory descriptions (or explanations) of something are complementary, and when they really are contradictory? "Material" and "immaterial," for example, are presumably in some sense contradictory predicates: when we state that God is immaterial, we imply that God does not have a body. How then are we supposed to understand the idea that human persons are *both* material and immaterial—or, as Jones says, "material-immaterial"? Unless we are given some explanation of this, all we are left with is the bare, unsupported assertion that humans *are* both material and immaterial and that this is true "somehow-I-know-not-how." Terms like "complementary" and "holistic," as Jones uses them, express this claim but do nothing more. In particular, they do nothing to help us understand how it is possible that the claim might be *true*.

I believe it would not be too wide of the mark to describe Jones's procedure in this last section like this: He has developed his two themes of holistic personhood and personhood as brain dependent, and he sees that there is a tension if not an actual inconsistency between them. In particular, there seems to be a conflict between mechanistic brain theories and holistic personhood. In seeking a resolution for this conflict he surveys several of the classical positions on the mind-body problem and finds them all unsatisfactory. Ultimately he resolves the problem by telling us that human beings are indeed holistic persons, that all of their personal functions are dependent on brains which appear to function mechanistically, and that there is no conflict because the mechanistic and the personalistic descriptions are complementary. In other words, he takes the problem with which he started, adds the word "complementarity" as a verbal embellishment, and presents the problem over again as its own solution!

Viewed as an attempt at resolving the mind-brain issue, Jones's effort must be judged a failure, but I would by no means wish to say this about his essay as a whole. In addition to the richness of the essay's detailed contents, I have already indicated my support for his two main themes of personhood as holistic and brain dependent. But now I want to add this: while the notion of complementarity leaves much to be desired when considered as a solution to the mind-body problem, this same notion has a great deal to recommend it when viewed as a *working strategy* for the Christian scientist, particularly for one engaged in brain research. Consider the situation of such a person. As a scientist she has, like any scientist, an obligation to the scientific community of which she is a part. With regard specifically to research, this implies that the research be conducted according to the best canons of scientific procedure and also that it be carried out in the manner which, in the researcher's considered judgment, is most likely to result in enhanced understanding of the given subject-matter—in this case, the human brain. Now it is just a fact (as Jones has indicated) that at present the effective and productive research which is being done on the brain is guided by mechanistic models and assumptions. So our scientist, if she wishes to make an effective contribution, will be well advised to "plug in" to the available mechanistic, neurochemical, and cybernetic models and pursue her research accordingly. This, of course, is just what has been done by such eminent Christian scientists as Donald M. MacKay and Sir John Eccles.

On the other hand, our scientist's obligations are not exhausted by her role as a member of the scientific community. She is also a citizen, a member of various groups and organizations, a friend, a family member, and—ultimately most important—a child of God. All of these roles involve her in a wealth of relationships, privileges, and obligations over and above the scientific ones. And—this is the crucial point—these relationships, privileges, and obligations simply cannot be described and interpreted within the restricted vocabulary and categories of mechanistic brain science. (This is obviously true from the standpoint of a participant, whatever one's view as to the "final" theoretical truth of the matter.) Rather, these human experiences must be described *and lived* in terms of the concepts and vocabularies of morality, of aesthetics, of religion, and of ordinary human relationships. This is the language, in Jones's terminology, of holistic personhood, or, as B. F. Skinner would say, of human "freedom and dignity."[7]

What then is our scientist to do? The only feasible answer, I think, is that she adopts what could be termed a strategy of complementarity. That is to say, when carrying on her scientific work, she pursues without stint the program of describing and explaining all aspects of human functioning through the concepts of mechanistic brain science. However, in other aspects of her life (including her personal relationships with her fellow researchers) she largely disregards these concepts and proceeds to live and understand her life along all the dimensions of holistic personhood. The two descriptions are, indeed, complementary: each describes (in principle) all of the same phenomena, but the descriptions are given for different purposes, in different contexts, and with different criteria for what constitutes an acceptable explanation.

The perceptive reader may have noticed an important omission in this description of our researcher's state of mind: What, in her view, is the *relationship* between the mechanistic descriptions of brain science and the personalistic descriptions of everyday life? Are they ultimately compatible and capable of being fitted together into a coherent whole? If so, how? If not, then how are the conflicts between them to be resolved? These would seem to be questions which cry out for an answer.

---

7. The somewhat dehumanizing tendency of Skinner's writings stems in large part from the fact that he really does want us to give up, in many respects, our ordinary ways of thinking and talking about human beings and replace it with the language of behavioristic psychology.

Our researcher, as we have described her, does not know the answer to these questions. She may, indeed, derive some consolation from the thought that quite possibly no one else does either. (Clearly, no solution to these problems has been able to win anything like universal acceptance. And it is at least arguable that this is not, as things stand, a matter for regret—that none of the currently available solutions has demonstrated its adequacy sufficiently to warrant universal acceptance.) More important is the fact that she is in a position to bear these unanswered questions without undue anxiety. That is to say that even though she does not know how the mechanistic and the personalistic descriptions are to be harmonized, she has good reason to be confident that the conflicts between them (if any) will not be such as to undermine the validity either of her scientific efforts or of her life and activities as a human being. Her adoption of mechanism as a working scientific hypothesis is fully justified by the considerations already alluded to.

On the other hand, her commitment to the concepts and categories of holistic personhood is warranted, not only by the illumination which these bring to her everyday life, but above all by the fact that God, the Creator of human persons with their brains and nervous systems, has spoken to us in these terms and that what God has said cannot be undermined or invalidated by what we may discover about the creation. Viewed in this light, her eagerness to engage in brain research may be seen as an attestation of faith: insofar as she believes that the God of truth has taught her to understand her life in terms of such notions as freedom, responsibility, guilt, forgiveness, and reconciliation, she is confident that none of this can be undermined by the truth that her scientific work may uncover.[8] (Conversely, the refusal to engage in such study may—I do not say it must—be evidence of a less than robust faith, a faith which in its heart of hearts does not fully believe that the Lord is "God almighty, Creator of heaven and earth, and of all things visible and invisible.")

I have dwelt on this at some length, but I believe the matter is of real importance. The scientific activities of Christians are, I think, often seriously hampered by the assumption that in order to engage responsibly in scientific research as a Christian one must possess more or less *ab initio* answers to the various issues that will arise between the Christian faith and the scientific discipline. On the one hand, this may lead to the proscription of certain areas of science as "anti-Christian" and "unbiblical." (This attitude may be justified in a few cases, if a discipline in

---

8. Our understanding of these matters might however be *modified* by scientific discoveries, just as our understanding of the biblical account of creation has been modified (whatever our specific views on the topic) by the discoveries of paleontology.

its current form is totally permeated by unsound and unbiblical assumptions. These cases, I am convinced, are few and far between.) On the other hand, the need to "have the answers" may lead to the premature acceptance of "accommodationist" solutions which "harmonize" Christian truth with the latest scientific wisdom in ways that may prove ultimately to be unsound. The strategy of complementarity injects a bit of Christian intellectual humility into the situation: we can accept, for the time being, that we do not know certain things and yet be confident that our ignorance in no way invalidates the other things that we do know, either because we have found them out for ourselves or because God has told us about them.

So there is a great deal to be said on behalf of complementarity. It is, all the same, not a way of answering questions but rather a way of postponing them. And while the strategy of complementarity may help us to see that we don't need to *have* answers to certain questions, it does nothing (nor should it) to quell the natural human impulse to *search for* answers. Finding answers to the questions about mechanistic brain science and holistic personhood means finding an acceptable solution to the mind-body problem. To this formidable task we now turn.

CRITIQUE OF MATERIALISM AND DUALISM

In discussing Jones's treatment of the brain-mind dilemma, I objected that the reasons he gives for rejecting central-state materialism and dualistic interactionism are not adequate. Since I also wish to reject these positions, it becomes incumbent upon me to produce my own reasons for doing so. Let us begin with materialism.

The hallmark of central-state materialism (also called mind-body identity theory) is its contention that mental states, events, processes, etc., are identical with states, events, and processes in the central nervous system, primarily the brain. (Behaviorism, in contrast, might be termed "peripheral-state materialism.") This general position has been developed and discussed in an enormous literature, and it comes in a number of significantly different versions.[9] Clearly it would be neither possible nor desirable to review here all of the objections that have been raised, the answers to the objections, the rebuttals to these answers, etc. Instead of attempting this thankless task I shall present here a single basic argument which, if it is sound, refutes central-state materialism in all its forms.

9. David M. Rosenthal, ed., *Materialism and the Mind-Body Problem* (Englewood Cliffs, NJ: Prentice-Hall, 1971) is a good selection of articles; an extensive bibliography will be found in Edgar Wilson, *The Mental as Physical* (London: Routledge & Kegan Paul, 1979).

In order to understand this argument, it is necessary to grasp the point that central-state materialism views the human being as a *mechanistic system*. The term *mechanistic,* as used here, requires some comment. It may tend to suggest the "clockwork universe" of Newtonian mechanics, but a mechanistic system need not be mechanical, as opposed, say, to electrodynamic or quantum-mechanical. Rather, it is a system whose states can all be explained and predicted solely in terms of *physical laws,* with no reference to "teleological" notions such as purpose, desire, goal, intention, final cause, and the like. A mechanistic system need not be strictly deterministic: many central-state materialists are quite happy to accept quantum mechanics with its implication of irreducible chance or randomness in the universe. What mechanism cannot accept is that events should happen "for a purpose," or "because they are supposed to," or in order to satisfy *normative requirements* of any kind. One can say that the electron swerved by sheer chance but not that it did so in order to avoid a collision or to make the world a better place for electrons!

Central-state materialism is committed to mechanism, because it is committed to the program of bringing all human life and behavior within the scope of a unified natural science, whose fundamental explanatory principles will be the laws of physics. Ultimately, then, everything that happens in the universe, from the explosion of a supernova to the erection of the Eiffel Tower and the care of a nursing mother for her baby, is explainable in purely physical terms with no reference to desires, intentions, or purposes.

On the face of it, this seems absurd. Leaving aside questions about the purposefulness of the universe as a whole (which are at issue between theists and others), how can it sensibly be denied that predators seek their prey because they desire to eat, or that humans perform their activities in order to satisfy the apparently unbounded variety of human desires, needs, and aspirations?

I believe it is absurd, but at this point the materialist—at least many materialists—will say that he has been misunderstood. In affirming that all human and animal behavior can be explained mechanistically, he has not meant to imply that it cannot *also* be explained in terms of teleological notions such as purpose, desire, and the like. On the contrary, both kinds of explanations can be used correctly in the appropriate contexts: they are, as MacKay says, "complementary." There is indeed a difference between human action and the fall of a meteorite, but this difference does not mean that human action lacks a physical explanation. Rather, the difference is that, unlike the meteorite's fall, the human action also can be correctly described as being the result of purposes, intentions, and desires.

In order to answer this it is necessary to show that, contrary to the mechanist's assertions, the claim that behavior is the result of mechanistic causes is *incompatible* with the claim that it results from purpose and intelligence. Rather than tackle this problem in its general form, I propose to focus our attention on one specific form of human behavior— the behavior that consists of accepting a belief as the conclusion of a rational inference. The point of inferential reasoning, I take it, is that it provides us with *warrant* or *justification* for the conclusions we reach. Of course such warrant or justification is crucial to any form of rational inquiry, including the inquiry which leads the mechanistic materialist to hold his view. Nevertheless, I shall show that if mechanism is true, then no one is ever warranted or rationally justified in accepting the conclusion of an inference.

The argument goes like this: We show that we are *justified* in holding a belief by showing that we have *justifying reasons* for the belief. In order for us to be rationally justified in believing as we do, it is essential that the justifying reasons should really be the *reasons why we hold that belief.* As Donald Davidson puts it, "The justifying role of a reason . . . depends upon the explanatory role."[10] This, after all, is the crucial difference between a reason and a rationalization: the rationalizer tries to justify herself by producing reasons for her belief or action, but we do not take her justification seriously once we realize that the reasons she gives are not her "real" reasons.

Now we can see *if mechanism is true, it is never the case that a person holds a belief because she sees that it is supported by good reasons.* Rather, my being in a certain belief-state, i.e., in a certain brain-state, is, like all of my other brain-states, completely explainable in terms of the physical laws which govern the behavior of my brain and nervous system. To be sure, the causal antecedents of my belief-state may include other brain-states which are identical with states of believing other things, things which may happen to constitute good reasons for my present belief. But *the rational connection between premises and conclusion plays no role in explaining my present state of belief.* Sometimes—not always, by any means!— the physical-causal connection between my earlier and my later brain-states may happen to correspond to rational relationships between the things that I believe. But that this is so is, on the mechanistic hypothesis, a piece of sheer luck,[11] relevant neither to the explanation of my

---

10. Donald Davidson, "Actions, Reasons, and Causes," *Journal of Philosophy* 60 (1963):690. In its original context, Davidson's point concerns the justification of actions, but it is equally relevant to beliefs.

11. At this point the mechanist is likely to reply that successful reasoning is not luck at all but is rather the result of natural selection. While this might explain reliable responses

beliefs nor to their justification. The fact is, that if mechanism is true, each one of us at any given moment believes whatever he or she is causally determined to believe, with the chain of causation going back past the beginnings of our individual lives and the beginning of life on earth to the cloud of gas and dust from which the solar system was formed . . . and on and on.[12] And if I sometimes have the inclination to say to you that my beliefs, unlike yours, are rationally justified, then my saying this shows that my own physical-causal history has caused me to say it but has no tendency at all to show that what I have said is true.

The argument just presented can be summarized as follows:

1. If mechanism is true, then no one ever holds a belief because he sees that it is supported by good reasons.
2. If no one ever holds a belief because he sees that it is supported by good reasons, then no one is ever rationally justified in accepting the conclusion of any inference.
3. So, if mechanism is true, no one is ever justified in accepting the conclusion of any inference.

This last proposition, I believe, constitutes a conclusive refutation of mechanism. If the mechanist rejects the antecedent, he has given up his position and we can now agree with him. If he accepts the consequent, he implies that he himself has no rational justification for accepting the mechanist position. And with this also we may cheerfully agree![13]

This argument points out a critical weakness of mechanism, and in doing this it also shows that in certain areas of human behavior mechanistic and teleological explanations are *not* complementary, as MacKay and others claim, but rather incompatible. I find it somewhat ironic that

on matters which are directly related to individual or group survival, it has very little relevance to the sort of questions philosophical controversies are concerned with. A particularly awkward case for the materialist is the matter of religious belief. Such belief, which in some form is universal among primitive humans, must to the materialist be conducive to survival or at least not inimical to it. Yet the materialist is committed to its being false.

12. If natural causation is not strictly deterministic, then *sufficient* causes of our present beliefs do not go back so far. But the injection of chance into the causal sequence does nothing to enhance its rationality.

13. While I hope this argument will carry some conviction as presented here, a rigorous development requires more space than is available. See the author's "The Transcendental Refutation of Determinism," *Southern Journal of Philosophy* (1973):173–83, and "Can Action Be Explained Mechanistically?" *University of Dayton Review* 9, no. 2 (1972):53–62. For a book-length discussion of arguments of this type see Joseph M. Boyle, Jr., Germain Grisèz, and Olaf Tollefson, *Free Choice: A Self-Referential Argument* (Notre Dame: University of Notre Dame Press, 1976).

MacKay's theory, to which Jones turns for refuge from the hard doctrines of materialism, should be subject to the same objection as materialism itself!

Yet another difficulty is that mechanism entails the denial of human moral responsibility. That this is so is beyond reasonable doubt, though it is often denied. For consider the following argument:[14]

1. No human being is responsible for the state of the universe one million years ago.
2. No human being is responsible for the fact that the state of the universe one million years ago has led to the events of today.
3. No human being is responsible for any of the events which take place today.

If (3) is false—and all of us act as though we think it false—then (1) or (2) must be false. But (1) is incontestable, and (2) is entailed not only by all varieties of determinism (since the connection between the past state of the universe and today's events is governed by deterministic laws over which human beings have no control), but also by a mechanistic doctrine which allows that, along with the laws of nature, chance and randomness play a part in the determination of events. For no human being can be responsible for what is due to chance. The mechanist must, therefore, accept the conclusion as true.

Central-state materialism, then, is unacceptable because it entails mechanism, but there is another objection to materialism which will seem even more evident to many Christian thinkers: materialism seems to be incompatible with the Christian affirmation of eternal life. If a person simply *is* a certain living body, then when that body dies and decays the person is no more. What could be more evident?

Certain theologians and philosophers, wishing to avoid a commitment to dualism, have claimed that the existence of a "soul" distinct from the body is *not* essential for eternal life. John Hick, for example, supposes that at some point after our death and (temporary) extinction, God *re-creates* us as resurrected persons, and our everlasting life goes on from there.

One's natural thought is that a person thus newly created after I have died could not be the *same person* as the one who died, no matter how similar in all respects. Hick seeks to overcome this objection by a series of hypothetical examples, of which the most interesting is the following: Our friend John Smith has just died, and his body lies before us. Then we

---

14. I owe this argument to Peter Van Inwagen. See his *An Essay on Free Will* (Oxford: The Clarendon Press, 1983).

learn that, just after John's death, an exact replica of John Smith has appeared, precisely similar to the original in all physical and psychological respects. (Hick even suggests that we compare stomach contents!) He says: "Even with the corpse on our hands we would, I think, still have to accept this 'John Smith' as the John Smith who died. We would have to say that he had been miraculously re-created in another place."[15]

Now Hick's story is at least intelligible on dualist presuppositions: one could simply say that God had for some inscrutable reason created a new body for John and caused his soul, after the former body's death, to be joined with and to animate this newly created body. But that is not Hick's view: his claim is that John Smith$_1$ and John Smith$_2$ are the *same identical person*, in spite of the fact that *no* part of John Smith$_1$ (in particular, not his soul, which does not exist at all as a separate entity) is a part of John Smith$_2$. Surely this is incoherent. If John Smith is identical with a certain living body, then it is an outright contradiction to say that that body is dead but the person still lives. The only way to avoid this contradiction is to hold that a person is not a concrete individual thing at all, but rather a *kind* of thing—something like a copy of today's newspaper—so that anything which is sufficiently similar to John Smith *is* John Smith. But this also is evidently absurd; it is what in philosophy is called a "category mistake."[16] This central—I think insuperable—problem stands in the way of any attempt to affirm eternal life while denying the existence of a mind or soul which is separable from the body.

These objections to materialism seem to have brought us back to the threshold of dualism, for two salient characteristics of the immaterial mind, on Descartes's view, are the facts that it functions rationally rather than mechanistically and that it is capable of surviving bodily death. If our reflections so far are on the right track, these same two characteristics must also appear in any acceptable solution of the mind-brain dilemma. Nevertheless, I agree with Jones that dualism, at least in anything like its classical forms, is to be rejected. I have characterized the reasons he gives for this as inadequate, so now I must state my own reasons.

These reasons are two, both revolving about the fact that dualism has difficulty in establishing a sufficiently intimate connection between bio-

15. John Hick, *Philosophy of Religion*, 2d ed. (Englewood Cliffs, NJ: Prentice-Hall, 1973), p. 101.

16. The category mistake is apparent when MacKay compares a person to a message on a chalkboard, which can be erased and rewritten any number of times, or to a computer program which can be programmed successively into a number of different computers (*The Clockwork Image* [Downers Grove, IL: InterVarsity Press, 1973], pp. 74–75). I would like to point out that messages and computer programs are also capable of any number of *simultaneous* "embodiments."

logical and psychological functioning. The first problem concerns the question of the souls of animals—in principle, a major embarrassment for much of the philosophy since Descartes. (In practice, the embarrassment has generally been avoided by ignoring the topic.) If dualism is true, then all sentient creatures must possess minds, or souls, in some sense at least closely analogous to that in which humans are said to possess them. Clearly it is out of the question for us to say, with Descartes himself, that animals are mere automata and have no feelings whatever. We can also rule out the occasionally heard suggestion that while in humans it is the mind or soul which has feelings, in animals it is merely the biological organs which have them. To admit that biological organs can have feelings without the aid of a mind or soul is to render the soul redundant also in the human case; it undercuts the philosophical motivation for accepting dualism in the first place.

While we can't follow Descartes in making animals into automata, we can appreciate the difficulties which led him to take this step. The difficulties of accounting for "animal soul" within the dualistic scheme are formidable. Presumably we do not want to have it that the beasts are immortal, but in the Cartesian scheme, at least, there seems to be no way of avoiding this that is not clearly ad hoc. There is also the problem of how the souls of animals originate. Presumably they cannot be replicated through biological reproduction. Traditionally the souls of human beings were held to be created individually by God, but it places a strain on one's credulity to affirm this in the case of slugs, gnats, and termites. The problem of the origin of souls is particularly awkward in the case of organisms which can be cut in pieces, each of which will develop into a complete organism (e.g., starfish). At the beginning of the process, there is one organism and one soul; at the end there are two organisms, and, presumably, two souls. How can we account for this? Did the knife which cut off a piece of the creature's body also excise a chunk of its nonextended soul? There is also the point that there does not seem to be any natural or plausible way to fit Cartesian souls into the story of biological evolution.[17]

The second major problem for dualism arises from the palpable fact of the *dependence* of consciousness upon brain processes, as illustrated by the commonplaces of everyday experience and also, more spectacularly, by cases of brain trauma such as those cited by Jones. The problem here is not one of logical inconsistency: there is nothing inherent in the dualist

---

17. For more on this objection, see the author's "The Souls of Beasts and Men," *Religious Studies* 10 (1974):265–377; and "Emergentism," *Religious Studies* 18 (1982):473–88. Somewhat similar points are made in Emmett L. Holman, "Continuity and the Metaphysics of Dualism," *Philosophical Studies* 45 (1984):197–204.

position which would force the dualist to deny that mental processes are correlated with brain processes in the way that we find them to be. But dualism has great difficulty in rendering this correlation intelligible—in explaining *why* the correlation should obtain. To be sure, dualism readily explains certain types of dependence. Clearly, sensory experiences must be mediated to the conscious mind via the brain; thus an impairment in brain function can deprive the mind of those experiences. It is universally assumed that memory is carried in some sort of brain traces, and if this is so then a disruption of brain function could deprive the conscious mind of access to those memories. (This of course creates difficulties about the memories—and therefore, on some views, about the identity—of the mind in a disembodied state. I will not pursue this problem here.) Obviously, also, brain misfunction could interrupt the communication between the conscious mind and the effector muscles, rendering voluntary bodily action impossible. But, on the dualistic view, why should *consciousness itself* be interrupted by drugs, or a blow on the head, or by the need for sleep? Why should reasoning, generally thought of as the distinctive activity of the conscious mind, be interrupted by such physical disturbances? The natural conclusion from the dualistic hypothesis would seem to be that consciousness should continue unabated during such times—deprived, to be sure, of fresh sensory input and of motor action, and perhaps also of some memories. It seems that by making mind essentially independent of brain rather than dependent on it, dualism deprives itself of a ready explanation for the kinds of dependency that we actually find. Presumably the dualist can contrive some sort of auxiliary hypothesis to account for this dependency, but I suspect that most such hypotheses will have a strong ad hoc flavor which is symptomatic of the artificiality of the whole scheme. Either that, or they will make mind dependent on brain in a way that undermines the independence which is the hallmark of dualism.

It is true that these two problems do not refute dualism in the way that our former arguments (if accepted) refute materialism. For many persons, however, they will generate enough intellectual discomfort to make the search for an acceptable nondualistic theory an attractive undertaking. Indeed, I would suggest that the more conversant we become with the facts about the brain dependence of persons, as ably displayed by Jones, the more we will tend to find traditional dualism artificial and implausible.[18] So in a way I do agree with him that dualism "misses the crucial and very intimate relationship *we*, as people, have to our bodies."

---

18. This may not be so for everyone. Presumably Eccles is tolerably familiar with these facts, yet he is an unrepentant dualist!

THE EMERGENCE OF PERSONS

The arguments against materialism and dualism not only provide a rationale for rejecting those views; they also serve to exhibit some of the constraints which an acceptable theory must satisfy. Such a theory must recognize fully the brain dependence of persons as this is shown both by common experience and by current research. And bare logical consistency is not enough; the brain dependence of persons should be an organic consequence of the theory and not merely an ad hoc accommodation. On the other hand, an adequate theory must do justice to the full richness and complexity of human personhood rather than forcing it into a Procrustean bed of scientific abstractions. A mechanistic theory, as we have seen, is inconsistent not only with our bone-deep convictions about human moral responsibility but even with the claim that this theory—or any theory—is accepted because it is seen to be supported by good reasons. For Christians, there is an additional requirement: an acceptable mind-body theory must enable us to make coherent sense of the affirmation of life after death.

How are these constraints to be met? Two fundamental questions which need to be answered concern (1) the nature of physical reality and (2) the origin of the mental either within or separate from the physical world. With regard to the first question, the standpoint of the present essay is an unabashed scientific realism. That is, the account physics gives of physical objects—in terms of molecules, atoms, protons, electrons, quarks, gluons, and the like—is taken to be, so far as it goes, an account of the true nature of these things. This contrasts with revisionist metaphysical theories such as Berkeley's phenomenalism or Whitehead's doctrine of "actual occasions." Such revisionist accounts are, in my opinion, inadequately motivated, though I cannot argue this here. While they do "save the phenomena" on which scientific theories are based they tend to empty these theories of explanatory force and leave them as mere computational devices. We may in the end have to deny that science can explain everything, but to deny that it correctly explains the very facts on which its theories are based is to indulge in unwarranted skepticism.[19]

The science of physics, however, offers nothing like an explanation of consciousness. So the question arises: What do we postulate as the source and origin of (created) consciousness? Here we must take a step beyond (present-day) science, but in what direction? Are we to say that, in addition to the intricate and fascinating properties of the ultimate

19. For argument on this point see the author's *Metaphysics: Constructing a Worldview* (Downers Grove, IL: InterVarsity Press, 1983), chap. 4.

constituents of matter as disclosed by high-energy physics, these constituents have other, as yet unknown properties which are relevant to the generation of consciousness? Or, are we to consider consciousness as something fundamentally alien to matter, able to animate it, or be infused into it (or however we do conceive this relationship) only *ab extra*?

Cartesian dualism, struck by the gulf between the mechanistic *res extensa* of seventeenth-century physics and the "rational world" of human thought and action, took the latter course. Even today there are eminent philosophers who find it utterly obvious that thoughts, pains, and other conscious experiences are nonextended and altogether different from any physical processes. [20] While this may seem persuasive when we contrast the higher reaches of human rational behavior with the inertness of brute matter (though even this gap has been narrowed considerably by computers), it has great difficulty in doing justice to the apparent continuity, with respect to conscious or at least sentient experience, between humans and other forms of life.

If this view is rejected, however, we must grasp the other horn of the dilemma and say that matter does, after all, have within itself the potentiality (at least) for sentience, awareness, or consciousness. It seems clear that this view enjoys considerable factual support, in the following sense: There are in nature a large number of physical-biological systems of different kinds, such that the evidence of sentient experience on the part of these systems is directly correlated with their organizational complexity (particularly in the central nervous system) and integrity of biological function. A scientific study of mind which takes its departure from such facts as these may or may not prove to be successful, but if it does not base itself on these facts, it will be unable to begin at all.

I am going to say, then, that the mental takes its origin from the physical. The physical phenomena of inorganic nature, so far as we can tell, give no evidence of being accompanied by any sort of sentience or awareness. But somehow the potential for such awareness exists in the physical stuff of the world, and actual awareness manifests itself when that stuff is organized and functioning in suitably complex organic systems. Somehow, then, the mental emerges out of the physical, and to mark this fact I propose to label the present theory "emergentism." [21]

Everything will depend, then, on the way in which this emergence is spelled out. My proposal is that we conceive of the mind, or soul (and

20. See H. D. Lewis, *Persons and Life After Death* (New York: Barnes & Noble, 1978), pp. 29–30.
21. For the concept of "emergence" which is involved here see "Emergentism," p. 476, n. 2.

corresponding phenomena among the lower creatures), on the analogy of the various "fields" (electrical, magnetic, gravitational, etc.) of physical science. Each of these kinds of field is conceived (in keeping with the scientific realist assumptions of the theory) as an actual concrete entity, produced in each case by a suitable configuration of matter, but nevertheless distinct from it. If for convenience we take the magnetic field as our analogue, we may say that "as the magnet generates its magnetic field, so the organism generates its conscious field."[22] Certain states and/or processes in a magnet cause there to be a magnetic field; similarly certain states and/or processes in a living organism cause there to be another kind of field—call it the "conscious field" or the "psychic field" or (perhaps most provocatively) the "soul field." Like the various physical fields, the conscious field originates from a generating physical object, but like those other fields it is distinct from that object rather than identical with it.

How does the notion of a conscious field help in meeting the constraints on an acceptable theory of mind? It is clear that this view has no difficulty recognizing what we have called the brain dependence of persons. If consciousness is a field generated by the organism—primarily, no doubt, by the brain—then one would naturally expect mental functioning to be closely dependent on the functional state of that organism and to be affected by changes in function due to fatigue, disease, chemicals, or brain lesions. Emergentism enjoys a clear advantage over dualism in these respects, and it also has the advantage of making intelligible the causal interaction between mind and body: two-way interaction between a field and the generating object is evident in the case of each of the physical fields mentioned. In this way the field analogy effectively rules our epiphenomenalism: a "conscious field" which merely registers changes in the generating organism but has no effect either on that organism or on any other object would be just as redundant and implausible as a physical field with corresponding characteristics.

Expanding on this last point, the field analogy offers a direct argument against certain kinds of mechanism. Mechanism in its standard forms—as presupposed by most versions of mind-body identity theory—aspires to account for the functioning of brains, and therefore of persons, entirely in terms of the laws which govern the microparticles of physics. Now these laws are set up without reference to the effects of conscious fields and are tested in experimental situations where there is no reason to expect such fields to be operative. Thus (from the standpoint of

22. Hasker, "The Souls of Beasts and Men," p. 272.

emergentism) it is no more reasonable to expect these laws to be sufficient for the explanation of brain phenomena than to expect the mechanics of particle-impact to account for the functioning of an electric motor.

The laws which account for electrical phenomena are still, in a broad sense, mechanistic. Accounting for the functioning of conscious fields, however, is equivalent to giving an account of the human person as a whole, and we have seen already that a mechanistic account of the person inevitably does violence to essential human activities. Thus we have a right to say that while the conscious field is generated from a functional configuration of physical particles, its functioning cannot be exhaustively explained or predicted either on the basis of the laws of microphysical particles or on the basis of yet-to-be-discovered laws of "mechanistic psychophysics." Rather, such an account must make room, at a fundamental level, for the teleological explanations of a humanistic psychology as well as for the normative principles of logic, ethics, and aesthetics. In short, the kind of explanation we require must enable us to *affirm* the multiple dimensions of "holistic personhood" rather than explain them away.

We have seen that emergentism is able to overcome many of the drawbacks both of materialism and of dualism. What of immortality? Doesn't the field analogy, which is apparently so helpful in illustrating the close connection between physical and mental functioning, also guarantee that the death of the body means cessation of personal existence?

It is important to be clear about what we expect of a mind-body theory in this regard. From Plato on, a great many philosophers have put forward philosophical proofs of the immortality of the soul, and many of these proofs have turned on the philosopher's doctrine concerning the soul's nature, i.e., on his mind-body theory. Such proofs have no proponents in contemporary philosophy, nor is their passing greatly lamented. For Christian believers, in particular, the hope of life eternal is grounded in the promises of God rather than in such philosophical proofs.

Even if we don't need a proof of eternal life, however, it is nevertheless of some importance that we don't include in our belief-structure other affirmations which *contradict* this belief. It will be recalled that our criticism of Recreationism was not on the grounds that this theory fails to *prove* life after death but rather because, given the assumptions of the theory, the notion of a future life for the person who died is incoherent, logically absurd. And so we can say this: an acceptable mind-body theory may or may not "prove" life after death (in the sense that immortality follows deductively from the premises of the theory), but it must at least exhibit a future life as an *intelligible possibility*, one which is *conceptually coherent* with the premises of the theory.

How does emergentism measure up on this score? To begin with, it is clearly the case that the physical fields of which we have knowledge require continuous support from the generating body in order to remain in existence. But that this is so is a matter of fact and not a truth of logic. Alternatives are readily conceivable. For instance, it is conceivable that a field initially generated by some physical object could thereafter become self-sustaining, so that it can continue to exist after the generating object has disappeared. Surprisingly, there is a plausible example of this within physics, in the recently developed "black hole" theory. According to Roger Penrose, "After the body has collapsed in, it is better to think of the black hole as a self-sustaining gravitational field in its own right. It has no further use for the body which originally built it!"[23]

Another possibility, perhaps even more relevant for our present purpose, is that when the generator ceases to function some other entity or agency takes over and sustains the field in being. Here the theological context has a bearing on what is possible: no doubt an almighty God could annihilate simultaneously all of the electromagnets in a particle accelerator and instantaneously replace them with others of an improved model, while causing the identical field to persist in being. Or God could simply grant to the field the power to sustain itself without a material generator. Perhaps there is no reason why God would do such a thing, but we think there is indeed a reason for God to be concerned with the continued existence of rational souls—and if God is so concerned, surely it does not lie beyond divine power to preserve them alive.

This then is emergentism's perspective on eternal life: the soul is not "naturally immortal," if that means possessing the guarantee of endless existence in virtue of its inherent metaphysical characteristics. It is, like the souls of the beasts, a product of biological functioning and liable to perish as they do—but for the power and wisdom of God who has purposed to keep us in being. Or if we do wish to speak of "natural immortality," we should interpret this as suggested by Austin Farrar:

> We might find the naturalness of the soul's immortality to lie in her relation with her Creator, not in her relation with the rest of the created world. Because other created things lack certain characteristics, it is natural they should be allowed to perish; because the human soul, or person, has these characteristics, it is natural God should conserve us always.[24]

23. "Black Holes," in *Cosmology Now*, ed. Laurie John (New York: Teplinger, 1976), p. 124.
24. *The Freedom of the Will* (London: Adam & Charles Black, 1958), p. 103.

It is time to sum up. Emergentism has revealed itself as capable of satisfying, to a high degree, the desiderata for an acceptable mind-body theory. It acknowledges freely and without constraint the brain-dependence of persons exhibited by current research. To be sure, it does not accept the mechanistic models which underlie this research as the final truth about the nature and functioning of human persons, but it allows full scope for the continued employment of these models so long as they continue to prove fruitful. (Even if the person as a whole does not function mechanistically, there may be—and apparently are—many subsystems in the brain and nervous system which do so function.) On the other hand, it rejects the dualist's vision of humanity as essentially bifurcated between the natural body and the supernatural spirit, while retaining the emphasis on humans as rational, moral, aesthetic, and religious beings which dualism sought to safeguard. And while it gives no guarantee of eternal life—leaving that to God—it does exhibit personal survival after death as an intelligible possibility. I suggest, then, that it merits consideration as an account of the persons God has created in the divine image.

Mathematics

COMMENTARY

Earlier in this volume Mouw questioned whether Skillen could build a biblical case for making justice the central norm in political life. This raises the broader question as to which values ought to inform Christians' attempts to act out their commitments not only in the sphere of politics but also in other spheres of activity. Heie proposes an answer to this question in the first of the two essays that follow. He also seeks for commonalities between his understanding of overarching biblical values and those mathematical values that underlie activity in the community of practicing mathematicians.

A clear distinction will be evident between the relative emphases given by Skillen and Heie to the roles of law and freedom in acting out the Christian faith. Skillen emphasized that all the diverse dimensions of life are structured normatively by divine ordinances. According to this view, the project of doing mathematics would primarily involve discovering those mathematical structures present in God's creation. In opposition to Skillen, Mouw questioned whether "laws" and "ordinances" and "norms" are such central features of God's relationship to creation.

The emphasis in Heie's proposal falls clearly within the spirit of Mouw's criticism. Heie emphasizes the freedom to create new forms of mathematics. This freedom does not ignore the mathematical structures inherent in God's creation (to oppose "creation" and "discovery" would violate the ecological nature of all knowledge, as proposed by Hodges). Neither is such freedom lawless (Heie proposes criteria for criticism of the results of such creative mathematical activity). But Heie's emphasis is clearly on the mathematician's free and creative response to his or her environment.

Heie proposes that mathematical activity is the expression of commitment to certain values on the part of members of the mathematical community. There is considerable room for pluralism of expression by different mathematicians, depending on the relative weights given to the various mathematical values. Heie argues that there is compatibility between a number of these values espoused by the mathematical community and certain biblical values such as freedom, creativity, beauty, and unified understanding of God's creation.

In his essay Chase proposes a view of mathematics that emphasizes its inherently irreducible pluralism. Nevertheless, while allowing for multiple mathematical approaches, Chase does argue that mathematics is not so much a free creation of the mathematical community (as Heie argues in part), but that it is in fact a replication of divine structures in the creation. Such submission on the part of the mathematician to the created order presupposes the value of humility (rather than freedom). As Chase states, "[Heie] seems to say that the value bounds in mathematics are self-imposed by the mathematical community, whereas in Christianity they are given by . . . God." Chase therefore reflects the same emphasis as Skillen.

In terms of the introductory taxonomy the central focus of this pair of essays is the exploration of commonalities in the value commitments between the mathematical enterprise and the Christian faith. Heie's approach is essentially compatibalist and pluralistic since he suggests that "the project of doing mathematics cannot help but be defined by those who have worked within the project over the years. . . . This does allow for gradual evolution in the understanding of the mathematical community as to the nature of its project . . . but one cannot choose to make abrupt radical changes in this self-understanding. One can only choose whether or not to enter the project of mathematics as it is currently understood by practicing mathematicians." Therefore, Heie does not see the role of a Christian mathematician as one of radically transforming the meaning of mathematics.

Chase, on the other hand, believes that Heie has not been sufficiently radical in his critique of the values of the mathematical community. In this respect he proposes that Christian thought is more congruent with views of mathematics that see it as discovery rather than free creation. He is revisionist or transformationalist to the extent that he rejects what has been a dominant view of the community of mathematicians (formalism) in favor of a less widely held view (much in the same way Hodges opts for a certain theoretical variant in psychology over against the wider community of psychologists).

Issues relating to the nature and possibility of knowledge have been raised in several of the earlier essays, especially the problem of discriminating between truth and error. Although Heie's paper deals primarily with a study of value commitments, he does make reference to epistemological assumptions. In particular, he views the traditional idealism versus realism debate in epistemology to be unfruitful. Rather, his starting point is an assumption that refuses to divorce a subject from the world. He believes that all knowledge claims are the results of interaction between the knower and the known and are therefore neither purely objective nor purely subjective in the common use of these words. However, Heie still wishes to use the word *objective* as referring to the existence of criteria for criticism or evaluation of knowledge claims.

Mathematics: Freedom within Bounds

HAROLD HEIE

> Art and conduct, science, philosophy and history, these are not modes of
> thought defined by rules, they exist only in personal explorations of territo-
> ries of which only the boundaries are subject to definition.
>
> Michael Oakeshott

It is all too easy for academicians to view activity within their chosen
specializations as divorced from the rest of life. In this paper, I will reject
such fragmentation. I will do so by reflecting on the integrative theme of
freedom within bounds; a theme that best captures the way in which I
believe my personal commitment to Jesus Christ ought to express itself in
all that I do, thereby giving coherence to all my varied activities in such
roles as mathematician, teacher, political independent, husband, father, and church member.

In brief, I will argue that all of my activities are informed by certain
fundamental value commitments; that within a given area of activity I
have a certain radical freedom to foster creatively the realization of the
pertinent values in a manner uniquely expressive of me; but that this
freedom of expression is bounded by the existence of certain criteria for
criticism presupposed by the nature of the activity. I will elaborate this
argument by considering, in order of increasing complexity, three types
of activities:[1] use of the classical laws of logic, the full scope of activities
labeled mathematical, and the area of discourse labeled as ethics. It is
within this last area of discourse that one can struggle with the question
of whether one ought to do mathematics. I hope to demonstrate that not
only is the doing of mathematics itself an exemplification of freedom
without bounds, but so is the decision to do mathematics.

---

1. I have previously argued that the concept of *freedom within bounds* illuminates our
understanding of scientific activities, at least as such activities are described by Thomas
Kuhn in *The Structure of Scientific Resolutions*, 2d ed., enl. (Chicago: University of Chicago
Press, 1970). See H. Heie, "Implications of Recent Developments in Philosophy of Sci-
ence for an Axiological Approach to Foundations of Mathematics," *Proceedings of the
Second Wheaton College Conference on Foundational Issues in Mathematics*, Wheaton, IL,
June 1979.

CLASSICAL LAWS OF LOGIC—WHO NEEDS THEM?

If anything appears to be of universal applicability, beyond any possible dispute, it is the classical laws of logic (the propositional calculus). In particular, few would question the certainty of the law of noncontradiction, $\sim[p \vee \sim p]$, which holds that a proposition cannot be both true and false at the same time (also referred to as the law of consistency). Just as certain (at first glance) is the law of excluded middle, $p \vee \sim p$, which states that any proposition is true or false (there is no neutral or middle ground between true and false).

As will be seen shortly, the law of noncontradiction is especially dear to mathematicians. Imagine then my initial chagrin when somewhere in my past readings I came across a book on Zen Buddhism wherein a Zen master is reported to have said to a disciple: "The grass is green. The grass is not green. . . ." The statements are an obvious violation of the law of noncontradiction. What was the Zen master trying to do by using language in this way that seemed so strange to my western mind? As far as I can tell, the master was trying to lead the disciple to some sort of "enlightenment experience" (satori), and the words he used were intended to help accomplish this.[2] If this was indeed the master's purpose, then his use of such language should be judged solely on the basis of the criterion of its instrumental effectiveness toward that end. In brief, I must know what a person is trying to do with language before I can tell how well that person is doing. (As obvious as this statement may sound, it is the root theory of meaning that informs this essay.)

Of course there are certain projects that presuppose the law of noncontradiction. The most prevalent such project is one that I believe every person must enter at times, namely, that of communicating propositional knowledge. If and when one chooses to enter this project, one must abide by the law of noncontradiction, for without this "project-defined rule" the project is nullified; it cannot be undertaken. The project presupposes this rule. There are times when even the Zen master must enter this project (e.g., when scheduling the next session with his disciple), and at such times he too must abide by this law.

The decision to enter the project of communicating propositional knowledge, and thereby to abide by its rules, is no doubt based on the

2. See R. C. Zaehner, *Mysticism, Sacred and Profane* (New York: Oxford University Press, 1961). Zaehner suggests that one of the normal prerequisites for that state described by Zen Buddhists as *satori* is that "the mind should be emptied of all conceptual thought" (p. 55). It is conceivable that language which violates the law of noncontradiction helps to accomplish this purpose.

obvious values that underlie this project (e.g., the value of being able to coordinate one's intentions as a person with the intentions of others) and the desire to realize those values. Once I have decided to enter this project I have great freedom in what I am allowed to say. The rules of the project (like the law of noncontradiction) serve as negative criteria for criticism that rule out my saying certain limited types of things that would invalidate the project (like, "The grass is green and the grass is not green."). But this still leaves me almost unlimited elbowroom for freedom of verbal or written propositional expression.

The status of the law of excluded middle (a proposition is either true or false) is a matter of considerable debate. Ernest Nagel suggests that this law (as well as the laws of noncontradiction and identity) "specify minimal conditions for discourse without confusion, for they state at least some of the requirements for a precise language." However, Nagel suggests that "these principles . . . are not *descriptive* of actual usage [of language]" because "everyday language, and to some extent even the specialized languages of the sciences, are vague in some measure, so that they do not entirely conform to the requirement set by these principles." For example, "if the term 'red' is vague, then there is a class of colors concerning which it is indeterminate whether the term applies to them or not, so that the principle of excluded middle fails in this case."[3] It appears that Nagel is setting up the law of excluded middle as an "ideal for precision" when involved in the project of communicating propositional knowledge, recognizing that there are times when this ideal is not attained.

There are projects, however, wherein the law of excluded middle cannot be given even the status of unattainable ideal; projects that presuppose the categorical rejection of this law; projects that require the use of multi-valued logics (rather than the two-valued logic—T,F— inherent in the law of excluded middle). For example, "undecidable" (in principle) appears to be a legitimate "third value" in the area of quantum mechanics.[4] Furthermore, multi-valued logics have been found useful for solving certain types of scheduling problems in the field of operations research.[5] Nagel has even hinted that it may be legitimate to pursue alternative multi-valued logics on aesthetic grounds, indepen-

3. E. Nagel, "Logic Without Ontology," reprinted in *Philosophy of Mathematics*, P. Benacerraf, ed. (Englewood Cliffs, NJ: Prentice-Hall, 1964), p. 315.
4. See H. Reichenback, *Philosophical Foundations of Quantum Mechanics* (Berkeley, 1946).
5. A. Rose, "Many-Valued Logical Machines," *Proceedings of the Cambridge Philosophical Society* 54 (1958):307–21.

dent of issues of immediate usefulness.[6] (Much more about that later.)

The purpose of the above discussion is to get my foot in the door by proposing that even the classical laws of logic are "project dependent." There are certain projects that presuppose these laws. Others do not. The starting point must be an understanding of the nature of a person's project. In other words, in the spirit of the "meaning as use" language theorists (usually traced to the later thought of Ludwig Wittgenstein), I start by asking how those pursuing a given project intend to use language within that project. Then, in the spirit of Kant's transcendental analysis, I seek to identify those criteria for criticism that are *presupposed* when one intends to use language in that particular way. Then, *if* one freely chooses to enter this project, these criteria for criticism are the "rules" one has implicitly agreed to live by. These criteria for criticism are negative in nature in that they weed out certain types of expression as inappropriate to the project being pursued. This leaves considerable room for freedom of expression within the confines of the boundary defined by these criteria.

On what basis does one choose a project? I believe such choices are made on the basis of one's value commitments and their perceived congruence with the values that underlie the various available projects. In the process of making such a decision, however, one has entered still another project, namely, the ethical project, which has its own criteria for criticism. (The plot thickens—but more about this project later.) Now that my foot is in the door I will attempt a more detailed analysis, using the approach described above, for that area of activity called mathematics.

THE PROJECT OF DOING MATHEMATICS

I will now venture a proposal on the intended uses (functions) of mathematical language as employed by members of the mathematical community; the value commitments that underlie these intended uses; and the criteria for criticism that are presupposed by these uses.

I view mathematical activity as the pursuit of and interpenetration between two primary functions, which I call the instrumental and aesthetic functions. The instrumental function has two components: first, the use of mathematics as a tool for applications in the natural and social sciences. A person who uses a portion of mathematics in this way is committed to the instrumental value of that portion as a means to

6. Nagel, "Logic Without Ontology," p. 317.

accomplish whatever functions are attributed to scientific activity (e.g., predictive reliability, problem-solving capability, unified understanding of the natural or social environment). The criterion for criticizing a portion of mathematics used in this way is obvious, namely, the effectiveness of the mathematical content as an instrument for accomplishing the intended scientific function.

A second component of the instrumental function is more elusive. It involves the use of abstract mathematical structures as a means toward achieving a unified understanding of the external world and the world of lived experience. (This component overlaps the first if one views one function of scientific activity to be the quest for unified understanding of the natural or social environment.) A prime example of this function is the abstract structure known as a "group," wherein a concise set of axioms can be shown to model diverse areas of experience ranging from aspects of musical composition to the rotation of plane figures and the symmetry of molecules. Again, since this second component is also of an instrumental nature (not in the crude sense), the pertinent criterion for criticism will be related to the extent to which such abstract structures are effective toward attaining a unified understanding of experience. Because this second instrumental component emphasizes the search for unification of apparently unrelated phenomena by means of a minimal number of principles, it closely interacts with an aesthetic function.

What I have called the aesthetic function of mathematics has been described by Raymond Wilder as follows: "[To provide] an aesthetically satisfying structure allowing of advances by creatively minded mathematicians."[7] The pursuit of this function reveals an underlying commitment to the value of creativity and to certain aesthetic values like beauty, harmony, and elegance. Commitment to such values seems to suggest certain criteria for criticizing the results of mathematical activity that concentrate on this aesthetic function. Stephen Barker proposes such criteria for criticism when dealing with axiomatic systems (axioms based on certain undefined primitives, and theorems deduced from the axioms using an appropriate theory of inference).[8] His criteria include simplicity, elegance (conciseness of primitive terms and axioms), richness (capturing as many as possible of the desired theorems in the mathematical field being axiomatized), and deductive power (capability of deducing a "rich" array of theorems from an "elegant" set of primitives and axioms). Another criterion for criticism that is essentially aesthetic

7. R. L. Wilder, *Evolution of Mathematical Concepts* (New York: John Wiley & Sons, 1975), p. 118.

8. S. F. Barker, *Philosophy of Mathematics* (Englewood Cliffs, NJ: Prentice-Hall, 1964), chaps. 2–3.

is the independence criterion, which stipulates that no axiom in the axiom set be deducible from the other axioms (failure to satisfy this criterion leads to a redundancy in the system which is aesthetically dissatisfying). Possibly the most compelling criterion for criticism of axiomatic systems has been that of consistency—the requirement that the system not violate the law of noncontradiction.

In light of the above considerations I propose the following thesis as a first step toward a philosophy of mathematics that seeks to make sense of the entire spectrum of mathematical activity.

> A major portion of mathematical activity is an expression of commitment to the instrumental and/or aesthetic functions (noted above) and to the values that underlie these functions. It is this commitment that roughly defines the mathematical community. In practice, there is considerable freedom for mathematicians to create their own expressions of such commitment. These expressions will reveal considerable pluralism depending on the relative weights one gives to the instrumental and aesthetic functions and the various values underlying these functions. But this freedom and pluralism are bounded by the existence of the criteria for criticism that are presupposed by these functions. The results of mathematical activity will be perpetuated in time to the extent that the mathematical community judges them as adequate in the light of these criteria for criticism.

I believe that my thesis ought to be judged by the extent to which it illuminates the field of mathematical activity, past and present. I will leave the greatest part of this critique to those having expertise in the history of mathematics. However, I will now propose two examples of how this thesis appears to illuminate significant areas of mathematical activity.

A central aspect of my thesis is that much of the freedom and pluralism of mathematical activity is due to the different weights that mathematicians give to the instrumental and aesthetic functions and their related criteria for criticism. Various developments in set theory provide a good illustration of this point, as will now be demonstrated.

As noted by Howard Eves and Carroll Newsom, "[Georg] Cantor had attempted to give the concept of set a very general meaning by stating: 'By a set S we are to understand any collection into a whole of definite and separate objects m of our intuition or our thought; . . .'."[9] But a theory of sets constructed on the basis of this concept leads to inconsistencies such as the paradoxes of Cantor and Russell.

Considerable mathematical activity has been motivated by the attempt to avoid the set paradoxes (to measure up to the criterion of

9. H. Eves and C. V. Newsom, *An Introduction to the Foundations and Fundamental Concepts of Mathematics*, rev. ed. (New York: Holt, Rinehart & Winston, 1965), pp. 298–99.

consistency). Barker notes four different approaches to the problem: "The intuitionists can avoid the paradoxes by abandoning nonconstructive axioms and definitions and the logical law of the excluded middle as well. Whitehead and Russell avoid them by narrowing the range of sentences in set theory that are to count as making sense [by use of a ramified theory of types]. Zermelo avoids them by limiting his assumptions concerning the existence of sets. Von Neumann avoids them by limiting his assumptions concerning elementhood."[10] Yet, as again noted by Barker, "Each of these approaches is able to preserve substantial parts of traditional set theory, yet none preserves all the laws of sets that might seem desirable."[11]

There seems to be a trade-off. This trade-off is particularly revealing when one considers the approach of Zermelo (and Fraenkel), which is to attempt a complete axiomatization of set theory to avoid the paradoxes. Robert Stoll provides a lucid blow-by-blow account, with some embellishment on my part: The desire for elegance suggests a minimal list of axioms. One starts with five: the axioms of extension, pairing, union, power set, and the axiom schema of subsets, "plus the temporary axiom that a set exists." But these axioms are too limiting, for "it does not appear that the axioms are adequate to prove the existence of an infinite set." And "the existence of the set of natural numbers [an infinite set] is essential for the theory of denumerable sets and for the theory of real numbers." Hence the axioms must be strengthened to include an axiom of infinity that provides for the existence of infinite sets. But the axiom system is still too weak. For "to develop a reasonable theory of cardinal numbers when they are defined as certain ordinals, the axiom of choice is required" (positing the existence of sets for which there are no rules of membership).[12]

But the axiom set is again too weak, for one cannot use it to "guarantee the existence of 'larger' sets than can be constructed on the basis of the earlier axioms—sets which must exist if a full-blown theory of transfinite ordinal and cardinal numbers is to be possible." One thus adds an axiom of replacement which now "provides for the existence of enough sets to reproduce all of Cantor's theory of transfinite arithmetic."[13]

But now the axiom system is too strong, for it allows for "the possibility of a set which is a member of itself,"[14] and it is this type of

10. Barker, *Philosophy of Mathematics*, p. 91.
11. Ibid.
12. R. R. Stoll, *Set Theory and Logic* (San Francisco: W. H. Freeman & Co., 1961), pp. 289–306.
13. Ibid., pp. 302–4.
14. Ibid.

impredicatively[15] defined set that leads to set paradoxes. Therefore we need a restrictive axiom (the axiom of regularity) that eliminates the possibility of impredicatively defined sets and the resulting inconsistencies.

The above drama (of sorts) is summarized by Barker: ". . . the problem, of course, is to introduce strong enough axioms so that the existence can be proved of enough sets to make possible the deduction of as many as possible of the desired theorems concerning sets, while yet keeping the axioms sufficiently restricted so that the paradoxes cannot arise. A compromise has to be struck, sacrificing some desired richness in order to preserve consistency."[16]

Is there room for differing compromises between the criteria of richness and consistency? Some would say no: you must make whatever sacrifice in richness is required to maintain perfect consistency. They take consistency to be the ultimate unyielding criterion for criticism. But is this propensity justified? Is the quest for consistency an aesthetic matter? It would appear that a body of mathematics does not have to be perfectly consistent to serve the instrumental function of mathematics for the sciences. Wilder makes reference to "the so-called 'working mathematician' (meaning one who is not a 'logician'!) . . . [who] may know that . . . [traditional set theory] conceals contradictions, but since his uses of set theory usually involve only the 'safe' portions of the theory, he justifies his methods by observing that they 'work.' Besides, he would not have time to set up a complete formalization."[17]

Has the "working mathematician" copped out? No! There is room for a mathematician to pursue the instrumental function of mathematics, as there is room for other mathematicians to pursue the aesthetic function, with some of the latter giving ultimate weight to a consistency criterion, while others are willing to temper that particular criterion in the light of various other criteria of an aesthetic nature. Different mathematicians can give differing weights to the instrumental and aesthetic functions, to the underlying values, and to the corresponding criteria for criticism.

A second area of mathematical activity that my thesis appears to illuminate is the program of the formalists. The formalist contends that all of mathematics consists of formal symbolic systems. This pushes the axiomatic method to its extreme. The standard axiomatic method starts

---

15. An impredicative definition of an entity E is one which defines E in terms of a class (set) of which E is an element.

16. Barker, *Philosophy of Mathematics*, p. 91.

17. R. L. Wilder, *Introduction to the Foundations of Mathematics*, 2d ed. (New York: John Wiley & Sons, 1965), p. 277.

with "mathematical primitives" and "mathematical axioms," with the logical apparatus (theory of inference) being taken for granted. As reported by Wilder, "[David] Hilbert [the major proponent of formalism] decided upon a *union* of the axiomatic and logistic methods. A reduction of mathematics to logic, even if successful, would still leave open the question of the consistency of that 'logic.'"[18] He did this by means of a formal axiomatic method which axiomatizes the logic being used at the same time that it axiomatizes the relevant "mathematical content." The long-range goal of this program was to show that all of mathematics could be reduced to one consistent formal axiomatic system.

Of course one must decide which system of logic to use. Hilbert decided on a First-Order Theory (Theory with Standard Formalization), meaning that the logical basis chosen was the first-order (restricted) predicate calculus. Stoll suggests that a possible justification for this choice is that ". . . it formalizes most of the logical principles accepted by most mathematicians and that it supplies all the logic necessary for many mathematical theories."[19] First-order mathematical theories are referred to as "elementary theories" (e.g., the elementary theory of groups).

Now a formal axiomatic approach requires a system of metamathematics, in the following way: A theorem about a formal theory is a metatheorem (e.g., "the elementary theory of groups is incomplete"—asserting [correctly] that not all the formulas of informal group theory can be proven from this first order theory). Metatheorems must be stated in a metalanguage (syntax language), which is a language used to discuss and study a formal theory (e.g., the English language).

How would one prove a metatheorem? Such a proof requires a system of logic (rules of inference), i.e., a metalogic. One could proceed by axiomatizing a chosen metalogic, thus formalizing the metalanguage. But then you need a metametalanguage to discuss the formalized metalanguage, etc. (infinite regress).

As reported by Stoll, Hilbert avoided this infinite regress by choosing an alternative that can be summarized roughly as follows: "In the metalanguage employ an informal system of logic [the metalogic] whose principles are universally accepted." But what is meant by "universal acceptance"? Apparently this refers to acceptance by the body of practicing mathematicians, for Stoll concludes, "In brief, metamathematics is the study of formal theories by methods which should be convincing to everyone qualified to engage in such activities."[20]

18. Ibid., p. 264.
19. Stoll, *Set Theory and Logic*, p. 375.
20. Ibid., p. 403.

Stoll provides a threefold elaboration on what Hilbert apparently thought his fellow mathematicians would find "convincing." First, the metatheorems of the formal theory "must be understood and the deductions must carry conviction." To help insure conviction, "all controversial principles of reasoning such as the axiom of choice must not be used." Secondly, "the methods used in the metatheory should be restricted to those called *finitary* by the formalists. This excludes consideration of infinite sets as 'completed entities' and requires that an existence proof provide an effective procedure for constructing the object which is asserted to exist." Finally, "it is assumed that if, for example, the English language is taken as the metalanguage, then only a minimal fragment will be used. (The danger in permitting all of the English language to be used is that one can derive within it the classical paradoxes. . . .)"[21]

Using the above metamathematical procedures, Hilbert's initial goal was to prove the "consistency of elementary number theory" (a metatheorem). This starting point was suggested by the possibility of the reduction of other portions of classical mathematics to that of elementary number theory by means of models. It was hoped that the restriction that all methods of proof be finitary might help insure such consistency. But, as noted by Stoll, "After some partial successes, the endeavor came to a halt in 1931 with the demonstration by Gödel of the impossibility of proving the consistency of any formal theory which includes the formulas of N [elementary number theory] by constructive methods, 'formalizable within the theory itself.'"[22] Hilbert's original program was doomed, since all the methods he was willing to permit in metamathematics were of this constructive type. As a result, the most that this program could yield were "relative" consistency proofs like: if elementary number theory is consistent (unprovable using Hilbert's metamathematics), then real number theory is consistent; if real number theory is consistent, then Euclidean geometry is consistent; if Euclidean geometry is consistent, then Hyperbolic and Elliptic geometries are consistent.

A version of the formalist program can be salvaged, however, if one relaxes some of Hilbert's restrictions on allowable methods in metamathematics. Gerhard Gentzen, a member of the Hilbert school, has given a proof of the consistency of elementary number theory, but he uses a nonfinitist metamathematical proof theory that Hilbert would not have found acceptable. Nagel and Newman give the following critique of Gentzen's work: ". . . these [Gentzen's] 'proofs' are in a sense pointless, because they employ rules of inference whose own internal con-

21. Ibid.
22. Ibid., p. 405.

sistency is as much open to doubt as is the formal consistency of arithmetic itself."[23] (Gentzen's proof uses a rule of inference that permits a formula to be derived from an infinite class of premises; a nonfinitistic metamathematical notion.) The major reason for Hilbert's insistence on finitary proof methods was to maintain reasonable assurance of the consistency of his metamathematical methods. It appears that Gentzen's work merely adds another if . . . then . . . clause at the beginning of the sequence of relative consistency statements: If nonfinitistic metamathematical methods are consistent (still questionable), then elementary number theory is consistent. Eves and Newsom express this conclusion as follows: "It now seems that the internal consistency of classical mathematics cannot be attained [proven] unless one adopts principles of reasoning of such complexity that the internal consistency of these principles is as open to doubt as that of classical mathematics itself."[24]

Another of Gödel's proofs shows that for any consistent formal system L which contains the natural number system, there are undecidable propositions in L. Therefore, for any axiom system for the natural numbers, if the system is consistent (unknown), then it is incomplete, i.e., there will be at least one statement F about the natural numbers such that neither F nor ~F is provable from the axioms.

The net negative effect of Gödel's proofs on the formalist program is then describable as follows: ". . . no complete axiomatic development of certain important sectors of mathematics is attainable, and . . . no truly impeccable guarantee can be given that certain important sectors of mathematics are free from internal contradiction. These are severe limitations of the axiomatic method. . . ."[25]

Viewed positively, the formalist program will be a lasting monument to beauty. It is a marvelous instance of the pursuit of the aesthetic function as it pushes the values of elegance, simplicity, deductive power, and richness to far-reaching limits. Its shortcomings merely reflect the fact that the levels of realization of these values that were originally envisioned were not attainable using the methods decided upon. For example, Gödel's incompleteness proof placed limits on the realization of deductive power and richness, and the compelling value of consistency appears to remain elusive. But this shortcoming should be tempered by Max Black's observation that "no science [biology, physics, chemistry, mathematics] which is still in the process of developing is more

23. E. Nagel and J. R. Newman, "Gödel's Proof," in *"Mathematics in the Modern World: Readings from Scientific American* (San Francisco: W. H. Freeman & Co., 1968), p. 229.

24. Eves and Newsom, *Foundations and Fundamental Concepts*, p. 336.

25. Ibid.

than partially self-consistent . . . and those sciences alone are completely consistent which, like anatomy, have degenerated into catalogues."[26]

In my own thinking, the formalist program possibly represents the premier example to date of the freedom of mathematicians to be creative, but always within boundaries defined by the criteria for criticism agreed upon by practitioners within the mathematical community, as the above rather lengthy account intended to portray. However, there is also a darker side to the formalist program; a side that disqualifies it as a full-blown philosophy of mathematics intending to capture the full scope of mathematical activity; a side possibly not intended by its founders, but one that seems to describe the mentality of some present-day disciples; a side that fits well with the general philosophical milieu of our times. This side finds its most radical expression in the statement, "Mathematics consists of games played with marks on paper."

This radical version of formalism attempts to divorce mathematics from the external world. Questions of whether abstract mathematical systems can be interpreted to correspond to external reality are bypassed. The main issue is whether one can create a purely symbolic system that is consistent. This approach is an example of a radical form-content dichotomy that I find suspect.

Even this radical version of formalism has a certain legitimate liberating effect. The aesthetic function in mathematics allows one simply to dream up a collection of primitives and axioms and then use them to construct an elegant, rich, consistent axiomatic system, independent of the issue of whether this system has explanatory power with respect to external reality. I argue strongly for the legitimacy of such activity on aesthetic grounds, but to argue that such activity is an exhaustive description of all mathematical activity is ludicrous. Consideration of the history of mathematics will reveal strong interactions between the construction of abstract mathematical systems and the attempt to find external models of such systems, thus suggesting close interdependence between the aesthetic and instrumental functions that I have had to separate up to this point for the purposes of discussion. In other words, the naive dichotomy between pure and applied mathematics is a myth. I will seek to elaborate.

It is true that some very significant abstract systems have been created with apparent disregard for the question of whether the system has external models. The creation of non-Euclidean geometries is the prime

26. M. Black, *The Nature of Mathematics* (Totowa, NJ: Littlefield, Adams & Co., 1965), pp. 2–3.

example. I reiterate the fact that I believe such activity is commendable on aesthetic grounds and must be encouraged (in directions I will suggest in the next section) as part of the freedom to create that I am espousing. In this mathematical version of the chicken-and-egg problem, however, it generally has been the models that first appeared, with abstract systems then being constructed in an attempt to unify diverse models taken from different aspects of the external world and lived experience. It is probably safe to say that those abstract systems that have the greatest chance of longevity within the mathematical community are those which combine aesthetic values with the capability of illuminating our understanding of the external world (e.g., groups).

Now in a real sense the mathematical chicken-and-egg (model and abstract system) debate is unfruitful. I view it as a special case of the traditional idealism versus realism debate in epistemology, which I also take to be unfruitful. I think it can be argued persuasively that even when a mathematician appears to be creating an abstract system "out of nothing," she invariably is reflecting her own vision of external reality, possibly years before those concerned with the instrumental function catch up to her. (The fact that mathematicians concerned with aesthetic values often create abstract systems that richly illuminate the external world ought to give one pause in reflecting about the ultimate nature of reality.) I believe that a mathematician's creations are neither pure creations of the mind nor the result of a passive reading of the external world. They are rather a result of interaction between these two poles. But I still view this debate on the psychology of mathematical discovery as relatively unfruitful in the present context because it concerns itself with the secondary issue of the genesis of the results of mathematical activity. The burden of this paper is to argue that the primary issue is that of evaluation rather than genesis, i.e., are there adequate criteria for criticizing the results of mathematical activity, whatever their source.[27]

---

27. A word is necessary on my rejection of the traditional epistemological dichotomy between idealism and realism. The classical debate is whether the "object" known or the knowing "subject" takes priority in the knowing process. According to strict epistemological realism, there is an "objective" world out there that can be known by a passive knower. According to strict epistemological idealism, a human as active knower creates conceptions of what the world is like independent of what is "out there." I reject both views. My starting point is a phenomenological assumption that refuses to divorce a subject from the world. I believe that all knowledge claims are the results of interaction between the knower and the known and are therefore neither purely objective nor purely subjective in the common sense of these two words. For an elaboration of my position on this point see W. A. Luijpen and H. J. Koren, *A First Introduction to Existential Phenomenology* (Pittsburgh: Duquesne University Press, 1969), chap. 2.

However, I still wish to retain use of the word *objective*; not as opposed to *subjective* in

FUTURE EXPRESSIONS OF MATHEMATICAL FREEDOM WITHIN BOUNDS

A feature of my main thesis which I value highly is its relative open-endness. Granted the existence of pertinent criteria for criticism, there is room for almost as much freedom of expression as a mathematician's imagination will allow. I will briefly note some directions that are emerging for future expressions of this freedom.

First of all, there is the ever-present quest for alternative axiomatizations of established abstract systems; axiomatizations which in the pursuit of elegance seek to minimize the required number of primitives and axioms. An inspiring past accomplishment of this type is Nicod's axiomatization of the standard propositional calculus that requires only one logical primitive (Sheffer's stroke symbol) and one axiom.[28]

A second area of future activity involves variations of Hilbert's formalist program. There is the continuing search for alternatives to Hilbert's metamathematical proof methods, a search which hopes to demonstrate that all of mathematics can be reduced to one consistent formal axiomatic system; a goal as yet unattained. Future activity in this area can also include formalizations of axiomatic systems wherein the embedded axiomatized logic is the second-order predicate calculus, yielding second-order formal theories, in place of the first-order (restricted) predicate calculus that formed the basis of the original formalist program.

---

talking about the genesis of knowledge claims (for I reject this dichotomy), but rather as referring to the existence of criteria for the criticism or evaluation of knowledge claims, independent of their genesis. Israel Scheffler uses the word *objectivity* in this sense when, speaking of scientific activity, he states that "the distinction between theory genesis and theory evaluation, between the context of discovery and the context of justification, enables us to say with considerable plausibility that objectivity characterizes the evaluative or justificatory processes of science rather than the genesis of scientific ideas" (*Science and Subjectivity* [New York: Bobbs-Merrill, 1967], p. 73). Karl Popper takes the same position in proposing that "the objectivity . . . of all science [rests] upon the criticizability of its arguments" (*Objective Knowledge* [London: Oxford University Press, 1972], pp. 136–37). Since the word *objective* is too often associated with the genesis of knowledge claims rather than with their evaluation, I propose that it may be better to use the word *rational* when referring to the existence of criteria for criticizing knowledge claims in any area of discourse. Therefore, knowledge claims that have passed the tests defined by the criteria for criticism in the area of discourse may be referred to as "rational knowledge" (which is unrelated to whether the knowledge claim resulted from intellectual deliberation or from feelings and intuitions).

28. See D. Hilbert and W. Ackerman, *Principles of Mathematical Logic* (New York: Chelsea, 1950), p. 29, for Nicod's Axiomatization as well as alternative axiomatizations proposed by Frege and Lukasiewicz.

Two further areas that seem to hold great potential for future activity have something in common, namely, they are expressions that dare to deny firmly established axioms in much the same manner as the creators of non-Euclidean geometries dared to deny Euclid's parallel postulate.

The first of these areas is non-Cantorian set theory. It is based on Paul Cohen's proof in 1963 that the continuum hypothesis is an independent axiom of set theory. Thus consistent axiomatized set theories may either include it or deny it, thus motivating the search for alternative set theories that include one or another form of the negation of this axiom.

The second area involves the creation of various multi-valued logics that deny the classical law of excluded middle. A number of such multi-valued logics have been proposed in the past.[29] Of course a typical reaction to the creation of a multi-valued logic is: "Granted that there is a consistent and complete way of using logical words that might be described as 'employing a 3-valued [or 4-valued, etc.] logic,' this alternative way of using logical words—alternative to the usual way—doesn't have any point."[30] How quickly we forget our history of mathematics, for as Hilary Putnam notes, "This objection . . . cannot impress anyone who recalls the manner in which non-Euclidean geometries were first regarded as absurd; later as mere mathematical games; and are today accepted as portions of fully interpreted physical hypotheses."[31] In fact, as already noted, certain 3-valued logics have already found limited application in such diverse areas as quantum mechanics and operations research. There is potential for much fruitful activity in this area.

MY ETHICAL PROJECT

If one grants on the basis of the above analysis that the project of doing mathematics is an exemplification of the concept of *freedom within bounds,* the question still remains as to whether one ought to enter the mathematics project. To discuss this question is to enter the "ethical project"—a project which attempts to provide normative answers to the questions What is of value? and How ought I to live in light of that which is of value? My understanding of this ethical project (which no one can avoid; for to attempt to avoid the project is to give an answer to these two questions) is again best captured by the idea of *freedom within bounds.*

29. See, for example, H. Putnam, "Three-Valued Logic," *Mathematics, Matter and Method Philosophical Papers,* vol. 1 (London: Cambridge University Press, 1975), pp. 169–73. For a more extensive survey see R. Ackerman, *Introduction to Many Valued Logics* (New York: Dover, 1967).

30. This common reaction is reported in Putnam, "Three-Valued Logic," p. 169.

31. Ibid.

Much elaboration is necessary, but limited space will allow for only an outline of my views on normative ethics, views that have evolved as a result of my commitment to Christianity.

The New Testament is clear about the centrality of attitudes in any Christian ethic. Christ taught that a person's deeds result from the good or evil that is "within" (Mark 7:21–23; Luke 6:45). I ought to be characterized by certain enduring attitudes regardless of where I am or what I am doing; attitudes of love (caring), kindness, patience, compassion, gentleness, peace, joy, and humility.[32] There are also certain attitudes that the Bible clearly proscribes, such as selfishness, pride, self-conceit, jealousy, envy, greed, indifference, and covetousness.[33]

But proper attitudes are not enough. (They are necessary but not sufficient conditions within a Christian ethic.) I can genuinely care for another person and yet do all the wrong things because I fail to understand that person's real needs. My caring and my expression of the other biblically prescribed attitudes must be guided by other biblical values. It is not possible to capture all the values that are explicitly stated or hinted at in the biblical record. I will merely note a few that I feel deeply about and that reflect not only my understanding of the Bible but also my experience with other persons.

Christ's teaching on the two great commandments of the law points to three values (Matt. 22:36–40). "Love of God" points to the value of *reconciliation with God,* the restoration of broken communion with God. "Love of neighbor" points to the value of *caring relationships between persons.* "Love of neighbor as yourself" points to a healthy self-love. To me this suggests the value of *personal growth* consistent with one's own unique abilities and talents; the fullest possible realization of one's God-given potential.

There are two aspects of personal growth that I believe to be implicit in the biblical record, thereby suggesting two additional values. The first is related to a person's ability to be self-directing. Personal choice is a fundamental human category. To be a person is to make one's own choices in life. One can indeed choose bondage (called "slavery to sin" in the biblical record [John 8:34–36]). But biblical teaching also claims that Christ can set a person free from such bondage. A redeemed person has been granted a radical freedom which can be used "as an opportunity for the flesh," but can also be used to love and serve others (Gal 5:13). I believe that *freedom to choose* is a biblical value. A second implicit

32. Gal. 5:22–23; Col. 3:12; Eph. 4:32; James 4:10.
33. Prov. 21:13; 1 John 3:17–18; James 3:14, 16; 2 Cor. 5:15; Gal. 5:26; Rom. 1:29; Luke 12:13–15; 1 Thess. 2:5.

biblical value is that of *creativity,* another basic human category. Persons are meant to be creative; to dare to look at old things in new ways; to dare to try out new ideas; to dare to try new solutions to old problems; to dare to express themselves in their own unique ways. I firmly believe that such creativity is part of the *imago Dei,* and the effect of the Fall was not to diminish this capability but to give persons the potential to express it in a destructive manner.[34]

The values noted so far can be termed "values of personhood." The Bible also hints at values of a more impersonal nature. God's judgment that the creation was "very good" (Gen. 1:31) suggests the value of all forms of *physical life* as well as the *inanimate world.* The biblical concept of truth is multifaceted and does not refer solely to the cognitive realm.[35] At least one aspect of such truth is the value of *knowledge:* having an adequate understanding of the nature of God's creation and my place within it. The apostle Paul admonishes us to give attention to "whatever is lovely, whatever is gracious" (Phil. 4:8), thereby suggesting the value of *beauty* as found in the creations of God as well as those of human beings. In the same passage Paul praises "whatever is just," which at least in part hints at the value of *distributive justice;* the concern for more equitable distribution of the other goods of life. The list could go on, but the above will suffice as at least a partial indication of the values I believe I committed myself to when I made a commitment to Christianity.

How, then, should I live? I view my ethical mandate as follows:

---

34. I view my position on this matter as consistent with that suggested by G. C. Berkouwer in *Man: The Image of God* (Grand Rapids: Eerdmans, 1962). Berkouwer distinguishes between two different aspects of the image of God. The ontic aspect of the image refers to certain ontological characteristics of humanity such as "the quality and structure of humanness, which is concentrated in man's reason and freedom, or in his personality" (p. 49). Berkouwer contends that "the Word of God never presents man in this isolated ontic aspect. . ." (p. 51). There is also a relational aspect of the image, which means that humans were created as beings in positive personal relationship to God. Berkouwer calls this "man's *conformitas* to God" (p. 50). Berkouwer suggests that this ontic aspect is not destroyed by sin. Humans are still human after the Fall. The effect of the Fall was that "man lost his communion with God" (p. 38). The relationship of human beings to God shifted from a positive to a negative relationship.

The implication of this position for my proposal is that sin does not obliterate humanness as characterized by attributes of personhood such as capacities for self-direction, reasoning, and creativity. The effect of sin is that it removes humanness from the context in which God intended for it to operate, namely, that of positive personal relationship to God. Some would argue that sin does diminish a person's ability to exercise ontic capacities. I believe that this is true to the extent that living outside of communion with God can have a detrimental effect on a person's motivation to exercise these capabilities or can cause a person to exercise these capacities in a destructive manner.

35. 3 John 3 speaks of truth in the broad sense of "the truth of your life."

Primarily motivated by biblically prescribed attitudes, I ought to perform those actions that bring about the realization of biblical values. In other words, I ought to be performing acts that help to bring about the reconciliation of persons to God; that bring about caring relationships between persons (including my own relationships with others); that foster the personal growth of others (as well as myself); that maintain and enhance physical life; that increase our understanding of God's creation; that show reverence for the inanimate world; that show appreciation for beauty and express beauty; that help bring about a more equitable distribution of goods to the world's needy and oppressed.

Of course my ethical mandate is as significant in what it does not say as in what it says. How should I enhance biblical values? There are so many. Where do I start? To answer these questions with a host of prescriptive rules would nullify my entire proposal.[36] The only guideline I can propose is that suggested by the parable of the good Samaritan and the entire life of Christ: I should start by responding sensitively to the needs of the persons I meet daily.[37] Outside of that, I am radically free; I ought to be creative. I should choose ways of enhancing biblical values that are uniquely expressive of me; ways that reflect my particular abilities and interests; ways that reflect my particular personality traits; ways that reflect my own personal biography; ways that reflect my own measure of faith, my conviction, without compelling evidence, that God wishes to accomplish some particular purpose through me.

This radical freedom is bounded. It is because I have come to love this freedom and wish to preserve it from the onslaughts of those fearful people who cannot handle it and wish to escape it, that I seek to define

36. Of course I do not wish to deny that the Bible contains numerous explicit and implicit prescriptions concerning actions, such as commands to "make disciples of all nations" (Matt. 28:19), to feed the hungry and thirsty (Matt. 25:35), and to practice hospitality (Rom. 12:13). Any such list, however, no matter how complete, can give no direction as to what I ought to be doing right this minute. The Bible was never intended to be used in such cookbook fashion. I believe that one can best make sense of the acts prescribed in the Bible if they are viewed as examples of deeds that enhance biblical values (e.g., to "make disciples of all nations" is to foster the realization of *reconciliation to God;* to feed the hungry and thirsty is to enhance *personal growth, physical life,* and possibly *caring relationships between persons;* to practice hospitality is to enhance *caring relationships between persons*). This view of biblically prescribed acts as a nonexhaustive list of examples allows much room for freedom and creativity as I seek ways to enhance biblical values.

37. Keith Miller, in *The Taste of New Wine* (Waco, TX: Word, 1965), presents the following perspective on the way Christ lived: "As I began to read the New Testament accounts I saw that Christ almost never 'went out of his way' to help anyone. He seems to have walked along and helped the people in his path" (p. 101). Such an approach cannot be viewed as an exhaustive description of ethical responsibility, for I do have responsibility toward those I may never meet personally. But it does appear to be the correct place to start.

its boundaries. The nature of the boundary is complex. A few examples will at best provide some clues. I cross the boundary when I perform acts that are actually destructive of the biblical values I claim commitment to (e.g., I should not gossip, quarrel, or create dissension since these acts are destructive of caring relationships between persons).[38] I cross the boundary when I perform apparently good deeds on the basis of biblically proscribed motives (e.g., knowing that I really ought to visit some person I know to be lonely, but deciding rather *only* to pray for that person because I'm really indifferent). I cross the boundary when I perform deeds that are in obvious conflict with the current body of empirical knowledge (e.g., withholding available medical treatment from my child for supposed "religious" reasons when there is good reason to believe that to do so will be destructive of physical life). I realize that the exact nature of this boundary can be debated; that is not my purpose here.[39] The present point is that there is a boundary, and the make-up of this boundary constitutes the criteria for criticizing my ethical decisions as I seek creatively to express my freedom to enhance biblical values. The criteria for criticism again serve the negative role of ruling out certain actions as inappropriate in light of my Christian commitment.[40] This still leaves me much room for freedom of ethical expression. The ethical project is the premier example of freedom within bounds.

---

38. 2 Cor. 12:20; Titus 3:9–10. Consistent with my argument in n. 36 above, I find it illuminating to view the many biblical proscriptions concerning acts as examples of acts that are destructive of biblical values. Such a view allows one to extend the biblical teaching to examples that are not mentioned in the Bible because they were not issues during biblical times. For example, I wish to proscribe the act of "brainwashing," despite the Bible's silence on this specific issue, because it is clearly destructive of the biblical values of *freedom* and *personal growth*. My view also allows for the more controversial possibility of modifying certain biblical proscriptions in the light of changing cultural contexts, but always on the basis of biblical values that are taken to be invariant. For example, I believe that certain biblical proscriptions of deeds were intended to apply only to the cultural context of biblical times. I would cite as examples the proscriptions that women should not wear "braided hair or gold or pearls" (1 Tim. 2:9) and that "women should keep silence in the churches" (1 Cor. 14:34). In such examples, careful study has to be given to the scriptural and historical context in an attempt to determine the reasons for these proscriptions. The task is to uncover the fundamental biblical values that are at stake. If this can be done, then possibly the original proscription will be seen to be no longer applicable, or to be in need of reformulation in the light of our present cultural setting.

39. A particularly difficult issue relative to this definition of the "ethical boundary" has to do with alleged cases of moral dilemma (tragic moral choice), wherein all the alternatives for action open to an agent are destructive of biblical values. Some would argue that such cases never exist; there is always a nondestructive alternative. But if there are genuine cases of moral dilemma (as I personally believe there are), then analysis of decisions "at the ethical boundary" becomes quite complex (see n. 41).

40. In terms of epistemological alternatives within philosophy my approach in this paper can best be classified as a form of Critical Rationalism that has strong affinities to the

WHY, THEN, DO MATHEMATICS?

I trust you realize by now that a prescriptive answer to this question is not forthcoming, at least not from my pen. I will, however, make two proposals that circumscribe possible answers to this question.

My first proposal follows from my portrayal of the mathematics project. Recall my suggestion that there are certain values underlying mathematical activity: the values of freedom and creativity; aesthetic values like beauty, harmony, elegance; the value of unified understanding of the external world (when mathematics is used as an instrument toward this purpose); the values inherent in the ends sought by those working in the natural and social sciences (when mathematics is used as an instrument toward these ends). Due to this plurality of mathematical values, there is significant freedom for the individual mathematician to create expressions of commitment to various combinations of these values. This mathematical freedom is bounded by certain mathematical criteria for criticism presupposed by the nature of the mathematical activity. (It may be helpful to think of an image of a circle representing mathematical activity with the circumference defined by the mathematical criteria for criticism; thus providing a boundary for the expression of freedom within the circle.) When pursuing the aesthetic function of mathematics the criteria for criticism include simplicity, conciseness, richness, deductive power, and consistency. When pursuing the instrumental function the criterion for criticism consists of instrumental effectiveness relative to the intended applications of the body of mathematics in question.

In light of the above view of the mathematics project I propose the following: If I choose to do mathematics, then I ought to attempt to work within the boundary for the mathematics project. My justification for this proposal is as follows: The mathematical criteria for criticism noted

---

view of Karl Popper, without the positivist overtones often attributed (erroneously, I believe) to his position. My views are definitely Popperian in the sense that I see criteria for criticism as serving the negative function of potential falsification (not verification) of knowledge claims made in a given area of discourse. For example, the criteria for criticizing the results of mathematical activity can, at best, weed out grossly inadequate results; they cannot prescribe the results that a given mathematician should work toward. That is a matter of freedom (within bounds).

In order to avoid misunderstanding I emphasize that I use the word *rationalism* in Critical Rationalism not in a narrow Cartesian sense but simply to reflect my position that rationality refers to the existence of criteria for criticizing knowledge claims, independent of the issue of the genesis of such claims (n. 27). The fact that a knowledge claim can be criticized makes the issue of the genesis of the claim a secondary one, thus allowing for a plurality of potential sources, ranging from the strictly cognitive to the strictly affective or intuitive realms, and thereby comprising another important element of the significant freedom (within bounds) that I am arguing for.

above are the standards established by the community of practicing mathematicians for distinguishing between "good" and "bad" mathematics (recognizing that this judgment will not always be easy to make, especially in light of the aesthetic nature of some of the criteria). As a Christian committed to excellence in all that I work at I ought to do mathematics that is judged to be of good quality by members of the mathematical community (i.e., mathematics that stands the test of the mathematical criteria for criticism; thus falling within the boundary for the mathematics project).

This very modest proposal does not yet address the most pressing question of whether I ought to choose to do mathematics. Such a choice is a decision made within the broader ethical project. Recall my suggestion that for me this ethical project is informed by commitment to biblical values such as the fruit of the Spirit, reconciliation with God, caring relationships between persons, personal growth, freedom, creativity, physical life, the inanimate world, knowledge, beauty, and distributive justice. Due to the plurality of biblical values there is significant freedom for me to choose ways to enhance these values that are uniquely expressive of me. This ethical freedom is bounded by certain ethical criteria for criticism (the boundary of the circle of ethical activity). These criteria for criticism proscribe actions that are destructive of biblical values; actions motivated primarily by biblically proscribed attitudes; and actions that are in obvious conflict with the current body of empirical knowledge.

My second proposal deals with the relationship between the mathematics project and the ethical project. Put simply: The boundary for the mathematics project must lie completely within the boundary for the ethical project. Thus I am not free to use mathematics for the purpose of enabling a corporation better to exploit its workers, for to do so is to step outside the ethical boundary (despite the fact that I will still remain within the mathematical boundary if the mathematics used is effective toward the intended destructive end).

It is important to note that my two proposals are again significant in what they do not say. They do not prescribe any particular actions, mathematical or otherwise, as long as I remain within the ethical boundary. I may choose to enter the mathematics project because of significant overlap between the values that underlie mathematical activity and biblical values (freedom, creativity, beauty, personal growth, unified understanding of God's creation). Thus I can freely choose to pursue mathematical activity as a way to enhance biblical values. I am also radically free not to make that choice, or to make that choice at some times in my life and not at other times. My ethical mandate is to choose ways to enhance biblical values that flow from biblically prescribed attitudes and are expressive of who I am. I cannot be more prescriptive than that.

Hold it, you say. Is there not a hierarchy of biblical values? Isn't it more important to "save souls" (enhance the value of *reconciliation to God*) than to create a new axiomatic mathematical system (enhance the values of *creativity, beauty,* and possibly *knowledge* in the sense of greater unified understanding of the world)? I am open to the possibility that there is such a hierarchy of values,[41] but I believe that it cannot be appealed to within the ethical boundary. My reasoning is based on the teaching of 1 Corinthians 12 concerning the "body of Christ." I believe that God's will for creation is the fullest possible realization of all biblical values. I believe further that this realization is to be brought about by the corporate efforts of the entire body of Christians, each making use of his or her own particular gifts and abilities (remembering of course that the "still more excellent way" (1 Cor. 12:31) than the exercise of any particular gift is the way of love—hence the ethical starting point that I previously suggested, namely, to respond sensitively to the needs of the persons you meet daily). Therefore, I am indeed radically free (within bounds) to choose ways of enhancing biblical values that are uniquely expressive of me. This includes the possibility of choosing to do mathematics.

WHAT ARE THE CRITERIA FOR CRITICIZING THE CRITERIA FOR CRITICISM?

The reader may now object that I have not pressed my search for criteria for criticism far enough. First of all, I have allowed the community of practicing mathematicians to define the mathematical criteria for criticism by means of which they judge the quality of their own work. Shouldn't this definition by mathematicians be subject to criticism (using some higher-order criteria for criticism)? I think not. The project of doing mathematics cannot help but be defined by those who have worked within the project over the years (if for no other reason than that it is the community of practicing mathematicians who decide which articles get published in mathematical journals as examples of quality mathematics). This does allow for gradual evolution in the understand-

41. It is conceivable that in cases of genuine moral dilemma *at* the ethical boundary (if such cases exist—see n. 39) an appeal would have to be made to a hierarchy of values in an attempt to determine the "lesser of two evils." Space does not permit further elaboration at this point. N. L. Geisler in *Ethics: Alternatives and Issues* (Grand Rapids: Zondervan, 1971) presents one possible outline of such a "hierarchicalism."

ing of the mathematical community as to the nature of its project and the pertinent criteria for criticism. But one cannot choose to make abrupt radical changes in this self-understanding. One can only choose whether or not to enter the project of mathematics as it is currently understood by practicing mathematicians.

A more cogent objection to my proposal is that my description of the ethical project and the corresponding ethical criteria for criticism is based on the unexamined starting point of biblical values (at least as I understand them). Should not this starting point be subject to criticism (again using some higher-order criteria for criticism)? There are at least three possible responses to this question. The first is that an unexamined starting point is unavoidable. To search for criteria for criticizing criteria requires further criteria for criticizing the second set of criteria, etc. (infinite regress). Therefore, I must consider my understanding of biblical values to comprise my presuppositions (control beliefs). Criticism of such presuppositions is impossible. I reject this initial response. No claim to knowledge can be viewed as self-authenticating. One must seek criteria for criticism of any knowledge claim (and at the same time avoid infinite regress).

The second and third responses are attempts at obtaining higher-order criteria for criticism of knowledge claims in the area of ethics (i.e., criteria for doing metaethics; the discussion of normative ethical systems). Both responses are further extensions of the concept of *freedom within bounds* that permeates this paper. Mercifully, limited space will allow me only to hint at these two approaches.

The first approach is to analyze the project of doing normative ethics (this metaethical analysis is not to be confused with what I have called "my ethical project" in the above text. That project is one result [mine] of doing normative ethics; other normative ethical proposals, Christian and otherwise, are possible). Again, in the spirit of Kant's transcendental analysis, one seeks to determine whether the very nature of the project of doing normative ethics presupposes certain criteria for criticism of the results of such activity.[42] If such criteria can be uncovered,

42. For one transcendental approach to justification of normative ethical principles see R. S. Peters, *Ethics and Education* (Atlanta: Scott, Foresman, 1967). Peters applies this method to ethics by attempting to determine "what any individual must presuppose insofar as he uses a public form of discourse in seriously discussing with others or with himself what he ought to do" (p. 43). Peters argues that any presuppositions so determined are justified unless one is not interested in asking the question "What ought I to do?", which he considers to be a position that is almost impossible to adopt (p. 44). Peters goes on to use this transcendental method to argue for the justification of the ethical principles of justice,

then they can be used to criticize my normative ethical proposal as well as alternative proposals by others. Again, these criteria for criticism will be negative in nature, allowing significant freedom for doing normative ethics, but within boundaries defined by pertinent criteria for criticism.

A second approach for doing metaethics is to suggest that any normative ethical proposal can be debated indirectly only as a portion of a broader metaphysical system. (Since a metaphysical system seeks to make sense of all aspects of reality, it must include beliefs concerning values and moral obligation.) The pertinent issue then becomes whether there exist criteria for criticism of the project of doing metaphysics. Some have argued, again using a transcendental approach, that the very nature of the metaphysics project presupposes certain criteria for criticism like consistency, coherence, and comprehensiveness.[43] Once again, these criteria are negative in nature, thus allowing significant freedom for doing metaphysics, but within boundaries defined by pertinent criteria for criticism.

Both approaches to metaethics outlined above view the project of doing metaethics as an exemplification of freedom within bounds. So is my proposed normative ethic (my ethical project, within which I may

---

respect for persons, liberty, consideration of the interests of others, and fraternity (pp. 49–53, 96, 105, 132, 146–47).

For a general description and criticism of transcendental approaches to justification in ethics see H. B. Veatch, "A Transcendental Turn in Ethics: A Possible Solution," *For an Ontology of Morals* (Evanston: Northwestern University Press, 1971), chap. 5.

43. These three criteria for debating the comparative merits of alternative metaphysical systems have been discussed by the following authors: Frederick Ferré, *Language, Logic and God* (New York: Harper and Row, Harper Torchbooks, 1961), pp. 159–66; Edgar S. Brightman, *Person and Reality. An Introduction to Metaphysics* (New York: Ronald Press, 1958), pp. 22–33; Ian G. Barbour, *Issues in Science and Religion* (Englewood Cliffs, NJ: Prentice-Hall, 1966), pp. 252–55; and Arthur F. Holmes, *Christian Philosophy in the 20th Century* (Nutley, NJ: Craig Press, 1969), pp. 226–40. Ferré, Brightman, and Holmes are discussing metaphysical systems and thus use the criterion of comprehensiveness as relative to all of experience. Barbour is discussing worldviews, and thus applies the criterion of comprehensiveness to a narrower range of experience, namely, all "the features (of reality) deemed significant as a framework for life-orientation" (p. 261). Holmes suggests that philosophical decisions about metaphysical questions are not solely based on the application of these three criteria. Such decisions are also guided by "personal commitments of an existential or valuational sort" (p. 230). He refers to this basis as the "demand for existential authenticity" (p. 237).

For two other proposals concerning criteria for criticism within the area of metaphysics, see J. Kekes, "The Rationality of Metaphysics," *Metaphilosophy* 4 (1973):124–39; and David Wolfe, *Epistemology: The Justification of Belief* (Downers Grove, IL: InterVarsity Press, 1983), pp. 66ff.

decide to do mathematics or something else) as well as the project of doing mathematics—or something else. The resulting potential for pluralism, compounded no less, will not be attractive to those who believe in a one-to-one correspondence between questions and answers. But I firmly believe that the idea of *freedom within bounds* (and the frightening baggage that accompanies it) maintains the dignity of God-created humanness by acknowledging that we now know only in part and makes possible that great venture of faith of freely choosing to serve God (within bounds).

Complementarity as a Christian Philosophy of Mathematics[1]

GENE B. CHASE

ALTERNATIVES FOR FAITH/DISCIPLINE INTEGRATION

There seem to be three approaches which have been taken to the integration of Christianity and mathematics. The first two seem to be inadequate; the third, difficult. They are what I shall call the applicational, the incarnational, and the philosophical.

The first argues that mathematics is useful for Christians in daily life. This could include such things as computer-aided instruction for Christian education or data analysis of Sunday school attendance records or numerical surprises in the Bible (sometimes bordering on numerology). The other side of the same coin is that Christianity is useful in mathematics: honesty in reporting statistics, humility in teaching mathematics, or thankfulness for the beauty of mathematics.

The second approach that has been taken has been the incarnational approach. I am both a Christian and a mathematician. I am a whole person. Therefore there must be an integration in me. A strong version of this view claims that "Christian" is a noun, not an adjective, so it is misleading to talk about Christian mathematics. Mathematics is neither Christian nor non-Christian. The St. Olaf College self-study (*Integration in the Christian Liberal Arts College*) illustrates this point when it talks about the context but not the content of mathematics being Christian. Mathematics is what mathematicians do; therefore, there is a Christian mathematics only insofar as there are Christians who are mathematicians.

The third approach is philosophical. One aspect of the philosophical approach is metaphysics: showing the relationships underlying superficially different views of reality—in this case, mathematics and Christianity. Because the philosophical approach is the broadest, I shall begin with an example of what I mean.

I know of a mathematician who attempted to argue that mathematics

1. I appreciate the hospitality of Dr. Robert Brabenec at three biennial conferences at Wheaton College, where I read an early version of this paper in 1981. Messiah College provided a sabbatical leave during which it was rewritten. The Summer Institute of Linguistics provided resources during that leave.

and Christianity are independent, but he lost his credibility when he positioned his thumb and fingers in the form of three independent vectors of a right-handed coordinate system as he spoke. To me, he was thereby proving the very thing that he had hoped to disprove. Even if the subject matter of mathematics and Christianity are disjoint, mathematics provides useful, interesting, beautiful ways of looking at the world. That mathematician who said that they were independent almost looked like he was about to orthogonalize them! The integration takes place at the metamathematical level. In that respect, mathematics is neither Christian nor non-Christian, but the metamathematics may inform or be informed by Christianity.

Actually I maintain as does Heie that a Christian philosophy of mathematics should not merely inform but also constrain mathematics. How we differ in this respect is the subject of a later section.

Thus we see a first example within metaphysics of the function of mathematics in a larger worldview: mathematics models reality. To paraphrase a statement made about M.I.T. "If you think that mathematics is hard, try real life." Mathematicians often express a happy surprise paraphrase a statement made about M.I.T., "If you think that mathematics is hard, try real life." Mathematicians often express a happy surprise that mathematics fits the world as well as it does.[2] A Christian are using analogies, albeit fine-grained ones. Analogies are important to Christians because Jesus used them frequently.

Within epistemology there is a second locus of integration: the axiomatic, deductive approach. Christianity is a reasoned faith. One can argue that this is so because of a marriage of Christian and Greek thought—Platonism via Augustine, Aristotelianism via Aquinas. Nonetheless, the marriage has not been barren. Christians regard a renewed mind as an essential part of maturing faith and apologetics as a legitimate activity.

Returning to the metaphysical aspect of the philosophical approach, I want to stress why I think that most of the deep thinking about the relation between Christianity and mathematics comes from the Reformed tradition of Christianity. What is there about the Calvinistic perspective that creates a favorable climate for discussion? I believe that the answer is a proper view therein of the relation between nature and

2. See, for example, R. W. Hamming, "The Unreasonable Effectiveness of Mathematics," *American Mathematical Monthly* (February 1980); J. T. Schwartz, "The Pernicious Influence of Mathematics on Science," *Proceedings of International Conference for Logic, Methodology and Philosophy of Science* (Berkeley, 1980); Eugene P. Wigner, "The Unreasonable Effectiveness of Mathematics in The Natural Sciences," *Communications on Pure and Applied Mathematics* 13 (1960):1–14.

grace, between common grace and saving grace. Questions of unity and diversity, Reformed theologians argue, are rooted in the Trinity. Christ can be Lord of all—even mathematics. It is truly possible to have a holistic view of life, in which one has integrated mathematics not only with a vague theism but with historic Christianity. I need to make this point emphatically because I shall be proposing shortly a complementarist viewpoint, which on the face of it might be viewed as a fragmenting rather than a unifying view of reality.[3]

Besides metaphysics, a philosophical approach must speak to the areas of ontology, epistemology, and axiology: What is there? How do we know? What is of value? These simple questions are at the same time the most profound questions that a philosopher can ask. Other authors have related the first two to mathematics and Christianity, but Heie is the first author that I know of who has related the third. How shall we compare these three questions in importance? If we value that comparison, there is some precedence of self-consistency for calling the third question the most important. Further, if one wishes to approach the matter from a Christian perspective, Scripture seems to stress the third question and take the answers to the first two as givens. I shall address the issue of values in my response to Heie, which follows a description of complementarity as a philosophy of mathematics.

WHAT IS COMPLEMENTARITY?

Complementarity is admitting two or more views which cannot be reduced to each other. On the face of it, they may even appear to be contradictory. Of course, they are not really contradictory, because the theory of complementarity proposes no common system to be available in which to discuss the supposed contradiction. The alternative to complementarity is reductionism.

3. From a historical point of view the appropriate sources for a complementarist philosophy of mathematics are as follows. Dutch Reformed theologian Herman Dooyeweerd painted the picture in broad strokes. He used the term "sphere sovereignty" to describe what it is for various disciplines ("spheres") to have complementary ways of looking at the same phenomenon. See for example his A New Critique of Theoretical Thought (Philadelphia: Presbyterian and Reformed Publishing, 1969). A Ph.D. dissertation by Dirk H. Th. Vollenhoven in 1918 detailed how that should be applied to mathematics in particular. Among contemporary writers, Vern S. Poythress and Willem Kuyk have provided readable accounts of complementarity as it applies to mathematics. See Willem Kuyk, Complementarity in Mathematics (Boston: Reidel, 1977); Vern S. Poythress, "Creation and Mathematics; or What Does God Have to Do with Numbers?" Journal of Christian Reconstruction 1 (1974):128–40 and "A Biblical View of Mathematics" in Foundations of Christian Scholarship, ed. Gary North (Vallecito, CA: Ross House, 1976), pp. 159–88. I have chosen instead a more personal approach, suggesting how I came to adopt the view myself.

As a simple example of complementarity between mathematics and a related field, consider the following example. How will you describe the relation between the following two sentences?

(a) $2 + 2 = 4$.

(b) $4 = 2 + 2$.

From the mathematical point of view, the question is simply one of whether the verb "equals" is symmetric. Since it is, the mathematician says that these two sentences "say the same thing," or that from one of the sentences we may derive the other by citing the symmetric property of equality as our grounds for the deduction. Neither statement has more primary status.

For the psycholinguist, however, the relation is much like the distinction between active and passive sentences: (a) asserts that the result of adding 2 and 2 is 4; (b) asserts that 4 can be broken down, among other ways, into the sum of 2 and 2. The first is compositional; the second is decompositional. Mathematicians do not make such distinctions, but children learning mathematics do. (Of course a mathematician *could* formalize this distinction. See Thesis 4 below.) The compositional form (a) is psychologically more elementary.

On the other hand, there are distinctions within mathematics that psychology does not make. One example for which this is true is in establishing the existence of irrational numbers. As Vinner and Tall put it,

> [T]he psychological need for mathematical realities cannot be satisfied within the restricted framework of mathematics. There are mainly two reasons for this. First, mathematics offers only relative existence. But what one needs [psychologically] is absolute existence. (One needs an unquestionable reality with which mathematics is associated. Mathematics establishes, for instance, irrational numbers *on* rational numbers, but in any reality we see one kind of object *at the side* of another kind.)[4] [Emphasis theirs]

The complementarist view emphasizes not only that different disciplines can provide complementary views of the same reality, but that the same discipline can view the same reality in complementary perspectives. This is the way that I actually do mathematics. For example, if I am modeling the classical predator-prey situation, I am free to see a signed digraph model, which relates the predator and the prey in a qualitative way.

4. Shlomo Vinner and David Tall, "Existence Statements and Constructions in Mathematics and Some Consequences to Mathematics Teachings," *American Mathematical Monthly* 89 (1982):752–56.

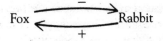

In this way, all that I need assert about the relationship between Fox and Rabbit is that an increase in the number of foxes results in a decrease in the number of rabbits, but that an increase in the number of rabbits results in an increase in the number of foxes. Or I may choose to use a pair of coupled linear differential equations, or if I am limited to a computer analysis, difference equations.[5] Instead of these deterministic models, I might choose instead to use a probability model. I do not find it helpful to discuss which is the better model when they are not refinements of each other, and even when they are, the best model depends on the purpose for which I am building the model. A variety of mathematical disciplines may apply.

Even within a given mathematical subdiscipline there are complementary perspectives. There are three mathematical approaches to probability: the measure-theoretic, the relative frequency, and the degree-of-believability. (The latter is sometimes called subjective probability, but since there is a mathematical formalization of it, "subjective" is a misleading term in this context.) When more than one of them applies in any situation, they give the same results, even though there is no way within mathematics to prove that they are equivalent, since they use incomparable terms in their axiomatizations.[6]

Christians in other disciplines have observed a principle of complementarity as well. Donald MacKay, communications theorist, calls reductionism "nothing-buttery." From the point of view of physics, the lights flashing across Times Square are "nothing but" flashing lights, but to someone who can read, they are a message containing news. The physical explanation is accurate but not complete. The informa-

5. Dooyeweerd makes a broad distinction between the numerical and spatial spheres. Kuyk relates this to the finer distinction between discrete counting and continuous measuring in the philosophical chapter of *Complementarity in Mathematics* (chap. 3).

6. Lloyd Montzingo seeks to relate probability to Christianity in a way that supports a complementarist philosophy in "Random Variables and a Sovereign God" in Robert L. Brabenec, ed., *A Third Conference on Mathematics from a Christian Perspective* (Wheaton, IL: Wheaton College, 1981), pp. 91–97. Various philosophers have attempted to argue why distinct theories of probability should give the same results. See Bruno deFinetti, *Theory of Probability*, 2 vols. (New York: Wiley-Interscience, 1974, 1975) and Karl Popper, *The Logic of Scientific Discovery* (New York: Science Editions, 1961).

tion-processing explanation is also accurate but not complete. One cannot reduce the message to mere physics.[7]

Linguist Kenneth Pike characterizes his linguistic theory (tagmemics) as

> a theory of the structure of human behavior which attempts to preserve the three perspectives within a single frame of reference, in a *complementarity* of perspectives which are static, dynamic, or relational. (The tagmemicist affirms that on occasion each must be used if the analyst wishes to capture certain aspects of the behavior of the analyst or of the native performer.)

Also, his theory

> insists upon the essentiality of static, dynamic, and relationship complementarity. This insistence, perhaps more than any other feature, currently differentiates tagmemics from other available theories of language or language within behavior[8] [emphasis his].

Whereas MacKay and other complementarists to whom I have referred are specifically attempting philosophy from a Christian perspective, Pike has not yet consciously developed an articulated Christian philosophy,[9] although he is as thoroughly Christian in his perspective as they. Pike's antireductionism was not framed as a Christian apologetic but was hammered out of the fabric of messy linguistic field data whose complexity he chose to face honestly.

As a youngster, I had some interest in chemistry. I regarded the real frontiers of biology for those concerned with foundational issues to be essentially chemical frontiers. I don't recall whether the further dependence of chemistry on physics was ever made explicit; perhaps I just felt it because the courses were sequenced Biology-Chemistry-Physics. As Bernhart says in criticizing reductionism,

> From one point of view (reductionistic) both physics and chemistry study some of the same subject matter. The main question of chemistry could be regarded as falling into a specialized compartment within physics. . . .

He then supports complementarity.

7. See Donald MacKay, *The Clockwork Image* (Downers Grove, IL: InterVarsity Press, 1974) for a popular account of these matters, as well as pointers into his more technical writings.

8. Kenneth L. Pike, "Toward the Development of Tagmemic Postulates" in *Tagmemics Volume 2; Theoretical Discussion*, ed. Ruth M. Brend and Kenneth L. Pike (The Hague: Mouton, 1976), pp. 91–127.

9. Pike, personal communication, 1982. Notwithstanding the fact that Vern S. Poythress calls Pike "the greatest living Christian philosopher," in *Philosophy, Science and the Sovereignty of God* (Philadelphia: Presbyterian and Reformed Publishing, 1976).

> But the best choice is to view them side by side in mutual dependence and mutual support. The two disciplines seem to me to be as different as they could possibly be, respecting the tremendous degree of overlapping and interpenetration.[10]

Likewise, as I studied physics it seemed to depend on mathematics as its foundation. Physics seemed to be describing the world in terms of quarks with colors and strangeness, in terms of spinors and group theory. Gone were particles and in their place were probabilistic wave functions. Physics was rooted in mathematics. So I decided to become a mathematician. Surely upon mathematics one could build a foundation for science. Within mathematics I studied in turn its foundations.

History is strewn with men who have sought in mathematics a certainty and a universality which no field of study can give—Plato, Leibnitz, and Alfred North Whitehead, to name just a few.[11] Complementarism explains why those attempts cannot succeed.

COMPLEMENTARITY IN MATHEMATICS: FOUR THESES

One discipline has always borrowed metaphors from another. For example, gravitational "attraction" was something like the attraction of a boy and a girl when the "chemistry" was right. The danger seems to be when the metaphor becomes master instead of servant. That is especially easy to do when the metaphor is drawn from mathematics, because mathematical models are the most precise of metaphors. We confuse precision with accuracy. We assume that the level of abstraction lends an immunity from criticism. We fall prey to the dangers of what Dooyeweerd calls "the pretended autonomy of theoretical thought," which he labels the "great idol of modern humanism." Mathematics as theoretical thought par excellence is not seen in complementary perspective with respect to other experiences and disciplines.

If one does not reduce mathematics to physics (as empiricists do), the most tempting alternative is to reduce mathematics to psychology. There is a sense in which all three classical approaches to the philosophy of mathematics elect this alternative. Intuitionism denies that

10. Frank Bernhart, "On the Four Color Theorem: Is the Proof Genuine?" Unpublished manuscript given as a talk at Wheaton College, June 1981.

11. In preparing the comprehensive bibliography *Bibliography of Christianity and Mathematics: 1910–1983* (Sioux Center, IA: Dordt College Press, 1983) with Calvin Jongsma, I did not think it accidental that references that are primarily personal testimony emphasize that they sought mathematics as a key to universal understanding. See, for example, Brian Stewart, "Playful Vocation," *Theology* 79 (January 1976):18–23.

which the mind cannot construct. Logicism reduces mathematics to what George Boole called "laws of thought." Even in formalism, seemingly the most immune from claims that mathematics is dependent on psychology, axioms are selected for their "elegance," "beauty," "appeal"—emotional terms, all of them.[12] When Barker presents a philosophy of mathematics which avoids the pitfalls of these extremes to get at mathematics as it is actually practiced, his view has its roots in developmental psychology.[13]

In short, because any philosophy which attempts to evaluate mathematics must stand outside it, the usual approach is to reduce the philosophy of mathematics to psychology. If, however, the critical foundational question of psychology is the mind-body problem, then those with an antithenistic bias are strongly motivated to reduce psychology to biology, bringing us full circle.

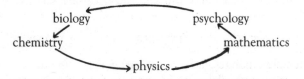

In just such fashion, modern searchers look for meaning in the way that they would look up words in a dictionary, scarcely realizing that the dictionary is by its very nature circular. This brings us to the first thesis of my complementarist philosophy of mathematics:

1. *Meaning is only found outside the system.* Reductionism avoids this issue by building larger and larger systems. This is especially clear in the formalist program. Metamathematics has been partially reduced to mathematics by arithmetization. Intuitionism, which has been set over against formalism as a philosophy of mathematics, has itself been formalized: The so-called formal system S4 of modal logic models intuitionistic proof theory.[14]

Another important example of the reductionistic program is the attempt by Alfred Tarski and his students to capture meaning within

12. Vern S. Poythress makes a closely related observation in "Mathematics as Rhymes" in Brabenec, *Third Conference,* pp. 29–42.

13. Stephen F. Barker, *Philosophy of Mathematics* (Englewood Cliffs, NJ: Prentice-Hall, 1964) and "Two Philosophical Problems About Mathematics" in Robert L. Brabenec, ed., *A Second Conference on the Foundations of Mathematics* (Wheaton, IL: Wheaton College, 1979), pp. 29–40.

14. It is important here to stress that the incompleteness theorems of Kurt Gödel and J. Barkley Rosser did not *verify* complementarity. They did deal a death blow to one narrow form of reductionism—the formalist program of David Hilbert.

mathematics. The Tarskian approach eliminated the intensional, configurational, situational, relational aspects of meaning by using the Axiom of Extensionality to guarantee that a set is "nothing but" its collection of elements. In so doing, the formalist was on safe ground. Recently, attempts have been made to capture intensional meaning in a formal way (for example, the late Richard Montague's grammar of a fragment of English or Dana Scott's lambda calculus models of computer programs and data). They capture more meaning, but still form a very small chunk of what we mean by meaning. Workers in artificial intelligence capture some intensional meaning in a network which has the freedom to model contradictions and to change dynamically. The networks can include meaning in the Tarskian sense and much more. But they still fall short.

How much we limit what we shall find by the very methods that we use! (Compare Hamming's first and second points: we see what we look for; we select the kind of mathematics to use.)[15] How then shall we choose our methods? I suggest that we admit a variety of methods, with their differing and complementary views providing different aspects of the whole truth.[16]

This brings us to the second thesis of my complementarist philosophy of mathematics:

2. *No single view of mathematics can be a final integration point for a philosophy of mathematics, nor can mathematics be such an integration point for the sciences. Any view of mathematics can be accurate but cannot be complete.* In the words of Willem Kuyk,

> The philosophy of mathematics necessarily employs a language which is a mixture of the natural language, and a formal language or a logical language, and by that nature, is open to inexactness and contradictions. It nevertheless may serve to glue the partial experiences of mathematician, physicist, and the general scientist together into a tentative unity.[17]

Davis and Hersh make a similar but stronger claim: mathematics itself is "fallible, correctible, and meaningful."[18]

I mean this claim more broadly as well. No viewpoint will be

15. Hamming, "Unreasonable Effectiveness," pp. 87, 89.

16. Compare Gene B. Chase, "Skolen's Paradox and the Predestination/Free-Will Discussion" in *A Christian Perspective on the Foundations of Mathematics* (Wheaton, IL: Wheaton College, 1977), pp. 75-82, and "On Kuyk's *Complementarity in Mathematics,*" in Brabenec, *Second Conference,* pp. 75-78, by the same author.

17. Kuyk, *Complementarity in Mathematics,* p. 161.

18. Philip J. Davis and Reuben Hirsh, *The Mathematical Experience* (Boston: Birkhäuser Boston, 1981), p. 411.

found, even in principle, this side of heaven that can unify all of mathematics. No "unified field theory" such as Einstein sought for physics, no overarching formalism such as Hilbert sought for mathematics, no comprehensive theory of mind such as wished for by Leibnitz and still pursued by workers in artificial intelligence. We shall always be limited in what we find by the tools we use as finite men and women.

Is then reductionism a straw man? To see that it is not, one need only turn to a recent article by one of the leading spokesmen in the field of artificial intelligence. Marvin Minsky, a mathematician in his own right, dismisses as merely a convenient fiction the notion of a "self" in these words: "Our self-awareness is just illusion. . . . [M]uch of what we 'discover' about ourselves by [self-awareness] is just 'made up.' "[19]

Why then do we believe this "illusion" of a "Single Agent," as Minsky calls the self? He says that to explain why it is that we believe this illusion, we must look at society.

> For then we realize how valuable to us is this idea of a Single Agent Self—no matter how simplistic, scientifically—in social matters of the greatest importance. It underlies, for instance, all the principles of all our moral systems; without it, we could have no canons of *responsibility*, no sense of blame or virtue, no sense of right or wrong. In short, without the idea of a Single Self, we'd scarcely have a culture to begin with[20] [emphasis his].

Minsky regards views of the mind that are not mechanistic as "simplified, . . . suitable only for practical and social uses, but not fine-grained enough for scientific work."[21] In this way he is able to dismiss out of hand any arguments to the effect that because machines cannot be self-conscious, they will not be able to think just like humans. For neither are humans self-conscious, according to Minsky. Consciousness can be reduced to mechanistic terms. I would agree instead with MacKay that information-processing models are capable of offering an accurate explanation of the mind, but only *an* accurate explanation and never a complete one, certainly not the most important one.

Whereas my first two claims about a complementarist philosophy of mathematics are explicit in the writings of others on complementarity, my final two points are not. The first is meant to dispel the myth of objective mathematics—its isolation from the personal, sub-

19. Marvin Minsky, "Why People Think Computers Can't," *The AI Magazine* 3 (Fall 1982):3–15.

20. Ibid., p. 12.

21. Ibid., p. 15.

jective mathematician. The second is meant to affirm that a mathematical view can always be taken. My first two theses emphasized the diversity of the various disciplines. These second two theses emphasize their unity.

3. *Because mathematics is personally structured, mathematical intuitions are trainable.* One must be careful to claim that something cannot be true because it is counter to one's intuitions. The intuitionist is on shaky ground, for whose intuitions are to form the basis for what is to be accepted mathematics? I have reason to believe that Kuyk has not given this point due consideration in his *Complementarity in Mathematics.* In discussing the ontological status of mathematical objects, he claims that he tentatively puts himself somewhere between Platonic idealism and an overly parsimonious constructivism. His middle-of-the-road set theory, allowing an axiom of countable choice, seems to me to be unnecessarily restrictive. I claim that you may extend your axioms as far as your intuitions allow, and that at least some few mathematicians (Polyá, Erdös, Solovay, or Michael Morley for example) have developed intuitions that extend beyond the countably infinite. I have seen my own intuitions grow and change as I have learned more mathematics. Thus my insistence that intuitions are trainable grows out of my experience. Mathematics is in complementary relation with the mathematician as subjective experiencer.

4. *No viewpoint of the world that "works" in practice can be excluded from valid consideration as a mathematizable (including fully formalizable) model solely on the basis of the contradictions some formalization of it makes with (other) mathematical entities.*[22] A classic example of this thesis is distribution theory. Roughly, a distribution is something that may not be a function, but whose integral is well defined. Dirac's delta function (O everywhere except at the origin where infinite; total area under the curve is 1) was used by physicists as a legitimate way of transforming data "because it works" before mathematicians recognized it as a legitimate object of study within a consistent system—not as a function, but as a distribution. Abstract mathematics that survives mere game playing holds more than a "what if" relationship toward axiom selection, as evidenced by Jacques Hadamaard in *The Psychology of Invention in the Mathematical Field.*[23] The Greek enjoy-

---

22. This is a philosophical extension of the theorem within mathematical logic which says that if a mathematical system has a model, then it is consistent. There is no branch of the real world (as if mathematics were not real!) that cannot be mathematized. Conversely, "Lobachevsky . . . held that there was no branch of mathematics, however abstract, that might not some day be applied to the phenomena of the real world." Stanley L. Jaki, *The Relevance of Physics* (Chicago: University of Chicago Press, 1967), p. 118. That is not thereby to say that the mathematics will explain what it describes.

23. (New York: Dover, 1945).

ment of conic sections was based on their interest in aesthetics, not their interest in modeling of practical problems. But (Heie calls it the chicken-and-egg problem) one might claim that the discovery of the conic sections was rooted in their concrete experiences, else why would they have no trouble with squaring or cubing but no ability to conceptualize the fourth power? Theirs was a geometry rooted in sense data.

This final thesis violates Kant's *a priori* view of mathematics. Mathematics stands in complementary relation with the other disciplines. That is, mathematics completes them by providing tools that will always apply. I do not claim that mathematics is unique in this respect, as did those during the Age of Reason who enthroned mathematics as queen of the sciences. Along with the Dutch Reformed theologians, I would affirm that every discipline can bring its tools and insights to bear on a situation.

So far I have not defended the position that complementarity represents a distinctly Christian philosophy. A brief review of my four theses will show that the position is indeed Christian in its roots. (1) Meaning is only found outside a mathematical system. The meaning of the created universe taken as a whole is found only in God who stands outside creation. (2) Mathematics is not a final integration point. To know everything about anything, you need to know everything about everything. (3) Mathematics is personally structured. It is a gift of God, whom we know in Christ to be personal. (4) Every possible discipline of study is mathematizable. The "surprising" applications of mathematics are less surprising but more full of wonder for a Christian who knows that in Christ all things hang together (Col. 1:17).

I see in complementarity a necessary concession to human finiteness. It implies not disjointness of efforts, nor relativism, but a mutual need for the work and viewpoints of others. "For now we see in a mirror dimly, but then face to face. Now I know in part, then I shall understand fully, even as I have been fully understood" (1 Cor. 13:12).

RESPONSE TO HEIE

In this section I shall turn briefly from my integrative theme of complementarity to summarize Heie's arguments, to support them where I can, to disagree with them where I must, and then to relate them to complementarity.

Heie has picked as his integrative theme "freedom within bounds."

By "freedom" he means two things: the freedom to choose to do mathematics at all and the freedom to do it for a wide variety of reasons, ranging from aesthetic to instrumental. (The latter describes mathematics as applied to other fields or as it contributes to unifying understanding.) His emphasis is on mathematics as a creatively free exploration. Christian and non-Christian alike are free in these ways, as a creation mandate, not as a redemption gift.

By "bounds" Heie means values that constrain those choices, values in the philosophical sense of criteria for criticism and judgment. There are bounds on the discipline—beauty and usefulness are two such criteria—agreed to by the community of mathematicians. There are bounds on the Christian mathematician as a person—ethical bounds—agreed to by the community of Christians. These include ethical constraints narrowly conceived—"Shall I solve ballistics problems for the U.S. Army?" They also include more broadly such things as good stewardship of natural talents—"Am I good at mathematics?" Or, my place in the Christian community—"Will my computer program speed the translation of the New Testament?"

I share four points of agreement with Heie:

1. I agree that integration of Christianity and mathematics is an important project (to use Heie's term) in which to engage myself.

2. I agree that the philosophical, rather than the applicational or the incarnational, approach is the right way to pursue integration. Heie has done an excellent job in marrying this to a personal testimony of how mathematics functions in his own life, but his approach is still basically philosophical.

3. I agree that a man is known by his commitments, bound by his values, and by definition lives within his "control beliefs" in the terms of Nicholas Wolterstorff.[24] That is no less true in mathematics than in Christianity. In both cases, one knows because one does (John 7:17), and we are talking about what the mathematician or Christian is doing as evidence of what he believes, and not what he may claim. I like, therefore, the way that Heie determines what are the values of these two communities.

4. Further, I agree that an integrative theme ought not to be self-defeating. This is not explicit in his paper, so I shall give three examples. Unqualified agnosticism is self-defeating because one cannot be consistent about it without being agnostic about one's own position of agnosticism. Denying the law of noncontradiction is also self-defeat-

24. Nicholas Wolterstorff, *Reason Within the Bounds of Religion* (Grand Rapids: Eerdmans, 1976).

ing because one cannot defend the denial of that law without an appeal to the law. In Heie's terms, to enter the project of propositional reasoning is to accept the law of noncontradiction. Finally, Heie chooses to value valuing in his paper. To do otherwise would be self-defeating, for—again in Heie's terms—"no one can avoid [the ethical project]; for to attempt to avoid it" is to give an answer to its questions.

What then is my objection to Heie's paper? Briefly, it does not go far enough. For Heie the mathematical community decides on the content and the values of mathematics. A Christian approach to mathematics selects those values which do not conflict with Christian values. Of course, Christian mathematicians are a part of the mathematical community which is deciding; still, it is the freedom for mathematicians to "do as you please" which receives the emphasis. Mathematics is what mathematicians do. The child who has been repeatedly disobedient to his frustrated parents is eventually forced into obedience by their final ultimatum: Do what you please! That to me seems to be the prescriptive force of Heie's proposal when applied not to the individual (who must do mathematics according to the rules of the mathematical community) but to mathematicians taken together. The two values of beauty and utility are not well defined enough to be very prescriptive.

Heie argues that many values of the mathematical community are also Christian values. He could argue more strongly from history that the connection is not accidental.[25] He allows for the amazing beauty and usefulness of mathematics, but his proposal does not account for it. Why is it that "there is nothing so practical as a good theory"? (This quotation is credited to Kurt Lewin, the psychologist whose attempt to use topology as an explanatory theory—field theory he called it—never really did get off the ground.) Heie does not say. In my opening remarks I criticized the incarnational approach (which says that mathematics is Christian only insofar as those who are mathematicians are also Christians) as being too superficial an integration. Heie narrowly escapes that criticism by refusing to distinguish between subjective and objective knowing.[26] Since I concur with that refusal, I can only ask for a greater emphasis on the content instead of the context of a Christian philosophy of mathematics.

25. Stanley L. Jaki, *The Origin of Science and the Science of Its Origin* (South Bend, IN: Regnery Gateway, 1979) and R. Hooykaas, *Religion and the Rise of Modern Science* (Grand Rapids: Eerdmans, 1971).

26. Heie, n. 27. Cf. Michael Polanyi, *Personal Knowledge* (Chicago: University of Chicago Press, 1974).

One way to get at the distinction between Heie's approach and mine is to compare the Dutch Reformed view of philosophy as exemplified by Dooyeweerd and the Thomistic view of philosophy. In the Dutch Reformed view, Christianity stands outside philosophy evaluating it and thereby constraining it. In the Thomistic view, philosophy is done to the point where the Christian view has been included, and then that view constrains the remaining discussion. Heie's view is more like the Thomistic view in that it does not provide a radical (that is, to-the-roots) critique of the mathematical enterprise but accepts it within the frame of reference of mathematicians themselves. From a complementarist perspective, it is clear why this will work to give a coherent explanation of mathematics, but it is not clear from a perspective of freedom within mere axiological bounds.

There are boundaries limiting the freedom of mathematicians, based on the specific nature of what it is to do mathematics (ontological and epistemological boundaries), beyond those provided by criteria for judging what is good mathematics. There are bounds on what is possible mathematics. We see what we have the tools to see. Mathematics has both amazing power and humbling limitations.

The greatest strength of Heie's proposal—celebrate it!—is that it is the first discussion of the philosophy of mathematics to give attention to values. He agrees with Karl Popper that judgments of value are not empirical statements but decisions, the outcomes of autonomous acts of mind. No mathematics without commitment! No "Sunday formalist"! In this respect, Popper seems to be a "co-belligerent" to a biblical view.[27] For the Bible also values decisions to follow God despite empirical data that might appear to point in another direction. Witness the Book of Job as an example. The Bible also puts highest emphasis on values.

Heie's view shares with complementarity a refusal to reduce mathematics to just a part of what it is. For Heie this follows from his commitment to creative exploration as an aspect of freedom. In contrast, however, he seems to say that the value bounds in mathematics are self-imposed by the mathematical community, whereas in Christianity they are given by an autonomous God. Heie fails to wrestle as much as I'd like with the givenness of much of our mathematical experience, albeit culturally given. That mathematics is developmentally ingrained limits freedom in ways not related to values, limits freedom in ways that Heie has at least not explored. Heie's value of "personal growth" is a thin thread on which to hang so much.

27. Francis Schaeffer uses this term to refer to two people who come from different philosophical bases but both agree to work together on a project on which they agree.

Furthermore, Heie's position shares with complementarity the feature of bounds that limit creative freedom. In complementarity, drawing as it does on the Dutch Reformed tradition, there are laws that God has created, laws that are as real as the entities that they govern. For Heie, the bounds in both cases are value commitments. For Christianity, such a conclusion is easy to justify, for the need for ethical decisions is obvious within the Christian life. It takes him many more pages, however, to argue that there are also value commitments for mathematics. What, Heie asks, are the criteria for criticism and judgment—for valuing—imposed by the mathematical community? He sees two such: the beauty and the usefulness of mathematics, a spectrum which includes a variety of classical philosophies of mathematics according as their proponents emphasize the beauty of mathematics (formalists) or its usefulness (constructivists).

A complementarist view is well within the freedom allowed by Heie's "open-ended" proposal with its "potential for pluralism." Conversely, humility is the value with which a complementarist would begin if she were to select an axiological starting point as Heie has done.

What is there? For the complementarist, mathematical objects are real but do not exist in the same way as physical objects like tables or legal objects like contracts. How do we know? For the complementarist, deductive and inductive reasoning are permitted, as well as analogical reasoning.[28] What of values? The question has not been addressed directly before by those seeking to develop Christian perspectives on mathematics. We are indebted to Heie for providing a map of the territory. An axiological approach stands in complementary relation to the ontology and epistemology of other approaches and is a valuable contribution to our understanding of mathematics from a Christian perspective.

---

28. Jean Piaget calls this "transductive" reasoning. Deductive reasoning goes from the general to the specific; inductive reasoning, from the specific to the general; transductive reasoning, from the specific to the specific. Piaget shows how this is a major mode of children's reasoning.

The Arts
COMMENTARY

Best's essay is an exploration of some of the ways in which the doctrine of God as Creator provides a pattern for artistic activity. Best makes the following points: (1) God does not create to prove himself, but to express freely who he is. So for human artists doing should be an affirmation of who they are. (2) God did not create copies of something already in existence; so nonrepresentational art is legitimate. (3) Creation is full of re-presentations rather than imitations; so traditional representative art is legitimate. (4) God does not engage in mere replication, hence imitation in art is not legitimate. (5) Creation reveals enormous variety that nevertheless reflects an underlying unity of personal style; so human creators are free to express their individual styles in changing and radically different ways. (6) God's creation unifies beauty and function, so the human artist should not view these in an either/or light. (7) God's creation does not reflect a hierarchy of aesthetic values. Certain parts of the creation are not more beautiful than others. So the human artist should not be elitist in favoring some forms of creativity over others. (8) God entered creation as a servant in Jesus Christ; so human artists must be willing to use their talents in ways that serve others.

Coppenger points out that Best's approach is an exercise in analogy. This approach, he argues, has both strengths and weaknesses. The weaknesses lie in the limitations of analogy. It does not logically follow from "God did it" that "we may (or should) do it." Coppenger further suggests a number of ways in which the limitations of the analogy may be clarified. The strength of an analogy is that it may give rise to fruitful hypotheses about artistic creation that can then be tested for their viability or legitimacy. Coppenger believes that it is helpful to regard Best's essay as a generation of hypotheses—"poet's work . . . bold, enjoyable, and provocative. It may even be correct, but we need the work of grammarians [criticism] to secure that judgment."

Coppenger makes a distinction between the Incarnationalists and the Calvinists, one wherein "the Incarnationalists emphasize the ways in which we are like God. The Calvinists emphasize the ways in which we differ from God." Coppenger suggests that these two camps will have different views of the work of the artist. The Incarnationalist artist will emphasize freedom to create, she will trust her intuitions and appreciate her passions. The Calvinist artist will regard herself chiefly as creature rather than bearer of the divine image. She will view the Incarnationalist's love affair with the imaginative possibilities of this world as idolatrous or self-serving. This distinction made by Coppenger bears similarities to distinctions implicit in the essays of Skillen, Chase, and Heie, in which Skillen and Chase give more emphasis to the ordinances of law emphasized by the Calvinists, and Heie gives more emphasis to the freedom to create emphasized by the Incarnationalists.

Coppenger thinks that Best's Incarnationalism can receive a stronger argument than Best actually gives by introducing the distinction between "you may unless we say no" (the position of some parents and Incarnationalists), and "you may not unless we say yes" (the position of other parents and some Calvinists). Using this distinction, Coppenger buttresses Best's Incarnationalism with the following reasoning: "As spectators we should honor the principle, 'They may do it unless God forbids it, God's behavior warrants ours unless God says otherwise.' So we should attend to Best's descriptions of divine behavior and assume that they are exemplary for some Christian artists. If God has done it, then the burden of proof should fall upon the one who claims that we must not do it." Coppenger's argument at this point bears similarities to Heie's theme of "freedom within bounds."

While both Best and Coppenger ground their remarks in ontological assumptions which Christians bring to the artistic enterprise, the strategy underlying both papers is an exploration of the relationships between the value commitments of the Christian and those of the artist. Both tend to see Christian commitment as compatible with a wide variety of existing and possible forms of artistic creation, though not necessarily compatible with all existing aesthetic judgments.

God's Creation and Human Creativity

HAROLD M. BEST

The purpose of this essay is to introduce a few ideas concerning the general bearing of God's creation on artistic creativity. The following statement forms the basis for the discussion: The doctrine of the creation provides the model, and God's actual creation provides the raw materials for human creativity.[1]

Some remarks are first necessary as to the meaning of creativity and its relationship to other kinds of doing. Creativity is the ability both to imagine (think up) something and to execute it. Making or shaping something without thinking it up is more properly termed crafting or fabricating. In creativity, imagination and execution are undertaken by the same person. In crafting, execution alone is undertaken. For example, an architect both designs (thinks up) a building and executes a plan; craftsmen then fabricate accordingly. In the meantime, the craftsman may well have to design and make a tool or think up a means for doing the fabricating, in which case he exercises creativity.

Technique and skill are means of executing a thought-up thing expeditiously, with efficiency, and if more than one is executed, with enough similarity to allow for interchangeability. Technology is the larger integration of technical means into an all-inclusive network of effectiveness. If technique and technology are means, skill is the degree of means necessary to accomplish a task. The more sophisticated the technology and the more advanced the skill, the more capability for similarity or subtlety. That which is mass produced demands similarity. That which is individualized demands subtlety.

Some activities demand highly developed skills: doing a coronary by-pass or hitting a fast ball; others demand less: using a socket wrench or playing a C major scale. By the same token, creativity can take place at a high level: composing a string quartet; or a comparatively low level: thinking up a paper clip. In each case, something has been thought up. The special quality lies in the thinking up, the imagining.

Creativity, technique, and skill are often confused, especially by those

---

1. This statement is drawn from a syllabus prepared by Arthur Holmes for an interdisciplinary seminar on creativity held at Wheaton College, Wheaton, IL, July 1980.

who should know better—educators, philosophers, and artists. Activities such as playing a musical instrument, painting, dancing, writing, learning a foreign language, and so on, are often termed skills. By contrast the study of history, literature, and the like, by being linked to conceptual and scholarly activity—the "life of the mind"—are implied to be different, perhaps superior. This is not only unfortunate but provincial.

If writing, for instance, consisted only of copying characters, it would then properly be termed a skill—penmanship. In a broad sense, penmanship may be defined as the skill of copying anything as closely as possible, whether simple or complex, whatever the medium. Copying an illuminated medieval manuscript, forging a Picasso, or attempting to imitate the way Horowitz plays Schubert are examples of penmanship carried over into various media at exceedingly difficult levels. Those who do only these things are craftsmen or technicians who, because of the exercise of consummate skill in the *context* of artistic creativity, may be thought to be artistic or creative.

But creativity is not just skill, however easily the two may be confused. If skill is the executor of creativity, creativity is the difference to be imagined, then executed. Thus, Horowitz must imagine the performance of Schubert differently from Rubenstein if he is to be considered creative. He must then possess the skill to execute this difference. If Rubenstein copies Horowitz, however difficult this may be, he is not creative but consummately skillful. There is, then, a difference between being musical and being musically creative.

Outside of the arts, a philosopher is only skillful if she can reason well and critique accordingly. She is creative if she imagines a new way of asking why or saying because, to which then the skill of reasoning becomes attached. In this sense, more philosophers are technicians and their work a collection of skills than is often thought to be the case. They may work skillfully within the world of ideas without necessarily having any of their own. Because they are working with ideas, they may think that this is different from playing, writing, dancing, or painting. Unless they are creative, imagining a difference, they along with others are craftsmen.

There is far more technology, skill, and crafting in the world of academia, as well as the arts, than is readily admitted, just as there is more creativity outside of the supposed creative areas than is first thought. There are creative people and technicians, better yet, poets and grammarians, in every discipline; creative philosophers and technician philosophers; creative musicians and technician musicians; creative historians and technician historians, and so on. There are poets and grammarians in all walks of life, not just literature and language. None of this is meant to imply that a given individual is a technician *only*, or creative *only*. Everyone, in some way, both imagines and crafts. The question is the degree to which one is more the technician or more creative, and vice versa.

This can only mean that the creative side of any mind and the technical side of any mind are special and necessary. It is obvious that God purposed it this way, for God thought up and crafted both kinds of doing, each important and each capable of exceedingly far reaches, each profoundly in need of the other. Humanity, not God, is in error for confusing the two, or worse, holding one or the other in suspicion. The imaginers are considered to be too impractical by the technicians and the technicians too pragmatic for the imaginers.

In the creational scheme of things, it is God, the All in All, who is both the supreme imaginer and the supreme technician, the consummate poet and the consummate grammarian, both the artist and the craftsman. God's creation is totally integrated at one with itself; that which is imagined "works." It may even be said that in the Incarnation both ways of doing were synthesized perfectly in Jesus, who was at once the poet-teacher and the craftsman-carpenter.

THE NAMES OF GOD, CREATION, AND CREATIVITY

Some of the most direct references to God's creatorhood lie outside the Genesis accounts, particularly the Psalms, prophets, and the all-important Christocentric passage in Colossians (1:15–17). However, the account of Moses and the burning bush (Ex. 3:1–14) articulates a dimension found nowhere else. Moses was the first person in recorded Scripture to ask God specifically who he was. The response was brief and profoundly mysterious—"I AM THAT I AM" (v. 14). God pointedly declared himself to be absolutely noncontingent, integral, and self-sufficient. The word *that* is crucial. It precludes sequence, contingency, self-evolution, and dependence. God is God: beyond this nothing can be added as to why or how God exists. God is eternally complete being God.

Even so, this is not God's whole name. Throughout Scripture, God gives himself a vast assortment of other names, each of which refers either to divine being or to divine acts. Those referring to divine acts also can be combined into one superior name: "I ACT THAT I ACT." Once again, there is noncontingency, complete sovereignty, self-sufficiency, and wholeness. All that God does is of divine choice, for divine reasons, and without exterior counsel.

God is not a divided God. Being and doing are not cause and effect, but aspects of each other. Hence, in eternal fullness, with all names as one, God is the "I AM THAT I ACT THAT I AM." God did not need to create, to imagine, to make things, or to act in order to prove anything, to authenticate his being, to bring credence to his authority, or to satisfy an unmet need. God is not the "I AM BECAUSE I ACT," or the reverse. Rather, God sovereignly chose to create and the creation is simply a satisfaction of choice. Had he not made the creation, God would still be fully acting within the infinity of himself. Scripture alludes to this when it speaks of the Holy Spirit searching out the things of God (1 Cor. 2:10). God is neither making new discoveries about the God-head nor putting on the finishing touches but eternally "at work" within himself, disclosing the fullness of himself to himself, and infinitely rich within these disclosures. The Trinity is eternally at work being the Trinity.

What does this mean to human creativity? Above all, it should mean that one does not create in order to be, to authenticate one's self, or to prove that one is. Humans are made after God's image. What God is infinitely, humans are finitely. God is the uncreated Creator, a human the created creator. Humanity was thought up and made, God was not. If God is the "I AM THAT I ACT THAT I AM," humanity is the "I am that I act that HE ACTS THAT HE IS." To be sure, this is a most awkward construction, but it is extremely necessary. It states that humanity is both entirely dependent and contingent but created to reflect in this state all that God is and does.

It is of prime importance that as with God being and doing are conjoined, so with humans, however much in our fallen condition we prefer to separate and sequentialize them. A man may assume that he is independent and noncontingent, that he has become like the gods; therefore he acts. Or, if he admits that there is a God whom he must please, he seeks to accomplish this by work of some sort—doing in order to become. When a man makes something in order to prove that he is, he belies the intended unity of his existence and perpetuates his split ways. When he makes something as a testament of his being—"I am that I do"—he reflects the union always intended for him.

The error of doing in order to become is as erroneous in salvation as it is in creativity. Jesus spent his years on earth teaching that doing in order to be was essentially evil and intrinsically worthless. The gospel is the message of becoming a new creation, a supernatural act and process by which humanity is both returned to contingency and to the reunification of being and doing. In this sense, the Epistle to the Romans and the Book of James are in counterpoint with each other: works without faith are useless, and faith without works is dead. The Christian is one who lives and does by faith. Faith is that which gives all things, lived and done, their proper substance and evidence. In light of this, the Christian's only option with what she is and does is to make an offering (Rom. 12:1), to make all an act of worship in place of an aid to salvation or to being. Human creativity then finds its fullest measure. Nothing is means; nothing is end. All is worship.

To be sure, unregenerate humans can make both beautiful and useful things and perform noble deeds. This is one of the benefits and mysteries of common grace. Common grace, however, does not justify. It only allows. Special grace, saving grace, both justifies and allows. Thus, humanity being declared right, now rightly makes. That is, personhood and creativity, being and doing, are wonderfully reunited. A person in Christ truly "is that he does."

THE CREATION, HUMAN CREATIVITY, AND COMMUNITY

God creates out of nothing, of which he is not, into something, of which he is not. Humans create out of something, of which we are part, into something else, of which we continue to remain a part. Creative humanity is not only utterly dependent and contingent on God for what we are and how we act, but on the creation itself in all of its natural potential, richness, material, and process. We are also dependent on the unique part of creation called fellow humans, on the diversity of human making called culture, and on the process and extent of human activity called history. Within these, we imagine and make. Without these, we are helpless. Our imagination and urge to shape depend on givens in order that we continue to be creative. We must have raw material, precedent, model, example, counsel. We must experiment, sketch, compare, reject, develop, synthesize, start over, refine, and review.

Thus, whether we know it and like it or not, human beings participate in a vast community of creativity, not just of people, but of everything. The network is rich and complex. Whether human creativity issues in rapaciousness (for humans can negatively imagine and shape) or usefulness, it is nonetheless within community. The more intelligent, the more gifted and creative a person is, the more she will take advantage of all that lies around her.

Had Beethoven lived in the Renaissance, he could not have composed the Fifth Symphony. His music did not appear out of nothing. It came from the loins of musical process as surely as he came from those of his ancestors. In order to express his own individuality he first needed Mozart; Mozart needed Haydn; Haydn needed the sons of Bach; they needed their father; Bach needed Buxtehude; Buxtehude needed his musical forebears, and so on, back through the lines, nuances, textures, and gestures to prototypical music. This musical lineage is then crossed with numerous communities and processes: societal, ecclesiastical, economic, political, geographical, procedural, and technological. Since the nature of human creativity couples imagination with context, it follows that great artists begin by following an example and end by setting one. So the process continues as long as humanity endures. Whether someone imagines a different thing, as with the best of the avant-garde, or imagines a thing differently, as with the best of conservatism, that person somehow participates in and contributes to all that surrounds him.

Artists can be deluded into imagining that they are somehow independent of their contexts—aloof from the very communities that made each one's particular creativity possible. There is a proper humility in the realization that no matter the level of creative genius, an artist's ability to create is related directly to her past and present surroundings.

THE IMAGINED CREATION AND HUMAN IMAGINATION

The doctrine of *creatio ex nihilo* is both familiar and necessary to our understanding of God. While attention is often focused on God's power in bringing things into being that previously were not, there is a preceding and equally profound mystery. Before the creation appeared, it had to be thought up. As simple as this is, it is still the great mystery; God thought up a giraffe, a cucumber, the overtone series, sexual reproduction, gravity, dolphins, and strawberries. God is none of these, and there were none anywhere to copy. There was simply no information except in God's own imagination that would give him an inkling as to what to make and how to make it. God thought up what was not.

Imagining what is not yet is of high importance for artistic creativity. In a very real sense, God was the first "abstract" nonrepresentationalist, for that which God imagined and made did not represent anything. Each thing made was, purely and simply, in and of itself and without reference.

A great deal is made over nonrepresentation, especially in the visual arts. Through a complex conceptual evolution, culture has been taught that art should imitate, that it should be a picture *of* instead of simply a picture. The result is often judged strictly on the basis of the artist's ability to imitate or somehow be "realistic." If the work "looks like," it is more acceptable than if it doesn't, quality notwithstanding. People and artists thus taught are robbed of the richness of creative expression. It may well be that this proclivity to imitate started with the fall, not of Adam but of Lucifer, who wanted to be "like the Most High." It may well be that the urge to imitate also comes from a lack of trust, a fear of newness or disturbance which covetousness generates. It is too easily forgotten that, in its summation, the creation is a vast, unsettling display, not just a collection of safe and beautiful parts. We don't become "used to" creation. Some of it lies beyond us; we shrink from it, for it disturbs us and tries our trust.

This entire matter is relevant for art. As long as we can see a barn or a daisy in a painting, there is security because we can *refer* to the "real" barn or the "real" daisy. When we see that which seemingly does not refer, we feel uncomfortable, perhaps even duped. Once again we choose that which is safe and comfortable. By contrast, artistic action finds its full merit and justification in the first day of creation when all was new and all was strange. The artist has an obligation to continue this precept of firstness. Creativity which refers or imitates so effectively that the perceiver has an equal choice between the imitation and the thing imitated is not creativity at all but replication, another form of technology.

At the same time, this does not mean that art need only be "abstract." There is too much greatness and originality in the varieties of representationalism which have appeared transculturally and transhistorically. The twentieth century is included, for we possess Andrew Wyeth, Edward Hopper, and many others whose work contains "recognizable" buildings and trees. These are in the same league as the nonrepresentationalists, as long as a careful distinction is made between imitation and re-presentation. This distinction can be illustrated as follows.

The creation was not only imagined but continued. That is, there was not just a first cactus, there have been countless others, no two of which were alike. Each re-presents the other. Re-presenting is a way of saying a thing differently, of saying it "in other words." The first tree was thought up; all others are re-presentations. Re-presenting, in the most profound sense of the word, is every bit as difficult as not re-presenting.

This is quite different from the Platonic concept of ideal and real, essence and accident. In the creational scheme, there is not one essential tree of which the rest are shadows. Each is essential, individual, and real. Form is not "out there" and content "right here." On the contrary, content is form and form content.

It is extremely important to remember that the artist does not paint things as they are ideally but as he sees them. If he paints a tree, the quality of the painting lies not in how well the tree is imitated, but in its imaginative re-presentation in the terms of the medium: shape, color, nuance, texture, confluence, and, above all, the artist's particular individual style—his capability for imagining a difference.

It is in this sense that the true artist sees the parallel between imitation and cloning and rejects it even as the scientist must. To the artist, imitation is dangerous in three ways: (1) It denies the individual worth of the thing imitated. (2) By consequence it questions the worth of the imitation. (3) It denies the individuality of the imitator and makes him an imitation of all imitators.

The question then is not, "Is the painting a tree?" but, "Is the re-presentation of the tree individually and stylistically unique?" Since style is essentially a matter of consistent individuality, there will be as many re-presentations of trees as there are imaginative individuals.

Furthermore, the uniqueness of personal style is far more critical than the procedure one chooses. Examples of this may be drawn from any of the arts, particularly the visual arts. However, one taken from music will suffice. At the end of the nineteenth century, particularly with the music of Richard Wagner, it was said that the process of tonality was ex-hausted. Then through the work of Arnold Schonberg, there was devel-oped a radical concept of organizing pitches, not around a single center, but in orderly relation to each other. The weight of this concept was such that every serious composer then and now has had to reckon with it. It is, to be sure, a predominate force in western music.

Even so, there were and still are a significant number of composers whose works utilize the tonal process, each of which shows striking originality. Why? Because of the prevailing importance of individual style over the system chosen. It is essentially dehumanizing to speak of individual style as system dependent. As long as there are no two cre-ative people alike, no artistic system ever need be exhausted. If an artist changes systems it is because her own thinking, not the system, is ex-hausted. In the meantime other artists may well find something more to say within that same system.

There are, after all, only two ways that an artist can show creativity. She will be either a conservative (she will still imagine within the system), or she will be avant-garde (her imagination will demand an-other system). Whatever else, profound and individual creativity re-mains the unchanging issue.

Three suggestions have been made thus far:

1. Since the creation was imagined and did not represent anything, the artist is free to imagine nonrepresentatively and nontradition-ally.
2. Since the creation is replete with re-presentations rather than imitations, the artist may re-present without imitating and remain free to continue traditionally.
3. In either case, individual style is of the essence.

The nature and extent of the creation are such that the first two suggestions may well be different ways of saying the same thing. That is, the only thing an artist can achieve, even the most radically nonrepresentational, is re-presentation. The artist is bound by his finitude and by the creation itself. He can never step outside of these. He is part and parcel of that which, in every conceivable texture, color, shape, density, nuance, and quality, has first of all been imagined by the uncreated Creator. Anything ever painted, sculpted, danced, or chiseled can only be a personal stylization and extension of something already in existence, whether seen or not yet seen by the artist, because all of this is in his "dust," and he is of the dust of all of these things. He can see into the creation without seeing all of it.

Thus we discover that a work of art initially thought to be nonrepresentational turns out to be quite like, say, the cross section of a cell under intense magnification, or the courting rites of a tropical bird. We see these and say, "How quite like this painting or that choreography," when in point of fact, we could say quite the reverse. It simply depends on which we see first, the art work or the creature, as to the order in which we say that the one looks like the other.

The foregoing stands in stark contrast to the ideal-real polarity found in Platonism, because realities only are the issue, each reality distinct and individual, each reality standing with all other realities. The creation is real, the artist is real, and the artifact is real. There is no ideal, hence no perfection, of which all else is a pale reflection. Excellence, not perfection, becomes the key word. In the broadest and most scriptural sense, excellence is the personal process of becoming better than one once was, not better than someone else is. Even in the heat of competition, others are not obstacles but models. They do not exist to beat or be beaten, but to stretch and be stretched. Excellence is also the process of showing a purposeful, qualitative difference among things. Not only must one improve one's self, one must also show a more excellent way.

In summary, the fact that creation was imagined offers these possibilities. *First,* God was the first nonrepresentationalist, the first to grant the creative person the possibility of continuing in this manner, albeit finitely. *Second,* there is nothing in the creation which remotely suggests replication or cloning. God could have proceeded this way but did not. Since God did not, we should not. *Third,* the true artist is thus directed not to imitate but to re-present. Endless variety is possible on the basis of endless individuality. Whether the subject matter is "abstract" or "representational" is of no particular relevance. By contrast, individual style is entirely relevant. Because of this, no particular system can ever be exhausted. The progress of the arts does not consist in the invention of new systems but in the on-going presence of individual vision, style, and imagination. True artistic value lies in the intrinsic quality of the work itself, not in its ability to imitate something outside of itself. It may refer but not replicate. *Fourth,* since it is impossible to step outside the creation, and since God has thought up more shapes and substances than humans ever can, all art is somehow re-presentative of something already in existence. Humans cannot outthink God; nevertheless, since we are made in the image of God and capable of participating most profoundly in the creation, we do not necessarily have to see something before we can imagine it. This is as close as one can ever come to creating *ex nihilo,* but how delightfully close.

THE CREATION, CREATIVE STYLE, AND VOCABULARY

The creation, at first glance, appears full of anomalies. Because there are lobsters and humming birds, deserts and rain forests, turtles and men, one is tempted to believe that there are a variety of creative opinions at work—a collection of deities, if you will—either having compromised with each other or having concluded their business in outright disagreement. How could the same Someone think up a hippopotamus, then turn around and imagine an orchid?

The answer to this affords another opening for the artist. There is but one God, one Author of all creation. God is changeless and proceeds unchangingly in all that he is and does. The creation, which God imagined, turned into handiwork, and called good, unites and coheres in Jesus Christ. Its astonishing variety, these supposed anomalies, issue out of oneness and singular consistency. In short, there is a common personal style, a unity of process, and a richness of vocabulary. For it is out of a singularity of process, the way things are personally and consistently done, that individual style issues. This singularity then allows for virtually limitless variety in vocabulary.

In the world of human creativity, Bach did not use one compositional process for writing fugues and another for minuets. He may have employed different compositional techniques or different formal approaches, but not different processes. His way of joining sounds remained personal and unique, as it does with all creative individuals, whatever their medium. Thus Bach's simple music, his complex music, his earthy music, his transcendent music—if you will, his hippopotomus music, his orchid music—all bear the same deep personal imprint.

An even more vivid example would be that of Picasso or Stravinsky, brothers in rampant shifts of vocabulary (critics erroneously call these style changes). The best in-depth analysis will always show that Picasso in his Blue Period is the same Picasso as in his Cubistic Period because Picasso is Picasso is Picasso. The same is true of Stravinsky in *Firebird, The Rite of Spring,* and the *Symphony of Psalms.* The same unchanging personal gesture is there, whatever the vocabulary. The supposed anomalies occur only in the superficial sense. In the deep sense, no one can change creative fingerprints. They always remain the same.

Critics spend too much time fretting over such shifts and changes, often with a suspicion that such varietal activity may indicate a lack of integrity and individuality or a series of stages leading to the final and ever important "Late Period." Until then, all else that the artist does is evidence that she is "trying to find herself." Of course she is finding herself. That is all she can ever do. She must find *all* of herself.

The creation itself tells us that multiple vocabularies are not an indication of creative schizophrenia or a compromise of personal style. Artists are often so afraid of trying something new that they end up with only dry, studied, even fearful works, overly complex, often lengthy and learned. Or they produce sketchy trifles, defended by being labeled "experimental."

Artists need not end up as slaves, afraid of their own creativity, afraid of lowering their standards, afraid of simply having fun, suspicious of the universe of variety. They simply must return to the creation and observe their Creator creating riotously, popularly, seriously, multi-idiomatically, lumberingly, elegantly, humorously, seriously, prickly, and smoothly. They must return to their easels, potter's wheels, pens, keyboards, and choreographic charts to do the same. If they do, and if they do so honestly and personally, if they put their minds and integrity of process to work, if they allow their imaginations, knowledge, and personal ways to vie with each other, the world will be all the richer, all the more pleasured, all the more disturbed. If the same God can make a cucumber and a sea horse, the same potter can make a cup and a free-form object, a poet can make a simple couplet or a complex drama, a composer a Scripture song or a symphony.

THE CREATION, INTRINSIC WORTH, AND FUNCTION

Any serious discussion of the arts is bound to include the subject of function or functionalism, wherein an art piece serves a purpose to which its specific aesthetic content may be subordinate. In western culture the concept has evolved gradually that art means itself, is inherently complete, and needs little or no exterior reference to justify or explain it. Within this there are the institutionalized settings for art: concerts, exhibits, museums, and theaters. Accompanying the doing of art is an equally enriched and fermentive world of theoretical study, scholarship, criticism, and social liturgy. It is this idea of art for art's sake—that is, art providing for its own functional independence—which has allowed western art to variegate and develop more rapidly than that of any previous culture. At the same time, this phenomenon has created increasing perceptual distances between the artist and the layperson. As artistic creativity has become increasingly specialized, the artist-specialist expects everybody to adjust to and to become literate in all of these changes as quickly as he does. Those who cannot or will not are thought to be uncultured or common. Those who try and fall short are considered to have poor taste. The artistic community then has no one to talk to but itself.

By contrast, the functionalist maintains that the arts need not be isolated and singularly prescriptive; they may be useful, at hand, at work, and more easily understood. They are meant to unite easily with other things and functions. Advertisers want music and art to help sell a product; the church expects its art forms to serve the liturgy, to help induce worship, or to prepare the congregation to receive the sermon. Within these and other contexts, art becomes a tool with which to do other things or to enhance their doing. It is neither an end in itself nor contextually independent. Purely and simply, it is means.

The division over worth and function need not be so great, and the proponents of each position must realize that they err. Ironically, high art participates in function in at least three ways. First, if art exists to be perceived for what it is, intrinsically is, then perceiving it, with all of the requisite skills and insights, is a function. It is in this sense that music functions as much to be heard; visual art, as art to be seen, and so on.

Second, even in the most "cultured" events there are accompanying activities and functions actually competing with or covering up the real "reason" for the art itself. A formal concert may function as a reason for wearing special clothing and jewelry, meeting friends, or showing one's cultural intensity. In a way, each of these functions has its own special worth; the concert itself may then only be background. There is also the concert hall. It, too, is an artistic event, perhaps a masterpiece, to be perceived in its own way and for its own worth. How then is it to be perceived during the concert? Does one ignore the building or the music, or does the building function with the music or the music with it?

Third, related more to the performing arts and an increasingly serious problem, performance itself may function primarily as a means of comparing performances. In this process the particular and intrinsic content of the art may be poorly understood and receive very little attention compared to the quality of the performance. The issue at hand may no longer be Beethoven's *Fifth* or Shakespeare's *Hamlet,* but Bernstein's *Beethoven,* Olivier's *Hamlet,* as compared to Solti's *Beethoven* and Nicholson's *Hamlet.* Performance for performance's sake pushes the perception of content into the background. It is in this sense that there may well be a classical Muzak. Not just the public but critics and students become so engrossed in performance alone that they are no longer deeply conversant with actual content aside from performance. The composer, just as much the specialist as the performer, continues in the background, increasing in distance from the performer as much as the performance world separates itself from the lay audience. No wonder the major symphony orchestras, opera companies, and theaters are locked into an almost static repertory. The ability to hear *in* the language has atrophied and has been supplanted by the narrower ability to listen for changes in the manner in which the language is spoken. In linguistic terms, phonetic hearing has superceded phonemic hearing.

The functional artist's most blatant errors lie in a preference for results at the expense of quality and immediacy at the expense of integrity. Artistic perception and use become a matter of repetition, conditioned reflex, even mind control. The artistic philosophy found within a totalitarian regime depends heavily upon the mandates of repetition. Artists are called to subordinate their art functionally to the aims and the ideals of the state. As strange as it may seem, the church is often guilty of the same philosophy when it controls artistic content and quality on the basis of results sought, moods set, and conditions preserved.

It is in this context that so-called witness art is suspect. Its basic weakness lies in its effort literally to mean the gospel—in a sense, to imitate truth—and of course it can't. Art cannot be preachment; it cannot be that singularly particular. Hence, witness art in its attempt to "mean" the truth, to preach the gospel, fails both itself and the gospel. In attempting to particularize itself enough to be "true," it generalizes the gospel itself. The very opposite should be the case. It is the gospel which has to be particular, whereas art at its best must mean many things at once. The arts can no more be an instrument of truth within the church than they can be an instrument of propaganda within the state, as long as the artist is devoted to honest, imaginative, and purposeful vision. Therefore, functionalism cannot mean enslavement or compromise, but coordination and servanthood.

Just as high art cannot escape function, functional art often turns out to possess intrinsic worth, either at the time of its function or separate from it. So it is with a great deal of the music we now listen to in our concert halls. It may well have functioned originally as dinner, church, or dance music. Objects and events can also drop into or out of function.

The ordinary Coca Cola bottle is now perceived by some to be an art object in its own right, even though it is available in seemingly endless quantity. Midwestern grain elevators, Shaker furniture, and other such useful artifacts also can be contemplated for their aesthetic worth, depending upon the way in which each is contextualized. Paintings and sculptures, artistically excellent in their own right, may well be integrated into interior decoration. In that context, they function along with that which has been designed for usefulness.

That worth and function can be united is shown in the creation itself. It is at once beautiful and useful. Each thing created has both intrinsic worth and functional value. There are not separate "Muzak" and "concert hall" creations. A sunset is beautiful, but it is also a consortium of usefulness: clouds holding moisture, light refracted and colored by an atmosphere to be breathed, reflections of things which in turn are useful and beautiful. The sun warms the earth, controls its weather, gives light, and, in its regular absence, allows cool and dark. However complex or extended anything in the creation is, it still functions. However simple and orderly anything is, it still has its own integrity and specific beauty, whether it is a molecule or an armadillo.

This assertion suggests something further. Did God make certain parts of the creation more beautiful than other parts? Is God's handiwork of unequal aesthetic worth? Does it suggest a hierarchy of values? Is a cactus less beautiful than an orchid, or a platypus than a bird of paradise? When we speak of the beauty of creation, we may really be speaking of our own favorite things, not the entire handiwork. We choose its parts the same way we choose a fugue, a sonnet, or a new dress. We in a sense imply that God's handiwork can be graded like a term paper. In so doing we overlook the generic wonder and beauty of creation, the sum of the essential wholeness and integrity of each created thing. We have no more ultimate right to say that a sunset is more beautiful than an artichoke than we do to say that classical music is more beautiful than jazz, or Gothic better than Bauhaus. The pursuit of excellence lies more in comparing Gothic with Gothic, Bauhaus with Bauhaus. Proceeding in this manner means participating generously and discerningly in as many categories of creativity as possible, in the same way that it means participating in the whole of creation, not just a few favorite things.

Participating widely in the arts is risky; one cannot simply rest in the security of the narrow world of a few masterpieces, in the security of being told what is good and lasting. One must sample new shapes, idioms, textures, and colors for which there is yet no critical opinion. Instead of hearing Brahms's *Fourth* for the hundredth time, as tempting as this is, one may need to venture into George Crumb or Appalachian folk, West Coast jazz, or tribal chant for the first time. The more diversified one is, the more discerning one eventually becomes. Those who live in the narrow world of regulated elitism may never know the wonder of the larger world of human imagination, with all of its risks, demands, and rewards. They may never know the difference between being told what is good and judging what is good.

Ideally, the ultimate aim of artistic action should be to see worth and function free either to separate or to unite at any given time. The danger lies in refusing their union *or* their separation. The former will most probably lead to snobbery, the latter to idolatry.

THE CREATION AND THROW-AWAY CREATIVITY

The concept of function and worth goes further. If a thing is intended to be used up quickly, it is not likely to be as carefully made as something intended to "last." There is throw-away technology—planned obsolescence, and throw-away art—faddism. Longevity is irrelevant; quality is in direct proportion to immediacy and a quick disappearance.

Interestingly enough, those who make art "for the ages" are as guilty in their own way as those who make art for the present, for each group overlooks the importance of its own contemporaries and surroundings. Throw-away artists litter the culture, futurists withhold themselves from it. The immediatist worships usefulness, the futurist, vindication. The immediatist says, "If it works it is good"; the futurist, "If it works it can't be good." In both cases, the victim is none other than the common people. Their creative sensitivity remains unshepherded. It is dulled by the immediatist and passed up by the futurist.

The creation also is meant to be used up. But in God's economy, the creation does not suffer from the values of the throw-away. God thinks and works differently. Roses wither and die, living things perish quickly, an apple which takes months to grow is eaten in a trice. Richly grained wood is burned in the fire, fire itself, in all of its beauty, is but an instant. Even though God's handiwork is used up, some more quickly than the rest, every speck of it is carefully and lovingly made. The rose, the earth worm, the mosquito, and the cabbage leaf are as lovingly constructed, richly variegated, and profoundly fascinating as a galaxy. There is no division of purpose. There are no two qualities of workmanship, one for the instant, the other for the ages. Being quickly used does not justify being sloppily made. The integrity of the Maker never changes with the transiency of the creature. There is no model whatsoever in the creation for a division between worth and function, or immediacy and timelessness.

When God makes something, from the very inside to its very outside, each part is finished. The interior is as finished as the exterior. A skeleton is not just a roughed-in framework, to be covered up eventually with "finish" work. The joints are finished as joints. Marrow is finished as marrow and flesh as flesh. In this sense, one can speak of something organically whole.

Humans, by contrast, often use exterior handiwork to cover up the roughness of interior work. The frame of a house is "rough" work; a person who does this is designated a "rough" carpenter. Joints are not precise, unfished wood is used, nails are not set, and so on. Then, specifically skilled people and specially made materials are provided to give finish. Thus, the "finish" work is not just handsome in and of itself, it also covers up a less crafted, less elegant workmanship. The rough work can be correct, even strong; the finish work is meaningful. It is not just correct and strong, but elegant. When all of the parts of something made, from the most interior frame to the most subtle outward detail, are exquisitely whole and carefully joined, one can speak of true, integral creative artistry.

Human creativity would regain much of its dignity if this example in the creation were followed. There would no longer be the crassness and cynicism of throw-away art, nor the pomp and pretense of art for the ages. Both are artificial, in that integrity is relativized. Each is end justifying means, the one in immediacy, the other in timelessness. The artist who will not bow to the god of immediacy may bow to the one of a distant future. Each is a kind of idolatry; the only difference is in the distance of the god.

By contrast, the stewardly and creative person invests time and energy intensely into the imagining and making of everything, because God alone is to be glorified and because God alone made it clear from the beginning that function, worth, usefulness, and lastingness are to be conjoined in the same stewardly purpose. Faulty and careless art may well issue in a surface attractiveness, in which the maker ignores the call to fine craftsmanship and ends up with something observed quickly or at a great distance. Surface art may find hiding places both in the avant-garde and in the traditional. In the avant-garde the force of the difference in vocabulary makes discernment difficult. Perhaps the best test of the avant-garde artist is in the demonstration of how imaginative and craftsworthy he or she was as a conservative. Here, the Stravinskys, Schonbergs, and Picassos stand out with force and integrity. They have earned the right to be revolutionary.

The surface art of traditionalism shows itself in cliché and formula, often sophisticated enough to go undiscerned and uncriticized. This art is bolstered by the masterpieces. It somehow looks or sounds just enough "alike" to pass muster, to fall in alongside greatness. The best test of the traditionalist is in the demonstration of a continued radical imagination within the bounds of the tradition. Here, the Bachs, the Brahmses, and the Wyeths stand out with the same force and integrity as the best tradition breakers.

THE CREATION, SIMPLICITY, AND COMPLEXITY

Just as there is error in separating worth and function, so there is in separating simplicity and complexity. What is simplicity? What is complexity? If complex means more and simplicity less, then Wagner's "Tristan und Isolde" is complex and Brahms's "Lullaby" simple. If complex means complicated and simpicity clear, then Karl Barth's writing is complex and that of C. S. Lewis is simple, or Notre Dame Cathedral complex and the Great Pyramid simple.

Which of these is better? More profound? Does complexity guarantee superiority and profundity, or does it simply provide a larger space within which these qualities must take place? Is Paul McCartney's tune "Yesterday" or one of Matisse's line drawings of lesser quality than Schubert's C Major Quintet or DiVinci's *Mona Lisa*? Which is more profound, the Golden Rule or the Epistle to the Romans?

Only if quality is carried out over a large expanse can complexity make a claim over simplicity. Even so, what is it about the *Mona Lisa* that sets it apart from another equally complex but lesser masterpiece; what creates the enchantment, the minute difference, but a detail here and a subtlety there? Except for these, it would be only less great.

Great art does not come about just by amassing detail. Great art is more a matter of exquisite timing and spacing of all its parts, whether few or many. This has nothing to do with complexity per se, but with process: the *how* and *when*. The *what* is anybody's property, the *how* and *when* the property of the truly artistic. There is only one note, the high F in the last phrase of Haydn's tune sung to "Glorious Things of Three are Spoken," which turns it from a good to a great tune. This note is a master stroke in the same way as certain singular gestures are in the *Mona Lisa*. The *Mona Lisa* is complex, the hymn tune simple. Each in its own way is great; each in its own way is a mystery. The one is distinguished from the other only by the expanse of quality. To be sure, carrying quality out over an expanse is a rare and precious gift, not to be taken lightly. It is rare only in the way a galaxy is rare. Even so, the galaxy is no excuse for overlooking the blade of grass. The blade of grass and the galaxy are different only in the expanse of quality. Each is made exactly the same way: simplicities are chained together in the one case to make something small, and in the other to make something large. It is their simplest parts, the elemental particles of matter, that are yet to be explained. This is the greater fascination.

Simple creativity is no less important to the whole of human creativity than the simplicities of creation are to their whole. This does not mean that only simplicity is to be preferred. The exclusive pursuit of simplicity may well be a sign of laziness. As elegant and enigmatic as the simple may be, its pleasure is for a comparatively brief moment and it is over. The complex, whether in the expanse of the creation or artistic creativity, demands discipline, extended attention, and profound memory. In turn it offers a different satisfaction, extended over the expanse of the thing made. The complete person needs both. It is a fallacy to assume that high culture should be singularly complex and low culture singularly simple. Just as the blade of grass dwells comfortably with the galaxy, so must the hymn tune dwell with the oratorio.

Something need not be difficult and inaccessible in order to be thought excellent, even though an excellent thing may be inaccessible at first. Inaccessible should mean only accessible with difficulty. Total inaccessibility would be a perfect reason for making nothing. In fact, total inaccessibility is essentially chaos, and chaos is pseudocomplexity. By the same token, pseudosimplicity is not instant accessibility but triteness. This occurs when simplicity is mistakenly thought to be a reduction of complexity. There is no reducing Bach's *St. Matthew Passion* down to a tune, nor is there any way of enlarging a tune into the *St. Matthew Passion*. A simple line drawing cannot be the reduction of a more detailed painting, because if it were, the lines would be structurally anomalous. Simplicity is not a plan and complexity its realization any more than a blade of grass is an outline for a galaxy. True simplicity is a quality, just as complexity is. Each must be itself and stand as itself. Both are difficult.

KENOSIS AND ARTISTIC CREATIVITY

Finally, just as in the creation and within human creativity the simple and the complex may be joined, so in the Incarnation. In point of fact, the Incarnation is the final model for the human being. *Kenosis* is the Greek word signifying emptying. It is used in the great Philippians passage (2:5–11) to describe the emptying of Christ to become man. This is not the place for the theological and doctrinal complexities of the Incarnation. Suffice it to say when Christ came to earth he somehow mysteriously limited himself as God, yet fully remained God, while being fully human.

In a way, God simplified himself. Yet this, as with so many simplicities, is the greater mystery. For all that the Incarnation means to the salvation of humankind, it means significant things for human creativity as well.

An analogy may help. If, before becoming human, Christ could be likened to an oratorio, in his Incarnation he became a hymn tune. In this, he lost nothing of his eternal character and excellence. Becoming a hymn tune was not a compromise, a dilution, or a weakening. Nor did it mean that Christ refuted being an oratorio. Rather, becoming a hymn tune was a uniqueness in itself, with its own wholeness and usefulness. It is in this way that we can once again say that a hymn tune is not a skeletal oratorio. Now we can say that it is an emptied oratorio.

There is a difference between putting something aside and losing it. Christ showed us this difference, and the true artist—may I now say the servant-artist—must likewise learn this well. The artist must come to experience the dignity, worth, and eventual joy of putting things aside, of emptying himself and taking the form of a servant. He must be able to move from the oratorio to the hymn tune, from the drama to the couplet, with grace, elegance, power, and imagination.

To lay aside is still to remain the same, as long as one's integrity, imagination, and sense of excellence are at hand. The lessons of simplicity and complexity, worth and usefulness, variety and unity, familiarity and strangeness, are corollary to the lesson of laying aside. The servant-artist proceeding this way has finally learned artistic wisdom. She has acquired the gift of functional integrity: the ability to maintain excellence, high purpose, and artfulness in the fulfillment of any creative task in any context to which she may be called.

Which is the greater mystery, that Christ is God or that Christ could lower himself while remaining God? Likewise, which is the greater mystery, that humanity is artistically creative or that in our creativity we may empty ourselves and still remain artistic? Servant-artists have their reward, just as Christ has his. Once the hymn tune has been written, the right to do another oratorio has been earned.

Creativity and Analogy: Some Limitations

MARK COPPENGER

Best's essay is not sham integration. He does not fashion theories and then christen them with vaguely religious terms. His Christian comment is not tacked on. Instead, his biblical and theological insights permeate his theories. Furthermore, his notes on the arts are not just shallow illustrations of his theology, for he knows the arts and he does them justice in his essay. Neither theology nor the arts gets shabby treatment.

Best's work is an exercise in analogy. He uses something familiar as a guide for understanding something less familiar. In this case, however, our comprehension of the familiar side, the explainer, is not much if any greater than that of the explained. That is to say we know little more about God's creative acts than we do about our own. So we have an analogy which is more provocative than illuminative. This doesn't mean that it's a bad analogy, for analogies can be prized for the fresh and careful thought that they generate as well as for the satisfying picture that they give us.

We often use humanity as a key to understanding God. Indeed God invites us to do so by calling himself father, shepherd, and comforter. Scripture gives us a variety of other earthly things to explain God's nature—bread, water, fire, wind. This progression from the things at hand to the things on high is natural. Best, however, leads us in the other direction.

The risks in both approaches should be obvious. As we move from humanity to God in explanation, we flirt with so anthropomorphizing God that we lose sight of his divinity and transcendence. When we move from God to humanity, we may well give human beings honor and privilege not properly ours.

Best, of course, has basic biblical warrant to pose and explore this analogy, for Scripture tells us that we have been created in God's image. We are similar to God in certain important ways. These are not spelled out in the Bible, so there is some freedom to consider just what they might be.

Now any analogy has positive, negative, and neutral or indeterminate components. There are ways that things are alike, unlike, and not clearly either. For example, when we say that God is a father, we know that he has a father's love (positive) but does not procreate as does an earthly father (negative). We are not, however, sure how "manly" as opposed to "womanly" God is (neutral). Does God manifest an earthly father's masculine personality traits to the exclusion of the feminine ones, or does God possess both in equal measure? This neutral or indeterminate zone provides room for the play of imagination.

In this essay, Best enters that zone. How much like God are we in our artistic ventures? How much like God should we be in these ventures? Does God's example rule out certain practices for the Christian artist? Does it require, suggest, or permit others?

Analogies are not so much true or false as apt or inept. The same holds true of metaphor and simile. For any two things in the universe or in history are alike in some respect. A Louisiana fishing license, Confucius, Gilbraltar, and a Babylonian's sneeze all have the property of existing after 2000 b.c. Furthermore, all are observable. We could go on, but the similarities among them are undeniable. Still, they don't make for fruitful analogy since the dissimilarities overwhelm us. A good analogy is a matter of degree. The composition of one thing is sufficiently like that of another to shed light on it. As we size up Best's analogical efforts, we must judge the degree of similarity, and so the aptness of the analogy of God and human beings as creators.

Recall, however, that there must be some dissimilarity or there would be no analogy at all. Instead, there would be identity. There must then be a healthy tension between the positive and negative components, or the analogy collapses. So Best has chosen to perform a sort of balancing act.

It would, I think, be helpful to contrast Best's analogical approach with three other prominent ways of thinking and arguing: deduction, induction, and the hypothetico-deductive method. The first moves with logical strictness from propositions to propositions. The second summarizes what it finds in a sampling of cases. The third is a combination of educated guessing and testing.

How might deduction serve to instruct the Christian artist? Certainly, any general directive to Christians would apply to Christian artists. For example, the Golden Rule may be particularized to the artist's situation, but Scripture doesn't give us general Christian prescriptions from which to deduce some of Best's more specific counsel. We do not find the verse, "All imitators are an abomination unto the Lord," from which we might deduce the maxim, "Artists should not be mere imitators."

This is not to say that there is no biblical warrant for Best's attack on imitation. It is just to say that the fit is often looser than that of mathematically precise logic. The Bible does not give airtight instructions for the range of artistic possibilities.

Deduction plays a role in Best's essay. Some of his adjustments follow necessarily from Scripture. The total picture, however, is only more or less probable rather than certain. This is no reflection on Best. Instead, it follows from the sketchiness of Scripture on these matters. This sketchiness is providential and not happenstance. For some reason or other, God chose to give us room to puzzle out the Christian artist's guidelines.

Deduction loves discrete, clearcut propositions from which to work, but any theologian who would try to build an irresistibly correct system of doctrine on a single biblical statement is more enthusiastic than wise, for Scripture is replete with modifying, balancing statements, which frustrate reliance on a single verse. Romans discredits "works" while James honors them. Some passages stress free will while others suggest determinism. Here we see the goodness of humanity and there we see our disgraceful evil. So the message of Scripture is often ill-suited for the sort of clean proof you find in geometry. It does speak unequivocally on some matters, e.g., the reality of the resurrection of Christ and his power and will to preserve beyond the grave the lives of his followers. But in many instances we are left to work without certainty.

Some might say we should restrict our Christian judgments to those matters which follow indubitably from Scripture, but this would serve to limit Christian counsel in many of our choices. This is simply unacceptable to the Christian who wishes to order Christianly all aspects of his life. If the Christian wants to be thoroughly Christian in his dealings with the culture, he must do some prayerful and studious guesswork. That's what Best shows us.

Induction also leaves us wanting. The inductivist must search for the common thread in all of God's words to those who would be artistic. That thread is terribly elusive. In Amos 6:5, musical improvisation is frowned upon, while it seems acceptable, even admirable, in Psalm 149:1. Of course, we must contextualize the passages to read them fairly, but to do so requires a theological framework which surpasses the simple induction it was meant to facilitate. In other words, biblical induction takes as much insight as it can give. As we seek to identify those cases through which the thread should run, we employ principles of discrimination which the thread was to reveal.

An inductive scientist may watch ducks year after year. In time she will be able to sketch their migration patterns. An inductive Bible student may, however, have difficulty in identifying the "ducks." She's not sure which passages to watch and which to disregard. If, for example, she wishes to record God's lasting instructions to women, she must set aside those passages which are strictly relative to the culture of the day. But to do so, she must have a general sense of what sort of shape a lasting directive would take. One must, in other words, take a leap of insight beyond the evidence in order to sort the evidence properly. Best has attempted just such a leap. He has ventured to identify the ducks for us, the passages and notions that bear watching, and he has done it by more than simple induction.

Finally, we should consider the hypothetico-deductive method. One begins by reading the data, whether they be the occurrences of aurora borealis or the varieties of biblical testimony. Then one formulates a hypothesis, an educated guess, about the truth which underlies the various data. From this hypothesis or theory one may deduce confirming and disconfirming tests: "If such is the case, then we should find (or not find) this and that." One then proceeds to check the theory against the facts. If, for example, the student of aurora borealis decides that the colorful patterns are caused by cosmic ray bombardment of the upper atmosphere, he will follow up with a series of instrument readings of electromagnetic activity, excitation of atmospheric molecules, and the like. The biblical theologian will instead see how his doctrine squares with the full body of biblical teaching. He may have begun by considering only passages containing a certain Greek or Hebrew word, but now he checks his theory against any and all passages.

The process of checking one's theory ought to be a merciless one. No stone should be left unturned. The most ominous and troublesome testimony should be heard. Hard questions should be forced upon the theory. If, in all this, the theory stands, there's warrant for allegiance.

Compared to confirmation and disconfirmation, to cross-checking and interrogating, the framing of the hypothesis is fun. Scanning the data, one is fascinated by the play of new patterns and gratified by fresh learning. And the actual hypothesizing can have a most romantic flavor—the flash of inspiration, the pacing, the flurry of notes, the bracing shift of perspective, the exultation of breakthrough. This is the realm of brainstorming, of dreaming, of new visions.

There is, then, in theorizing both the imaginative and the prosaic, the thrill of the hypothesis and the fearful grind of the testing. The hypothetico-deductive method calls for both the poet and the grammarian, to use Best's apt expressions.

Best's essay is largely poet's work. He gives us an analogical hypothesis. Analogies make perfectly acceptable hypotheses, even in physics, e.g., light is a wave. His theory is bold, enjoyable, and provocative. It may even be correct, but we need the work of grammarians to secure that judgment. While the essay does trace some implications of the basic model, it does not test them all. It does some of the deductive work of the hypothetico-deductive method, but it does not grill these deductions. It simply presents them. This is not to demean the essay, for Best covers a lot of valuable ground within his allotted space. It is just to say that the program, as it appears here, is incomplete. Hard questions remain to be asked. Certain Scripture passages beg attention. Grammar follows poetry.

Best's work, then, properly goes beyond simple deduction and induction. It stands as the guess in the guess-and-check method. It is a good strategy so far as it goes, but it leaves important work to be done.

In Best's comments on skill in the introduction, you may note special words of counsel for the philosophers. It is not accident that he chose philosophers instead of historians or chemists. Philosophers are peculiarly eager to perform vivisection on each new artistic work and notion that comes along. Here he gently suggests that there is more to scholarship than vivisection, and that each discipline should balance its grammatical work with both its own poetry and an appreciation for the poetry of others.

The friction between art and philosophy sometimes comes at the point of establishing the primacy of word or image. In light of some current research, it may focus on brain hemispheres. There may be, as it were, a hemisphere for grammar and a hemisphere for poetry. At any rate, the integration of grammar and poetry is, on a Christian liberal arts college campus, as trying as the integration of faith and learning. I will at times perform the grammarian's task, pressing and questioning Best's notions. I hope also to supply contrasting notions to show Best's own in clear relief.

Before giving specific attention to the subsections of his essay, we should bring to mind another distinction, that of the Incarnationalist and the Calvinist. Best draws on both traditions. The two categories are fuzzy, and each has perversions and misapplications which are hard to detach from the true item. Still, it is important to sketch the contrasting notions. I will employ them repeatedly in my response.

All Christians know that there are ways in which we are like God and that there are ways in which we are unlike God. We are created in God's image, but we are not ourselves gods. The distinction, then, is primarily one of emphasis. The Incarnationalists emphasize the ways in which we are like God. The Calvinists emphasize the ways in which we differ from God. Both sides have valid points. The Incarnationalist looks, of course, to the Incarnation, to Christ's assumption of humanity, to God in flesh. In contrast to gnostic teaching, earthly bodily existence is honorable; it was, after all, good enough for God to enter it. So we may appreciate rather than denigrate our own human passions and circumstances. God chose to join us in earthly sorrow, anger, discomfort, friendship, danger, hunger, humor, relaxation, travel, labor, and rest; and we may identify with God in Christ in encountering this world.

Furthermore, we know that God is incarnate today, in us, for his Holy Spirit resides in our hearts, serving as guide and comforter. We do not need to leave this earth to find God, for God speaks within us, and we bear the stamp of his will in our natural consciences.

As artist, the Incarnationalist is candid and exuberant. She appreciates her passions, trusts her intuitions, and communicates readily with nonbelievers, who themselves bear some image of God. She sings, cries, laughs, and embraces less self-consciously than those who find our earthly frame suspect. Bearing God's image, Christ's flesh, and the Holy Spirit's presence, she makes a place for herself in the culture.

On the other hand the Calvinist sees humanity primarily as creature. God is sovereign. God foreknows, ordains, and judges our actions. God chooses, separates, quickens, and equips us for service. He hates pride, dissolution, and an independent spirit. In great numbers of people, God finds his image hopelessly marred. God sees the abuse creation suffers and commissions radical renewal of its every aspect.

Where he finds creation unspoiled, the Calvinist celebrates, for the handiwork of our Creator is good. He does not sit easy with unbelievers, because their minds are both godless and hostile toward God. He knows that, as God's handiwork, he enjoys valid passions and faculties, but he is equally aware of the incursions and delusions of the evil one.

The Calvinist is not her own. She is bought with the price of Christ's blood. Submission and loving service are her standards, and she trusts in God's grace rather than her own wits to keep her true. The Atonement and not the Incarnation is stressed. In her judgment, the artist should regard herself chiefly as creature rather than as bearer of the divine image.

Calvinist art is generally more sober and modest than Incarnational art. The Calvinist artist gratefully receives God's gifts of color, rhythm, ingenuity, community, labor, wildlife, and government; he then records, reports, and affirms their unspoiled manifestations. He quietly and confidently depicts the family at home, the fruit of field and vineyard, the play of clouds and boats above and on the sea, the forms of flora and fauna, the postures of people at worship. His work is not so much photographic as conservative. It is content to dwell upon the created order rather than to magnify or adjust it. It is humble art.

The Incarnationalist picks up where the other leaves off. She sees what lies before her and considers ways to embellish and refine it. Her enthusiasm for musculature and color leads her to imagine a perfect physique and a riot of color. She gives us halos and backgrounds of gold leaf, a grander-than-life statue, a dreamlike landscape, and a sensuous gathering of romantic figures. She pushes nature's themes beyond the commonplace, and she does not limit her attention to those matters which can be handled with dignity, restraint, and quietness. She is fascinated with the full range of phenomena and with the materials they provide for fantasy and intrigue. She has fun with the possibilities.

The Calvinist considers the Incarnationalist's behavior unbecoming. It's as though they both received lamps as gifts; one places his strategically beside a chair for reading; the other puts the shade on his head and sings a whimsical song into the bulb as though it were a microphone. Calvinists don't wear lampshades on their heads.

The Calvinist uses springs to make scales; the Incarnationalist uses them for a trampoline. The Calvinist bakes bread, the Incarnationalist makes chocolate eclairs. One keeps old bottles for storage use; the other shatters them to fashion a kaleidoscope. One shuns extravagance; the other applauds it.

To the Calvinist, the Incarnationalist's love affair with the imaginative possibilities of this world is idolatrous or self-serving. To the Incarnationalist, the Calvinist's reluctance to fantasize is pitiable. One feels that the other ignores proper bounds; the other feels that those bounds are artificial and ill-conceived.

One seeks to glorify God, the other to glory in the image of God. One finds enjoyment in service; the other finds service in the enjoyable. One admires; the other dreams.

The sacraments play a role in this controversy. The Catholics maintain that the elements in communion actually become the flesh and blood of Christ. For this to occur, the duly ordained priest in good standing must perform the ceremony of the Mass. The consumption of the elements then serves as a means of grace. This view of the proceedings reinforces the Incarnationalist conviction that God affirms and enters our fleshly state, thus identifying with us continually. It also encourages a sort of earthiness in the congregation. Since this occasion for grace is supervised by an official of the church, a distinction is drawn between the sacred and secular professions. The sacred are those which oversee the holy things. The secular are mundane, not characterized by fastidious attention to a consecrated regimen. The artist, not being a priest, is not constrained to work at sacred projects.

The Calvinist rejects this view of the sacraments and so the sacred/secular office distinction. We are all to be priests in the sense that each act should be a pleasing sacrifice or offering to God. The artist does not slip from secular to sacred work and back again, for all work is properly sacred. This does not mean that it is strictly work within the specific programs and services of the congregation and denomination. Rather, all work should be directed toward bringing God's fallen creation in line with his directions.

To summarize, let me simply say that Incarnationalists are generally more "worldly" and more inclined to trust their instincts. They have more respect for human wisdom and are not as comprehensively pious. They are fonder of imagination. And they are less impressed than Calvinists with the Fall.

THE NAMES OF GOD, CREATION, AND CREATIVITY

Best's prose in this opening section will put a strict grammarian's hair on end. For example, there's the part about God's disclosing "the fullness of himself to himself." Does this mean that there are things that God doesn't know about himself? Apparently not, because earlier in the sentence, Best rules out God's making "new discoveries about the Godhead." But what is disclosure if not a revelation of something hidden? This is confusing.

Then we have the eye-popping extensions of "I AM THAT I AM." The theme is challenging enough without the variations, so the grammarian grumbles and interrupts.

This is not the place for a long discourse on writing style, but a few remarks are in order. The typical American professional philosopher in our century has been tutored in the ways of British philosophy. Its watchword is clarity. Its enemies are muddle, semantic inflation, and pompous or romantic obscurity. Mysteries are to be solved, not celebrated and preserved. The empiricist's demand for sensory meaning is honored. The obscure and ponderous tomes of German scholarship are cast aside in favor of the ordinary-language essays of the men and women of Oxford.

Despite the resurgence of continental philosophy, the influence of existential and phenomenological talk, and the fact that British philosophy has gone to seed in the obscurantist wranglings of symbolic logic, the demand for clarity is still strong. We all remember graduate seminar scoldings in the name of clarity.

When those who have been coached in precision encounter those from disciplines more fond of expressive speech, the meeting is not always a happy one. While both may integrate their own faith with their own learning, it's difficult to get joint statements of integration from the language groups.

In the popular mind, philosophers are masters of aphorism, pithy and provocative statements not far removed from *Poor Richard's Almanac*.

For example, we all know some version of the proverb, "Those who ignore history are condemned to repeat it." It seems fitting for philosophers to generate this sort of thing.

Professional philosophers, however, blanch at this job assignment. They consider aphorisms too neat and simplistic to be valid, and they are suspicious of clever turns of phrase, of snappy "one-liners." Their disdain for them mirrors the musicologist's aversion to advertising jingles.

So Best's aptitude for aphorisms is troublesome. Consider these samples:

> Nothing is means; nothing is end. All is worship.
> . . . great artists begin by following an example and end by setting one.
> The immediatist says, "If it works it is good"; the futurist, "If it works it can't be good."
> Just as the blade of grass dwells comfortably with the galaxy, so must the hymn tune dwell with the oratorio.

The winsome force of these observations is the stimulus for the grammarian's objections. They are so captivating and memorable that they can serve as substitutes for rigorous inquiry. They're wonderful when they're right but awfully hard to counter when they're wrong. Simplicity is so seductive.

What then shall we say of Best's style? Do the philosophical grammarians have the last word? Yes and no. There is a time to be artful and a time to be prosaic. Certainly Scripture provides us with a model of aptly divergent styles. When fetching imagery or paradox bears truth and quickens the reader, it may serve. When the lively image and intriguing puzzle sidetrack the inquirer, then prose may be right. Hard proof calls for one sort of discourse, the impression of ideals another. Or, perhaps, varied forms variously serve identical purposes.

Some topics allow more precision than others. Just as it would be folly to compute IQ to the sixth decimal point, it would be irresponsible to round off all engine tolerances to the nearest inch. The lesson in all this is that each expression must be weighed on its own. Does it advance or retard understanding? Does it neatly summarize or blunt needed inquiry? Does it engage or impose mystery?

It is, of course, caricature to treat philosophers as grammarians and Best as an aphoristic poet. Many philosophers enrich their essays with artful expression, humor, and imagery, and Best gives us a generous portion of hard-nosed reason, of down-to-earth argument. However, a distinction persists.

As we consider integrative strategies we should not overlook style, for style determines what moves one is able to make. It colors the final product of inquiry and makes cooperation with other Christian scholars more or less feasible. Since different styles may prove fruitful, it is good to take an "innocent-until-proven-guilty" approach to the particular writings. No blanket condemnation or approval will do.

So what shall we say about God's self-disclosure without self-discovery? I find that particular notion unhelpful if not downright contradictory. As for "I AM THAT I AM," etc., let's give it some slack for the moment. As mysterious as it may be, it's undeniably biblical at base.

Working from God's name, Best argues that just as God's acts are an integral part of his being, so should ours be. God does not try to prove or gain anything and neither should we.

This is not an idle matter, an exercise in academic posturing. It touches the working life of Christian artists most persistently, for these brothers and sisters are constantly on trial. Their public often insists upon edifying and innocuous art—Sunday school illustrations, stirring hymns, family movies and plays, inspiring biographies. If their work is perplexing, their consecration is quietly questioned. If they dare to employ something downright illicit in their compositions—the nude figure in painting and sculpture, swearing in the script of a play, or jazz and rock patterns in music—they are rebuked and shunned.

Art professors on a Christian college campus are frequently under fire. If they are not charged with sins of commission, their sinful omissions—their failure to do real good for Christendom—is carefully noted. "After all, how can this one keep cranking out abstract color patterns when the world's going to hell? And what good is that one doing with his atonal mishmash? Doesn't he see his responsibility to shore up the spirits of the saints?"

It is in the face of such audience response that Best writes. God's acts are not justificatory. They lie squarely within his nature and are free expressions of his spirit. God does not create in order to assuage his guilt for having sat around for ages without making new things. God does not curtail his work for fear he'll make a bad impression. God does not strain to be pleasing or well received. He pleases when it pleases him. And God doesn't lose sleep over the reception he's getting. God is unaffected, self-assured, and coordinated in spirit and deed.

Recognizing that we are not ourselves gods, Best nevertheless finds in God's model some guidance for us. As we are in God, in fellowship and synchronization with God, our own deeds and thoughts are continuous with his. We do not give exemplary service in order to validate ourselves and to gain seats in the throne room. For no one of real importance is keeping score. As beings with new natures, we are simply called to be natural. Our godward and God-infused actions will follow their proper contours. Our aim is to be holy (not to perform acts popularly seen as holy) and then to let the chips fall where they may. So to the nasty question, "What do you think you're *doing*?" the Christian artist answers, "*Being* a Christian." God would answer the same question, if at all, with, "Being God."

Is Best on target? I believe so, though his point is easily misapplied. He has strong support in the biblical doctrine of justification by faith. Righteousness is not based upon perfunctory acts, but upon a quality of heart. Furthermore, hypocrites, those whose behavior does not match their inward beings, are castigated in Scripture. When the fruit of the Spirit is listed, we find, not accomplishments, but graces—peace, kindness, faithfulness, etc.

The Book of James stands, though, as a warning. The heart is capable of enormous self-deception. We may suppose our hearts to be worshipful, but our behavior may undercut this supposition. If we ignore the estimations of others, the impact of our efforts, we may well miss important clues to the quality of our inward beings. There are circumstances in which our most godly service is in slavish attention to the agenda of another. Consider, for instance, the New Testament's instruction to literal slaves, even those with harsh masters. And Christ, whose being we should mirror, was a suffering servant.

The artist is not exempt from the duty to love her neighbor as herself. She must be mindful of the other's needs and consider ways to help. A faith which is no more than a matter of personal enjoyment and sweet contemplation of God is sub-Christian. This truth, however, must not be used to bludgeon the artist into immediately accessible and gratifying work. There is surely a place for brainstorming and for lonely quests. Technology needs pure physics; the practical needs the not-clearly practical. There is no telling what use humanity and God may make of strictly exploratory efforts, but it is certain that without them beneficence will be denied some valuable tools. Love can underwrite daydreams as well as cups of cold water. Necessity is not the mother of all invention; leisure and play are also sources of fresh and helpful notions. Best must not be read as an apologist for willfulness and insensitivity to the opinions of others. Rather, he holds that these opinions are not the last word in determining the artist's projects.

He does not so much base his argument upon the Creator/creator analogy as demonstrate the analogy itself, for he shows on both sides the inappropriateness of justificatory works. He takes two familiar principles of Scripture—the sovereignty of God and righteousness by faith—and links them in a fresh way in support of his thesis that God's model is pertinent.

His comparison of God and humanity has an Incarnationalist look about it, but it would be a mistake to think that here he has rebuked the Calvinists with their talk of duty. For they, above all, would deny validation by works. Although there are Calvinists who would stifle imagination and demand quick results, there are others who are quite content to give the artist a great deal of slack. They do not insist upon immediate payoff or even on payoff at all; rather, they insist only upon a gracious and submissive heart, as opposed to a spirit of self-aggrandizement and indifference to the plight of humanity.

So, properly qualified, Best's position should not be that troublesome for the Calvinist. And properly construed, the Calvinist position should be tolerable to Best. This is frustrating for those of us who would draw distinctions, but it is not surprising. Important and enduring systems of Christian thought did not become so by totally ignoring vital features of Scripture and human experience. Love, obedience, imagination, appreciation for beauty, reverence—these all find support in both Calvinism and Incarnationalism. It is again, and finally, a matter of emphasis, of arrangement. One highlights responsibility, the other imagination.

Although Best does not say so in this paper, he chooses "Creationalism" over Calvinism and Incarnationalism. He finds in the doctrine of creation equal emphasis on our God image and our creatureliness. In his judgment, we err if we fail to maintain a balance between the two. His essay, when taken as a whole, shows this reluctance to join either of the two rival parties.

THE CREATION, HUMAN CREATIVITY, AND COMMUNITY

The doctrine of creation *ex nihilo* marks a point of disanalogy between the Creator and creators. This is no problem for the Incarnationalist since, as said above, every analogy contains some disanalogy.

In accepting this doctrine, Best stands against two foes, one ancient and one modern. The former may be identified with Platonism. It was Plato's conviction that there were eternal, immutable Forms or Types through which all things were made. The Form of the tree, for example, preexists all individual trees and outlives them all. It is the essence, the concept, the standard of treeness. On this model, God could only create on the basis of these Forms. The divine task was to instantiate the eternal Ideas.

Since the time of Christ, this theory has surfaced repeatedly in one form or another and has caused some serious strife. Among Christian philosophers, the controversy centers upon what is called the problem of universals. Each side has charged the other with impiety. The realists (who claim that universals or archetypes are real) claim that nominalists (those who say that only particular things are real) are materialists (those who accept only the reality of the material world). They call them relativists (deniers of fixed truth) and find their opinions at odds with belief in God's created order.

The nominalists, on the other hand, find the realists beset with foggy fictions. They warn that these universals would rival God's sovereignty and eternality. Realists respond that universals have existed as mere possibilities in the mind of God, or that God created them as well and so is not answerable to them.

Thus the controversy proceeds. As esoteric as it seems, the issue may make an important difference in one's theology. If God is obliged to work with given materials, whether physical or intellectual, then he is in the same fix as we. If God is constrained or carried along by established patterns, then he is not as independent and all-powerful as many suppose.

I am enough of a pragmatist to believe that a dispute that makes little practical difference is not worth having. I suspect that the realist/nominalist controversy can be so exposed. Whether trees are created similar to one another or to an ideal model, they still come out recognizably alike. And whether God's designs are co-eternal with his mind or are subsequently framed, he still does what he wills.

I do, however, think that Best is correct in maintaining a difference in kind between God's creative acts and ours. For God's have none of the cultural and physical limitations ours face.

The more typically modern controversy concerns not God's bondage, but our freedom. Some modern and contemporary artists presume to be "gods" at work. They believe their missions and their accomplishments to be utterly original. They are, in their own estimation, obliged and able to be free, bringing absolutely new things into existence. Best is correct in assailing this conceit. He shows the web of artistic dependency and insists upon the Creator/creator distinction.

One pertinent topic he does not discuss is that of inspiration. Given that the artist does not fashion things *ex nihilo*, where does he get his ideas? Do the wheels of his mind, laden with cultural data and innate dispositions, spin out various combinations of these resource materials? Does the Holy Spirit plant germinal notions or place full-wrought concepts into the mind of the artist? Beside the question of what occurs lies the question of facilitation. If ideas are gifts from God, how do we seek those gifts? Does God reward prayer, hard work, and desperation? Or does he hand them out inscrutably? If the workings of the mind generate ideas, how might these operations be encouraged? How does one stimulate and assist the brain or mind for creative work?

Both perspectives may be Christian. One thanks God for an image; the other thanks God for image-producing equipment.

THE IMAGINED CREATION AND HUMAN IMAGINATION

Here Best continues to treat themes set out in the second section, creation *ex nihilo* and anti-Platonism. In this section, he first puts his full weight on the Creator/creator analogy. He trusts it to support his claim that artists should not be imitators. In doing so, he clearly sides with Incarnationalists as over against Calvinists.

God, he notes, did not imitate objects at Creation; he invented them. There was "firstness" in God's acts, and his subsequent work is "representative" rather than imitative. God's example should be honored by earthly acts of originality. His works were innovative; ours should be no less.

The Calvinist will quite correctly object to the form of this argument. We cannot move directly from "God did it" to "we may (or should) do it." There are too many counter-examples in Scripture for this reasoning to succeed. God commanded Abraham to kill his son; we are not free to demand such tests of faith. God instructed an army to kill every living thing in a Canaanite town; we have no moral warrant to make such an order. God demands that we worship him; we are not free to demand that others worship us. The creatures do not have all the privileges of the Creator.

This is not to say that Best's conclusion—we ought to create and represent rather than imitate—is wrong. It is just that his method of reasoning falters. It's obvious that this is a serious difficulty for his essay, for his analogy. It seems that at the crucial point in the game, the point at which the divine model is at stake, the Calvinists hold the strong hand. The differences between us and God are too great for us automatically to justify our behavior by his. Much as parents and children have different rules, God the Father and his children often operate differently. "Do as I say and not as I do" applies. Of course, God often does as he says, but this is not necessarily the case. He does, in Christ, offer exemplary servanthood. But he demands penitence when he himself has none.

Without a supplementary principle or argument, the analogical argument cracks when Best leans on it. There is, however, a way to strengthen it. We should look more closely at the relationship between the earthly parent and the child.

Sometimes a child should emulate her parents; sometimes she should not. She should not try to drive the family car, but she should pick up her parent's honesty, patience, and charity. (Let us assume that they display these qualities.) Of course, the child may find it difficult to decide which of her parents' acts are appropriate for her. Should she also drink coffee, light fires, use the power mower, and pinch mommy on the bottom?

The family policy will favor one of two rival forms. They are, "You may unless we say no," and, "You may not unless we say yes." Following the former, parents lay down both general ("Be kind to animals." "Don't use others' property without permission.") and specific ("Don't try to move our television." "Put your crayons on the second shelf when you're through with them.") rules. When the child is faced with a new possibility, she reviews the rules, exercises her basic sense for danger and offense, and then goes ahead if the coast is clear. There are risks here, but there is also great chance for growth in ingenuity and competence. She may live to regret bathing the cat and disassembling her prize toy, but she may also hatch a new design for the family Christmas card or trap the mouse that's been worrying mother. When her parents discover her new work, they are apt to encourage her, even when the results are less than grand and she's made something of a mess. They're proud that she struck out on her own.

On the other hand, there are the parents who insist upon permission for fresh ventures. The child's agenda is passed down to her; she knows that "Daddy did it" does not form even the beginning of an excuse. She is reminded continually that she is a child and that she should wait upon parental prescriptions. She knows that if she sets up a successful lemonade stand without her parents' encouragement, she will be in trouble, regardless of the quality and success of the enterprise. Her parents will not be tickled at her initiative; they will read dangerous tendencies therein.

The first approach has an Incarnationalist flavor while the second is a bit Calvinistic. The former emphasizes broad leeway within the rules, the latter favors step-by-step guidance. Which one is correct? Both are, but in different respects.

Scripture teaches children of the Heavenly Father to consult him in all our decisions. We are told to be continually in prayer, to be ever sensitive to God's leading. Since God is always there, there is no good reason not to ask permission and leading. There is no proper occasion for strictly independent projects. And there is no time when God doesn't care what we do so long as we don't break a basic rule. God's concern is comprehensive. So the Christian artist should seek God's guidance for his day's efforts, both in the pages of Scripture and on his knees. He is, in his own estimation, a living sacrifice to God. He is not his own, for he has been bought with the blood of Christ.

He does not expect God to give precise direction in each situation, but he does approach all his choices prayerfully. He considers the missions and commitments to which he has been divinely called in a variety of ways. He prizes the stewardship of his resources and capabilities. He is alert to the nudgings of the Holy Spirit.

This is not, however, the last word. There is a place for the principle, "You may unless Father says no." This one should guide the "critic." While the Christian artist should try to find his peculiarly given task among the multitude of basically moral options, the critic (in the sense of lay, moral watchdog) has no business trying to tell him which task is his. The critic should, instead, focus upon clear departures from God's universal instructions. The critic should not suppose that the artist is being pretentious or willful when he elects to do things the critic would not have chosen to do. The critic gives the artist the benefit of the doubt within God's moral limits and does not presume to condemn the other's understanding of God's personal will for his life.

This, then, is where we may best profit from Best's analogy. As spectators we should honor the principle, "They may do it unless God forbids it; God's behavior warrants ours, unless God says otherwise." We should attend to Best's descriptions of divine behavior and assume that they are exemplary for some Christian artists. If God has done it, then the burden of proof should fall upon the one who claims that we must not do it.

In sum, the Calvinists are right to say that "God does it" does not imply "we may do it." The Calvinists are also correct to stress careful attention to God's leadership in all aspects of our lives. But the Incarnationalists are better critics because they do not presume to judge another's piety and consecration, apart from the most general moral guidelines. They understand that soul searching is best left to the individual whose soul is being searched.

Best's model is thus more useful to critics than to artists. It can enable the artist to follow God's leading more freely, but more importantly, it serves to neutralize some censors.

Let me use one other analogy to make clear the difference between artists' and critics' rules. Some believe that in sexual matters, anything goes so long as God's rules are not violated. One must avoid homosexuality, marital frigidity, fornication, cruelty, adultery, incest, etc; but there is still room for sensual exploration and invention. Others insist upon a more cautious manner. They attend to procreation and make sure not to defraud the spouse sexually. But they don't find scriptural encouragement for the exotic, so their manner is quite guarded.

The former group quite correctly defends the exotic from the critics. They champion the freedom available in sexual matters. They drive the critics back to the basic moral norms and warn them to come no further in their judgments.

The latter group, however, has an important word of counsel: just because it's morally permissible does not mean it's personally appropriate. Within the freedom given us, we must still act responsibly. For example, although a certain sexual practice may be an option for Christians in general, it does not follow that it is right for every Christian couple. Each couple should be free from outside condemnation but anxious to choose prudently from among the options which are available to Christians.

The same distinctions apply to every area of Christian life. There are things God forbids (e.g., murder). There are things which God permits but which are not right for me (e.g., becoming a missionary to Zimbabwe). Then there are things both which God permits and which are right for me (e.g., teaching at a Christian college in the 1970s).

As we consider Best's analogy, we will not find instructions for specific artists. Instead we will find general areas of permission for them which we as critics should respect. I believe Best would accept this, for on one occasion he said that worldviews don't produce artists or generate specific projects for them; rather they produce a context within which they may work.

Now, let's return for a brief look at Best's attempt to buttress his argument. He supplements the analogy with an argument which links imitation with disrespect. This case needs more work to be persuasive. How exactly does imitation deny the individual worth of the thing imitated? What insult does a diamond suffer when I produce a Zircon? This seems to be more flattery than disrespect. Is cloning the key? Do we demean the person whose uniqueness we would erase? Perhaps there's a point here, but it's not clear how this carries over to nonhuman things. If there is any disrespect to the object of imitation, it would seem to be vastly outweighed by the honor accorded it. After all, we make more artificial roses than artificial seaweed.

This grammarian's work is nasty business, but another claim bears attention—"There is nothing in the creation which remotely suggests replication or cloning." It seems, on the contrary, that there are billions of instances in which replication is not merely suggested but shouted; cell mitosis and the formation of common molecular structures give us a host of examples.

In light of all that's been said, we must conclude that there is no obligation to refrain from imitation (unless we intend to deceive), for God is not necessarily our model. Besides, it's not clear that God refrains from imitation in every case. The most we may conclude is that abstract art is an option for Christian artists. God has worked nonrepresentationally, and he's not forbidden us to do so. Christian critics then have no cause for ruling this manner of work unacceptable. Each Christian artist must, in turn, decide whether abstract work is right for her in light of God's guidance for her life.

Best's third section has virtues to offset its faults. Notice, for instance, his irenic spirit at work in the defense of both abstract and representational art. The patrons of these two styles are frequently at each others' throats. One side objects to obscurity and apparent lack of skill. The other blames artists for being copycats and sentimentalists. Best makes room for work in both contexts. First, he argues that God worked from no precedents, used no models; he was an abstract artist of sorts when he made the first sunset. Second, representational painting can be stylistically fresh, showing a new vision of something already about.

Best's impulses are good. Throughout the essay, he tries to mediate disputes, showing both parties to be correct in important respects. He chooses a both/and approach over an either/or approach—both in form and function, both intrinsic and extrinsic worth, both simplicity and complexity.

While each conciliatory gesture must be judged on its own merits, the conciliatory spirit is a rare and laudatory one in Christian discussions of the arts. Best shows that he's heard the best thoughts of the rival parties, that he's done his homework, and that he is inclined to accept good notions when he hears them.

In the technical sense, God was not an abstract artist. Best would agree with this; his choice of expression here is designed to address the words of the lay critic. The abstract movement in art took the opposite of God's approach. It sought to move beyond the particular objects of nature to the more fundamental patterns and entities. Its artists distilled from (hence the "ab" in abstract) experience what they understood to be the more general features of reality. They saw this as a purifying move.

God, on the other hand, did not work from an array of objects, discerning essences in the concrete. God created concretely; he made particular things. So it is more accurate but less striking to say that God was the first nonrepresentational artist. It is this wording that Best chooses for his sectional summary.

Finally, Best touches but does not explore a difficult topic in the arts, excellence. He associates it with stretching and differentiation, but, presumably, not all that stretches and differentiates is excellent. For instance, Nazi pageantry, architecture, decoration, film, and painting extended themes as old as Imperial Rome and was clearly distinguishable as a genre. Nevertheless, it is more tawdry and pretentious than excellent. Best may mean something more refined by "stretch" and "differentiate," but it's not clear what.

Of course, there is no shortage of writers eager to help him with his definition. Some tie excellence to a collection of aesthetic features, e.g., rhythm, organic unity, balance. Others look to payoff for the viewer—Does it sustain contemplation? Does it give pleasure? Does it fascinate? Some base it upon the artist's frame of mind, upon the nature of the creative experience itself. Still others refuse to analyze it, insisting that excellence is an irreducible, clearly discernable property in its own right. Since Best does not spell out his choice on this matter, we will let things stand with this thumbnail sketch of the options.

THE CREATION, CREATIVE STYLE, AND VOCABULARY

Calvinists picture the contemporary artist as an arrogant devotee of newness. Not content to represent the created order, this artist seeks freedom, knocks over all boundaries, and projects an alternative reality. The Calvinists counsel a more submissive spirit.

It is, then, interesting to see Best's estimate of this artist. Instead of crashing through old frontiers, this artist seems to be cowed by his own precedent. Instead of enjoying praise for bold departures from his norm, he's charged with vacillation.

Now a Calvinist might argue that imagination is fine per se, but that in this age of radical experimentation and flux, we simply throw gasoline on the fire when we encourage imagination. We should temper rather than celebrate it.

Best, however, suggests that artists are more commonly stodgy and fearful, and we would do well to encourage boldness and flexibility. Whether an artist shifts from or to a more traditional manner of work, she should have the courage of her artistic convictions. Best's claim that God's multifarious work is pertinent to our case is well taken. God's creation shows dazzling variety, and God does not demand narrowness of us. We may take this as permission to be flexible in our choice of projects.

On the other hand, Best's claim that there is a common personal style in all God's creation is puzzling. It may be there, but it's hard to say just what this style might be. Best doesn't tell us. Perhaps Best means a careful attention to detail or to both form and function. Perhaps he means that there are repeated applications of certain basic engineering principles, such as those in hydraulics and aerodynamics.

At any rate, it doesn't seem to be crucial. So what if there are shifts in style? Or, if one cannot alter his stylistic fingerprints no matter how much surface variety there may be in his work, then what use is there in either encouraging or discouraging stylistic integrity? If unity of style can be traced throughout something as varied as nature, then is the notion of style so broad as to be useless?

THE CREATION, INTRINSIC WORTH, AND FUNCTION

In this section, Best makes a nice point, but he leaves the grammarians new reason to fret. He sketches the battle lines in the form/function war and notes that both totalitarian regimes and the Christian community favor preachy, strictly functional art. He then shows that both the beauty of creation and the institution of high art are functionally laden. His aim is to repudiate ideologies which are indifferent to either form or function. Again, he shows a conciliatory rather than a partisan spirit.

It's interesting, though, that he doesn't claim a mandate for Christian artists always to integrate form and function. After all, God's creation is so integrated: all has beauty; all has function. But Best concludes that form and function should be separated freely or joined at any time. How can this be when the divine model shows nothing but union?

To continue in the role of grammarian, I don't see the problem in claiming that one part of creation is more beautiful than another. Can we speak meaningfully of beauty when we maintain that a hyena is as beautiful as a gazelle, that a baboon is as beautiful as a tiger? Wouldn't it be better to say that every aspect of creation is admirable or engaging rather than beautiful?

His treatment of "witness art" is also puzzling. Why exactly is the gospel particular and art general? "Whosoever will" seems to be quite general, and certain art (e.g., satire) can be deadly particular. As before, Best's fundamental observation is helpful, but his subsequent discussion raises problems.

THE CREATION AND THROW-AWAY CREATIVITY

This is a lovely and edifying section. It should serve as an antidote to slapdash commercialism in art. Best's "rough work"/"finish work" analogy is apt and memorable.

God does indeed demonstrate the ideal in his creative work, but we must not forget the difficulties in moving from the divine case to ours. God suffers no limits in time, materials, intelligence, or power. So God's products, whether pancreas or willow tree, are "finish work." We do not, however, enjoy God's powers and resources. We are often compelled to "make do," to "jerry rig." We are not always in a position to insist upon the very best. There are deadlines to meet, publics to be served, shortages for which to compensate.

The artist who only does "finish work" may, on occasion, neglect a proper task. A composer should be willing to scratch out a silly and utterly forgettable song for a party. A painter should be willing to spend a few moments on a publicity banner whose usefulness and quality are strictly limited. An instrumentalist should be willing to play without the best equipment if the situation dictates. That which is apropos is not always finely crafted, though even within the realm of improvisation there are degrees of excellence.

The point to the divine model is not, then, always to do perfect work. Rather, we should always do the best we can with the resources and time that we have. This is what God did, though, of course, he had no limits. We have fewer resources and should be content to do less marvelous work when necessary. It is unbecoming for a finite creature always to be "above" rough work. By way of analogy, there is a time both for the "meatball" surgery of the battlefield and for the refined and cautious work of the peacetime operating room. The battlefield surgeon who insists upon working deliberately and delicately is as irresponsible as the peacetime surgeon who does a rush job.

THE CREATION, SIMPLICITY, AND COMPLEXITY

Best's case is strong here because he deals in permission rather than obligation. Creation shows both simplicity and complexity. Who are we, then, to disparage either? Both involve artistic excellence.

In thoroughly Christian fashion, he attacks the cult of inaccessibility. He observes that "total inaccessibility is essentially chaos," so we may not say that all motion away from the popular is good. I might add that Christian artists intent upon the cryptic are hard put to show wherein they serve with love.

KENOSIS AND ARTISTIC CREATIVITY

The lesson of this section might be better tailored to the preceding section. In that one, Best gave simplicity and complexity equal value. In this one, he suggests that the move from oratorio to hymn is a step down, albeit an acceptable one. Wouldn't it be better to say that the emptying can occur when the artist moves from the arena in which there are personal comfort and honor to that in which there are dangers and difficulties? For some, hymns are the realm of heavenly security and sure esteem. Their servant mission might take them to the foreign territory of the oratorio.

At any rate, Best's application of Philippians 2:5–11 is an important one. Although he highlights the Incarnation, his message of servanthood is quite Calvinistic. The Calvinist would, I think, press him at one point. Best seems to say that one may move in and out of the servant mode while on earth. The Calvinist would insist that Christ retained the form of the servant unto death, that his exaltation or refilling was eschatological and not periodic.

I hope that my appreciation for Best's project is clear. I believe that God's example is important for artists, but that it must be tailored for human use. Best has helped us see God's work with new clarity. We must decide what to make of it. Perhaps my comments will help in this task. [1]

1. A helpful book on concerns related to Best's essay and my response is Nicholas Wolterstorff, *Art in Action* (Grand Rapids: Eerdmans, 1980).

Philosophy

COMMENTARY

In his essay Evans addresses a problem that has been common property of the philosophical community for millennia, namely, "Why be moral?" Evans interprets this as a request for reasons that justify doing one's moral duty. After criticizing several perennial responses to the question, he elaborates a version of what he calls the "popular" answer, divine rewards and punishments. While admitting that certain versions of this answer are philosophically defective, Evans argues that adequate conceptions of God, heaven, and human nature make the popular view defensible. By conceiving the relationships between the concepts of morality, God, and heaven as fundamental and internal (he explains and uses the word *intrinsic*), Evans seeks to show that to choose morality may be conceived as choosing God.

Evans summarizes his argument as follows:

1. Rewards which are intrinsic to an activity provide a reason to perform that activity which in no way despoils the character of the activity.
2. If heaven is understood as the enjoyment of the presence of God (both in this life and afterward), and God is understood as the ontological realization of that love which is the heart of moral striving, then heaven provides a reason to be moral.
3. If God has created every human being with a need for himself, then every human being has a reason to be moral.

Therefore, Evans concludes that divine rewards can provide a reason to be moral.

In his response Reid suggests that there is another way to conceptualize what it means to be moral, and therefore another possible response to the question "Why should I be moral?" Reid suggests that Evans is overly preoccupied with the language of duty and that the Christian theist needs to complement Evans's concerns with an equal concern for the "language of virtue," meaning a concern with those attitudes, inclinations, and dispositions that ought to characterize the Christian.

Reid claims that Evans misses this emphasis because of an incomplete set of theological beliefs that form the presuppositions for his position. In Reid's view Evans restricts himself to those beliefs common to all theists without going on to include those beliefs that are specifically Christian.

Reid claims that this larger set of theological presuppositions suggests an alternative answer to the question "Why should I be moral?" The foundation of the moral life is Jesus Christ. He exemplifies "the life of a distinct human personality with characteristic virtues: reverence, faith, hope, self-giving love, forgiveness, thanksgiving, joy, and peace." Reid goes on to assert that *"knowing* what it is to be moral and *becoming* a morally worthy person are inseparable from a personal trust in Jesus Christ."

In terms of the introductory taxonomy, Evans's paper provokes some interesting observations. The philosophical enterprise accepts substantive (or ontological) disagreements as a matter of course. Such disagreement is simply grist for the philosophical mill. In this sense there is no such thing as the transformation of substantive assumptions in philosophy proper. There are, however, historically identifiable traditions in philosophy which have their own shared substantive assumptions and favored ways of arguing.

Now it appears that both Evans and Reid find the methodological assumptions of philosophy proper compatible with their Christian faith, and both enter into the philosophical fray with ontological assumptions that may not be popularly shared by other professional philosophers. Yet each of these writers espouses a different tradition in ethics. Evans's tradition emphasizes moral *duty,* while Reid's emphasizes moral *character.* This indeed leads them to differing reasons for being moral, and in both cases those reasons are articulated in terms of the wider tradition in ethics which they represent. Having identified the features of these approaches which our authors find compatible with their faith, it is important to note that each seeks to transform his tradition to some extent by taking seriously theistic or Christian elements that are not necessarily shared by other philosophers in that tradition. In this respect Reid's conclusion that the Christian's reasons for being moral lie in personal trust in Christ transform more radically the ethical tradition he reflects, both in substance and in the nature of justification, than is the case for Evans.

Could Divine Rewards Provide a Reason to Be Moral?

C. STEPHEN EVANS

THE QUESTION AND TYPES OF PHILOSOPHICAL ANSWERS

The question "Why should I be moral?" embodies a philosophical quandary which moral philosophers from Plato to Baier, Gewirth, and Donagan have attempted to resolve. To most people it appears that doing one's moral duty sometimes requires a person to act in a manner contrary to self-interest. Why should the individual be willing to sacrifice self-interest in such a case?

A variety of types of answers have been presented in response to this question. One type of answer consists in denying the legitimacy of the question. One's moral duty is precisely what should be done without question. To demand a reason for being moral is to be immoral. I shall term this line of thought the "autonomy response." The trouble with the autonomy response is that it appears to imply that moral action is irrational or nonrational, since no reason for such action can be given. An alternative version of this answer insists that to say that an action is moral *is* to give the reason for performing the action and that the question "Why be moral" is therefore meaningless. It is difficult, however, for the individual who is contemplating a moral action which will cost him severely to see what is meaningless about wondering why he should perform the action, even though he already understands that the action is his moral duty.

A type of response which I shall designate the "eudaemonistic response" consists in arguing that morality and self-interest are only apparently divergent, or only divergent in the short run. Morality really is in the individual's interest ultimately. The trouble with this line of thought is that it does not appear to be true always. Even if following morality generally does benefit the individual, it is not hard to think of cases in which doing one's duty seems to lead to a net loss of well-being for the agent in question. In addition to this problem, the eudaemonistic response appears to collapse the distinction between moral action and self-interested action. To many philosophers, notably Kant, the person who is moral only because she thinks morality will "pay off" is not truly moral.

A type of answer which I shall term the "altruistic response" claims that we may have a nonegoistic reason for following morality. Prichard, for example, holds that the desire to do what is right provides a reason for being moral, and he denies that acting on such a desire is acting egoistically.[1] Francis Hutcheson claims that humans have natural feelings of benevolence or goodwill to others, and that these feelings are not grounded in self-love.[2] Such feelings therefore provide a nonegoistic reason for moral action. I think that Prichard and Hutcheson are right in arguing that actions based on such desires are nonegoistic in character, but there are still problems with this type of response.

Let us assume that it is true that moral people have a desire to do what is right and have natural feelings of benevolence for others. This might give them a reason for acting morally. However, two serious problems are left: (1) In addition to their altruistic inclinations, moral people, like everyone else, also have selfish inclinations. The existence of the altruistic inclinations may provide a reason for acting morally, but the existence of the selfish inclinations will also provide a reason for acting immorally. No reason to prefer the moral reasons to the immoral reasons has been given. (2) The desire to do what is right and feelings of benevolence are noticeably lacking or diminished in very evil people. Hence, on this account, they have little or no reason to be moral. This theory implies therefore that moral people have reasons for being moral, but immoral people do not; hence, immoral people cannot be charged with acting unreasonably. If one believes that moral obligations hold for all, this seems to be an undesirable result.

Other types of answers than these three are possible, but these are probably the most common. I do not here claim to have shown that any of these answers is unsatisfactory. (Indeed, I shall argue that there is a satisfactory eudaemonistic answer, which embodies the most important features of an altruistic answer.) However, none of the three appears to be without difficulties, and we may safely conclude that the question "Why be moral?" is a deservedly troubling one.

THE "POPULAR" ANSWER: WHY PHILOSOPHERS REJECT IT

In the face of this perplexing situation it is surprising that philosophers have not paid more attention to the answer which the "average" person

1. H. A. Prichard, "Duty and Interest," in *Moral Obligations and Duty and Interest* (London: Oxford University Press, 1968), pp. 224–26.
2. Francis Hutcheson, "An Inquiry Concerning Moral Good and Evil," in *British Moralists, 1650–1800*, ed. D. D. Raphael (London: Oxford University Press, 1969), pp. 268–78.

gives to the question. I think it would be admitted by skeptics and religious believers alike that most people who believe in God (and the great majority of people do) believe that one of God's main "functions," so to speak, is serving as a moral judge. God is supposed to reward the virtuous and punish the vicious. If this belief is true, then it certainly would appear to provide a reason of sorts to be moral. This would be a eudaemonistic answer in that it would imply that ultimately it always is in the best interest of the individual to be moral.

Why have philosophers found this popular answer uninviting? One reason sometimes given is that it is claimed that belief in God is not psychologically effective. Divine rewards and punishments, coming after death, seem so far away that they frequently fail to deter even believers from doing wrong. It is difficult to say how psychologically effective belief in God as moral judge is in producing moral behavior, but it does not matter very much because this point is logically irrelevant. The question as to whether God's existence provides an adequate sanc-tion to produce moral behavior is logically distinct from the question as to whether God's existence makes moral action reasonable. Since human beings do not always behave reasonably, God might well provide an excellent reason for moral behavior even if most people continued to behave immorally.

A second criticism of the popular answer is that it is undesirable to make the reasonableness of morality depend upon God, since many people do not believe in God and some even find belief in God to be positively unreasonable. No doubt it is true that many people would prefer a nonreligious reason for being moral. However, the existence of this preference does not guarantee that it can be satisfied. In any case, even atheists might find it interesting to consider the question as to whether God would provide a reason for being moral *if* God existed. This sort of question is a standard form for many philosophical issues. True, people who do not believe in God may not be as interested in this question as others, but that is a psychological fact about them. The question retains whatever intrinsic interest it may have for skeptics and believers alike. And it must not be forgotten that most people do believe in God and find it reasonable to do so. It cannot therefore be claimed that the question of whether God provides a reason to be moral, if God exists, is an esoteric one with no living interest.

Also, it ought to be noted that one type of reason often given for belief in God is the moral argument. It is obvious that the question of whether God's existence provides a reason to be moral may be relevant to the success of some forms of this argument. (I do not claim that this factor alone would determine the success of the argument.) Therefore, to fail even to consider whether God provides a reason to be moral on the grounds that belief in God is unreasonable is an unreasonable procedure. It amounts to refusing to consider what *may* be evidence for the truth of a belief on the grounds that we have no evidence for the truth of the belief.

The third reason frequently given by philosophers for rejecting God as an answer to the question "Why be moral?" seems to me to be the most serious and substantive. This is the general problem with all eudaemonistic answers, which is that they appear to reduce morality to self-interest and thereby collapse the distinction between moral and nonmoral or even immoral behavior. This objection is weighty because its roots lie in the religious tradition, which often has insisted that truly moral behavior is behavior which is done with no thought of a possible reward. The moral person is the one who does what is right regardless of the personal outcome. This seems to imply that God could provide a reason to act morally only at the cost of undermining the moral character of the act. If God's existence is to provide a reason for being moral, this difficulty must be surmounted.

INTRINSIC AND EXTRINSIC REWARDS

To deal with this problem it must be remembered that this difficulty is a general one which applies to eudaemonistic answers in general. So, before attempting to decide whether God could provide a reward for moral action which would not compromise the character of the action, let us ask the more general question of whether any type of reward could provide a reason for moral action while leaving the character of the action unsullied.

If one looks at human action in many areas, rather than just morality, a distinction can be drawn between two types of rewards. Imagine two young people who are both seeking to become concert pianists. These two musicians are equally talented and have worked equally hard at their profession. Their motivations, however, are different. The first pianist wants to be a concert pianist because of the money, fame, and adulation such a position will bring him. The second musician is simply in love with music. She derives intense satisfaction merely from playing beautiful music well, and wants to be a concert pianist because she knows this will challenge her to continue to grow toward her maximum potential as a musician.

Both of these musicians can reasonably be described as seeking personal rewards through their endeavors. The rewards, however, are of different types. The first musician's reward is extrinsically or externally related to the musical activity which is supposed to lead to the reward. The second musician's reward is simply the satisfaction gained from the activity itself. This reward is internally or intrinsically related to the activity in question. Similar examples from other fields can be given. Think of the contrast between a young man who truly loves a woman and gains pleasure from pleasing her and a man who hopes to make his fortune by marrying the daughter of a rich family.

To generalize, one can distinguish between intrinsic and extrinsic rewards. A person who is motivated by an extrinsic reward is not truly devoted to the activity by which he hopes to gain the reward. He regards that activity as a mere means. The person who seeks an intrinsic reward is in a different position, however. The satisfaction the lover of music knows will be gained from music does not mean that the lover is not truly devoted to music but the very reverse. It is only because she truly cares about music that she can gain the satisfaction.

This distinction is equally relevant to moral action. Clearly there is a great difference between a person who takes deep personal satisfaction simply from living righteously and the person who thinks that a moral life will lead to an external reward, whether that reward be thought of as this-worldly social popularity, or dancing girls in an after-life paradise. The reward which is intrinsic or internal to moral action in no way takes away from the merit of the action. In fact, we regard a person who acts virtuously *and* takes satisfaction from so acting as morally superior to someone who performs a duty grudgingly. It is Kant's failure to take full account of this that leads some people to find fault with his theory. Perhaps the point of people like Prichard and Hutcheson is similar to this. Someone who gains satisfaction from moral action itself does indeed have a reason to be moral. Morality is clearly connected with personal happiness without moral action being reduced to self-interested action. Someone who acts morally because of the intrinsic rewards of the moral life in no way regards morality as simply a means to an ulterior end. The happiness gained is because of a true devotion to duty.

GOD AS INTRINSIC REWARD OF MORAL ACTION

I have argued that we must distinguish between intrinsic and extrinsic rewards for moral action, and that an intrinsic reward provides a reason for acting morally which does not compromise the purity of the moral life. Does this have any relevance to the question of whether God could provide a reason to be moral?

On the surface the answer may appear to be No. Many religious believers hold that the rewards and punishments which are the result of moral and immoral actions consist largely of after-life experiences. God is conceived as an agent who rewards the virtuous (heaven) and punishes the vicious (hell) with external-type sanctions. Heaven has streets of gold and hell contains a lake of fire. On such a reading heaven and hell do not seem to be connected internally with the moral life and the rewards and punishments God provides seem to be extrinsic to morality.

However, a deeper look at the religious tradition reveals that this is a superficial view. The theologian and the saint agree that what is truly blessed about heaven is the experience of being present with God, an experience of which the believer is supposed to have foretastes even now. It is not dancing girls or streets of gold but God's presence which makes heaven desirable. Conversely, what is truly horrible about hell (or extinction) is that human beings are cut off from God's presence in such a state. Fire and brimstone are rightly to be interpreted as symbols of the misery of being separated from God. God is not just an agent who arranges heaven and hell for deserving creatures. Finding God *is* heaven; losing God *is* hell.

Why is God's presence a reward and his absence misery? Surely most believers would respond that it is God's character which makes his presence a reward, meaning by character particularly God's holiness or righteousness, though not limiting the concept to that. Furthermore, the religious believer does not regard the connection between God and righteousness to be external or contingent. God is essentially and necessarily good, and as Creator is the ultimate source of all goodness. Someone who wishes to be morally good and wishes a relationship with God does not want two externally and contingently related things.

This point is well illustrated in the New Testament in the first letter of John. The writer of this letter tells us that God is not merely loving but love itself. "God is love, and whoever lives in love lives in God and God lives in him" (1 John 4:16). "If someone says 'I love God' yet hates his brother, he is a liar" (1 John 4:20). "Dear friends! Let us love one another, for love comes from God. Whoever loves is a child of God and knows God. Whoever does not love does not know God, because God is love" (1 John 4:7–8, all refs. TEV).

Admittedly, it is difficult to understand and interpret these sayings. However, the philosopher who wishes to evaluate a religious tradition must accurately represent that tradition. Without raising the metaphysical question of whether it is proper to think of love as an ontological principle identical with God, one can take the writer of this letter to be making at least the following claims: (1) God is himself essentially loving in his character. (2) God is in some sense the source of all human love. (3) A person who loves fellow human beings thereby becomes more like God and more able to commune with God and enjoy God's presence. (4)

Someone who loves thereby draws closer to God, whether knowingly or not. (5) Someone who truly draws closer to God necessarily becomes more loving.

The love which is discussed here is, I believe, an active concern for the well-being of others, not a mere sentimental feeling, and this sort of love can plausibly be argued to lie at the heart of true moral character. If this is so, then the claims made in John's letter, taken collectively, may be read as implying that the rewards and punishments which the religious believer seeks and fears are not extrinsic to morality after all. The chief reward for moral action is the experience of God's presence. God's presence is a reward because the truly moral person is the one who values righteousness supremely, and God is both the source of righteousness and its highest exemplification. From the believer's perspective, the individual who truly loves God necessarily loves righteousness, since that is God's essential character, and the individual who loves righteousness necessarily loves God, even if he does not know this. One might say that the personality of the latter is such that he necessarily *would* enjoy God's presence if such an experience were possible.

From this perspective divine rewards and punishments are no longer arbitrary or contingently connected with moral activity. God can and ought to reward the just with heaven because they are the only ones who can enjoy heaven. To an immoral person God's presence would be torture. In fact, hell is perhaps best defended as an expression of divine mercy. Though to the righteous being separated from God, the source of all righteousness, is a horrible fate, to someone who hates virtue separation from God, who is pure love, might be a kindness which would spare the unrighteous the greater torment of experiencing God's overwhelming goodness.

The critic might respond at this point that, however closely linked God and moral righteousness might be, they can still be distinguished. Doing one's duty is one thing; enjoying the presence of God after death another. By this the critic means to imply that the connection between God and an eternal happiness still retains an element of contingency. Someone who is moral because she hopes to see God is still externally motivated. The response to this requires several points.

First, it is always possible analytically to distinguish a reward from the action which leads to the reward. This is possible even in the case of an intrinsic reward, but it in no way despoils the character of the action that leads to the reward. Striving to become a great musician and finding satisfaction in the process are distinguishable, and the connection between the two is contingent in some senses. For many people no such connection exists. However, someone who *does* find that the attainment of musical excellence leads to happiness certainly has a reason for striving to achieve that excellence which in no way undermines his commitment to music. The reason this is so is that making fine music and enjoying that activity form a natural whole or unity.

Implicit in our foregoing account is the claim that enjoying God's presence and acting morally also form such a natural whole or unity. What this means is that the moral agent who finds moral action satisfying is already enjoying "a taste of heaven." Heaven must be understood as a continuation and intensification of experiences which occur at times in human life already. Thus the individual who is striving to act according to love *and* finds this satisfying is, whether she is fully aware of this or not, already encountering God's presence and enjoying it. And that is "heaven," as we have defined it.

At present it appears to us that moral action and heaven are two contingently connected events, but the individual *should* see this reward as part of a natural whole with moral striving. In an after-life heaven the individual will actualize righteousness continuously and will clearly understand that in doing so he is getting to "see God." At this point, perhaps, the *appearance* that moral action and heaven are arbitrarily connected will vanish. With a deeper understanding of righteousness and the unity of God and righteousness, the individual will realize that moral activity on earth and the satisfaction it provided were the *beginnings* of a process which has now reached its fulfillment. He now sees that taking satisfaction in goodness was, all along, taking satisfaction in God.

In summary, my response to the objection is that the connection between heaven and moral action, though contingent in some senses, is by no means arbitrary. Heaven, understood as the enjoyment of God's presence, is already experienced when an individual takes joy in goodness. The ground of this is the believer's conviction that God and righteousness are not contingently connected. God *is* love.

To say that the individual may experience tastes of heaven in the here and now is by no means to depreciate the after-life reward, however. For heaven in the traditional sense is still the culmination of the process. This hope of a full realization of what is only tasted in this life gives true meaning to the moral life, a true "reason to be moral." The satisfactions of the moral life can now be valued, not only for their own sake, but as evidence that the individual is properly preparing for an eternal life which exhibits those qualities and possesses those satisfactions.

For the believer these connections are not fully grasped as long as we "see in a mirror dimly." For the believer, too, heaven and moral action can appear to be arbitrarily conjoined. But she struggles to believe what she thinks will one day be clear: that when one chooses love one chooses God, and that finding a life based on love satisfying is to be satisfied by one's Creator. God's presence can be conceived as a reward which is internally connected to the activity which leads to it. Heaven in the sense of an after-life reward is not a "wholly other" experience, but the culmination and completion of a process which has already begun and which clearly forms a "natural whole" with moral action.

CREATION: GOD AND HUMAN NATURE

At this point I believe a secular humanist might respond that my argument, even if successful, does not show that God provides *the* reason for being moral, but only *a* reason. My argument that God provides a reason for being moral rests on the notion of an intrinsic reward for moral action. I have tried to show that God's presence may be conceived as such an intrinsic reward, and that it is reasonable to think of the experience of God's presence as the outcome of moral action. This certainly does not establish that an intrinsic reward for moral action must be conceived in this way. A nonbeliever who takes intrinsic satisfaction from living a moral life would appear to have a valid reason for moral action, and she would appear to have this whether or not God exists.[3]

This humanist point is sound. People who take satisfaction from living morally do have a reason for living morally, regardless of the truth of any religious doctrine. Problems still remain, however, for such a view. These are the problems which arose in connection with the altruistic view of why one should be moral. It is true that a person who finds the moral life satisfying has a reason to be moral, but only the virtuous person finds the moral life to be such, at least on the surface. Essentially, people who truly want to be moral seem to have a reason for being moral, but people who do not want to be virtuous do not. Even people who want to be moral and therefore have a reason to be moral may also want to be immoral and therefore have a reason to be immoral.

Is the religious answer to the question "Why be moral?" superior here? As I have sketched out that answer, it might appear to be in the same predicament, since God is conceived as an intrinsic reward for moral action, whose presence is a reward only to the person who loves virtue. So it would seem that God provides a reason to be moral only to those who care about morality.

What this problem makes clear is that if God is to provide a *superior* reason to be moral, his existence cannot be conceived as just "one more fact" in a universe which otherwise resembles that which the naturalist

3. However, it should be noted that on the religious view the satisfaction gained from moral living will be eternal in character, since the moral life itself is eternal, which might imply that the believer's reason for moral action is superior to the reasons of those who believe that the moral life and its intrinsic satisfactions are only finite in character.

accepts. However, within the Jewish and Christian traditions it is obviously inappropriate to consider God's existence as such an isolated fact. The concept of God is the concept of a being who created the heavens and the earth and who made human beings in his image to commune with him. To discuss the existence of God is therefore also to discuss whether the heavens and the earth have the characteristic of being dependent on God for their existence, and whether human beings, by virtue of their nature, are intended to resemble God in his righteousness and commune with him.

If it is true that humanity was created to glorify God and commune corporately with him, and that therefore human purpose includes as an essential element moral activity and the communion with God and one's fellows which is the satisfactory end of such activity, then it is eminently reasonable to hold that human nature is such that *true* human happiness and well-being is always bound up with the moral life in the long run.[4] The immoral individual may not desire the presence of God, but that attitude is foolish and unreasonable, for it cuts the person off from the happiness and well-being for which his own created nature is suited and was destined.

In short, if the Judaeo-Christian God exists, then this entails certain universal psychological truths. Finally and ultimately, happiness cannot be gained apart from experiencing God, and one cannot experience God's presence without a concern for moral righteousness. In this way, I believe the popular view is correct that God, if real, provides a universal reason to be moral, a reason valid for everyone and valid at all times and therefore superior to that offered by the secular humanist. When it is seen that the truth of God's existence entails certain other truths about human nature, it is clear why God's existence makes moral action reasonable. Of course, assuming that God does exist, the person who does not believe in God might not realize that the moral life is reasonable in this way, but that would merely be a defect in the person's knowledge.

In conclusion let me try to summarize the points I have made and connections I have drawn:

1. Rewards which are intrinsic to an activity provide a reason to perform that activity which in no way despoils the character of the activity.

4. The religious believers may here take the contentions of people like Hutcheson and Prichard that there is a connection between moral action and satisfaction which is not egoistic as best explained by the fact that human beings are God's creatures. The psychological links between happiness and an altruistic life which are empirically evident at least help to make believable the claim that such links are ultimately universal.

2. If heaven is understood as the enjoyment of the presence of God (both in this life and afterward), and God is understood as the ontological realization of that love which is the heart of moral striving, then heaven provides a reason to be moral.

3. If God has created every human being with a need for himself, then every human being has a reason to be moral.

In response to this, the humanist might still claim that there is some universal psychological connection between moral action and happiness which holds independently of any religious doctrine. Presumably, one would have to show empirically that it is impossible for an immoral person to be happy and conceptions of happiness which allow for such a possibility are mistaken. Such an undertaking may be possible, but I am skeptical that such a psychological thesis can be defended unless it is given some kind of theological or metaphysical grounding.

Of course the psychological thesis which underlies the religious tradition here must be open to empirical testing as well. It is appropriate to examine the lives of saints and sinners, as well as one's own experience, to decide whether true happiness is connected with moral activity and communion with God. My own convictions are that such a psychological thesis can neither be conclusively proven nor disproven empirically. However, someone who had independent reasons to believe in God, and also believed that humanity was created in God's image, might well make a reasonable claim that the empirical evidence is at least consistent with the belief that her ultimate happiness is linked to the development of her moral character. To the extent that this line of action actually brought that person happiness and fulfillment, one could reasonably judge her belief to be, at least in part, empirically confirmed.

Is There an Alternative Reason to Divine Rewards for Being Moral?

MALCOLM A. REID

It is widely believed by lay people that philosophers spend much of their time reconsidering perennial, very general, and quite mystifying questions of dubious importance. The question "Why should I be moral?" would almost certainly be regarded by Evans's "average" person as a particularly choice example. Evans clearly agrees that it is an ancient philosophical quandary,[1] but he does not think it is a question either uninteresting or unimportant.[2] He thinks that the question "Why should I be moral?" should and can be answered.[3] Furthermore he has undertaken to elaborate and defend the superiority of what he takes to be *the* answer, namely, that if God rewards the virtuous and punishes the vicious, then that belief is itself a sufficient reason to be moral. The central aim of his essay is to show that divine rewards, properly understood, provide a better reason for being moral than does any other reason.

1. Plato did not pose the question "Why should I be moral?" but asked, "Why should anyone be just, courageous, etc.?" or alternatively, "Is it rational to be just, courageous, etc.?" Both Plato and Aristotle and later many Christian moralists not only argued that it was rational but that these virtues and others were together necessary if human beings were to flourish, or achieve eudaemonia. While Plato would have agreed with Evans that reasons can be given for being virtuous, he would not (1) have given Evans's reasons, nor (2) would he have agreed that "being moral" is primarily a matter of finding out our duties and doing them. Cf. William Frankena, *Thinking About Morality* (Ann Arbor, MI: University of Michigan Press, 1980), pp. 12, 78.

2. Many moral philosophers would agree with the judgment of Tom Beauchamp that the question "Can the claim that one ought to be moral be justified?" is one of "the three most general and important metaethical questions." The other two are, "Can answers about what is morally good and right be justified?" and "What are facts and values, and what role do they play in moral justification?" *Philosophical Ethics* (New York: McGraw-Hill, 1982), p. 305.

3. Not all philosophers believe that this question can be justified by advancing non-moral *reasons*. For example, Beauchamp, following Sartre, suggests that our decisions about normative moral issues may in the end be based on "whether we have a sufficiently strong *desire* to live the moral life—a stronger desire than to live some alternative form of life" and that it "may not be a rationally defensible desire at all" (ibid., p. 332). He, therefore, rejects the self-confessedly unprovable claim of William Frankena that rational persons would choose to be moral if they had a comprehensive view of the nature and consequences of living a moral life (*Thinking About Morality*, pp. 82–94).

In the present essay I will not argue that Evans's project fails. I think that if any theist holds as true just that set of beliefs about the existence and attributes of God and about God's relationship to and intentions for humanity that Evans identifies, then divine rewards are a reason for anyone to be moral. I will argue, however, that there is a different, although not necessarily contradictory, reason that the "average" *Christian* theist could give other than "divine rewards." It is both possible and important to do this because the set of religious beliefs upon which Evans relies are precisely not those beliefs *within* the larger web of Christian theistic beliefs that distinguish a *Christian* worldview from one that is *theistic,* yet not Christian. This is not to say that the view Evans has presented is sub-Christian, let alone non-Christian. Neither is the case. So far as I can see the beliefs he identifies are all major strands of that larger web. But there are other strands that anchor the web, beliefs that center on the life, death, and resurrection of Jesus Christ and on his reconciliation of humanity to God that might suggest to the "average" Christian a different answer to the original question, "Why should I be moral?"

In addition to these theological matters there are philosophical considerations that at this point lead me not to propose a different reason for being moral but to interpret what it means "to be moral" in a way that is different, though again not necessarily contradictory, to the understanding that Evans seems to have. I say "seems to have" because in claiming this difference I wish to acknowledge that I am less sure of what his view is. Specifying, in part at least, a general conception of what it means *to be a theist* was a necessary part of his project in a way that specifying a general conception of what it means *to be moral* was not. Nevertheless, I will try to show that a particular conception of what it means to be moral pervades Evans's essay, although the alternative view I wish to stress may also be present. Before proceeding to develop these alternative views it may be helpful first to set before the reader my interpretation of the sort of strategy Evans has employed. In doing so he has shown himself to be as exemplary in his vocation as a philosopher as he is faithful to his commitments as a Christian.

I

My analysis of Evans's strategy will have a broader and a narrower focus. In the first instance we will want to see how it is possible for Evans to be both a philosopher *and* a Christian in ways that would be recognizable, even if not in all respects acceptable, to philosophers who are *non-Christian* and to Christians who are *philosophers.* This will provide a context for looking at how this integrative intent is actually carried through in the way in which he has posed and answered a particularly knotty philosophical question.

The essay by Evans gives clear evidence that as a *Christian* philosopher he has not failed to acknowledge the fact that he holds substantive metaphysical assumptions that are different from those held by non-Christian philosophers. He is everywhere conscious of and anticipates possible objections posed by "atheists," "secular humanists," or "naturalists." It is hardly possible to be a Christian philosopher and not to be aware of such differences, though it is quite possible, and in fact not unusual, for a Christian philosopher to fail to engage his non-Christian colleagues in productive dialogue. This may happen for a number of reasons. He may think that there are few or no substantive factual or axiological assumptions which they both share; few canons of rationality held in common to which he may appeal in explaining and seeking some adjudication of their differences; few conclusions reached by non-Christian philosophers on any epistemological, ontological, or axiological problems that he could affirm. Such self-isolating denials may leave Christian beliefs intact, but they make it difficult to conceive of how such a person could function as a participant in contemporary philosophical discussion at any level. Denials of this kind often arise out of the belief that only in this way can specifically Christian affirmations be kept free from secular compromise. Evans's essay is free of such defensive denials. Theistic beliefs are self-consciously affirmed and clearly articulated, but they are introduced into a pattern of thought that *any philosopher* would accept as a fairly common sort of philosophical argument.

Philosophical questions are simultaneously intellectually interesting and baffling not just because a number of plausible answers may be given to them but even more because disagreements break out about what the question itself means or whether it "means" at all. This is certainly the case with the question Evans has set himself to answer. When persons ask, "Why ought I to be moral?" are they asking themselves why they ought to act morally as opposed to immorally, or are they looking for a nonmoral reason why they ought to live moral lives or strive to become persons of good moral character? These are logically different questions. In the first, "ought" is construed morally, in the second, nonmorally. Both ways of interpreting the question seek justification for being moral. In the first, rational justification is sought in terms of rules, principles, ideals, etc., that are *internal* to a normative moral system; in the second, rational warrant is sought in relation to beliefs that are *external* to any or all moral theories. Adopting Salmon's (1966) useful distinction, when we advance moral beliefs internal to a moral system (as when we say that this act is forbidden by this rule) we have provided *validation* for that belief: when we propose nonmoral beliefs as a reason for being moral we are seeking some form of rational *vindication* for morality itself. Evans's project is to provide a nonmoral reason why, for any individual, moral demands should take precedence over self-interest in those cases where each indicates different courses of action. He wants to explain why people should *always* act morally, especially in those cases where self-interest induces them to do otherwise. Evans is fully alert to the fact that the success of his project in large part depends upon how convincingly he has shown that an appeal to "divine rewards" is not, as some non-Christian philosophers have argued, merely a disguised appeal to self-interest. [4] Complicating things further is the claim of some philosophers that the most serious issue regarding the question "Why should I be moral?" is not whether a certain answer to it is correct but whether it is itself a meaningful question. [5] Evans is convinced that it is and that ordinary people too are concerned to know whether there are any good reasons for them to adopt a moral rather than an egoistic point of view. For him, however, the main controversy *is* over "whether a certain answer to it is correct."

We need now to look more closely at how Evans's essay is instructive for understanding the constructive task of the Christian philosopher. How does Evans set about integrating Christian beliefs with his discipline? First, he does not try to show that Christian beliefs entail the rejection of any answer given by a non-Christian philosopher. The brief criticism he offers of what he takes to be the three most common answers offered by philosophers does not depend upon the truth of specifically Christian beliefs. Non-Christian philosophers have said as much. For example, Evans could have argued that a doctrine of sin understood as total depravity entails the denial of the claim made by Pritchard and Hutcheson that people have nonegoistic natural feelings of benevolence. He chooses instead to argue from our common experience of each other that since natural benevolence is neither a single nor universal condition in all people, it must fail to provide a reason for everyone to be moral.

---

4. Cf. the essays by John Hospers, "Why Be Moral?" and Kai Nielsen, "Why Should I Be Moral?" in *Readings in Ethical Theory*, ed. Wilfrid Sellars and John Hospers (Englewood Cliffs, NJ: Prentice-Hall, 1970), pp. 730–68.

5. That the question is meaningless has been argued by H. A. Pritchard in his famous essay, "Does Moral Philosphy Rest on a Mistake?" Stephen Toulmin, in *An Examination of the Place of Reason in Ethics* (London: Cambridge University Press, 1950), and Jean-Paul Sartre, in *Existentialism is a Humanism*, each argue in rather different ways that no nonmoral reason actually succeeds in providing the desired justification for being moral.

Second and more significantly, Evans shows that his own "divine rewards" theory is in fact a version of the traditional eudaemonistic answer, which is preserved from degenerating into egoism by incorporating an essential feature of the pure altruistic answer. This approach is significant because it shows that a Christian philosopher is able to affirm and incorporate the results of other philosophical inquiries into his own theory construction.

Still, this cannot be all there is to integration. We need more than a coherent combining of these two theories to tell us how the new theory would achieve the desired integration with the larger web of Christian beliefs. This is the crucial issue. Evans evidences a fine sensitivity to it at those points where he anticipates a reason non-Christian philosophers would advance for rejecting God as an answer to the question, "Why be moral?" (pp. 295, 298–99, 301).

This tactic is important to his overall strategy for at least two reasons. It quite obviously serves to sharpen our awareness of the fact that any appeal to central theistic beliefs must elicit objections from the non-theistic philosopher. It also functions to alert the Christian philosopher that not just any sort of appeal to God will succeed in avoiding the general problem with eudaemonistic theories, namely, that morality is just egoism. To do what is right merely because God will reward us is not to do it because it is right but because we want the reward. Egoism triumphs; but worse, the unity of the nature of God and divine freedom are compromised. God's omnipotence as a dispenser of extrinsic rewards is recognized, but there is no recognition of the fact that, for the Christian, morality is ultimately justified in relation to the essential goodness of God. Evans has set himself the delicate task of showing that the popular "divine rewards" reason can be construed in such a way that it avoids both the morally objectionable consequence of reducing moral reasoning to a mere matter of self-interested prudential calculation and the theologically damaging outcome of regarding God as simply instrumental to human satisfaction.

Each of these unwanted consequences will be avoided, Evans argues, (1) if there is a real distinction to be observed between intrinsic or internal and extrinsic or external rewards, and (2) if divine rewards are understood as internal to and never external to moral motivation and action. In moral terms this distinction amounts to establishing the difference between that person who takes satisfaction from having lived morally and the person who lives morally in order to obtain rewards (like honor or wealth) that are external to the moral act. When God is conceived as a reward for being moral, it is not because he promises future rewards to the moral and future punishment to the immoral, but because God is himself, by virtue of his righteousness, a present reward for being moral. Evans is well aware that a logical distinction of this kind does nothing to establish the truth of the latter claim. It is here that he acknowledges his acceptance of just those metaphysical truth claims that are among the basic beliefs that distinguish a theistic from a naturalistic worldview. These are at least four: (1) God exists; (2) God is essentially and necessarily good; (3) God is the ultimate source of all goodness; and (4) God has created human beings such that they are moral beings who ultimately cannot find true satisfaction except as they love all that is morally good. This last belief does not, of course, entail that everyone whose acts are habitually or usually morally good will actually or necessarily experience happiness as a concommitant satisfaction in this life. This may not happen for a number of reasons. First, even among theists "happiness" may be variously interpreted.[6] Second, someone may be quite clear theoretically that "when one chooses love one chooses God, and that finding a life based on love satisfying is to be satisfied by one's Creator" and yet experience evils, not at all of her own making, so severe that such satisfaction must be of the nature of a "conviction of things not seen."

Finally, it is worth emphasizing that Evans is not content to argue that "divine rewards" as he defines that notion is merely one among a number of different but generally adequate reasons that might equally well satisfy anyone seeking a sufficient nonmoral reason for being moral. His is a stronger thesis. The theistic answer is *superior* to any nontheistic answer. He maintains that this is true even if one grants, as he does, that anyone who finds living morally satisfying has a reason for being moral regardless of the truth or falsity of theistic beliefs.

What does Evans present to support the truth of this strong thesis? How plausible is his case? He is quite clear that it won't do for the theist to give a similar reason to the one just mentioned. That is, he cannot rest content with saying that fellowship with God provides a reason to be moral only to those who care about morality. This move would fall victim to the criticism he has already advanced against the pure altruist answer, namely, that the vindication it offers for being moral is less than universal. Anyone who does not want to be moral has no reason to be so. To avoid this development Evans now emphasizes the importance of the last two of the four basic beliefs mentioned earlier. That God exists and

6. The word *happiness* is notoriously ambiguous: Among other things it has been taken to mean (1) "getting what you want," (2) "experience of joy or delight," and (3) "contentment or peace of mind." The language Evans uses to describe his intrinsic divine rewards version of eudaemonism accords with (2) and (3) and even with (1) so long as it is not understood egoistically.

that God is essentially good are necessary but not sufficient conditions for making good the claim that God is *the* reason for being moral. It is necessary to add that God is the creator of all contingent reality and that God created human beings such that they "are intended to resemble God in his righteousness and commune with him." Only when these two beliefs are added is the popular view of "divine rewards" providing *the* reason for *anyone* being moral given a clear explanation and an adequate justification. For now it is recognized that to believe in the God of Hebrew-Christian revelation is to believe that God created the nature of every human being such that only in fellowship with him can we become perfectly good and completely happy.

II

I turn now to the task of making good my claim that there is another way of conceptualizing what it means "to be moral" other than the one that seems to be implied by Evans's use of moral language. My purpose here is not to deny the legitimacy of such language but to stress an alternative and complementary sort of moral discourse; one that in some important respects is more congruent with the different answer I will propose to the original question, "Why should I be moral?"

It is of considerable importance first to notice how Evans typically uses the terms *moral, duty,* and *virtue.* At the beginning of his essay he seems to assume that being "moral" is primarily a matter of doing one's "duty," that persons who do their "duty" qualify as "virtuous" persons, and, to close the circle, that such "virtuous" persons are those who are "being moral." Consider the following representative passages:

> Even if following morality generally does benefit the individual, it is not hard to think of cases in which doing one's duty seems to lead to a net loss of well-being for the agent in question. . . . we regard a person who acts virtuously *and* takes satisfaction from so acting as morally superior to someone who performs a duty grudgingly. . . . Someone who acts morally because of the intrinsic rewards of the moral life in no way regards morality as simply a means to an ulterior end. The happiness gained is because of a true devotion to duty.

Here "following morality" is clearly understood to be equivalent to "doing one's duty." Furthermore, those who do their duty grudgingly or devotedly "we regard" as having acted "virtuously," though we also judge the devotedly dutiful person to be "morally superior" to the grudgingly dutiful person. The performance of the duty is sufficient to qualify it as a virtuous act. The evaluation of the dutiful act as virtuous is separable from any evaluation of the moral quality of the attitude or disposition that a person may have toward doing the dutiful act. "Why should I be moral?" is construed as equivalent to asking "Why should I do my duty?" and to have done one's duty is to have acted virtuously.

Evans understands his original question in this way for the most part, though there are indications toward the end of the essay of a different, though not necessarily a contradictory interpretation.

> It is true that a person who finds the *moral life* satisfying has a reason to *be moral*, but only the *virtuous person* finds the *moral life* to be such, at least on the surface. Essentially, people who truly want to *be moral* seem to have a reason for *being moral*, but people who do not want to *be virtuous* do not. . . . God is conceived as an intrinsic reward for moral action, whose presence is a reward only to the person who *loves virtue*. So it would seem that God provides a reason to *be moral* only to those who *care about morality* (p. 300, italics added).

In this passage "to want to be moral" and "to want to be virtuous" is to want the same thing: to "love virtue" and "to care about morality" are identical. Asking "Why should I be moral?" is now equivalent to asking "Why should I be virtuous?" It is not just that "moral" and "virtuous" are now used interchangeably but that to which each refers is different: it is what *persons* are morally, or what they want to *be* rather than what they *do* or what they *ought to do* that is in view.

Evans's "average" person is, I think, as at home making moral judgments about what *people* are like as about their individual *acts*. They will say that Uncle Joe is "kind" and "humble" and just as readily that his peevish criticism of a neighbor yesterday was both unkind and arrogant, quite "out of *character.*" "He wasn't his old *self*, I wonder what got into him."

It is not my intention to try to show that Evans understands "being moral" exclusively as a matter of "doing one's duty." If he did he would not have pointed out correctly that we judge people who do their duty gladly as morally superior to those who do so only grudgingly. I do contend, however, that he tends to think of morality as primarily about actions rather than about persons. I wish at least to question the idea that normative morality is co-extensive with a theory of moral obligation, so that virtues are just those traits which correspond to the principles of duty recognized by the theory.[7] Additionally, I would argue for a narrower use of *virtue* than Evans. In the second of the two passages quoted earlier, he speaks of a dutiful act as virtuous independent of any evaluation of the moral quality of the agent's attitude or disposition toward it. Not to associate moral virtue with duty aids conceptual clarity. It allows

7. William K. Frankena, *Ethics*, 2d ed. (Englewood Cliffs, NJ: Prentice-Hall, 1973).

us to reserve the use of the word *virtue* and cognates for references to any beneficial trait, tendency, disposition, or habit that a person possesses or wants to possess.

Modern moral philosophers debate the relative merits of interpreting the moral life principally or exclusively either as a matter of formulating and justifying principle(s) and rules that ought to guide human actions or as a matter of determining what qualities of character we ought to acquire if we are to fulfill ourselves as human beings.[8] The first approach takes human actions as the main focus, and the question "What ought I to do?" is to be answered either by providing a rule to be followed or by pointing out that a rule already accepted prescribes a particular action. This is a morality of principle(s) and rules: "it is concerned only with what people do or fail to do, since that is what rules are for."[9] The second approach focuses on the moral worth of persons and not simply on the way their actions did or did not fulfill rules enjoined, say, by the utility principle, or the moral law. The question "What ought I to do?" is to be answered either by providing a virtue, such as saying, "Be compassionate," or, "Be patient," or simply by saying, "Be like X" (where X is either an ideal sort of character or even an actual person who is taken as having actualized the ideal). When either answer is given the original question is not really understood to be asking about what act I should perform; it becomes a question about what sort of person I ought to be or become.

The distinction between being and doing should not obscure obvious connections between each. It is not merely the trivial fact that persons cannot just *be*, or that their moral qualities are shown to others through their acts; it is also (as both Moses and Aristotle in their own ways

8. Beauchamp, *Philosophical Ethics*, pp. 146–79. Beauchamp argues generally for viewing each as offering a "worthy perspective" on the moral life, while Alasdair MacIntyre in *After Virtue* (Notre Dame: University of Notre Dame Press, 1982) argues cogently that post-Enlightenment versions of an ethics of duty as represented by Kant and Mill have failed (chaps. 5 and 6) chiefly because they have no conception of a telos that transcends the sum of particular actions or practices that establishes what is good for a whole human life. The older tradition of a virtue ethics had, and any later version requires, a historical understanding of the moral life as having a "narrative unity" and a concept of social "practices" with goods internal to them. It is precisely the loss of such an understanding of human life that has led to the dominance of individualistic ethics of obligation, and loss of any understanding of the virtues as excellences that, functioning together, have the consequence of perfecting each person in relation to each other (chaps. 15 and 16). Stanley Hauerwas has developed and defended an ethic of virtue as the most adequate model for understanding Christian moral experience in *Vision and Virtue: Essays in Christian Ethical Reflection* (Notre Dame: Fides, 1974) and other works.

9. Bernard Mayo, *Ethics and the Moral Life* (London: Macmillan, 1958), cited in Beauchamp, *Philosophical Ethics*, p. 152.

recognized) that the moral qualities that together constitute their characters are formed by acting habitually in certain ways.[10] But there is a weakness in thinking of morality as exclusively or even primarily a matter of acting in conformity to moral rules and principles. It may lead theorists to ignore the moral tendencies, dispositions, or attitudes that people possess antecedently and subsequently to any of their individual acts. On the other hand, theorists may recognize their importance but fail to show how such good or bad qualities of persons are coherently related to a clearly articulated theory of moral obligation.

It is generally agreed that recent normative moral theorists in the English-speaking world at least, whether consequentialist or nonconsequentialist in approach, have tended to think that an ethic of obligation exhausts the domain of normative thinking in ethics. Those, like William Frankena, who deny this nevertheless believe that an ethic of obligation is primary.[11] I have neither the occasion nor the inclination to address the much-debated issue of whether an ethic of obligation or of virtue is primary. That debate may only obscure what seems to me to be the real issue that provoked it, namely, the problem of getting clear about what is the scope and character of morality. That is easily *said* but, as Frankena has observed, "it is not easy to get clear just what the truth is in this matter—or even just what the issue is."[12] But even if one is not clear about the best way of understanding the relation between obligation and virtue (mutual exclusion, complementarity, or dependence), perhaps there are plausible reasons for believing that a conception of morality that focuses exclusively on human *acts* and the principles and categories of deontic ethics is unable to do justice to significant features of a Christian understanding of the moral life.

The language of obligation, whether utilitarian or deontological, has as its fundamental concern the moral ordering of relations between persons or groups rather than the moral ordering or formation of the internal tendencies, interests, or dispositions of individual selves. The evaluative categories that we call (or at least people like us once called) virtues and vices are used to articulate this aspect of our moral experience. The moral language of the Scriptures is not limited to judgments about what is obligatory, permitted, or right to do but includes moral judgments about the intentions, tendencies, and dispositions that together are the marks of the characters of persons. The man who does not kill another cannot be accused of doing what is prohibited, but he may

10. Cf. Deut. 6:4–7 and *Nichomachean Ethics*, Book II, 1 and 4.

11. "Prichard and the Ethics of Virtue" (1970) in *Perspectives on Morality: Essays of William Frankena*, ed. Kenneth E. Goodpaster (Notre Dame: University of Notre Dame Press, 1976), pp. 148–60.

12. Ibid., p. 159.

yet be judged a bad person because he has allowed anger, bitterness, or envy toward another to fester in his consciousness (Matt. 5:22). The Scriptures speak not only of specific duties that we owe to ourselves, to others, or to God, but also of passions and desires like self-conceit, lust, jealousy, and hatred that "those who belong to Christ Jesus have crucified" (Gal. 5:24) and other good passions and desires like peaceableness, patience, kindness, and humility that characterize the life of those who have "put on the new nature, created after the likeness of God. . ." (Eph. 4:24). The language of obligation seems ill-fitted to articulate these good and bad passions. If this is so, then it fails to do justice to an important feature of Christian moral experience.

It may be objected that it is one thing to argue that room should be found in moral philosophy for considerations of personal virtue as well as interpersonal obligations but quite another thing to have tied it so closely to the moral requirements of a particular faith. So far as I can tell I have not claimed that *any* ethic *must* find a place for the language of virtue—though such a case might be made.[13] What I have claimed is that a Christian ethic must do so.

On this general issue of the place of the language of virtue in Christian ethics, it is of some importance to note again the transition Evans makes from talking about "being moral" as a matter of "doing one's duty" to talking about it as equivalent to "being virtuous." It occurs in the final section, in which Evans is not addressing (as he was in the previous section) the idea of a righteous God as the intrinsic reward of moral *action* but the idea of God as the Creator of *beings* who by virtue of this fact are necessarily dependent upon him for the happiness that alone can satisfy them. Here, as earlier, in order to arrive at a specification of the "divine rewards" answer, Evans found it necessary not only to stress the essential goodness of God but also to insist that our creation by God entails certain truths about human nature. Put shortly, every human being is created with a need for God and that fact about everyone provides *the* best reason to be moral.

All this seems to me to be what a clear-thinking theist must say, and in saying it Evans has specified theological claims that provide a sufficient reason why anyone should be moral. The possibility of giving a different reason is open to *Christian* theists because they are bound to think about the moral life in relation to a much more complex set of theological beliefs; beliefs that center on the significance of the life and destiny of Jesus Christ. While a Christian ethic must begin with the claim that God is essentially good and continue with the further claim that he has

---

13. Cf. Stanley Hauerwas, "Obligation and Virtue Once More," in *Truthfulness and Tragedy* (Notre Dame: University of Notre Dame Press, 1977), pp. 40–56.

created human beings with a need for fellowship with himself, it does not end with them. It must add to these a belief about human rejection of just those claims; a conviction that this covenanting God was incarnate in the person of his Son whom men and women called Jesus; a claim about the reconciliation of men and women to God through his atonement for their sin; and an assurance that through confession of sin and faith in Christ freedom and power to live a fully human life (marked by just those virtues that comprised the character of Christ himself) is given. The Christian maintains that these beliefs are true and together they provide a foundation for a distinctive conception of the virtuous person. This at least seems to be the way the apostles understood the grounding of the moral life in the whole story of redemption.

If this is the case then Christians who ask, "Why should I be moral?" might reply by appealing to the revelatory and redemptive significance of Jesus. They would see his life and death as both a revelation of the essential goodness of God and the actualization of a fully human life: one that was completely faithful to the moral demands of God. What they receive in this revelation they might say is not in the first instance a fundamental moral principle or new rules but moral goodness personified and exemplified in the story of a life that moves from birth to transfiguration, crucifixion, resurrection, ascension, and Pentecost. It is the life of a distinct human personality with characteristic virtues: reverence, faith, hope, self-giving love, forgiveness, thanksgiving, joy, and peace.[14] Thus such Christians may say that the foundation of the moral life is Jesus Christ. To realize that one is reconciled to God through redemption from alienation effected by him, such Christians may say, is at the same time to acknowledge not only that one ought to be moral but that *knowing* what it is to be moral and *becoming* a morally worthy person are inseparable from a personal trust in Jesus Christ. This conclusion is without doubt controversial. It depends upon the truth of two premises about the exemplarity of Jesus: First, that human beings are unable to discern with sufficient clarity what it means to be morally good; second, that Jesus was unique in possessing such discernment. I have not tried to warrant the truth of either premise but any attempt to do so will entail a move away from strictly ethical matters to the larger issue of how warrant is to be provided for the whole web of beliefs that is the Christian faith.[15]

14. Keith Ward, *The Divine Image: The Foundations of Christian Morality* (London: SPCK, 1976), p. 86.

15. An exploration of the conditions under which warrant for any set of beliefs, religious or not, is possible is provided in David L. Wolfe, *Epistemology: The Justification of Belief* (Downers Grove, IL: InterVarsity Press, 1982).

PART III
Conclusion

Faith-Discipline Integration: Compatibilist, Reconstructionalist, and Transformationalist Strategies

RONALD R. NELSON

Asked if he believed in infant baptism the honest catechumen responded, "Believe in? Man, I've *seen* it done!" So it is with readers of this volume. The reality of Christian learning can never again be a mere creedal nicety. We've seen it!

But what have we seen? Braving our way along labyrinthine paths of scholarly argument, pushing our way through an often lush undergrowth of disciplinary detail, some of us have spotted few familiar landmarks. Although our essayists have called attention to the larger issues of strategy, we have sometimes found the jousting between allies to be the more interesting spectacle. The time has come to look back on the rugged terrain over which we've come, take our bearings, and give thought to future lines of march. To such, at any rate, the reader is invited.

Taking a cue from the introduction to this volume we can identify three approaches to Christian learning. Let us call these the *compatibilist* vision or strategy, the *reconstructionalist* vision or strategy,[1] and the *transformationalist* vision or strategy. As I would define these, the first places a premium on the effort to locate and to integrate *compatible* elements indigenous both to the scholar's Christian faith and to his discipline. The second, conscious of the radical demands of Christian commitment and seeing no substantial common ground between faith and a given discipline, believes that complete *reconstruction* of the discipline is the necessary condition for valid Christian learning. The third approach shares with the first a concern for a measure of common ground between faith and discipline. There is a recognition of at least some shared assumptions and concerns. But with the second approach, the third wants to do justice to the sovereign and comprehensive claims of Christ. It therefore perceives the need for disciplinary *transformation*.

---

1. Reconstructionalism has been used in reference to a generic strategy that finds expression in various Christian circles. Though it would encompass at least some of what goes under the banner of *The Journal of Christian Reconstruction* (Vallecito, CA), it is by no means synonomous with that movement.

Working from within the discipline as it is presently constituted, a transformationalist strategy will strive toward the radical and integral fulfillment of faith's vision for the discipline, i.e., its ultimate subjection to the lordship of Christ.

Before giving more detailed attention to these particular strategies of Christian learning, it will be useful to sketch out briefly the notions of "discipline" and of "faith."

A discipline is a specialization of human interest directed toward the exploration of some sphere or dimension of reality. There are, as it were, two sides to this interest. There is the spirit of inquiry that animates the scholar, call it curiosity, a desire to know, active intelligence, or imagination. There is also the questionability, the intelligibility, or meaning of the sphere or dimension of reality that is being explored. Whether we think, say, of the musician searching in imagination for a musical metaphor that will give utterance to his emotional experience; or of the mathematician puzzling over ways of operating on the entities, real or possible, which intrigue her; or of the psychologist hunting for the patterns of human behavior encoded in his computer printout, each is making a disciplined inquiry into a sphere or dimension of reality that he or she regards as amenable to such inquiry. Each discipline gives its particular shape to the fluid spirit of inquiry. Each develops its own heuristic, that is, its own principles and methods of discovery. Each devises and revises its own special categories, its own conceptual system. Each claims the prerogative of formulating its own criteria for judging the validity of what is put forward by scholars in the field. Each has its own sense, diffuse and debated though it might be, of what the integrity of the discipline requires.

To be sure, in thus understanding themselves, the disciplines are subject to a variety of dangers and complications. There are the ever present temptations toward disciplinary isolationism, reductionism, and imperialism. The world of scholarship is replete with examples of individual scholars, indeed of whole generations, who have succumbed to one or more of these temptations. Yet it is precisely amidst such dangers that each discipline aspires to be a self-directing, self-correcting community of scholars. To add a relevant complication to this picture we must note that there are bound to be wide differences of conviction among scholars in any given discipline regarding fundamental values and beliefs. Such convictions invariably will originate in what we might call the scholar's extradisciplinary life. These convictions, as the history of any discipline will testify, exert themselves in a variety of conscious or unconscious ways within the affairs of the discipline.

The Christian faith is a response to the mercy and love of God in

Christ Jesus. There are, as it were, two sides to such faith. There is the revelation from God, what he has made known of himself and his ways. So Christians speak of the undoubted truths of their faith, of the things most surely to be believed. Faith, in this sense, has a propositional *content*. It is expressible in creeds and doctrines. There is also faith as loving obedience toward God. Such faith is the deep, centered *act* by which the believer entrusts himself and his future to the will of God. In its intentionality such faith reaches beyond this world into transcendent mystery, but it pertains nonetheless to that which is of this world, to that which is proportionate to humanity's finite understanding. Faith in its two sides gives the believer deep convictions about humankind and the cosmos, their divine ground, their corruption, and their redemption. Faith orients the believer toward the tasks of life, perchance those in the service of an academic discipline, with a desire to do all to the glory of God.

Inasmuch as the project of faith-discipline integration raises a host of subtle and complex problems, in the introduction to this book Wolfe has set forth a criterion for the separation of spurious from genuine integration. As he puts it, "*Genuine integration occurs when an assumption or concern can be shown to be internally shared by (integral to) both the Judaeo-Christian vision and an academic discipline.*" The process of integration, he says, involves bringing together such *assumptions or concerns* "in an interesting and informative way."

By calling on scholars to identify the shared assumptions and concerns internal to both their faith commitments and their scholarly pursuits, Wolfe's canon implicitly recognizes that integration is not so much an achievement, not so much the synthesis of a new compound, as it is the recognition of a reality. For scholars who are convinced that in Christ "all things hold together" (Col. 1:17), it remains for them to dis-cover, however proleptically, that ultimate coherence to which Scripture points.

Wolfe's manner of conceiving the integrative enterprise resonates primarily with what we've called the compatibilist and the transformationalist strategies. Insofar as the Christian scholar identifies assumptions and concerns integral to both her faith and her discipline and links them in ways requiring no radical revision of either, she may be counted among the compatibilists. Insofar as the assumptions and concerns of faith are exercised in such a way as to exert a radical influence on how the scholar conceives of her discipline, and insofar as the scholar is still committed to working within the discipline as presently constituted while striving to realize an alternative, i.e., Christian, vision of the discipline, she is among the transformationalists. Wolfe would expressly exclude a reconstructionalist strategy from the pale of Christian learning, at least insofar as his canon for genuine integration is concerned. Despite Wolfe's stricture I have chosen to give cursory attention to the reconstructionalist position. As a strategy reconstructionalism is not without its popular appeal. I dare say it is what many lay people hope (and some academics fear) Christian learning is all about. Be that as it may, both in what it affirms and in the problems it confronts, reconstructionalism serves to highlight important emphases and issues for the enterprise of Christian learning.

In what follows I will first comment on some features of the compatibilist strategy that have hitherto been largely overlooked in these pages. Next I will call attention to certain distinctives of a reconstructionalist strategy as I understand it. Then I will make a case for a transformationalist approach, bringing to light concerns that in my view have not as yet received adequate attention in the realm of Christian learning.

I

In the compatibilist approach to Christian learning the integrity of both faith and discipline are in large measure presupposed. The scholar's task is one of showing how these shared assumptions and concerns can be profitably linked. In Wolfe's phrase, "Integration is the process by which two often very differing visions are related in an interesting and informative way on the basis of one or more shared presuppositions." Two features of the compatibilist approach call for particular comment. The first arises from a theological question. Given the Christian understanding of the transcendent sources of the content of faith and given the deleterious effects of sin on human noetic capabilities, how can the presence of faith-compatible assumptions and concerns *on the side of the discipline* be explained? The second, closely allied matter relates to compatibilism's implicit acceptance of the claims of disciplinary communities to be self-directing and self-correcting.

The understanding of integration commended by Wolfe and exemplified by the compatibilist strategy carries with it an implicit theological cargo. This is not necessarily a criticism, but it does call for acknowledgment and does invite comment on possible ways of accounting for this freight. The Christian faith is grounded in a revelation from God. It provides to humanity truths about the world not otherwise available. Inasmuch as the integrative enterprise as envisaged by Wolfe requires the identification of comparable and compatible concerns and assumptions emanating both from within the circle of faith and from within the discipline, one is faced with the problem of accounting for the presence of these faithlike assumptions and concerns *within* the discipline. The more central to the Christian faith these assumptions and concerns are, the more acute the problem becomes. That is, the commonalities that require a recognition of truth consistent with a general theism or a broad concern for the value of personhood will be less problematic than one's requiring a rather complex body of Christian doctrine or extensive reference to scriptural data. In any case, if we have to do with the integrating of disciplinary concerns and assumptions with those stemming from faith, even if it be only a matter of the discipline asking the perceptive question which faith answers, it is incumbent that there be some accounting for the conditions of this possibility. There are various routes open; one's choice among these may well depend on the theological tradition within which one stands. In what follows, no attempt will be made to look at all the possible approaches; rather, a few observations will be offered as a way of broaching the general issue.

One could appeal to the notion of general revelation. All human beings in that case do potentially know some truths of the faith apart from those given on more privileged occasions of relevation. This appeal has some merit and would account for some elements of commonality. General revelation, however, has usually been understood to provide only the most elementary of truths and therefore leaves the integrative enterprise standing at a fairly jejune level. Moreover, some interpretations of general revelation would argue that human sinfulness is such as to render the knowledge of divine truths received through general revelation all but nugatory.

One might have recourse to the claim that the disciplines, in the western world at any rate, have been largely shaped under the influence of the Judaeo-Christian tradition. This approach, however, would not only serve to account for the potential for integration on the disciplinary side, it would render the project of integration somewhat superfluous since the marriage, as it were, has already taken place historically. While there might be some value in periodically reiterating the marital vows, the scholars anthologized in this volume do seem to be claiming something more substantial than that for their efforts.

Some Christians will account for the apparent prescience of a given discipline in matters consequential for faith by appealing to what has been called God's "common grace." This doctrine explains not only God's restraint of the more devastating consequences of sin on human affairs but also his bestowal on humanity of the temporal structures of marriage, the family, the state, and fruitful labor (including the arts and sciences). Common grace is said to equip men and women for developing the potentialities of the world and for performing works of "civic righteousness." In this light one can see how it might be that the concerns of a discipline, quite apart from specifically Christian influences, would exhibit those insights which make integration possible. The logic of the matter was put well by John Calvin, who is often credited with first deriving the idea of common grace from Scripture.

> In reading profane authors, the admirable light of truth displayed in them should remind us that the human mind, however fallen and perverted from its original integrity, is still adorned and invested with admirable gifts from the creator. If we reflect that the Spirit of God is the only foundation of truth, we will be careful, as we should avoid offering insult to him, not to reject or condemn truth wherever it appears.[2]

An appeal to common grace, however, does not lay all problems to rest. The doctrine has been controversial even within the Reformed tradition where there are differences of opinion concerning the nature and extent of common grace and its relationship to the "saving grace" of Christ. Still, it does offer one avenue of response to queries that must arise concerning the theological status of the "integratable" elements one identifies within a discipline. The point is not to air this matter exhaustively here but to observe how germane it is to the integrative enterprise, especially for scholars of a compatibilist persuasion.

Yet another issue presents itself in reference to the compatibilist school—that of disciplinary *autonomy*. What is meant here by autonomy? Recall the generic notion of an academic discipline provided at the beginning of this essay. If what was sketched there approximates reality, it is evident that inherent in the idea of a discipline is that of a self-directing and self-correcting community of scholars. Such disciplinary autonomy is widely acknowledged to be the ideal even if its *de facto* realization is denied. Compatibilism has no difficulty with this understanding of disciplinary autonomy. After all, it will be said, who but those in the kindred circle of the initiated and proven can comprehend and take responsibility for the arcane affairs of a discipline—be it physics or physical education? Compatibilists only claim that their discipline, its penchant for autonomy notwithstanding, in some respects does operate from assumptions and does generate truths that resonate with those of the Christian faith. The agenda of these scholars includes bringing into creative relationship such elements of their discipline and of their faith. To colleagues who do not share this faith or whose conception of autonomy precludes the very recognition of discipline-relevant ideas apart from the certified tradition of the discipline, such faith-discipline integration may be the occasion of great scandal. The compatibilist, however, con-

---

2. John Calvin, *Institutes of the Christian Religion*, II, ii, 15.

vinced of the truth of his faith no less than of the integrity of his discipline, is prepared to break ranks with such members of his guild in these matters, if need be.

Since he expressly affirms the notion of disciplinary autonomy (at least as regards mathematics) as the compatibilist understands it, we can profitably relate our discussion at this point to Heie's essay. His approach is impeccably Wolfeian. He tells us that he chose to enter the "mathematician's project" in the responsible exercise of the freedom he enjoys as a Christian. In that measure his doing of mathematics is contextualized by his faith. But, having thus entered the mathematician's project, he is committed to exercising his freedom there in conformity with the values inherent in that project. It is the mathematical community alone that is competent to define the mathematical project and therefore to formulate the criteria of criticism by which mathematical work is to be judged. There is a common denominator—a kind of isomorphism of integrals—between Heie's faith and his vocation as a mathematician; both are instances of "freedom within bounds." Moreover, values that he affirms as a Christian prove to be congruent with values integral to his work as a mathematician.

What Heie affirms, however, Chase questions. For Chase and his complementarist approach, Heie's position amounts to having the mathematical community decide on the content and values of mathematics and leaving it for the Christian to select those mathematical values that do not conflict with Christian values. This, says Chase, is like telling the mathematical community, "Do as you please!" He would, for his part, want the mathematician's autonomy to yield to the "laws God has created" for mathematics. This dispute between Heie and Chase serves to illustrate the importance of the issue of disciplinary autonomy. We cannot pursue the matter into greater depths now but would simply note that the compatibilist strategy per se is not at war with disciplinary autonomy.

We must not think of disciplinary autonomy in a way that is too simplistic. A person involved in a given discipline obviously has many other dimensions to her life. It cannot be denied that these dimensions, be they religious or philosophical beliefs, political or ideological commitments, cultural or avocational interests, may have a large impact on a scholar's disciplinary pursuits. Such beliefs, commitments, or interests will often be the source of insights, questions, and concerns that in some fashion relate to the discipline. The sensitivity an academic has to particular issues and the verve with which she pursues them may be largely extrinsic to her discipline. This entire volume witnesses to this phenomenon. We have seen, however, that frequently when concerns to which scholars are made sensitive by virtue of their faith are brought into the realm of their scholarship, they will argue their cases on the grounds and with the warrants that are indigenous to the discipline. We see this phenomenon at work in two ways. We observe scholars claiming that certain positions which they know to be *incompatible* with their own faith commitments are also problematic within their discipline's larger frame of reference. Conversely, we see the case being advanced for the essential *compatibility* of faith positions with disciplinary positions.

Notice, for instance, the arguments Hasker mounts against the materialist and the dualist approaches to the mind-body problem. He makes no appeal to foundational Christian certitudes in this refutation. His case rests on warrants that are meant to have force with any scholar treating the question in an open-minded way. Such a procedure is not limited to those employing a compatibilist strategy. The same kind of observation could be made relative to Skillen's criticisms of the "reductionism" of Karl Deutsch. He attempts to show that Deutsch's analysis is simply unequal to the complex human reality that the political scientist seeks to understand. (So far as I can see, Skillen, in critiquing Deutsch's "starting point," is not *simply* arguing from his own Christian presuppositions. He wants to show that Deutsch's position is inadequate for coping with problems that ought to concern all political scientists.) A similar point could be made concerning the line of thought Clark and Gaede put forward respecting the excessive and reductionistic claims sometimes made by sociologists of knowledge. They point to various fallacies, which are fallacious not because they make problems for Christian belief but because they involve moves which are illogical, inconsistent, or arbitrary. Christians may take comfort from this chastening of sociological pretensions, but so must sociologists of any stripe insofar as they want to promote the growth of sociological understanding.

II

The second general approach to Christian learning which we note has been called the reconstructionalist strategy. The shortest route to understanding the distinctive character of reconstructionalism is to continue with the theme of autonomy raised in the previous section. One will find among the advocates of reconstruction that the problem of disciplinary autonomy is crucial. There are well-thought-out concerns at stake here. Implicit in the Christian faith is what we might call its "totalitarianism" (taking that word in its strictly etymological sense and eschewing its political associations). There are two related sides to this totalitarianism. Adherents to the Christian faith have responded to the call to love

God with *all* their hearts, souls, minds, and strength. The one who claims this allegiance is the source of *all* things; nothing ultimately evades God's will. In the light of such claims one might well ask about this "autonomy" which the disciplines presume to claim, whether as a regulating ideal or in actual fact.

One will find, therefore, that in some Christian quarters charges are leveled respecting "the logic of the self-appointed autonomous mind." Autonomy means "self-law" and stands, we are told, over against "God's law," namely, that given in Scripture. Reconstructionalists are likely to view assertions of disciplinary autonomy as clear evidence of human attempts to do without God. It is construed as a yielding to the primeval temptation, "You will be like God" (Gen. 3:5). The call is sounded to form a firm line of battle at the point of "antithesis" between belief and unbelief in the arena of scholarship. Academicians of this mind are quite likely, doubtless motivated by their sense of obligation to the total claims of Christ, to view the compatibilist scheme of integration as a manifestation of nefarious "synthesis."

The alternative to which they point is a radical reconstruction of the disciplines on what they discern to be fully biblical foundations. The categories and epistemological presuppositions for any and all academic disciplines are to be found, they say, in the concrete revelations of the Old and New Testaments. We may take as illustrative of such an approach a book of essays that appeared not long ago under the title *Foundations of Christian Scholarship.*[3] In the introduction to this volume, the editor tells us that the essays will show that "each academic discipline is utterly bankrupt epistemologically." "Each contribution" in his book "is offered on the assumption that all forms of secular knowledge have been constructed on foundations of epistemological sand." Eschewing the "'baptized secularism' of modern Christian colleges" the several authors offer "a thoroughly biblical set of foundations for Christian scholarship."

Without a doubt the most influential application of a reconstructionalist strategy in our time has been in the field called "scientific creationism." Christian scholars of this persuasion have drawn attention in a most appropriate way to the naturalistic assumption implicitly, if not always explicitly, operative in many accounts of physical and biological evolution. They advocate, by contrast, a "Bible-believing" basis for the sciences. To get an idea of the way in which proponents of scientific creationism envisage the reconstruction of the science of geology, con-

---

3. Gary North, ed., *Foundations of Christian Scholarship: Essays in the Van Til Perspective* (Vallecito, CA: Ross House, 1976), pp. vii–ix.

sider the following paragraphs from the "Summary and Conclusion" of a volume titled *Scientific Creationism.*

> There seems to be no possible way to avoid the conclusion that, if the Bible and Christianity are true at all, the geological ages must be rejected altogether. Neither the day-age theory, the gap theory, nor any other theory is capable of reconciling them with Genesis. In their place, as the proper means of understanding earth history as recorded in the fossil-bearing sedimentary rocks of the earth's crust, the great worldwide Flood so clearly described in Scripture must be accepted as the basic mechanism.
>
> The detailed correlation of the intricate geophysical structure of the earth with the true Biblical framework of history will, no doubt, require a tremendous amount of research and study by Bible-believing scientists. Nevertheless, this research is urgently needed today in view of the world's increasing opposition to the Biblical Christian faith.[4]

Here is a proposal for disciplinary reconstruction indeed. The various "strategies" pursued by scholars in the present volume are more aptly styled "headlong retreats" by comparison. Insofar, however, as these reconstructionist scholars seek the foundations of the science of geology or of other modern disciplines in the details of Scripture, they are open to serious challenge respecting the intent of the biblical text. In this connection John Calvin's comment on the relation of biblical language and concepts to the discoveries being made by sixteenth-century astronomers has a relevance far beyond the controversies of his day. Speaking of the references in the first chapter of Genesis to the sun and the moon as the "greater" and the "lesser light," he says, "Moses does not subtilely descant, as a philosopher, on the secrets of nature. . . ." Rather, he wrote in a "popular style." Astronomers, by contrast, "investigate with great labor whatever the sagacity of the human mind can comprehend."

> Moses makes two great luminaries; but astronomers prove, by conclusive reasons, that the star of Saturn, which, on account of its great distance, appears the least of all, is greater than the moon. . . . If the astronomer inquires respecting the actual dimensions of the stars, he will find the moon to be less than Saturn; but this is something abstruse, for to the sight it appears differently. Moses, therefore, rather adapts his discourse to common usage. . . . Let the astronomers possess their more exalted knowledge; but, in the meantime, they who perceive by the moon the splendour of night, are convicted by its use of perverse ingratitude unless they acknowledge the beneficence of God.[5]

---

4. Henry M. Morris, ed., *Scientific Creationism* (San Diego: Creation Life Publishers, 1974), p. 255.

5. John Calvin, *Commentaries on the First Book of Moses Called Genesis*, 2 vols. (Grand Rapids: Eerdmans, 1948), 1:87. Bernard Ramm gives contemporary expression to Calvin's point: "The language of the Bible with reference to natural things is *popular, prescientific,*

In effect, Calvin is saying that if one wants to know the science of astronomy one should go to the astronomers, not to Moses.

That Scripture has a formative role to play in the pursuit of Christian learning is obvious; such is not the issue at stake here. What is at issue is whether or not the problem of disciplinary autonomy is adequately met by appealing to the Bible to establish foundations for particular disciplines as reconstructionists are wont to do. This is not the place to develop an adequate hermeneutic, and certainly the citation of Calvin's authority on a single issue does not settle the array of questions that need to be faced. The root of the matter, as has often been said, is the discernment of that which Scripture *intends* to teach. This is a matter, I would suggest, which needs more careful consideration not only by reconstructionalists but by Christian scholars of other persuasions as well. To recognize this need is not to detract from the laudable objective of the reconstructionalists to be loyal to the totalitarian demands of faith as they understand them. To an alternative way of responding to those demands, however, we now must turn.

III

Recalling the notion of a *transformational strategy* suggested in the Introduction, we note that it presupposes "some legitimate insight in the disciplinary assumptions to begin with" and an aim to remake or transform a discipline "into one with a Christian orientation." Martin's essay, "Toward an Epistemology of Revelation," strikes me as among the clearest instances of a transformationalist approach in this sense. He finds that the discipline of human psychology has lost sight of *the* issue which should be central to it—namely, the knowledge of persons. He finds Hodges's paper representative of this problem. It is clear from the latter portion of Martin's paper that it is his Christian faith that alerts him to the issues of the personal dimensions of epistemic processes and of the personal ground of reality (with its coincidence of intelligibility and opacity). He thinks within a Christian horizon. He therefore points to the need to develop (i.e., transform) psychological study in ways that will "make room for persons." But notice how Professor Martin leads up to this conclusion. He does so by pursuing his questions through vast

---

and *non-postulational*. It is the terminology of the culture prevailing at the time the various books were written. It is a matter of the Spirit of God speaking through these terms so that (i) the terms are not themselves thereby made infallible science, and that (ii) the theological content is in no wise endangered." *The Christian View of Science and Scripture* (Grand Rapids: Eerdmans, 1954), p. 76.

thickets in the realm of philosophy, thickets wherein various philosophical-psychological schools have built their homes. He shows us the inadequacy of each of these positions for the development of an epistemology of personal revelation. He does this not by building his case on explicitly Christian presuppositions but by lines of thought he means to be compelling for any psychologist interested in the integrity of the epistemic foundation of the discipline. A compatibilist, with an eye on disciplinary autonomy, would find this all very laudable, but in suggesting as he does that psychology as it stands is fundamentally flawed, Martin has pointed toward the need for a transformation of the discipline of psychology itself.

In the discussion of transformationalism which follows I will be calling attention to some features of one version of such a strategy. In so doing I will not be focusing on any particular discipline. If my comments therefore suffer from a certain abstractness, it is to be hoped that they will be found the more pertinent to a wide variety of disciplines. I have tried to clarify an approach that could prove useful to the many scholars for whom the identification of relevant concerns in the conceptual content of faith for integration with their disciplines has seemed problematic.[6] While a plurality of strategies, as has been suggested elsewhere in this volume, is no doubt to be desired, we also have need of an approach with a very comprehensive relevance to the world of scholarship. I would not say that I've provided the definitive specifications for such a strategy. I will be satisfied if my comments serve to suggest promising directions for further reflection.

6. Comment surrounding Nicholas Wolterstorff's *Reason Within the Bounds of Religion* (Grand Rapids: Eerdmans, 1976) is instructive in this connection. While acknowledging that "the Bible cannot function as a black book of theories for the Christian scholar," Professor Wolterstorff urges Christians to test the theories in their field by subjecting them to the truths of the faith. Wolterstorff writes: "The Christian scholar ought to allow the belief-content of his authentic Christian commitment to function as control within his devising and weighing of theories" (p. 72). Professor George Mavrodes of the University of Michigan reports that he has had occasion to study Wolterstorff's book with a group of Christian professors, many of whom have international reputations for their research achievements. To illustrate their problem with Wolterstorff's thesis, Mavrodes writes, "We could not think of, nor does Wolterstorff supply, plausible examples of (say) mathematical conjectures or chemical theories which we might reject because of our Christian commitment, nor of new research experiments in astronomy which that commitment might suggest." Mavrodes concludes that while the Christian professor may not want to leave his faith outside the door of his laboratory, he may well find that there are fields in which he is not able to bring it in. "Could we say, perhaps," concludes Mavrodes, "that the best thing to do would be to leave the door open?" *Reformed Journal* 27 (July 1977): 4-5. I would suggest that while the open door is a good thing, it is not the only recourse for these scholars.

We can begin by stating as briefly and unequivocally as possible the rationale from a Christian standpoint for the transformationalist vision. The Christian faith makes a total claim upon the lives of believers. Their Lord is the Creator and Redeemer of all things. To enter by faith upon the path of discipleship to Christ is to move into a relationship that brooks no rivals, no divisions of allegiance. Such relationship is constituted by *conversion,* by a radical *transformation* of one's self and of one's world. As the apostle Paul put it, "If any one is in Christ, he is a new creation; the old has passed away, behold, the new has come" (2 Cor. 5:17). One has changed sides in a spiritual struggle of cosmic proportions. Though the victory is assured in Christ's resurrection of the dead, one is engaged in a battle which demands to be waged on a front as wide as all created reality. It is a fight in which, through the power of the cross, the believer is challenged to "destroy arguments and every proud obstacle to the knowledge of God" and to "take every thought captive to obey Christ" (2 Cor. 10:5). The Genesis mandate to subdue the earth and to have dominion over it is now to be obeyed with renewed strength and fidelity and in the confidence that the kingdom of God will yet come on earth as it is in heaven. Nothing less than the transformation of the creation is in view. So far the reconstructionalist and the transformationalist are likely to be in agreement. But now a parting of the ways arises.

A transformationalist strategy requires some measure of commonality between faith and discipline. To make the point in a more concrete and personal way we can ask what the believer and the nonbeliever, engaged in the same scholarly pursuit, have in common. I propose to answer that by suggesting that we give consideration first of all to the structure and dynamism of cognition as exhibited in the disciplines generally. The faith concerns which are integral to all cognition will be made evident in due course. Then we will consider how faith, as arising from Christian conversion, can work a transformative influence on the cognitional process.

Returning to the definition of a discipline given at the beginning of this essay, we would say that the academic disciplines are specializations of humanity's native desire to know. They explore diverse spheres of reality through methods and with conceptual tools that are suited to those spheres and which commend themselves to the practitioners of a given discipline. Disciplines exhibit the multiple differentiations of which human consciousness is capable. But knowing, for all of its varieties, is not so various that its essential *conditions* cannot be specified. To get a handle on what it is finally that faith must transform in *any* of the specialized branches of learning, we will do well to attend to those conditions. To do this in a fully adequate way would involve us in matters far too complex for development in the present context. We shall have to be content here with an outline of the bare essentials. In this and much that follows I will be drawing selectively on the thought of Fr. Bernard Lonergan, adapting his ideas to my purposes.[7]

Knowing is the activity of coming to the conclusion that such and such is so. The activity of knowing, however, as reflection by the reader on her own knowing will verify, is not a single act; rather, it is a structured set of operations. It is not simply attending to the data of one's experience or to the data of one's consciousness. As Scripture has it, one may "hear but not hear." Nor is knowing the simple matter of having an insight into the data of one's experience. Insights, at least on some occasions, are "a dime a dozen"; they may or may not be valid. To be sure, if there is to be knowledge there must be insight. Understanding must intervene, catching the point, seeing the meaning, discerning the pattern in the data. Yet attending to the data of experience and intelligently grasping the point do not of themselves constitute a complete instance of knowing. What is understood may or may not be true. Therefore, if to know is to posit that thus and such is so, there must be judgment—the evidence must be weighed and evaluated. To judge without understanding is presumption. To understand without judgment is to leave the question of truth or reality undetermined.

Experience, understanding, and judgment are not automatic operations. They are intentional, highly personal acts of the conscious person. If one is to know one must be attentive to one's experience, one must make intelligent inquiry into that experience, one must make reasonable judgment vis-à-vis what is understood. An imperative of personal responsibility supervenes at every point in the knowing process. The commandments to which all would-be knowers are subject are, Be attentive! Be intelligent! Be reasonable! Be responsible!

There are, as it were, four levels of consciousness involved in cognition. Each has its appropriate activity and quality. There is the *empirical*

---

7. Bernard Lonergan, a late member of the Society of Jesus, held academic posts in Toronto, Rome, and Boston. His major works were *Insight: A Study of Human Understanding* (New York: Philosophical Library, 1970), hereafter cited as *Insight*, and *Method in Theology* (New York: Herder and Herder, 1972), hereafter cited as *Method*. For a discussion of Lonergan's epistemology in relation to that of Kant see Giovanni Sala, S.J., "The A Priori in Human Knowledge: Kant's *Critique of Pure Reason* and Lonergan's *Insight*," *The Thomist* 40 (1976): 179–221. For discussions of Lonergan's thought in relation to various modern thinkers including Dewey, Dilthey, Gadamer, Ricoeur, Heidegger, and Rahner see Philip Meshane, ed., *Language, Truth, and Meaning: Papers from the International Lonergan Congress, 1970* (Notre Dame: Notre Dame University Press, 1972). For an indication of the variety of fields in which Lonergan's thought is being fruitfully applied by scholars see Matthew Lamb, ed., *Creativity and Method: Essays in Honor of Bernard Lonergan, S.J.* (Milwaukee: Marquette University Press, 1981).

level. This pertains to some data of sense, as when we taste, smell, touch, see, or hear, or to some data of consciousness, as when we imagine or experience our own intellectual or emotional states in some fashion. There is the *intellectual level.* In the data of sense or of consciousness, through inquiry, one sees some pattern, some clue, some definition, some significance. The basic question at this level is, "What is it?" There is the *rational level.* What has been understood may or may not be the case. One must ask, "Is it so?" and arrive at a judgment by reflecting on the data, weighing the evidence, comparing what has been experienced with what has been understood. This structured progression from experience to understanding and judgment requires the willful collaboration of the self. Hence, there is a fourth level of consciousness, the *level of responsibility and decision,* which transcends and sublates the other three. At this level the knower is concerned with his own operations, purposes, and possible courses of action. One must decide whether or not one will attend to the relevant data of experience, exercise one's powers of intellect as fully as possible, and employ one's powers of judgment with full recognition of the constraints of reason. In short, one must decide whether or not to be responsible toward the norms inherent in the structured set of operations we call knowing.

Knowing is not only a self-directing process, it is also a self-transcending process. It wants to make true judgments, to specify *what is so.* In the measure that one is responsible toward the imperatives of the cognitional process one achieves such self-transcendence. In Bernard Lonergan's words, "When we seriously affirm that something really and truly is so, we are making the claim that we have got beyond ourselves in some fashion, somehow have got hold of something that is independent of ourselves, somehow have reached beyond, transcended ourselves."[8] Such cognitive self-transcendence is the goal, ever renewed as new questions arise, of the desire to know which animates the academic disciplines. The Christian and the non-Christian alike are subject to the inherent constraints of cognition and are responsible for self-transcending judgments if they are to be contributors to the ongoing life of their disciplines. Though the Christian will understand those constraints and that responsibility as flowing from her life as a creature before her Creator and the non-Christian may well deny this root of the matter, both are nonetheless subject to the same state of affairs insofar as they would be knowers. Our initial picture of disciplines as communities of scholars responsible for the advancement of understanding through their collective labors can be seen in the background here. We also have a basis on

---

8. Bernard J. F. Lonergan, *A Second Collection,* ed. William F. J. Ryan and Bernard J. Tyrrell (Philadelphia: Westminster Press, 1974), p. 167.

which to appreciate the positive stance which the compatibilist takes toward disciplinary autonomy. The picture, however, is as yet incomplete.

Before treating the relationship which Christian conversion has to the self-directing, self-transcending character of knowing, it will be of value to take note of two characteristics of the desire to know which call attention to its intrinsic spiritual depths. As we shall see, by virtue of the potential limitlessness of the desire to know, the scholar, whether a Christian or not, bears implicit witness to the question of God. Also in connection with this same desire to know, the scholar shows himself to be entangled with the pervasive surd of sin.

First then the unrestrictedness of the desire to know, evidenced in the dynamic of the scholarly disciplines (and in no small measure in the play of positions and counter-positions in this present volume),[9] points toward the question of God, if not to the very fact of God's existence. There is no conceivable limit to which we may submit the spirit of inquiry. To try to limit questioning is immediately to raise the question of the legitimacy of the limit, and to raise that question already takes us beyond the proposed limit. Inasmuch, then, as questioning, if authentic, aims at understanding, and inasmuch as the human sense of the questionableness of reality is unrestricted, questioning we must say aims at, intends, complete understanding. But though human capacity to question is unrestricted, clearly our capacity to understand is limited. It is limited to what we can experience and to that which is proportionate

9. Think for instance of the drive for intellectual cogency evident in Hodges's dictum that "even the claim that rationality is embodied in comprehensive criticism cannot avoid critical scrutiny" (p. 123). Or recall Heie's remark as he engages us in a quest for criteria for criticizing the criteria of criticism: "No claim to knowledge can be viewed as self-authenticating. One must seek criteria for criticism of any knowledge claim . . ." (p. 228). The interplay of ideas between the essays also exemplifies a driving spirit of inquiry. Remember, for instance, how Hasker challenges the adequacy of Jones's complementarist solution to the mind-body problem and how he argues for an answer based on emergentism. Recall how the search for an intellectually satisfying epistemology leads Martin to question the cogency of the direct realism and post-empiricism advocated by Hodges and to plunge beyond realism and idealism to find a theory of knowledge that does justice to the demands of a psychology of persons. While Skillen calls into question the fundamental assumptions of some of the leading practitioners in his field of political science, Mouw sets the radically different ideas of John Howard Yoder over against Skillen's. We could easily go on in this manner through the whole volume of essays. The dialectical play of position and counter-position is fascinating, but more than gamesmanship is involved. There is a deep passion for advancing human understanding through disciplinary scholarship. This is, of course, a penchant which these Christian scholars share with members of their respective disciplinary guilds who may not be professing Christians. Such questioning and challenging is the life-blood of the disciplines.

to the grasp of our finite minds. Human beings *aspire* to complete understanding but know our *grasp* to be limited. To speak of complete understanding, of understanding everything about everything, of an unrestricted act of understanding that would correspond to unrestricted questioning, is to speak about that which would be the prerogative of God alone. Thus does humanity's imperious drive to understand bear witness, however inchoately, to our native orientation toward God. Though God is beyond everything humans can grasp by immediate knowledge, God can be dimly perceived to be the ultimate satisfaction of our unrestricted questioning. God alone could ground and fulfill the intelligibility to which humanity has limited access and for which we have an unlimited hunger.[10]

By attending to the potential unrestrictedness of the scholar's desire to know, we have pointed to the presence in the human spirit of an orientation to the divine source of all intelligibility and meaning. The effectiveness of that orientation, however, may well be questioned, for rarely has deliberation on the foundations or methodology of any discipline brought to light the transcendental significance latent in the questioning process. If the drive to understand has the implications we have suggested here, an awareness of God, at least as to his "eternal power and deity" (Rom. 1:20), would be commonly confessed within the academic world. Effectively, it would seem, the spirit of inquiry is corrupted in some manner. In the apostle Paul's words, "men . . . by their wickedness suppress the truth" (Rom. 1:18). Elsewhere in this volume, Hodges alludes to the effects of sin on the desire to know in this way, "The biblical promise to 'seek and you will find' does not imply that everyone seeks." The Bible also reveals, he says, that humans "stifle" the truth. (It is important to recognize in this connection, however, as Heie suggests, that human freedom and creativity, marks of the *imago Dei*, were not so much diminished by the Fall as thereby given the potential to express themselves in a destructive manner.) Therefore, the desire to know, which fuels the disciplines, is subject to profound corruptions and distortions. There is not only a desire to understand, there is also a flight from understanding. This flight is evident in the "blind spots," in the short-circuiting of the questioning process, in the deeply rooted personal and group biases of scholars and scholarly communities. The impact of such epistemic malfunctioning could perhaps be illustrated in terms of such theories as the "central-state materialism" which Hasker critiques or the "stimulus-response" view of politics which Skillen finds in the thought

10. I have presented Lonergan's line of thought in this regard only in a very compressed and truncated fashion. See further *Insight*, pp. 634–86, and *Method*, pp. 101–3.

of Karl Deutsch. Only the suppression of highly relevant questions regarding the nature of human persons renders such positions tenable.

How then does Christian faith serve to promote the transformation of the spirit of inquiry which we have identified as central to disciplinary pursuits? It will be useful in entering into this issue to recall the distinction drawn in the first pages of this essay between faith as the *content* of belief and faith as the *act* of belief. The former is the dominant notion of faith in most of the essays in this volume. It stresses the cognitive or conceptual side of faith. Thus we have seen how Christian convictions about personhood, justice, values, and epistemology can be brought into fruitful interaction with disciplinary concepts. The compatibilist strategy lends itself especially well to this sort of integration. In what follows we will be concerned primarily with faith in its more act-oriented meaning. Here faith is understood as a verb rather than as a noun. It has to do with the conative side of faith, faith as the striving, intending, valuing, venturing behavior that flows from a primary response to God. The model of such faith is Abraham. He, we recall, left his native city at God's behest. Not knowing where he was going he went looking for a city "whose builder and maker is God" (Heb. 11:10). Faith as *act* is a matter of not knowing where you are going but going anyway because of your confidence in the faithfulness of the One who calls you. I am not speaking here of some vague faith in faith or of some general commitment to the search for absolute truth. The God and Father of Jesus Christ is the object of the Christian's faith; she trusts her life, not least of all her life as a scholar, to this One and to no other. Our attention below will be on this trust in God which is expressed in love and obedience (though to be sure also in believing *what* God has revealed).

Granted the exigence for self-transcendence in the intellectual processes we call the disciplines and granted the proneness of our hearts to deny the unfolding of that exigence in the name of our egoistic biases and fears, what shall we say is the remedy for our predicament? What is it that would actuate human capacity for self-transcendence, rendering it effective even in its latent desire to know God? The answer is found in *loving* God with all one's heart, soul, mind, and strength (Mark 12:30). "As the question of God is implicit in all our questioning," says Bernard Lonergan, "so being in love with God is the basic fulfillment of our conscious intentionality." What would be the character of such love? It would be love without qualifications, conditions, reservations, or restrictions. It would be a love of someone transcendent, someone supreme in intelligence, truth, and goodness.

> To be in love without qualifications or conditions or reservations or limits is to be in love with someone transcendent. When someone transcendent is my beloved, he is in my heart, real to me from within me. When that love is

the fulfillment of my unrestricted thrust to self-transcendence through intelligence and truth and responsibility, the one that fulfills that thrust must be supreme in intelligence, truth, goodness.[11]

While the normative thrust of a human heart is to bring a person to the knowledge of God for which he was born and lives, and while the normative pattern of operations (experience, understanding, judgment) through which a man knows anything, in its unrestrictedness, is meant to lead him to the knowledge of what is truly so, it is by virtue of what he truly loves that a man may or may not adhere to that normative thrust and may or may not follow the transcendental precepts of that pattern (Be attentive! Be intelligent! Be rational! Be responsible!). The desire to know at the root of humanity's intentional consciousness is, as we have suggested, essentially if not effectively unlimited. It is oriented, in the unrestrictedness of its questioning, to inquire about everything. Insofar as love is directed toward that which is truly ultimate, namely God, the unrestrictedness of the spirit of inquiry has free expression. It is bound only by the constraint of its own reality-intending orientation. Insofar as love is "biased," directed toward any object of concern other than God, human openness of spirit is in that measure restricted, and the native thrust of the desire to know is in that measure suppressed. The desire to know can have the unrestricted expression which is native to it only if one's unconditional love is congruent with that unrestricted expression. From the Christian's perspective, loving God without restriction is a capacity given to humanity by God. Such love is a gift; it serves to redirect and to fulfill the created spontaneities of human intellect, of our desire to know. Grace, say the theologians, perfects nature. As Herman Bavinck puts it, grace repairs the injuries inflicted on nature by sin. "The God who created and provides for us is the God who renews us after his image. Grace indeed triumphs over nature but it is not in conflict with nature."[12]

God's gift of his love profoundly affects all of one's intentional operations; it makes effective the self-transcending orientation of consciousness. The receipt of such love initiates one's conversion. It places one within a new horizon. In Lonergan's words, the unrestricted love of God "dismantles and abolishes the horizon in which our knowing and choosing went on and it sets up a new horizon in which the love of God will transvalue our values and the eyes of that love will transform our knowing."[13] This notion of horizon and its relation to values and knowledge warrants our consideration.

11. Lonergan, *Method*, p. 109.
12. Herman Bavinck, *The Doctrine of God*, trans. and ed. William Hendriksen (Grand Rapids: Eerdmans, 1951), p. 329.
13. Lonergan, *Method*, p. 106.

In a literal sense the horizon is the line formed by the meeting of the earth and the sky, delimiting what can be seen from what cannot be seen. In a metaphorical sense the horizon is the boundary, as established from a determinant standpoint, delimiting what is known or of interest from what is unknown or not of interest. We all inhabit a variety of horizonal fields in this metaphorical sense. For instance, thinking of the academic disciplines, we could say that chemists, psychologists, and historians each in some measure live within a different horizon. Each group has different interests and a different sphere of knowledge. These differences are not necessarily basic. They do not set up mutually exclusive horizons. Each disciplinary group knows about the others and recognizes a need for these others. Such horizons are complementary and are relative to special interests. We will refer to such disciplinary horizons as *relative horizons*. The notion of horizon may also refer to a more basic distinction among knowers. One's horizon in this sense determines one's fundamental orientation in life, one's orientation to matters of ultimate truth and values; in short, to God. Such matters determine one's *basic horizon*.

The passage from one basic horizon to another is a matter of *conversion*. One whose horizon is not determined by such conversion does not have the same capacities for knowledge as one whose horizon is so determined. As the apostle Paul says, "The unspiritual man does not receive the gifts of the Spirit of God, for they are folly to him, and he is not able to understand them" (1 Cor. 2:14). Conversion, then, has profound implications for a person's conscious and intentional operations. As Lonergan puts it, "It directs his gaze, pervades his imagination, releases the symbols that penetrate to the depths of the psyche. It enriches his understanding, guides his judgments, reinforces his decision."[14]

Scholars engaging in a given discipline share a common relative horizon. They are trained in the specialized operations requisite for entry into that horizon, and they attend to the portion of the world of meaning that is the object of that discipline's attention. But these same scholars may operate from out of a variety of radically differing basic horizons. Because these differences of basic horizon exist among scholars working in the same discipline, and because differences in basic horizons affect the cognitional process in its most fundamental operations, it becomes possible, even mandatory, for the impact of basic horizons on disciplinary pursuits to be made explicit. This explicitation of basic horizons is a matter of bringing into the light the most elemental values and concerns

14. Ibid., p. 131.

of the individual scholar or of the community of faith to which the scholar claims allegiance. We have here the basis within a disciplinary guild for the *dialectical clarification* of positions arising from different basic horizons, though held by persons specializing within the same relative horizon. Insofar as such dialectical analysis can bring into the open the conditions of the possibility of the least cognitional bias and of the fullest self-transcendence, it invites migration from one basic horizon to another.

We have already said that insofar as disciplinary methods are distorted by the personal and group biases to which cognitional process in general is subject, there is a concommitant flight from understanding, a failure to acknowledge or to grasp in clarity the meaning structures that are con-stituitive of created reality. The disruptions, conflicts, and suffering which enter human life through the effects of bias-ridden scholarship are manifold and pervasive. For scholarship, no less than other areas of human culture, falls prey to a "reign of sin."

We have suggested, too, that insofar as scholars in the same discipline work out of different basic horizons (different in that their lives are directed toward different objects of faith and love), this will affect pro-foundly the degree to which they adhere to the imperatives of attention, intelligence, and reason. In disciplinary scholarship, sin is primarily a refusal, grounded in what one ultimately loves, to follow the moral imperatives of attention, intelligence, reason, and responsibility. The relevance of Christian belief to such moral rebellion and impotence is seen in the fact that the death of Christ for us releases us from the need for self-justification which is at the root of the ideologies that bias disci-plinary enterprises.

The transformationalist strategy of faith-discipline integration, we said above, affirms common ground between faith and discipline, but it also affirms the objective of transforming the discipline into a Christ-honoring configuration. The foregoing discussion would suggest that the common ground is precisely the structure and dynamism of cognition and of the moral imperatives which are ever operative there. The inte-gration of faith with an academic discipline in this connection means the transformative action of faith on the desire to know which motivates the discipline. Such faith has a curative and liberating effect on that desire. We are speaking here of the effect of faith on the "heart," or on what Lonergan also calls the fourth level of consciousness. The first three levels are the levels of cognitional activity: of experiencing, of under-standing, and of judging. The fourth level, which sublates and controls the other three, is the human subject on the level of existential inten-tional consciousness. It is the human heart in its responses to values, particularly those that are discerned by faith. Without such faith, values originate with humans and terminate with such good as humans bring about.

> But in the light of faith, originating value is divine light and love, while terminal value is the whole universe. So the human good becomes absorbed in an all encompassing good. . . . [N]ow human concern reaches beyond man's world to God and to God's world.[15]

It is by faith then that one not only responds to the love of God and comes to a knowledge of God, but one also finds one's self to be within a horizon determined by God's love. One begins to live for the values ensuing from the love of God, including the value of believing those things God has revealed through his Word to his people.

Insofar as Christian scholars are undergoing conversion (though it may begin abruptly, the ensuing process is lifelong), insofar as conversion is effective in their individual lives and in their collaborative efforts, there will be the possibility of disciplinary transformation. It follows from a responsiveness to the values integral to the Christian horizon; it follows from fidelity to the imperatives of cognition. What shape it will take within any particular discipline cannot be prescribed *a priori*. One thing is sure, however. Only as Christian scholars are themselves transformed through God's Spirit will they have a transforming impact on the concerns and assumptions of their disciplines.

We are left with the question of how to account for the fact that persons whose cognitional operations are not consciously under the sway of the redeeming love of God contribute so positively and massively to the achievements and ongoing labors of the various academic disciplines. I should myself have recourse here primarily to the doctrine of "common grace." If humans are not as wrongheaded as they might be, or if the cognitive process often works effectively for them despite their infidelity to its imperatives, then the restraint of this sin is due to the gracious influence of Christ, "the true light who enlightens every man," the "light [which] shines in the darkness and [which] the darkness has not overcome" (John 1:9, 5). Nor would I rule out the answer which Lonergan suggests, namely, that there can be effective love for God, prompted by his grace, before God is known.[16]

15. Ibid., p. 116.

16. Ibid., pp. 105-7, 340-41. Dag Hammarskold's testimony in *Markings* (New York: Knopf, 1965), p. 205, may well illustrate the phenomenon in question. "I don't know Who—or what—put the question, I don't know when it was put. I don't now even remember answering. But at some moment I did answer yes to Someone—or Something— and from that hour I was certain that existence is meaningful and that, therefore, my life in self-surrender, had a goal."

What are the chief points of comparison among the three integrative strategies we have been considering? The compatibilist strategy seizes the opportunity to bring together shared assumptions and concerns integral both to a discipline and to faith. In so doing there is a danger that the compatibilist has not recognized adequately the radical claims of faith on all of life and hence on the discipline as a whole. The reconstructionalist has correctly seen that the integration of compatible elements drawn from a discipline and from one's faith does not constitute a sufficiently comprehensive strategy from the standpoint of faith's totalitarian demands. Such a scholar, therefore, seeks to rebuild a discipline on a foundation of revealed truths and strives to avoid the compromising of that foundation with the materials of "apostate" thinkers. The transformationalist shares the reconstructionalist's vision of a wholesale reformulation of a discipline into a fully Christ-honoring configuration but also recognizes with the compatibilist that the discipline as constituted may have dimensions that commend themselves to integration with faith's assumptions and concerns. She does not, however, with the compatibilist simply seek to focus on those "Christian" elements already present, so to speak, in the discipline. The transformationalist recognizes that conversion to Christ puts a whole new light on existence, and this light alerts her to the values and realities that must be made integral to the *essence* of her discipline. The ultimate goal is nothing short of the total translation of the discipline into its rightful place among the treasures of God's kingdom.

The view taken in this essay is that such transformation has not been made easy for the Christian scholar by virtue of revelations from on high. Development of disciplinary insights, knowledge, if you will, of the laws which God has decreed for the several spheres of reality, comes with the hard work of attention, insight, rational deliberation, and judgment. This is the labor from which will arise the disciplinary transformations we seek. The transformationalist, as I have depicted him, will draw the theory and practice of his discipline toward recognition of a Christian understanding of the prerequisites for effective adherence to the cognitional norms implicit in the discipline. That Christian faith is the condition of the possibility of sustained adherence to those disciplinary norms bespeaks both the scandal and the power of the gospel of Jesus Christ, "in whom are hid all the treasures of wisdom and knowlege" (Col. 2:3).

What are the chief points of comparison among the three integrative strategies we have been considering? The compatibilist strategy seizes the opportunity to bring together shared assumptions and concerns integral both to a discipline and to faith. In so doing there is a danger that the compatibilist has not recognized adequately the radical claims of faith on all of life and hence on the discipline as a whole. The reconstructionalist has correctly seen that the integration of compatible elements drawn from a discipline and from one's faith does not constitute a sufficiently comprehensive strategy from the standpoint of faith's totalitarian demands. Such a scholar, therefore, seeks to rebuild a discipline on a foundation of revealed truths and strives to avoid the compromising of that foundation with the materials of "apostate" thinkers. The transformationalist shares the reconstructionalist's vision of a wholesale reformulation of a discipline into a fully Christ-honoring configuration but also recognizes with the compatibilist that the discipline as constituted may have dimensions that commend themselves to integration with faith's assumptions and concerns. She does not, however, with the compatibilist simply seek to focus on those "Christian" elements already present, so to speak, in the discipline. The transformationalist recognizes that conversion to Christ puts a whole new light on existence, and this light alerts her to the values and realities that must be made integral to the *essence* of her discipline. The ultimate goal is nothing short of the total translation of the discipline into its rightful place among the treasures of God's kingdom.

The view taken in this essay is that such transformation has not been made easy for the Christian scholar by virtue of revelations from on high. Development of disciplinary insights, knowledge, if you will, of the laws which God has decreed for the several spheres of reality, comes with the hard work of attention, insight, rational deliberation, and judgment. This is the labor from which will arise the disciplinary transformations we seek. The transformationalist, as I have depicted him, will draw the theory and practice of his discipline toward recognition of a Christian understanding of the prerequisites for effective adherence to the cognitional norms implicit in the discipline. That Christian faith is the condition of the possibility of sustained adherence to those disciplinary norms bespeaks both the scandal and the power of the gospel of Jesus Christ, "in whom are hid all the treasures of wisdom and knowlege" (Col. 2:3).